ECHOES

IN THE

DARKNESS

Books by Joseph Wambaugh

FICTION

THE NEW CENTURIONS
THE BLUE KNIGHT
THE CHOIRBOYS
THE BLACK MARBLE
THE GLITTER DOME
THE DELTA STAR
THE SECRETS OF HARRY BRIGHT

NONFICTION

THE ONION FIELD
LINES AND SHADOWS
ECHOES IN THE DARKNESS

ECHOES
IN THE
DARKNESS

Joseph Wambaugh

A PERIGORD PRESS BOOK

WILLIAM MORROW AND COMPANY, INC.

New York

Library of Congress Cataloging-in-Publication Data

Wambaugh, Joseph.
    Echoes in the darkness.

    1. Murder—Pennsylvania—Philadelphia—Case studies.
I. Title.
HV6535.U63P488   1987   364.1′523′0974811   86-23708
ISBN 0-688-06889-8

Printed in the United States of America

6 7 8 9 10

In memory of the missing and the dead:
S.R., K.R., M.R., E.H., S.H. and J.V.

Author's Note

I first became involved with the so-called Main Line Murder Case in 1981, when it was already two years old and still unsolved. I traveled to Pennsylvania and interviewed many people, one of the most memorable being William Bradfield with whom I dined in Philadelphia. Another was Sergeant Joseph VanNort of the Pennsylvania State Police who invited me to his mountain cabin for a weekend to discuss the investigation.

Convinced from all I learned that this case of murder and disappearance would never be heard in a court of law, I decided to abandon the book and return home. Sergeant VanNort tried to convince me that I was wrong, and in the end, I was.

In 1986 I was back in Pennsylvania on the same case, interviewing more people and attending a murder trial involving well over a hundred witnesses. The Main Line Murder Case is probably unique in the history of American law enforcement. A team of police investigators was assigned to a single investigation and worked it every day from early summer 1979 to early summer 1986. They worked on nothing else for seven years.

Since two of the characters in this true story are named Susan, I've elected to refer to Susan Myers at all times as "Sue." I've changed the names of two peripheral characters. This was done to discourage frivolous litigation, which is, these days, a by-product of nonfiction.

Acknowledgments

Many thanks to all who shared with me the private thoughts and secret knowledge without which I would not have attempted this book.

Gothic: a late 18th century and early 19th century style of fiction characterized by historical and picturesque settings, an atmosphere of mystery, gloom, and terror, supernatural or fantastic occurrences, and violent and macabre events.
—*The Random House Dicitonary*

I mate with my free kind upon the crags;
   the hidden recesses
Have heard the echo of my heels,
   in the cool light,
   in the darkness.
    —EZRA POUND

Prologue

There was always a taste for Gothic in the original colonies, particularly in that historic territory that lies west of Philadelphia, and east of Lancaster where Amish farmers still resist the 20th century.

Schoolchildren of the commonwealth of Pennsylvania are told that the springtime explosion of red, white and blue on the mournfully lovely countryside was caused by the sacrifice of Revolutionary dead. The tulip is *blood*-scarlet, the dogwood *bone*-white, the iris a *visceral* blue. Thus, the flora is a memorial to the patriots, or so the schoolmasters say.

The haunt of history is everywhere. "The Main Line" of the Philadelphia commuter train slashes east and west near the old battleground where soldiers wrote of corpse-eating wolves that could outhowl the wind. Local schoolchildren envision bloody footprints in the snow, and gaunt specters with ice-locked muskets, their feet wrapped in rags, led by General Washington who denied himself shelter so long as his starving soldiers had to sleep in the wilderness.

It's a land of splendid trees. When William Penn arrived in 1682 he marveled at the trees: black walnut, cedar, ash, hickory, sassafras, beech. The oaks are formidable: red, white and black. Some trees, 250 years old, are local treasures. There are ancient

15

buttonwoods, yellow pines, firs and red maples. And of course, there's hemlock.

A great oak still stands that was used as a gibbet after the Battle of Brandywine where in 1777 Washington suffered a defeat. The wretched victims of the gibbet were spies, or so their executioners claimed. Their white dangling bodies turned iron-gray and then black against the colorless sky and parchment leaves of that hanging oak.

Not surprisingly, it's a land of antiques and collectors. Tables in Main Line mansions and manor houses are often made of split slab, with round legs set in auger holes. Ancient nails of all kinds are treasured collectibles, some shaped like tiny piano mallets.

This was a land of forges and furnaces. Iron was always cherished. "There is an abidingness about iron," a settler wrote, "and most things made from it." It's impossible *not* to feel this abidingness along The Main Line.

Youngsters from all over America come here to attend prestigious prep schools and academies. For higher learning there's Swarthmore, Haverford, Villanova, Bryn Mawr and others, as well as several seminaries marked by split-rail or white-pine or iron gates, surrounded by native trees that turn bronze and fiery during Indian summer. The trees lie side by side with pretty autumn flowers whose names are sinister: red-hot poker, white snakeroot. It's hard to miss the taste for Gothic.

One can be lulled by a sense of the "abidingness" on suburban roads, especially on cloudy days when vivid colors are muted, and cheerful light shines from a Georgian mansion, a French château, a colonial manor house. There's something reassuring about the craft and labor that's turned so many ancient carriage houses and barns and stables into enduring homes of brick, stone and cedar. But just past any turn in the road, there might be another kind of structure made of the local moss-green stone called serpentine. A slated spire or iron-gray vaulted arch might loom suddenly. It'll only be a church or public meeting house or a distant manse, but the medieval stone undermines the pastoral in this heartland of Friends, as the English Quakers were called.

Perhaps the Gothic Revival was inspired by the mercenaries who brought the warrior arts. German professionals taught the citizen soldiers the value of cold steel at the end of a musket.

Bloodied French veterans scoffed at tales of Lafayette's gallantry. They massacred for *money*. In the early days native Indians were never certain whether they should murder *for* the invaders or risk being murdered *by* them. In the land of patriots and Friends there were always pitiless renegades. They were as medieval as serpentine stone.

But even with their taste for Gothic the locals were bewildered by the series of irrational and "evil" events that destroyed many lives and led to the most massive homicide investigation Pennsylvania had ever experienced.

1

The Poet

"I wasn't the first colleague to fall for Bill Bradfield, not by a long shot," Sue Myers said. "He had a way. He was intense yet boyish. He was articulate and erudite but wasn't afraid to show affection. He might suddenly just put his arm around your shoulder when he was talking ever so passionately about something as mundane as a lesson plan for advanced students. He was handsy, but it seemed so natural. Some people found it endearing.

"He dreamed of visiting the *sacred* places that T. S. Eliot and Ezra Pound visited when they toured Europe," she remembered. "I never pretended to understand Pound's poetry. I attempted to read *The Cantos,* but I couldn't decipher them. I thought Bill Bradfield was the most brilliant teacher I'd ever met. He was interested in art and music and literature. He was interested in everything. The students loved him, and pretty soon so did I."

The newspapers never got her age right when they wrote about her. Sue Myers was older than reported. Born in May, 1940, she was seven years younger than William S. Bradfield, Jr.

Sue Myers met William Bradfield when she came to teach at Upper Merion Senior High School in the fall of 1963, and within a year they were lovers. But being the lover of Bill Bradfield had its drawbacks. Newspaper accounts in later years would refer to him as the "Rasputin" of Upper Merion, but if so, somebody must've misplaced the mad monk's rampant glands. Sue Myers was a virgin when she began dating Bill Bradfield and thought for several months she might *remain* one.

"He never made me feel he was after a sexual fix," she said. "We hardly did more than kiss for a long while."

When she first dated him he wore a hand-me-down suit that had belonged to a dead uncle, yet on his wrist was a top-of-the-line Omega. When he was away from home he'd stay in places where at night the wallpaper wiggled and shimmied, yet once he ran out and bought seven pairs of Nettleton shoes because someone told him they were good. He kept Sue Myers so confused it was literally months before she thought she understood his marital status. And *then* she was wrong.

He was a whole lot of work, this teacher. She'd learn about him, but a little at a time.

One of the things she learned early was that Bill Bradfield was the only son of a retired corporate executive who owned a nice piece of land and a 19th-century farmhouse near Downingtown. His father had worked for Western Electric and had been transferred often in his career. Bill Bradfield told her that he'd been enrolled in thirteen different schools before entering Haverford College in the heart of The Main Line, considered part of the "Little Ivy League," along with Colby and Amherst, and sister schools like Swarthmore and Bryn Mawr.

It was always painful for him to recall his boyhood relationship with his father. It seemed young Bill Bradfield could never perform any task well enough to suit an aggressive, overachieving businessman. One day the boy was determined to do an expert job of trimming the hedge in their yard. He dug a hole, and after measuring precisely, planted a pole at each end of the hedge to mark the desired height. Then he tied a string between the two pencil marks and trimmed the hedge as "flat as a table top." He'd labored for hours, and when he was finished he nervously awaited his father's judgment. The executive pointed out that his son had forgotten to take into consideration the terrain, which sloped twelve inches from one end of the hedge to the other. Put an egg on *this* table and you'd better like omelets.

"Bradfields never forget," Sue Myers said. "Bill grew to be a *very* unforgiving man."

Bill Bradfield stood six feet three inches tall and weighed two hundred pounds, with a chest and shoulders he'd developed as a college wrestler. He had brooding blue eyes, shaded by overhanging eyebrows that often caught bronze highlights when he cocked his head in a dreamy pose. His gaze was so intense it could transfix, so his blue eyes were variously described as "poetic," "icy" or "hypnotic," depending upon his moods.

He had coppery blond hair and in the early days of their relationship, a romantic D. H. Lawrence beard that could look like a clump of seaweed when he was in his "active" phase.

His active phase, according to Sue Myers, took place in the spring. "The juices would flow," she said, and he'd become about as predictable as a Chinese earthquake.

Sue Myers was more than a foot shorter than her secret lover and weighed a little over a hundred pounds. She was a brunette with a small mouth and grayish teeth and dark self-conscious eyes that darted like a pair of hummingbirds.

She was *not* a dreamer. Sue Myers was a practical woman who knew her limitations and couldn't believe that she was being chosen by (it would become an Upper Merion cliché) the most "charismatic" teacher in the district. She was only modestly attractive, but Bill Bradfield had never been known to pursue beautiful women. In the true Romantic spirit, he said that he sought "the beauty of the soul."

One of the first things anyone ever learned about Bill Bradfield was that he was crazy about Ezra Pound. Early in their love affair he told Sue Myers how it had happened.

Unable to get his academic bearings in his undergraduate days at Haverford, Bill Bradfield read a book that altered the course of his life. It was *ABC of Reading,* by Ezra Pound. Like all of the poet's work, it was obscure, arcane, filled with Greek, Latin and classical allusion. The young man didn't understand the book but was deeply moved by it.

He learned that Ezra Pound was still confined at St. Elizabeth's mental hospital in Washington, D.C., having barely escaped a charge of treason for lending support to Benito Mussolini. Before Pound was released, Bill Bradfield visited him and managed to ingratiate himself. He ran errands and visited the Library of Congress on Pound's behalf. He was, in a sense, on the scene when

Pound wrote his most famous work within the walls of the asylum. While Ezra Pound was studying Confucius and writing *The Cantos,* Bill Bradfield wanted to help his master escape and to hide the poet in the Bradfield attic.

Sue Myers was never certain how the undergraduate's plans ran aground, but the upshot was that Bill Bradfield returned to Haverford inspired to complete his undergraduate and graduate degrees and pursue a life of contemplation and poetry. Though born and raised a Quaker, he was, through Pound's influence, deeply interested in Catholicism and the writings of Thomas Aquinas. From then on, when asked his religion, he would say, "I'm a Quaker-Confucian-Catholic."

Sue Myers always believed that he would never have chosen her if she hadn't been a virgin. Bill Bradfield always spoke of chastity, and celibacy was one of the things he admired most about the Roman Catholic clergy.

In later years, she would often say, "The fact of the matter is, Bill Bradfield would have been *much* happier as a monk."

But he was far from monkish back in those days. Sue Myers had to endure many other women but he would always vow to repent. And she would forgive.

"When he talked of love to me," she recalled, "I felt I was the *only* person in the universe for him. When he'd hold me, I was convinced of it beyond all doubt."

Alas, there were several other teachers at Upper Merion equally convinced. Bill Bradfield sought the soul of one of them but had settled for her body when her husband found out about it and warned Bill Bradfield to desist at once.

The next thing the husband knew, the former college wrestler came crashing through his front door and chased him down the hall while the wife, wrapped in a towel, stood screaming. According to the police report, Bill Bradfield punched the husband twenty times, breaking his nose, thereby adding injury to insult, as he bellowed, "Never interfere with me again!"

He was charged with aggravated assault and battery, but charges were dropped after he agreed to turn over $500 in bail money for the victim's medical expenses.

Sue Myers heard all the stories, but she wanted this man. She intended to marry him and have children with him. So they talked of living together, but he had one little caveat: their arrangement would have to remain *secret*. She said she'd consider it.

There was a very good reason for the secrecy, he told her. The school district might charge them with moral turpitude if it was found they were living together out of wedlock.

And when she suggested that they could easily eliminate that problem, he had a lot of complex and confusing reasons why marriage could not take place. Not yet.

In the first place, he confessed, he was already "sort of married." *Twice.* And he had children by both ladies. It seems that he'd met Fran in college, and being young and inexperienced, he decided to live with her, a daring decision at that time. There wasn't sufficient thought given by either of them, he had to admit in retrospect. There had been other things occupying him: a martyred poet locked in an asylum, for instance. Anyway, they had two boys, Martin and William, born a year apart. When the boys were five or six, Fran left. (He was very vague about this part.) And then along came Muriel.

She wasn't as pretty as Fran, and of course she wasn't his intellectual equal. She was tall and thin and had a long angular face. Not a great housekeeper either, but she was a born mother, and his two lads needed a mother. He and Muriel struck a bargain and entered into a living arrangement. Another "common-law" marriage, so to speak. Part of the agreement required that he sire another child for Muriel. She wanted to bear a child with "his looks and brains." So David was born.

All of the kids lived with Muriel in a house he owned in Chester County. He saw to their support, but he still wasn't *actually* married, he said. But it was his nature to be "spiritually married," joined by conscience until the boys were old enough to make their own way. So he asked Sue Myers to be patient and remain a secret lover until a better time.

Sue Myers was nothing if not patient. Not many people ever knew they were lovers. He always claimed they were "close friends." It took an extraordinary capacity for secrecy to pull this off over the years. It took an extraordinary capacity for *obedience* on the part of his half-pint Sancho Panza.

••••

The most memorable time in their life together, Sue Myers would later say, the year that marked a profound change in their relationship, was the sabbatical year of 1972–1973 when they finally realized their dream. They began a pilgrimage to Europe to see all the *sacred* places of Ezra Pound.

Sue Myers had tried to prepare for the intellectual onslaught by studying *The Pound Era* by Hugh Kenner, but to her the poet's work was about as lucid as a polygraph chart. She was informed at the last minute that he had decided to bring along his two eldest sons, now restless teenagers. And she had to promise not to make a single slip in word or deed by revealing to his sons that she was anything more than another faculty member who happened to be traveling to the same places. By then, they had only been lovers for *eight* years.

The highlight of the journey was to have been an audience with the Master, if they could arrange it. But at the first stop, London, they got the horrendous news: Ezra Pound had died in Venice, literally in the arms of his mistress.

Bill Bradfield went off alone to make grief noises. When he returned he could only say, "A *fellow* poet has died!"

And that death set the stage for a maniacal tour of the sacred places. The disciple wanted *relics.* The four of them—Bill Bradfield, Sue Myers, and the two boys—careened around the Continent in a rented Volkswagen bus while he hungered to see every site where the bard had so much as walked.

They rattled into Rapallo where Pound had been arrested at the close of World War II for treasonable collaboration with the Fascists. They tracked down a former friend of the poet who still lived in the same house she had occupied as a child when she was Pound's neighbor. The woman couldn't speak English but managed to understand Bill Bradfield's Spanish.

She revealed to him a treasure trove. Her house was filled with books by and about Pound, and photos, and memorabilia. It was a day of joy!

They found a prison compound near Pisa and visited Ezra Pound's former cellblock as other pilgrims visit Lourdes. Bill Bradfield clipped a piece of the barbed wire that encircled the now defunct compound and treated that snippet like a sliver from the True Cross.

They met and lunched with the man who owned the property where the camp had been. Bill Bradfield assured him that his land would be very valuable, after Ezra Pound attained his rightful place in the world of letters. He advised the man to build a grand monument, a tribute to the poet.

But the simple Italian said, "My roses are a tribute. It is enough."

Venice, of course, was a challenge. They went to every lodging, every restaurant, every bar that Ezra Pound had frequented.

She *really* worried in Austria, when they got to the very doors of a castle occupied by the poet's daughter. But by now, Bill Bradfield had lost some of his heat. His blue eyes weren't quite as bright, and after some urging, he agreed that Pound's daughter wasn't likely to receive two Pennsylvania schoolteachers and a couple of kids, even if he *could* convince her that he had known her old man back in Washington.

Sue Myers was thirty-two years old by then, and felt fifty when they finally arrived at a tiny Austrian town mentioned in *The Cantos*. The Austrian town had prospered during the Great Depression when its mayor had created and issued his own money. He dated the currency and decreed that it would depreciate in value each and every week it was *not* used; therefore, the money circulated and people traded vigorously for it.

Ezra Pound had immortalized the town as a tribute to Mussolini and he'd made the grandiose generalization that what worked on the village level could work on a national level. Indeed, on a *global* level.

At the entrance to the village there was a little bridge bearing a plaque written in German. Sue Myers was finally able to contribute something to the intellectual business at hand. She'd studied German in college and could translate.

Bill Bradfield was excited to discover that the plaque was a testimonial to the mayor whose economic brainstorm had saved the village. The daughter of the mayor was still alive, and thrilled him even further by giving him pieces of the old money to add to his collection of Pound memorabilia. She also graciously showed them her father's library and it was just as Ezra Pound had described it! She even had an old photo of the poet holding a neighbor's baby.

Well, that was about it. He had the rusty barbed wire, the dated money, and several other relics. Sue Myers had anemia and frazzled nerves and was being driven nuts by his bored teenagers.

She'd fought with the older boy relentlessly for ten months. The younger had a crush on her and that was almost as bad. Whenever they'd arrive in a new town, she'd slip them some lire or francs or pesetas and tell them to get lost until it was time to move on.

Bill Bradfield, after concocting the elaborate cover story to explain Sue Myers to his sons, had stuck to it. He was always reassuring them that she was nothing more than a colleague from the English department who happened to be going to Europe, and that they'd pooled their bucks. For a time the boys *wanted* to believe that two grownups could share the sleeping quarters in the Volkswagen bus while they slept outside in a tent.

Unfortunately, the younger son's crush on Sue didn't wane, and one day he found some birth control pills in her luggage. A *year's* supply. He felt betrayed. Finally, he caught them in bed together in Granada, Spain.

"The boy never forgave me," Sue recounted. "I've heard Bill Bradfield reminisce about every slight he'd suffered in his lifetime. He remembered every toy he didn't get as a child. The Bradfields don't forgive."

And then *she* made a discovery: Bill Bradfield had letters awaiting him at various destinations. Letters from several women. After finding and reading them she knew that he'd been encouraging them all along the way.

She was heartbroken. There had been other affairs during their years together, but she thought that somehow when they returned from Europe it would be different.

"I *hated* springtime," she always said. "He'd get so active."

Sue Myers was certain she'd have a mental breakdown if she didn't get home to the States. But now she knew that he'd be as active as before with all the cryptic notes, and a secret post office box, and ringing phones that went dead when *she* answered.

She vowed to get out. She wanted to be married and have children. Her kiddie clock was ticking in her ears.

As always, he begged forgiveness and made new promises. This time he pointed out that since he was a poet like Ezra Pound, his

2

Prince of Darkness

She'd heard that the new principal had arrived at Upper Merion Senior High School, but where the devil was he? And who was the tall army officer roaming around the corridors in full uniform?

Ida Micucci had a whole lot of questions that went unanswered during the first days of Jay C. Smith's tenure at Upper Merion, though one of them got answered pretty fast. The tall army officer *was* the new principal. Jay Smith was a staff officer in the U.S. Army Reserve, but why he felt he needed to wear his uniform to school on his first day was a mystery. It was probably the most innocuous of all the mysteries that would trouble the principal's secretary from that day until her retirement.

It took a full week for the new principal to walk into her office and introduce himself.

"You're never seen such a pair of eyes in all your life," she said often. "There was no *feeling* in them. You might think you've known a few people with cold fish eyes, but not like his."

They were *not* fish eyes. They were eyes that newspaper editors

27

in later years loved to isolate for effect. They were referred to as "reptilian," but that was not correct either.

Jay Smith was tall, middle-aged, with receding dark hair, a weak knobby chin and a rubbery sensual mouth. He was *not* an attractive man. Some thought that Jay Smith looked like an obscene phone call.

Ida Micucci hated to admit that his eyes scared her, but then she was too busy disliking Jay Smith to be all that scared. For starters, no one could ever find the guy. He'd come to school and enter his office and *vanish*. When he'd eventually reappear after people went looking all over campus for him, he'd never apologize. He'd simply enter the office and tend to his paperwork. By late afternoon he'd lock his office door and refuse to come out.

Ida Micucci was annoyed from the start. She knew that sometimes a school principal had private business that needed closed doors, but Jay Smith would lock his door nearly every day as a matter of policy. He did not want to be disturbed unless it was urgent.

Being several years older than her new boss, Ida felt it was up to her to put this principal in his place. She gave it a try from time to time and was just about the only one at Upper Merion who ever did. For one thing, she'd turn him down when he came around with army paperwork that needed typing. He was going for colonel then with a good shot at becoming a general before he retired.

She'd say, "No, I'm far too busy to do the *army's* work." And he'd simple turn and walk quietly away.

It became apparent though that neither Ida nor anyone else was going to put him in his place. He had a quick mind and a sharp tongue and wouldn't hesitate to draw blood if he was crossed.

He could speed-read and remember whole chunks of books. He virtually memorized the yearbook, and astonished students by addressing them by name. He loved using arcane words on troublesome faculty members when they bothered him with petty problems.

One of those troublesome faculty members was Bill Bradfield, whom Ida liked as much as she disliked Jay Smith. Ida thought that Bill Bradfield was handsome and manly and she liked the way he'd come in and give her a hug and a smile and a cheery hello.

Sometimes Bill Bradfield as teachers' representative had occasion to start ragging the principal about a teacher who'd received an unsatisfactory notice and thought it unfair.

Jay Smith would simply fix him quietly with those eyes and say something like "I find your reasoning a bit *periphrastic.*"

Bill Bradfield would have to scamper for a dictionary, thereby leaving Jay Smith to do his customary vanishing act.

One semester the principal gave Ida an unsatisfactory notice and she marched straight into his office and told him that she'd never received an unsatisfactory notice in her entire career and she was not about to take one without an explanation, a *written* explanation.

Jay Smith sat there and stared vacantly with those eyes and nodded and wrote his explanation. The report indicated that by bringing in candy every day and putting it on her desk, Ida Micucci was encouraging teachers to loiter around the principal's office. And furthermore, Ida Micucci was attracting "bugs and other vermin."

That did it. Jay C. Smith had a very angry senior secretary on his hands. And one day he called her in and apologized for the report. And not just a few times. He apologized every time he happened to glance at the candy jar. She thought he was going to spend the remaining years of her career apologizing.

He'd be handing her something to type six *months* after the bugs-and-vermin report, and he'd suddenly say, "Please forgive me, Ida."

But he never apologized to another soul for anything. And pretty soon, he got tired of dumping words like "sesquipedalian" on his unfortunate faculty. He started *inventing* words for the likes of Bill Bradfield when he dared to match wits with Jay Smith.

Once when the teachers' representative came reeling out of Jay Smith's office unable to find a word like "ransmigrifold" in *any* dictionary, the principal sat and chuckled mirthlessly and finally had to share his secret.

"I'm *inventing* words for them, Ida," he informed his secretary. "Those pseudo-intellectuals need the exercise that I provide."

Jay Smith would bring his *trash* to work. Nobody could believe it at first, but it was so. He'd bring bags of trash from home and transfer it from his car to the school Dumpsters. Even the custodians were asking what the hell was going on! Didn't they have garbage pickup in his neighborhood?

And that wasn't all that the custodians were wondering about. They noticed him hanging around school at night when everyone else had gone home. *Late* at night. Once, a janitor saw the principal strolling out of his office on the way to the lavatory. It wouldn't have caused concern except that Jay Smith was wearing nothing but *underwear*.

Then there was the matter of his meeting and greeting prospective teachers. One of them was a new member of the English department, a young woman, recently widowed.

Jay Smith had a full, smooth speaking voice and always enunciated crisply. His most dulcet tone was reserved for attractive women.

"Do you use Warriner's *Grammar*?" he asked the young widow as she squirmed a bit. Many women reported feeling that his eyes were always asking lewd questions.

"Yes, I do," she answered, just as his phone rang.

"One moment, my dear," he said and picked up the telephone.

And the teacher started wishing for silver bullets because he was transformed!

"This is *Colonel* Jay C. Smith," he snarled. "And we *will* bivouac at oh five hundred, do you understand?"

Bang went the telephone and just that fast the wolfman disappeared.

It was a velvet frog who said, "Yes, my dear, it's a *very* good grammar book and I'm delighted to see that you think so."

And there was the "stress" question. Every teacher at Upper Merion, new or old, had to get used to the fact that Jay Smith seemed to have a perverse need to shock.

For example, he'd sometimes gravely ask a prospective teacher what kind of birth control she used, as though her diaphragm was at least as important as Upper Merion's football schedule.

To the user of Warriner's *Grammar*, he said, "As a young widow, perhaps you could tell me how you handle your sex life."

She answered, "Discreetly," and the chill in her voice made him conclude the interview.

He dealt with male teachers in a similar fashion. To a new English teacher named Vincent Valaitis who had the face (and the worldliness) of a Vienna choirboy, Jay Smith said, "Young man, just remember one thing, English literature is nothing more than fucking and sucking."

The twenty-four-year-old teacher thanked the principal for the insight and got the job.

◆◆◆◆

A change took place at Upper Merion Senior High School. It was gradual at first and then it gained momentum as the years passed. It became clear to the faculty that their principal would let *them* run their classrooms pretty much as they wished. This meant that traditions like a dress code went out the window for students and for some teachers.

Faculty members like Bill Bradfield came to class in down vests and jogging shoes. And without a dress code Bill Bradfield grew his beard into a John Brown Raiding Harpers Ferry model. His mustache hung over his mouth so long and ragged that Sue Myers practically needed a machete for a kiss. And the kisses were coming less frequently since their return from Europe.

Jay Smith eventually took a sabbatical to complete work on his doctorate in education at Temple University. But whether he was present or on sabbatical, the principal was ever the subject of gossip.

For example, there were the "open mike" episodes so called because Jay Smith would, when in a garrulous mood, deliver messages to the students over the public address system. The students loved it, particularly after he returned from Temple University as *Doctor* Jay Smith. The messages got longer, more rambling, and sometimes wiped out the first period.

He would say things like "This is your principal speaking. There is a new regulation for gym clothes. You may wear yellow bottoms and blue tops. [Long pause.] Or you may wear blue bottoms and yellow tops. I trust that this will please authoritarians in the faculty and not displease libertarians. But I have one caveat:

in the winter it shall be the duty of each and every student to be encased in warm underwear."

Dr. Smith hated to be troubled by picayunish disciplinary problems. Once, the-widow-who-handled-sex-discreetly stormed into his office to complain about some students who were racing cars up and down the parking lot, and tossing Frisbees around the corridors, and sunbathing on the roofs of their cars with ghetto blasters turned loud enough to shatter her zircons.

And Dr. Smith's response? "I have *no* time for overreacting menopausal women, my dear."

When she retired from Upper Merion and had time to reflect, Ida Micucci could only picture Jay Smith in a black suit. The same black suit, she thought at first. But she eventually came to realize that it *wasn't* the same black suit because sometimes his sleeves would be two inches shorter than at other times. When Ida could bear it no longer she said, "Where in the world do you *get* those black suits? They don't fit!"

He just slid those eyeballs in her direction and showed her a grin like an ice pick, and said, "You may not believe this, Ida, but I get *all* my clothes at the Salvation Army."

She believed it all right. But despite his secondhand rags, he was clean. Was he *ever*. The man would wash his hands fifteen times a day. He ran to the john so often that Ida thought he had a bad bladder until male faculty members reported that he'd only wash his hands. Around the faculty dining room they said that Dr. Jay Smith washed his hands more than Dr. Kildare.

Dr. Smith seldom fraternized with faculty or staff on or off campus, but once a year he might show up at a soiree. One of these was a party given at the home of a teacher who'd been taking belly dancing. She was pretty good, and after everyone had enough to drink she slipped into her harem costume for a little demonstration.

Fueled by martinis, all the male teachers started clapping, and when the music started she came slinking in. Two of the younger female teachers happened to be standing in front of Jay Smith when the belly dancer permitted the men to slip dollar bills inside her costume as she shimmied.

Jay Smith moved close enough behind the young women for them to feel his hot breath on the napes of their necks and asked,

"What does one do when a portion of one's anatomy gets *hard?*"

And the young teachers started gulping their drinks and jabbering inanely to each other and pretended not to have heard, afraid to turn around and see a pair of eyes that looked like the eyes of a . . .

They *all* had trouble describing the eyes of their principal. "Amphibian" came to mind, but that wasn't precisely correct either.

There were constant cryptic phone calls and messages from women to Jay Smith, and that was just one of the many things bothering his secretary. Worse than that were the chemical odors in his office. Ida got so that she'd creep in after his solitary closed-door session in the late afternoon and she'd smell something medicinal, something chemical.

And when he went out he always looked as though he'd been asleep. His black suit would be more rumpled than usual and his hooded eyes seemed to have a glaze on them.

Ida's husband finally said he was getting sick and tired of hearing all the crazy stories. He got so he was accusing *her* of being crazy.

"Would you like to meet the wife of a school principal?" Ida asked her husband. "A man with a doctorate? A colonel in the army reserve? We'll take a little drive down to the dry cleaner's where she works, and take a gander."

Many a male customer took a gander at Stephanie Smith when she had her back turned. What they'd see was a voluptuous woman in hot pants and white plastic boots, with dyed hair teased and sprayed to the point of fracture. From behind, Dolly Parton. From the front, a hook-nosed hag from *Macbeth.*

But she was kind and sweet and friendly. Ida Micucci, after she got over the shock, really liked Stephanie Smith.

Stephanie called everybody "hon." She was several years older than her husband, and like him had grown up poor in West Chester. She'd worked very hard all her life and helped put Jay Smith through college. It took about three minutes to get to know her intimately, and from then she was all heart and loyalty.

If Jay Smith was about as forthcoming as *Pravda,* his wife Stephanie delivered more gossip than the *National Enquirer.* She was constantly threatening to leave her husband, or doing it and returning home when she had a change of heart. And she'd give anyone the blow-by-blow whether it was wanted or not.

"Take a look, hon!" she said to Ida one day before the secretary could escape from the dry cleaner's.

"Oh, I can't look at private letters!" Ida protested, but curiosity drew her toward the documents that Stephanie was holding.

"He *always* keeps his basement apartment locked," Stephanie confided. "He won't let nobody down there. Not me and not our daughters. But I broke in!"

Ida read a few paragraphs of Jay Smith's "love letters" reportedly to be sent to a professor's wife at a nearby college. They were all about collies and Dobermans. Nothing that would have shocked the Marquis de Sade, but Ida Micucci got queasy.

"*Please,* Stephanie, I already know more about your husband than I *want* to know!" she said, rushing out of the cleaner's.

Ida not only liked and pitied Stephanie, but she also pitied Jay Smith's daughters. The elder was named Stephanie for her mother, and the younger was called Sheri. They were both troubled girls, and for a time, young Stephanie was a student at Upper Merion. Ida talked often to her.

It was common knowledge that young Stephanie was a drug user, and as time passed, she dropped out of school and was rumored to be involved in prostitution to support a heroin addiction. Jay Smith's was not a happy family.

Young Stephanie caused her parents so many problems that Ida wanted to pity the principal himself, but he was a hard man to pity. Sometimes she wanted to join him in the faculty dining room where he sat alone, his face nearly in his plate, holding a fork as though it were a dagger. He'd stab at his food and shove it begrudgingly into his rubbery mouth as though it were eat or die. Ida Micucci decided she could never pity Jay Smith.

On another of her trips to the dry cleaner's, Ida again begged Stephanie Smith to stop the onslaught of bizarre information concerning her principal. She didn't want to hear any more about Dr. Jay's theories on animal husbandry. *Then* it became clear what Dr. Jay Smith's eyes resembled! Not fish, not reptiles though the eyes were very lightly lashed and a bit hooded. But at certain times, in his more sardonic moments, when the eyebrows lifted to form two perfect S's across his high forehead—in those moments the irises slid back and she noticed that his eyes were Tartar, and tilted. And if you simply elongated the pupils, gave them a vertical squeeze in your imagination, it was abundantly clear that Dr. Jay C. Smith had the eyes of a *goat*!

◆◆◆◆

The references to cloven hooves and leathery wings and sulfurous odors *really* took off when Vincent Valaitis and another teacher happened to see Dr. Jay coming out of his little hideaway late one afternoon. There were already plenty of rumors about him hanging upside-down and making piles of guano for the janitor, but *this* was too much.

A radiator leak was causing a cloud of steam to gather at the feet of the principal who was dressed in his black suit, and was busy wrapping his black raincoat around himself like a cloak.

It was *too* Gothic, especially for an imaginative lad like Vince who had a taste for fantasy and science fiction and horror stories. There was Dr. Jay, a tall figure in a black cloak stepping out of a mist with the eyes of a goat. Only one thought was possible: what in hell *is* this guy, *really*?

Vince thought he had the answer. He turned to his friend and in his most excited Dungeons and Dragons whisper said, "Now I *know* who he is. Alive and well in Upper Merion. That, my friend, is the prince of darkness!"

Some of the whispered gags grew a bit urgent when one night a mysterious fire almost burned down an entire wing of the school. They never learned the source of that blaze. Vince and others offered a theory, only half in jest: given whose principality this was, could the fire have been caused by spontaneous combustion?

3

Renaissance

Those who didn't know her very well joked that she'd been created by Nathanael West, and she did indeed resemble a pen pal in *Miss Lonelyhearts*. But a psychotherapist and good friend of Susan Reinert's took pains to refute the image.

"Susan was *not*," the psychologist said, "in spite of her appearance or what others say, mousy or passive. She was quiet and reserved, but strong."

Still, the word "mousy" couldn't be avoided in any discussion about Susan Reinert. She had a high-pitched voice, and squeaked like a rodent when she got excited.

Susan Reinert was thirty-three years old when William Bradfield and Sue Myers were settling in their apartment near Phoenixville, and Jay Smith was enjoying his new title of "doctor."

Susan was even more petite than Sue Myers, and was definitely *not* attractive. She wore oversized glasses with dark plastic rims, an effect that accentuated a large blunted nose. Her lower lip protruded, pushed out by big gapped incisors. Her dark hair was always worn in short sensible styles. Her clothes were conservative and sensible. She was a quiet, sensible English teacher at Upper Merion Senior High School, but she was a woman living in a liberated era in a *most* liberated school wondering what was missing in her life.

Susan's marriage had been unsatisfactory for quite a while, and if she never wrote a letter to Ann Landers, she did write painfully and intimately to herself. She began keeping a secret diary, and it was full of loneliness, confusion, guilt and regret:

> To use sensitivity jargon I'm going to try to get in touch with my feelings. I feel like I'm losing my mind. I need help and I can't find it. I don't know what I want to do!

Susan Reinert was trapped between duty and uncertain desire at a time when American women were attacking every male bastion from the firehouse to the boxing ring.

In that same diary she asked and answered various questions:

> Why do I keep plugging away at this marriage? Answer: Because I'm afraid it's the only one I'll ever have, and if I cannot live with Ken, who really is not all that bad, then there must be something wrong with me.

◆◆◆

In the early years of their marriage, Ken Reinert had served as a navigator on a B-52 bomber, and his bride lived with him at air force bases. Susan and Ken had a baby girl and a year later a boy. It was not a particularly easy life with two babies, but they were busy and young and didn't mind.

The former air force captain later said of those times, "There was a lot of killing in Vietnam and I know I caused some of it, but I honestly can't say I hated my tour of duty. It wasn't like being a marine and risking your life in some rice paddy. Up there in that B-52, I was, well, just so far *above* the killing. I have to say death didn't mean a lot to me then. But when I was finished I wanted to settle down somewhere and live quietly and watch my children grow and never think of killing, not *ever* again."

All her life Susan had revered her father, William Gallagher. Some of her intimates wondered if any man could live up to her father's image. Prior to his untimely death, William Gallagher had run a small-town newspaper in western Pennsylvania where Susan grew up with her older brother, Pat. Their mother had been a schoolteacher, and young Susan had been the kind of girl who always knew where she was going. It was a natural and inevitable progression from the Future Teachers of America to a master's degree at Pennsylvania State University. She hadn't given serious thought to any other profession.

Upper Merion was one of the wealthiest school districts in Pennsylvania with the advantage of being a suburb of Philadelphia. It wasn't that the students were as affluent as those in the nearby Main Line prep schools and academies, but the district had an excellent tax base and there were prosperous business interests within the Upper Merion boundaries. It seemed like a good place to teach, and it was only a short drive to their home on The Main Line.

It was a very active time for the young Reinert family. The growing children and Susan's duties in the English department kept her extremely busy, and Ken got himself a good position with a Philadelphia bank.

The kids were a happy surprise. Though no one had ever called Susan Reinert pretty, her kids were very handsome. They were also bright and active—and polite, which was to be expected. The Reinert grandparents, who lived thirty minutes away, couldn't get enough of their grandchildren. This family had every right to believe that life would be orderly, quiet, predictable.

••••

Impending middle age didn't do Bill Bradfield any harm in the mid-1970's. He stood tall and vigorous, his powerful chest and shoulders without a sag. His hair remained coppery and his brooding blue eyes glowed as boyishly as ever when the mood was upon him.

Sue Myers served and obeyed and taught her classes and kept her secret about being his live-in companion. He pretended to be residing in Downingtown with his parents, if anyone inquired. Bill Bradfield had more secrets than the Politburo.

Under the laissez faire administration of Dr. Jay Smith, a teacher like Bill Bradfield could take the bit in his teeth. Soon, he was not just teaching English but had small groups of advanced-placement students dabbling in Latin and Greek. In fact, he stopped referring to himself as an English teacher. When asked, he would say, "I'm a teacher of English, Latin and Greek."

To Susan Reinert he was Byronesque. She didn't know what to believe about the many rumors of romantic trysts with other teachers, but she simply could not bring herself to believe the more insidious gossip about "involvement" with a few of his gifted students.

Susan Reinert felt that a man like this would always be the target of jealous gossipmongers. His way with students and teachers was wholesome, she believed. He touched people with his hands as well as his inquisitive probing mind because he was an affectionate man, a *natural* man.

Meanwhile, the diary entries of Susan Reinert were growing more troubled. "Where does responsibility enter? I don't seem to be convinced that it's right to do something just because I want to. I'm so tired of crying."

One day in 1974, a colleague named Sharon Lee and some other teachers got into a friendly dispute with Bill Bradfield about the value of American literature.

"It's all second rate," he maintained. "One page of Homer is worth the whole of it."

When Sharon Lee objected, Bill Bradfield said, "Pick a book from your list. *Any* book."

"Okay, *The Great Gatsby.*"

"Let's meet and discuss *The Great Gatsby,*" Bill Bradfield challenged.

Susan Reinert volunteered to host the literary shoot-out in her home.

It wasn't all that serious an event, as it turned out. Everyone had drinks. There was some literary jargon and critical theory tossed around and Bill Bradfield bashed American literature. No one later remembered much about what Bill Bradfield had to say on the subject, though they never forgot the *way* he'd said it.

"He'd come up to within inches of you," a colleague later reported. "He was tall and big and he'd intimidate you with those piercing blue eyes. He was so *intense* he could sometimes be spooky."

So the evening went pretty much as expected, with Bill Bradfield spooking some and charming others.

Whether Bill Bradfield was a truly gifted teacher with an ability to inspire, as some argued, or a glib and clever scholastic hustler, as others maintained, he had a decided effect on his hostess, Susan Reinert.

She was seen hanging on every word he uttered that evening, and, as always, Bill Bradfield uttered plenty of them. She confided to a friend that *this* guy was truly a Renaissance man.

And there was poor Ken Reinert already getting puffy beneath the eyes even though he was at least a decade younger than Bill Bradfield. Ken almost never read poetry. He didn't know a damn thing about Ezra Pound. He liked to watch television.

Sharon Lee, the teacher who had proposed the *Gatsby* debate, was single and attractive. Susan Reinert was married and unattractive. Bill Bradfield never stalked attractive women. One of his more critical colleagues said that Bill Bradfield could smell insecurity and loneliness the way a pig smells truffles.

Late that evening when most of the guests had gone and Ken Reinert was in bed, Sharon Lee was in the kitchen getting an ashtray. When she returned a bit too quietly she found Bill Bradfield leaning over the chair of Susan Reinert and whispering softly in what she would later describe as "an intimate position."

Sharon Lee coughed discreetly and Bill Bradfield jumped up and returned to his chair.

An already shaky marriage was reeling. These two teachers had forgotten American literature and *The Great Gatsby*. This looked more like a Main Line replay of plodding Charles against worldly Rodolphe, with Susan Reinert, of course, Madame Bovary.

••••

Susan soon began seeing a psychologist named Roslyn Weinberger, who provided emotional support. But the marriage was finished. Susan herself described that frantic school year in a diary entry:

> Sunday, November 17th. What a year this has been. First Ken's accusations of unfaithfulness, requests for divorce, bad scenes in bed, stormy silences (plus my contribution to problem by fear of revealing true feelings), then Mother's serious illness. Finally growing attraction to Bill and accepting Sharon's suggestion to see Ros as could no longer cope. A year of crisis.
>
> Finally told Ken that children and I would leave. He then decided he would go but fought it all the way. He calls in a.m., p.m., and tells me he can't cope.
>
> Have gotten sterner about his not calling or coming over but hardly a day goes by without my hearing from him at least once.

Yesterday, he asked same question: Was he competing with Bill? Did I love Bill? What was extent of contact with Bill?

Susan Reinert confessed to one intimate friend that she was now the secret lover of Bill Bradfield, and that within five years, after he was emotionally and financially secure, they would be man and wife. He had a secret "five-year plan" for both of them, she said.

But the children were suffering from the family rupture, and their mother was only too aware of their pain:

> One good thing, Karen and Michael have been to Ros and will go again. Although Karen's temper tantrums and refusals to go to dance class and Michael's crying have increased, they seem to be handling situation. Teachers say everything O.K. with them at school. Other crisis: Ken discovered note to Bill. Still don't know what he thinks he knows. Told him what Ros advises regarding nature of relationship and need to grow. It's taking its toll on me.

As the school year neared an end, Susan Reinert wrote Bill Bradfield of her feelings:

> May 2d. It's been one year since I left Ken, taking Karen and Michael with me. Some things are better. The divorce is over. K & M are more relaxed. Some of my anxiety is gone, but I'm not happy. I don't have what I want nor does it seem likely I will get it. I feel very isolated. Missing you and resenting restriction caused by Sue Myers. And by you.

♦♦♦♦

The apartment that Sue Myers shared with Bill Bradfield suited him very well. It was in a colonial-mansion-cum-apartment-house, a fine old building with columns in front and dark shutters.

He still maintained a cordial relationship with his "common-law" wife Muriel and his youngest son who lived on his property in Chester County. Sue Myers estimated that he saw them once every three or four months.

Sue Myers knew by now that the "purging" he said he'd received from their Ezra Pound pilgrimage had not changed him. There were still the odd-hour phone calls and hangups, still the notes and other evidence she'd pick from his pockets when he was asleep.

The romantic affair that wounded Sue the most involved a former teacher who said she was leaving the school district to pursue advanced degrees. During one of Sue's night-prowling raids she found a letter from the woman that had been addressed to *herself* at his secret post office box. It was a Bill Bradfield ruse Sue would come to learn only too well.

Reading it, Sue was devastated to discover that the woman had gone off to give birth to *his* baby. Sue confronted him, in tears. He confessed, and begged forgiveness once again.

But this time Sue was heartbroken enough to get out and did—but returned after he begged and promised never to be unfaithful again. Sue was by then in her mid-thirties. She went home feeling like her womb was full of baby rats.

The Reinert affair was something else altogether.

"By the time I realized he was involved with Susan Reinert, I thought I was getting numb to it," Sue recounted. "But Susan Reinert awakened something in me, or spawned new feelings. I wasn't just so much jealous or brokenhearted, I was *outraged!*"

Even when Sue Myers discussed it years later, a diagonal stress line popped across her brow: "I even *hated* her voice. That screechy whiny voice of hers was like fingernails on a chalkboard. It made me want to *scream.*"

The little clues were there for her. Sue Myers could always detect provocative Bill Bradfield glances, and more tellingly the *return* looks he'd receive from women at school.

"Not *her!*" she yelled at him one day in the corridor of Upper Merion. "Damn it, *not* Susan Reinert!"

"What in the world are you talking about?"

"She's downright homely, for God's sake!" Sue Myers said, trying to check the tears. "She's got nothing to offer. *Nothing!*"

"Get hold of yourself," he told her. "Your imagination's out of control. We'll talk when we get home."

Sue Myers explained it at a later time by saying, "With the others, with all the others, I could see *something* in them, something that might've attracted him. But not with Susan Reinert. To me, she was an *insult.* The final personal insult. Maybe my spirit did go absolutely numb after her, I don't know."

Sue wanted to believe him when he told her how silly she was to think he would so much as entertain a thought about mousy

Susan Reinert. But then Susan Reinert began to penetrate the Great Books "inner circle."

The Great Books Program, conceived by Mortimer J. Adler, was introduced to Upper Merion by Bill Bradfield. It was a program for self-education in the liberal arts, the concept being that a group of people from the community might educate themselves by meeting twice a month and discussing some two hundred of the Western world's greatest books. They might all read a selection from Descartes or Aristotle or Voltaire and attempt for two hours to address a question posed by Bill Bradfield posing as Plato. It was seminar oriented and that appealed to Bill Bradfield, who was a seminar group leader.

The seminar was cost-free and could be accomplished with library books. Bill Bradfield devised a similar program for the advanced students at Upper Merion, and other teachers quickly became sold on it when they saw the kids discussing Rousseau, Kant, Aristotle.

"Whatever else he was," Sue Myers said, "Bill Bradfield was an *inspiring* teacher."

He allowed certain faculty members to become a part of the Great Books inner circle that administered the seminar for the advanced students. But there were some, outside of the circle, who tried to denigrate their accomplishments. One teacher claimed that an advanced student of Greek tutored by Bill Bradfield, and given straight A's, was later discovered to know about as much Greek as the delivery boy at Spiro's Deli in Philadelphia.

Susan Reinert wanted to belong to the Great Books inner circle. Sue Myers wanted to strangle her with her own pantyhose. Sue found herself peering through campus windows, glaring at Susan Reinert with her quick hummingbird eyes.

One of Bill Bradfield's lifelong idiosyncrasies was the need to *save* things. He'd rathole memos, notes, letters, bills, receipts, many of which Sue Myers would eventually locate and use against him. She sometimes thought that the goofy complexity of his methods and his pack rat collections were designed so that she *would* catch him. She thought it enhanced the *risk* and made his conquests sweeter. She wondered if he was building a Bill Bradfield Memorial Library.

One afternoon she crept by his empty classroom and saw the

corner of a letter protruding from the pages of a book. Sue peeked around the corridor, and seeing that all was quiet, sneaked in and read the letter—and found herself gasping. She later described the note as "obscene" and said she'd never heard a woman describe portions of her body in such a way. She reeled back to her homeroom.

A letter by Susan Reinert would later surface that was either the one Sue read or a version of same:

> It's eight o'clock. I'd like to go to bed so I could turn off my head and body. I am miserable. I didn't hear from you for so long I actually lost most of my physical desire for you for the only time I can remember. But your visit with certain promises rekindles it, damn it. All day today I kept hearing you say that it's not as bad for you. That you can go for days putting me out of your mind! That you have no chance to call me! Knowing that you don't suffer like this is maddening. By now I'm very short tempered. I yell at Karen and Michael and I hurt like hell.
>
> This morning I awoke with aching pubic area and erect nipples as usual. My breasts yearned to brush up against your chest. My legs wanted to curve over yours. My arms wanted to be around you with my hand rubbing you, tracing your face, touching your hair. My wetness desires to cover your penis, and rub up and down against you, to pulsate with delight as we move together. Enough writing. Writing it down isn't working. I want you more not less, and I'm more upset at that.

Sue Myers staked out Susan Reinert's homeroom. When Susan arrived, Sue Myers took her aside and whispered through clenched little teeth, "You bitch! You whore! You leave Bill Bradfield alone or I'll . . . I'll make public the contents of your filthy note!"

Now one might think that a grownup schoolteacher wouldn't get in a tizzy if Upper Merion discovered that she woke up with hard nipples and a yen for a Renaissance man. But Susan Reinert had a terrible fear that her former husband would seize any pretext to take her children away from her. The fear was unreasonable. Their relationship was affable. Ken had remarried and had never offered such a suggestion, but still it was preying on Susan's mind. Perhaps someone had planted the obsessive idea. Someone she trusted.

••••

At about the same time that Susan Reinert was writing to Bill Bradfield, the prince of darkness was composing a love letter of his own. And Stephanie Smith, the wife of Dr. Jay, was almost as snoopy as Sue Myers. One evening when Jay Smith was not at home Stephanie managed to break into the locked basement apartment again and this time found a swingers' magazine with a certain page clipped. The swinging couple on that page were offering to share themselves with any other congenial couple who might write to their post office box. The man in the picture was wearing briefs and had his back to the camera. When Stephanie saw it, she was convinced the swinger in the picture was her husband.

She also found a letter and showed it to her best pal at the dry cleaner's.

The friend nodded and clucked sympathetically when Stephanie said, "I work my buns off so he can get a doctorate degree! Where's he wanna work? Sodom and Gomorrah?"

> Lovewoman,
> We've been working, loving, fucking, and smoking for over a year now and I thought on your graduation a status report is in order. As we agreed, our relationship is sexual. I love your blowjobs and get red hot seeing my cock in your mouth and my cum—you call it lovejuice—seeping from your lips and you licking up each drop.
>
> Your lovecock, forever
>
> P.S. Got some special cocoa butter cream for your asshole so it won't be sore.

Jay Smith just *loved* to talk dirty. In another letter he wrote:

> No matter what we've done, I still love your blowjobs the best, and get red hot looking in the mirror watching my cock go in and out of your precious lips. When my juice drips down your chin and you lick it up and in that sweet Southern accent say, "Good to the last drop," I throb about ten extra times.
> Even though I got your ass virginity and we'll do some fistfucking this summer (Where did you get the idea of fistfucking?) I prefer your mouth to your cunt or your asshole.
> We share sex only with ourselves. No two-timing. I don't count our spouses, but nobody else. I'm not like your husband so if you fuck around on me I'll beat your ass instead of fucking it. Really!
> Now to some areas we disagree on. Marriage. I still don't want to

marry you even tho I love you more than any woman (my love for my wife is special so it doesn't count). I like being with you even when it's not fuck-suck. But you still tend to fib a little and like to practice deception.

I'll raise this issue again: your husband. We should level with him. Even if you say he's a momma's boy, he should accept the situation. You told him about you and your brother and he still married you. Incidentally, if you go down South, don't go out alone with your brother. Your lust for him is not healthy. Tongue kissing sneaked into open bussing is okay, but if you dress up to cock-tease him you're going to get him hard again and have to suck it off again or at least jerk it off. Don't do it even if it gets you off big.

Your husband forgave you once. I won't. No brother sex. Period. Your husband accepts your stupid flirtations. The past indicates he could accept our fuck-suck. He might even join us in our work. Think it over again. I want to meet him. I don't mind sharing your pussynality with him so why can't we be open? My wife will accept it if it's open. From the way you describe his fucking we could help him. Don't spread your legs so wide and keep them high. It makes your cunt tighter, also . . . Shit, that's his problem for now. But we should include him in. Soon. Don't needle him. Love him good. Keep his balls empty. Well, that's a long report, but I thought I'd review some highlights. Let's take vacation days next week or so.

I love you. Always will.

Your lovecock, forever

Stephanie Smith jumped right out of her disco boots and dressed like an aggrieved wife and ran to a divorce lawyer. She was really steamed because "lovewoman" was the wife of a college professor and had always been described by Jay as a perfect lady.

Stephanie wasn't the only storm on Jay Smith's horizon. It seemed that he had a few compulsive habits. The local township police had been called on more than one occasion when a merchant spotted Dr. Jay shoplifting merchandise. Because he was a prominent educator, the shopkeepers on each occasion had decided not to prosecute, and the police had kept it quiet.

There's some evidence that the U.S. Army Reserve Command got the reports because Colonel Jay Smith took an early retirement before he could fulfill his life's ambition of becoming a general.

When Stephanie Smith started making those visits to the divorce lawyer, she had lots to say about her husband, and she didn't restrict her tales to her attorney. She told her friend down at the dry cleaner's that Jay Smith owned a devil costume and some weird dildos.

When that information became public, Jay Smith claimed the costume was a Chinese waiter's getup, but Stephanie knew they don't wear horns and a tail when they stir-fry your wontons.

So pretty soon, a lot of folks were hearing rumors that the old prince of darkness must be some *special* kind of party animal! As it turns out, they didn't know the half of it.

4

The Courier

The Sears, Roebuck store in St. Davids is situated in a nice part of The Main Line. St. Davids residents have a train station and live close to good schools. It's not far from the village shopping of Wayne, and Wayne looks like an American town from the Frank Capra movies of the 1940's.

Villanova University is close by St. Davids and a Villanova sophomore happened to be working as a part-time cashier in the Sears store on Saturday, August 27, 1977. She was at the Ticketron counter, selling tickets and money orders. When she returned from lunch at 1:50 P.M. she found a line of waiting customers, as well as a tall middle-aged armed courier who was standing one counter down. He wore what looked to her like the uniform of the Brink's security company.

"Just a minute," the student-clerk said to the courier, and hurried to the back to fetch the day's receipts.

There was a deposit slip for a large amount in checks and there was another for $34,073 in cash. The young woman brought the bags as well as the Brink's logbook for the courier to sign. The courier signed the name "Carl S. Williams" and received the bag of checks and money.

Five minutes later, the young woman was interrupted by yet

48

another Brink's courier who insisted that *he* had come for the day's deposits.

"But you were already here," the confused cashier informed him.

••••

It was Vincent Valaitis who had hung the prince-of-darkness jacket on Dr. Jay. Vince believed in The Demon in a very real, Roman Catholic sense. And though he didn't truly think that Jay Smith was of The Legion, he realized that none of the teachers in the Catholic schools he'd attended all his life had prepared him for a principal like *this* one.

Vince was a tall lad with a firm jaw and wide shoulders. He looked like an athlete without being one. He wore eyeglasses and was called "Clark Kent" by the Upper Merion students because he bore a resemblance to the television superhero.

At twenty-four Vince Valaitis looked seventeen, and most of the teachers thought he was a new student. He was an avid trekkie, and besides *Star Trek,* he adored any TV show, film or book about fantasy, horror or science fiction. When he attained enough seniority he hoped to teach a course in film literature. Vince had a collection of old movies and encouraged the students to read Tolkien. He was crazy about Gothic movies like the silent classic *Nosferatu.*

Bill Bradfield was charmed by Vince Valaitis. He said that Vince reminded him of himself at that age, so enthusiastic and bubbling with ideas and energy. Bill Bradfield did not add "naïveté," because it is doubtful that even as a child Bill Bradfield was *ever* as naïve as Vince Valaitis.

For Vince, it was a great honor to be admitted into Bill Bradfield's inner circle so readily, and to become a friend of the unquestioned leader of the English department.

"I learned right away to give him latitude," Vince Valaitis said. "I didn't press him with questions. He was incredibly fascinating and different. There were so many secrets about him. Like where he lived. A simple enough question for anyone else."

One day at school, Bill Bradfield placed his hand on Vince's shoulder and in his own conspiratorial style said, "Vince, there are certain things about me that I don't reveal, but though we've only known each other a short time, I count you as one of my *true* friends."

And so one afternoon over lunch Bill Bradfield revealed an episode in his past. It seemed that during the revolution he'd gone to Cuba on a mission for the government. He met some Castro guerrillas who took him to the harbor in Havana to show him *yanqui* ships loaded with munitions. All at once somebody started shooting at suspected saboteurs. Everyone dashed for cover.

"I'll never forget the moment because I was wearing expensive alligator shoes," Bill Bradfield chuckled, while the astonished Vince Valaitis tried to keep his chin off his plate.

"There were always those touches," Vince said later. "You could never doubt any part of his stories because of the little touches that were so convincing, like the alligator shoes."

Bill Bradfield came up choking on seawater, he said, and found that he was inside a military compound. He had to get away pronto, and though he had never committed an act of violence in his life, he had no choice but to garrote a Cuban guard and make his escape. Before returning to America he helped the Castroites blow up that ship in the harbor. But that was another story to be told later.

Vince was asked not to talk freely about this part of Bill Bradfield's past because there were still dangerous people who might resent his having been a young revolutionary. And while Vince was crossing his heart and hoping to die or something, Bill Bradfield revealed yet *another* secret that would require even more discretion. He cautioned that it should never be revealed to a living soul, particularly not another soul at Upper Merion.

Bill Bradfield said, "I want you to come to our place for dinner tonight. Mine and Sue's. I live with Sue Myers, and no one can know. We'd be fired if the district found out."

Vince had only a few seconds to chew on that one when Bill Bradfield said, "I want to assure you that my relationship with Sue is not and never has been sexual. By the way, how do you feel about chastity?"

And Vince, who'd had about as much sexual experience as his *Star Trek* hero, Dr. Spock, started wondering where *this* conversation was going.

Bill Bradfield said, "I respect so much about you. Your mind is incredibly receptive, and I admire that you're a devout Catholic. I've spent a great many years in contemplation of the teachings of Thomas Aquinas. I respect chastity most of all. I think the Church is correct in urging young men to remain absolutely chaste until marriage. I hope you agree."

"Of course," Vince reassured him. "Of course I do. In fact, I almost entered the seminary. I thought very seriously about becoming a priest."

"Well, well," Bill Bradfield said. "That's admirable. I want you to know that the relationship between Sue and me is one of friendship. We have a lot in common and I care for her deeply, but only in a platonic sense."

It's not certain if at this time Bill Bradfield had learned a few things about Vince Valaitis. For one, Vince still wore a scapular around his neck, a practice that most Catholics had abandoned a generation earlier. Moreover, he carried at all times a set of rosary beads. Most Catholics who still did that lived in convents.

A dinner invitation to the apartment occupied by Sue Myers and Bill Bradfield represented the best thing that happened to Vince at Upper Merion.

"I felt tremendously flattered," he admitted much later. "I was honored."

Bill Bradfield had painted three Chinese characters on the white interior wall next to needlepoint hangings that Sue had done. He explained to Vince that the writing was from the Ezra Pound translation of Confucius.

It said, "Day by day, make things new," and pertained to Pound's advice that all translators should try to turn a translation into a poem in the new language. Bill Bradfield was trying to turn his life into a new kind of poetry.

Privately, Bill Bradfield revealed a little more about his Cuban adventure. He had been forced to spend a short time hiding out in a bordello. The prostitutes made passes at him, but he resisted. His traveling companion was a friend named Tom. The prostitutes left Tom alone after they were told he was homosexual.

Vince managed to amuse Sue and Bill Bradfield when the talk turned to their principal, Dr. Jay Smith. Vince told them the prince of darkness story and they laughed. He *didn't* tell them that he had an overpowering urge to draw his rosary and point that crucifix like a six-gun every time the principal passed his way.

Pretty soon Vince was relaxed and enjoying himself immensely. He flashed his trekkie's bunny tooth grin after Bill Bradfield made a startling suggestion.

"I was simply bowled over," Vince Valaitis remembered. "Bill Bradfield asked me if I'd like to live in their building. There was a vacancy coming up and he thought I'd make a fine neighbor."

He didn't need coaxing. Soon Vince was moving in downstairs, getting all settled with a videocassette recorder, his collection of fantasy films and his brand-new tombstone that had been chiseled out of granite for someone named Mary Hume.

When he'd had a chance to buy that tombstone, he couldn't resist. After all, this was his first real home away from home other than an apartment he'd shared with a roommate, and anybody who adored Dracula movies should have a tombstone in his living room. Vince Valaitis was exceptionally happy.

Before long, Vince was aware of Bill Bradfield's scheme to sail to Barcelona on an oceangoing sailboat. He got to see all the specifications that Bill Bradfield had obtained by mail, and it was even hinted that Vince might be considered as a shipmate on that dream voyage. Nobody commented when Sue Myers said he could take *her* place because she'd rather be a cabin girl on the poop deck of the *Andrea Doria*.

The fantasy trip to Barcelona was nothing compared to the most ambitious scheme to date: the Terra Art store. This one scared the hell out of Sue Myers but it was mostly her idea.

Bill Bradfield had decided that there was money waiting to be made in a retail store in the Montgomery Mall. What the mall needed, Sue decided, was a store offering arts and crafts, the things she enjoyed. Bill Bradfield wasn't frightened by the huge money investment. It seemed like a sure thing because it was a franchise operation and had an established factor of name recognition.

He'd never seemed to care much about the world of commerce, but this was a way to achieve his plan of someday having the economic security to cruise the Meditteranean on the trail of Odysseus. That would require a whole *lot* of money for a gaggle of schoolteachers.

Sue Myers agreed to supply most of the labor and Bill Bradfield mortgaged the house he owned in Chester County and put up $40,000. Vince threw in his nighttime labor. A corporation was formed with Bill Bradfield as president, Sue Myers as secretary, and Vince Valaitis as treasurer with a salary and 5 percent of the business.

The store opened its doors on the very day that a bogus Brink's courier pulled a major theft at the Sears store in St. Davids. Vince and Sue did all the actual work at the store and business was all right at first.

The Christmas season was also pretty good but there were some disturbing signs that the shoppers at Montgomery Mall had not been spending their lives waiting for gimcracks. Still, Vince was well paid and was happy with the arrangement.

When Bill Bradfield had occasion to take time off from school Vince often took over his class. Bill Bradfield would leave a lesson plan even for a one-day substitute, a *detailed* lesson plan complete with a laboriously drawn seating chart. He wanted to control the class even if he wasn't there.

Vince wished that Bill Bradfield was less serious, and even hinted to the older man that there were things in life that could not *be* controlled.

••••

It had been a prosperous holiday season for the Sears, Roebuck store in Neshaminy Mall. The bags containing the receipts were bulging on Saturday afternoon, December 17, 1977. The cash total alone was $137,798.

It was nearly time for Armored Motor Service to make its daily pickup, and the assistant head cashier waited impatiently. Sears was running short of one-dollar bills and silver coins.

At 2:00 P.M. the assistant head cashier was finally handed an identification card by one of her clerks who told her that the courier had arrived. The woman took the courier's identification card to the back office to compare the name with a list of Armored Motor Service couriers on the office wall. For security reasons, the names and signatures of all couriers were posted.

The courier's name, Albert J. Wharton, checked out with the name on her list, but she decided to use a little more caution because of the August theft at the Sears in St. Davids.

She compared the signature of Albert J. Wharton on the card with the signature of Albert J. Wharton on the posted notice. They had *not* been written by the same hand.

The assistant head cashier walked out of the back office and examined the uniformed courier. He was fiftyish, a tall man with glasses.

"Did you bring our money?" she asked. "We ordered coins and one-dollar bills to carry us over a few days."

He shook his head and said, "Had a very heavy demand today. Had to put it on another truck."

The courier seemed calm and controlled. But the woman had worked at that store for seven years, and the couriers had *never* needed a second truck.

"Just a few minutes," she said, and went back to her office.

The armed courier looked at his watch and began to pace outside the cashier's office. A minute passed, then another. Even if the courier heard the call going out over the Sears public address system he probably wouldn't understand it.

"Eight hundred call for operator thirty-nine," the voice announced.

It was directed to the store security officer and meant trouble in the cashier's office.

The cashier would later say, "There was something about his face. It was *not* a common face."

That uncommon face was suddenly damp with sweat. The courier looked at his watch once again.

"You can't go in there!" one of the cashiers yelled from the outer office as the courier suddenly vaulted the half wall and ran toward the inner office where the assistant head cashier awaited the arrival of the Sears security officer.

He slammed into another clerk knocking her to the floor as he burst into the office.

"I want my card!" he warned, stopping before the assistant head cashier. "I don't have to *take* this type of treatment! I'll just go back downstairs and send sombody else up! But I *want my card*!"

The frightened woman didn't get a chance to reply and perhaps couldn't have, as she gaped at that uncommon face. The courier snatched the card from her hand, turned and bolted out.

During his escape, the courier pushed people out of the way and hurtled daringly down the moving steps of the escalator. The courier did not get the money. Not this time.

"The composite police drawing never got the eyes right," one of the witnesses later complained to police. "There was something about his *eyes*."

••••

Things in the Upper Merion crucible had been simmering for three years and were bound to boil over.

The confrontation took place in the teachers' lounge. According to Sue Myers, she lost her temper and kicked Susan Reinert in the shin. According to Susan Reinert, it was a knee in the thigh coupled with a warning that sounded like "If you care for yourself and your kids you'd better leave Bill alone."

That afternoon a sobbing Susan Reinert called her therapist and said, "How do I handle something like this with Karen and Michael? I don't want to scare them, but I think they need to take necessary precautions. What do I tell them? Should I say to beware of any woman who comes up and tells them she knows Mommy from school? I really *fear* this woman!"

Susan Reinert had stopped seeing Roslyn Weinberger on an individual basis by then, but still telephoned and still attended group therapy. The group was not composed of the kind of people with whom Susan Reinert had shared her life. They were *not* Great Books advocates, nor English teachers, nor even college graduates necessarily. They were ordinary working folks, and they had lots of advice when Susan Reinert brought them her tale complete with contusions.

One of the group members asked, "How much *more* are you going to expose yourself to, Susan?"

"Well, I don't know," she answered. "You see she works with me and . . ."

"We're not talking about *her*," another one muttered.

"This guy means you no good," still another informed her.

"He's a manipulative son of a bitch!" yet another piped up.

"Whether he does or doesn't leave the other woman, you can do better than *this* bullshit!" still another pointed out.

"But I think you have the wrong idea," Susan Reinert squeaked. "You don't understand. He really does have *lovely* qualities. And he's been with her so long he just doesn't want to run out on her when she's so unstable and needy. He's just waiting for the proper time to get her out of his life!"

••••

Sue Myers wasn't in such hot shape herself after the fight, not emotionally. It had all come to so little, this life with Bill Bradfield, all the years and sacrifice and patience, all the promises of marriage and children of her own. It had come down to fighting like alley cats in the faculty lounge.

"Susan Reinert pursues me," Bill Bradfield swore to her. "The woman's neurotic. She's looking for a stepfather for her children and somehow she's chosen me!"

"You're lying!" Sue Myers said. "Even when you were in New York studying Latin last summer, her number showed up on our phone bill. Why're you so cruel as to bill those calls to *our* phone? Do you *like* to torment me?"

"I don't see her in the way you think!" he said. "I felt sorry for her. She's pathetic. Sure, I've called her. I've given her advice because she begs me for help. My God, I wouldn't have anything to do with a woman like that, not in the way you imply. She's not even an adequate teacher. I can't even stand her absurd politics!"

Sue Myers had heard a good deal on *that* subject. Her "absurd politics" meant that Susan Reinert was not politically conservative enough to suit Bill Bradfield. Now that Ezra Pound was long dead, his greatest living hero was William F. Buckley, Jr. In fact, he once went to a *National Review* dinner in a new suit he bought for the occasion.

One afternoon, Sharon Lee, who'd arranged the *Great Gatsby* party, received a very strange visit in her homeroom from Bill Bradfield. He was visibly distressed. His brow knitted anxiously. His blue eyes ached with concern. Though he had never told a living soul that he'd had any sort of romantic involvement with Susan Reinert, he did admit to Sharon Lee that he was a friend and adviser to the troubled woman. And in that Sharon Lee was

Susan Reinert's close friend, Bill Bradfield wanted her assistance.

"I know I can trust you to make Susan understand," he said. "Tell her to stay *away* from Sue Myers. I'm concerned for her welfare. I fear that Sue Myers is insanely jealous. She might actually do harm to Susan Reinert." And then he added, "Or even to her *children*."

Susan Reinert wondered if *any* man was worth it all. She made up her mind to tell Bill Bradfield that he had to choose between Sue Myers and herself, and must do it at once. On the other hand, she told her friend and fellow teacher Pat Schnure that Bill Bradfield could not just simply walk away from Sue Myers without properly preparing the way, and that there was a reason for this. It seemed that he'd experienced a great loss in his own life and couldn't bear to make others suffer loss without easing it as much as possible.

There had been a girl in Annapolis with whom he was desperately in love. She was diagnosed as having terminal cancer. The disease ravaged her quickly and one day when he went to her family home to see if the prognosis was at all hopeful he was told that God had taken her suddenly and mercifully.

By and by, in the throes of despair, he found himself in the place where they'd first kissed. Theirs had not been a sexual love. It was pure and chaste. On the very spot where they'd vowed their fidelity, he experienced a *catharsis*, he said. He wept as only poets weep. And he was whole again.

This man, Susan Reinert informed her friend, was worth waiting for. He swore that the wait would be a short one.

She dabbed a little more liniment on her bruises and decided to be patient.

5

Mr. Chips

Sue Myers often worried that Bill Bradfield would never see himself as half the success in academia that his father had been in the world of business. Yet she found him to be talented as well as inspiring. True, he was sometimes erratic, always eccentric, frequently late or absent while doing a dozen *other* things unrelated to his job, but that ability to inspire was a gift, she believed.

But their sex life was diminishing even more. He was so often away on conferences, or seminars, or lectures, or various other outings that she frequently found herself alone, listening to the kiddie clock running down.

Added to this was a brand-new worry for a frugal, mature, sensible schoolteacher. She was facing something she hadn't given a serious thought to in her entire working life. Sue Myers faced the possibility of financial disaster in the Terra Art store.

Bill Bradfield, who had hardly set foot in the store while she was working two jobs, told her that she was silly to worry so soon. He said that he would never risk their economic future. It just takes businesses a while to get going, he assured her, and the art store *was* her idea, after all.

She wondered if this dangerous refusal to bail out now was some sort of unconscious attempt to score a little victory in the world of commerce. To prove something to the old man who still doled out money to his son on special occasions.

Sue Myers always thought that instead of loving his parents as he claimed, Bill Bradfield hated them. It gave her night sweats because it seemed to relate to the real danger of financial ruin for both of them. On top of all this were recurring fantasies that at this very moment as she lay suffering, he might be in the bed of Susan Reinert. Yet he swore that he couldn't bear the woman, and in *that* he seemed truthful. She was sure that he actually despised Susan Reinert no matter what he did with her.

Before Sue had started growing numb trying to understand and anticipate the moves of Bill Bradfield she used to wonder about his feelings toward women in general. He had once told her a strange story about his friend Tom, a drama critic who'd lived with him and his first common-law wife, Fran.

Bill Bradfield had decided that his common-law affair with Fran should come to an end and so he persuaded Tom to attempt a seduction of Fran. If Tom could manage to get Fran in bed, Bill Bradfield was going to take some pictures with a hidden camera and force Fran to leave the relationship quietly. It was a strange and disturbing story, particularly since Tom the seducer was homosexual.

Bill Bradfield's most extravagant need was for that oceangoing sailboat, but Sue had long since believed that to be just another symptom of the child in him that had originally attracted her and was making her crazy. As she now had to face impending middle age without an economic safety net, she started tallying up the emotional debits and credits. His inconsistency revealed itself in every facet of life.

One of their cars was a Volkswagen. He had decided that he was going to take care of the VW to save money. He couldn't replace a light bulb yet he bought a full set of expensive metric tools. He never turned a bolt.

There was the world's most expensive tennis racquet that never played a single match. And a set of Latin grammars he *had* to buy because he thought their friend and neighbor Vince Valaitis should learn Latin. They were never opened.

He had five thousand books in that apartment, and more stored away in the attic. Most had never been opened.

"I seldom saw him read," remembered Sue Myers. "And I mean during our *entire* time together."

Then there was the piano. Sue Myers was able to trace that one to his childhood. It seemed that his family had sent his sister to the Peabody Conservatory to study music. Young Bill Bradfield got jealous and decided that he too had musical talents. He was positive that his parents would buy *him* a piano for his birthday. What did he get? A toy truck.

Now a $3,000 Stieff piano was sitting in the living room of their apartment. Bill Bradfield called it proudly a "Southern Steinway," and said it had antique quality. He had lessons for a while. He said it took him back to the good old days in the Haverford College glee club. He was determined to learn to play.

One day the music stopped and he never touched the piano again. That's the way it was for Sue Myers with Bill Bradfield: either symphony or silence and nothing in between.

As she lay alone in her bed and thought about all this and faced the prospect of financial ruin, it suddenly occurred to her: That old piano in the living room had cost more than her car! *She* had to cough up three thousand bucks because when *he* was a little boy his old man had bought him a goddamn toy truck!

••••

And while Sue Myers was facing a bleak economic future and a worse emotional future, Susan Reinert was doing her own sort of tallying. Bill Bradfield had never told a single person that he had so much as dated Susan Reinert.

And so Susan Reinert began engaging in a curious exercise. In addition to diary entries to herself, she began writing letters to *him,* most of which were never mailed.

The references in the letters made it clear that they were meant to be read, and *were* read, but it seems that most were read during his visits to her home. It was a curious ritual: writing one's thoughts as they occur, as one waits, unable to meet or talk on the telephone. Then when they did meet, to have him read and discuss the letters. It was curious but consistent with the obsessions of the man who needed documentation of *everything.*

There were letters filled with her frustration over his inability

to appreciate her as a professional, and of being deliberately misunderstood, letters full of self-pity.

> To accuse me of judging your religious search as palaver ranks as
> one of your cruelest remarks. And regarding the department
> chairman, you have always undervalued me as a professional. You
> would, I presume, turn down my name immediately, firmly and fi-
> nally, not letting it get to the stage of nomination.
> You never praise me except for my body and cooking. I'm not
> as simple as you might think. If I were, I might be content to let
> one day a month, or one day a summer be enough. It's not. Being
> with you only makes me want to be with you more—to have our
> separations be the natural ones required for our separate selves,
> not the lonely ones imposed by you. I can't turn myself off for
> five years. I'm not apologizing for that. I wish the intensity of the
> hurt didn't match the intensity of the passion, but I accept that
> next to God, Karen and Michael, you are the center of my life.
> Somewhere I became deluded into believing I was that important
> to you.
> I can't make you love me. I guess you're used to being loved by
> women. No man except my father has ever loved me for very long.
> I'll stop trying. If you ever decide that spending time with me is
> worth making some changes, let me know. I'll try to keep from
> drying up.

She frequently threatened to break off their relationship, and
would, but after a short while she'd relent.

The literary allusions for his mind were always coupled with
appeals to his belly.

> Visions of Prufrock, your hair, my dark private place, Andrew
> Marvell, nuns, come drifting in. Saturday I felt an integral part of
> you! Treat yourself to a nice dinner, please. Plan on roast lamb ra-
> tatouille when you return here. You can help me pay the phone
> bill later.

••••

Meanwhile back in the principality, the old prince of darkness
was letting the school go to hell. An "open class" policy was unofficially instituted at Upper Merion, hence student absences often
went unreported.

When a guidance counselor complained to Jay Smith that this
didn't seem to be the way to run a school, Dr. Jay replied, "You

should consider getting *out* of education. There're other ways to make money, you know."

When the surprised guidance counselor asked to what ways Dr. Smith was referring, the principal arched those brows and showed him a grin like an eel and said that he knew a guy who made some nice pocket change by running ads in the local newspaper offering to silence guns. Then he laughed and left the guidance counselor gaping.

Jay Smith was more entrepreneurial than Henry Ford. To another dissatisfied staff member he said, "You don't need this job anyway. You live on a farm, don't you? You should raise dogs. Men can never sexually satisfy a woman. If animals can help the blind they can be surrogate sex partners."

Jay Smith's "open mike" monologues to the students were becoming more frequent, less coherent. The kids loved to bait Dr. Jay by sending questions to the principal's office. Sometimes he could ramble on through two periods.

And by now, the principal's secretary was getting to know more about his family than she *ever* wanted to know. Ida Micucci knew that his eldest daughter Stephanie was a strung-out junkie, living at various times with other addicts in the area. The young woman was in and out of rehabilitation programs. She would often call her father, but end up telling Ida how much she needed money.

Sometimes she'd come into the office to get money from her father, money she said was to be spent at fashionable beauty salons in Valley Forge, but which probably went up her nose or into her arm. And if her father wasn't there, the young woman would sit and complain to Ida that while her husband Edward Hunsberger was locked up for his own narcotics addiction, Jay Smith was trying to push her into a relationship with someone else. She asked if Ida had any influence with her father.

And of course Ida would have to say that God Himself had no influence with Jay C. Smith, and the secretary's heart would ache for the poor girl. She felt even more pity for his other daughter Sheri, a sweet but deeply troubled youngster. She wished that Sheri would get out of that house and go to live with one of her uncles.

And so it went. Ida would take all the strange phone calls from strange women, and watch Jay Smith in his black suit go to wash his hands twenty times a day, and smell the strange chemical smells in his office after he left. Moreover, people were reporting thefts from their desks lately. There was a thief about, but Ida figured a desk burglar was small potatoes around here.

Then, despite all her attempts *not* to be drawn into the troubled life of her boss, Ida learned that the entire Smith household was disintegrating. As if the addiction of young Stephanie and her husband Eddie wasn't trouble enough, Jay Smith's wife discovered she had terminal cancer.

So Ida Micucci went on trying to pity her boss. And in his own strange way he sometimes surprised her pleasantly.

Once, Ida happened to tell Jay Smith that she liked stuffed cabbage. Two days later when she got home from work, Ida discovered a *vat* of stuffed cabbage on her front porch, enough to feed the Philadelphia Eagles.

When holidays came, she'd discover presents in her car. No notes, no acknowledgments necessary.

At times like these when he was weathering such tragedy, she truly wanted to pity him. But whenever she tried to commiserate for the elder Stephanie's illness or young Stephanie's drug problems, she'd search his eyes for signs of sadness or pain. She never say anything but Pan leading a nymph to perdition. He was a very hard man to pity.

Susan Reinert occasionally brought her children Karen and Michael to the principal's office when she had a late class. Jay Smith didn't like the idea. One day after they left Ida said to him "Boy, if all kids were only as nice and polite as those two!"

He slid his eyes in her direction and said, "I don't like teachers bringing their damn kids around school. We're not here to babysit."

"You'd have to like *those* kids," Ida Micucci retorted.

"I don't like *any* kids," Jay Smith replied.

And because Ida was the only one who ever tried to get in the last word with Dr. Jay Smith, she said, "How can you be a school principal and not like kids?"

He turned and went silently back to his office and closed the door.

During the tenure of Jay Smith, Ida discovered that she was losing respect for teachers in general.

"They could all see what was happening to our school," she said later. "They were so scared for their jobs they said nothing. I'll never feel the same about the profession after my experience working for Jay Smith."

And though it wasn't her place to administer discipline, one day Ida got sick and tired of all the cowards she perceived them to be. She stormed into Jay Smith's office and said, "Do you know that there're students smoking dope in the parking lot? Are you going to do something about this or *not*?"

And Jay Smith sat back in his chair and folded his arms and slid his eyes onto her, and with a look of amusement said, "What do you want me to do with them, Ida? *Kill* them?"

••••

The elder daughter of Jay Smith wrote a very troubled letter to a former boyfriend that winter, a letter that ended up in the hands of local police. In the letter, young Stephanie expressed an irrational fear of her father. She had come to believe that her father had somehow induced the rapid growing cancer in the stomach, intestines and lymph nodes of her mother. The terrified young woman concluded that perhaps her mother's illness had been induced through toxic substances in her food.

The letter said in part, "So much cancer in such a short period? No way. I'm afraid I'll kill myself if anything else happens!"

And then there occurred the strangest event of all in the legend of Dr. Jay C. Smith. Young Stephanie and her husband Eddie happened to stop at the home of his parents, Pete and Dorothy Hunsberger in North Wales. The Hunsbergers, like the Smiths, had suffered a lot because of the addiction of Eddie, their only child. Eddie was a handsome young fellow and an avid reader. His parents knew he had potential. The Hunsbergers had never stopped hoping that perhaps he *could* conquer the addiction, and Eddie seemed to be making some strides in rehabilitation this time. The reason he came to them that Saturday in February, 1978, was to complete his income tax return.

Their son customarily visited once a week. The last words that Dorothy Hunsberger ever heard him utter were "We'll be back a little later."

He and young Stephanie walked out the door and were never seen again. Except by Jay Smith.

After weeks of frantic inquiries, Dorothy Hunsberger told police that Eddie's father-in-law, Dr. Jay C. Smith, was the last person to see the couple.

Jay Smith had told Dorothy Hunsberger that the young people had suddenly decided to head out for California because Eddie discovered there was a warrant out for his arrest, a warrant for writing forged drug prescriptions.

"But I've checked with federal, state and local authorities!" Dorothy Hunsberger told police. "There *aren't* any warrants for Eddie."

The last message she ever got from Jay Smith regarding their children was given during a phone call near the end of that school term. He said, "Well, the kids are finally in California."

The last she ever heard on the subject from the *wife* of Jay Smith came in a terrifying phone call that she at first chalked up to delirium from cancer drugs.

The elder Stephanie said to Mrs. Hunsberger, "Oh, my God, I hope Jay didn't do them in!"

♦♦♦♦

Ida Micucci thought her prayers had been answered. The school received word at the last faculty meeting of 1978 that Dr. Jay Smith was leaving the principal's office for a position in the Upper Merion administration building. That's what they heard publicly. Privately, there were rumors that the district administrators had gotten wind of some of the shoplifting complaints that local merchants and police hadn't kept totally quiet.

At that last faculty meeting, Bill Bradfield arose and gave Dr. Smith a *glowing* testimonial. He spoke extemporaneously for five minutes. And he organized a retirement dinner.

While Sue Myers and Vince Valaitis and Susan Reinert and Ida Micucci and almost everybody else around the school were feeling relief, Bill Bradfield was comparing Jay Smith to Albert Schweitzer. When Bill Bradfield got through, you'd think that Upper Merion's foremost expert on poodles in your waterbed was *beloved.* It was a reprise of *Goodbye Mr. Chips.*

One of the people ever so grateful to see him go was Pat Schnure, Susan Reinert's closest friend in the English department. Pat was tall and willowy with dark hair and turquoise-blue eyes. Bill Bradfield had once made a minor pass at her, but she was far too pretty for his efforts. When Pat had occasion to drive her principal home one day she felt his eyes slide over her like a steamy wet cloak.

He said things like "Pat, it's not easy being a fellow like me in the company of a beauty like you. You see, I'm aware that I'm not attractive, but it doesn't mean I don't have *needs.*"

Trying not to jam the gas pedal through the floor, Pat said, "Gee, wasn't that a swell lunch?" and anything else that popped into her head to change the subject.

"Tell me, Pat," he said, "do you like to have your body *relaxed?* Through massage for instance?"

She started shaking a little, but then he said, "You know, there are *other* ways to make money. You could have a second career if you wished."

And as she was getting ready to say, "Gosh, thanks, Doctor Smith, but I'd make a lousy masseuse," he *totally* surprised her by saying, "You should consider a security job. I see you as a very fine security officer. What do you think of that?"

6

The Gunman

As the school year of 1977–1978 and the tenure of Dr. Jay C. Smith drew to a close at Upper Merion, there were a lot of plans being made by Bill Bradfield and his friends. Vince Valaitis had become gradually aware of a lessening of contact with Bill Bradfield while he and Sue Myers tried to keep the Terra Art store from bankruptcy.

When he did see Bill Bradfield, the older man was always complaining about having been wrong to take on the responsibility of "helping" fellow teacher Susan Reinert, who he said was constantly bothering him for advice or money loans.

"She's *so* pathetic and needy," he told Vince Valaitis, "I can't bring myself to just ignore her, but I wish she'd leave Upper Merion and go away."

Vince was by then twenty-six years old, and not as frequently mistaken for one of the students. But most of the faculty still found the young teacher refreshing and fun. A couple of minutes into one of his excited monologues on horror flicks and the other grownups felt like taking him to a monster movie and feeding him jelly beans.

He was the kind of guileless young guy who wasn't ashamed to say, "Sure I've had a sheltered life but it was a *nice* shelter."

Vince Valaitis was so loyal that he'd kept his sandbox pals from kindergarten. Vince could make you worry that with a checkbook in his pocket he might someday meet a guy with an honest face and a pinkie ring selling timeshares in Atlantic City. People just wanted to protect Vince. He looked more vulnerable than Liza Minnelli.

At one of the end-of-term soirees, Susan Reinert, who'd had a drink or two, sat at Vince's feet and put her arms around his knees and told him how good-looking he was, which of course was true, and how much she liked him, and of course *everybody* liked him.

But Vince got nervous about the pass and reported it to Bill Bradfield who said it only went to prove what he'd been saying all along, that Susan Reinert was a frustrated neurotic who would jump into bed with *any* man in order to find a husband.

Vince knew that Susan Reinert did not always have an easy time of it financially and once when she was hard pressed he gave her money to buy Michael a cub scout uniform. But Bill Bradfield warned his young friend to stay away from that sex-starved creature, even though he knew that Vince Valaitis had a sex life like Saint Francis of Assisi. Warning him to stay away from Susan Reinert for fear of being ravished made little sense, unless viewed as a tendency of Bill Bradfield's to keep certain people apart, for reasons of his own.

Another of Bill Bradfield's coterie was a young fellow a year older than Vince. Bill Bradfield had seen a great deal of Christopher Pappas over the years, but he usually arranged it so that Vince Valaitis and Sue Myers were *not* part of his social life with Chris.

Chris was not as easy to get to know as Vince Valaitis, but in his own way, he was another young man who some thought needed protection. Chris was of medium height, sturdily built, and looked Sicilian, though he wasn't. He was soft-spoken, unassertive, and was a *very* introspective young fellow. His parents were Greek-American and proud to have forebears in the country that had produced Socrates, Plato, Aristotle. His father was an assertive, self-taught house builder with clever hands and a perfectionist's temperament. Chris spent his life trying and failing, or so he perceived *his* father-son relationship.

He'd been a student at Upper Merion, and along with his

brother had wrestled on the team that Bill Bradfield helped to coach. When he graduated from high school in 1968 he was an unhappy lad, insecure, plagued with self-doubts. He was good with his hands but would never be as good as his father, and more than clever hands was expected from him.

His grades and test scores were too low for the local colleges and universities, but Chris heard that Kansas State University wasn't so competitive. He enrolled, got accepted, and in his words "went to college just to be going." He majored in political science because he had to major in something. His first year was disastrous, but in his second he took a course in philosophy. At first it had to do simply with being Greek, but soon it changed his life. He stayed at Kansas State for five years, and probably owed his degree to classes in philosophy.

"Philosophical ideas had an impact on me," he said. "At last I realized that it *was* possible to figure things out."

As long as he could remember, he'd seen himself as a disappointment to his father. He'd been a very slow reader all his life and believed himself to be slow in every way. His grasp of philosophical concepts started to persuade him that perhaps he wasn't totally inadequate, but he was by no means a confident young man even after he graduated and returned to visit old friends and teachers at Upper Merion.

He began driving a school bus for the township, and was still looking for direction when Bill Bradfield urged that he enter Cabrini College and work toward a teaching certificate. His former teacher also encouraged Chris to sit in on his Great Books Program to see what advanced students could accomplish given the proper motivation.

Chris Pappas listened and pondered and followed Bill Bradfield's advice. He did attend Cabrini as well as St. John's in Santa Fe, New Mexico. He got the certificate and returned to Upper Merion as a substitute teacher and also taught kids with learning disabilities and emotional problems. He was a good choice for a job that required compassion.

During the year that he was a substitute teacher, Chris Pappas became very close to Bill Bradfield.

"You remind me of myself when I was your age," Bill Bradfield told him. "We're similar, you and I. We've both had to deal with overpowering fathers who believed the only right way to do things was their way. We've always felt very little sense of accomplishment in our fathers' eyes, haven't we?"

Chris confessed that he'd been such a worrier all his life that he'd developed a stomach ulcer at the age of *ten*. Now *the* scholar of Upper Merion began telling him that he had a *superior* mind, and that one way to prove something to the ghosts of one's childhood is to prove something to oneself. Bill Bradfield demonstrated that the way to achieve self-satisfaction and self-esteem is through duty and service. Chris trusted Bill Bradfield to guide him.

Chris Pappas was as decent and likable as Vince Valaitis, and, in his own way, even more vulnerable. He listened attentively whenever Bill Bradfield extolled the teachings of Thomas Aquinas and pointed out to him that Catholicism proved that one is not enslaved by *obedience* to higher authority; one is set free by it.

At the time Chris had a friend named Jenny who was several years younger, but he and Jenny were no more than friends. And Jenny had a best friend named Shelly who was eighteen years old and one of Bill Bradfield's gifted students. Shelly was a sturdy industrious girl who reminded Chris of a flouncing Pennsylvania German milkmaid, bursting with energy and opinions and a need for approval.

Soon, Shelly started wearing a Greek sailor's cap like the one Bill Bradfield wore. And after listening to Bill Bradfield on Catholicism, Shelly became convinced that she should begin taking instruction to convert. It wasn't long until Sue Myers was peeking out of her classroom window watching Bill Bradfield greeting the girl with a kiss. For a teacher, that could be a dangerous little maneuver on any high school campus, even one with the laissez faire policies of Dr. Jay Smith.

Neither Susan Reinert nor Shelly seemed as threatening to Sue Myers as a woman Bill Bradfield had been seeing on and off for a few years, a woman from Annapolis.

Rachel had originally come to Upper Merion to talk to Bill Bradfield about his advanced students as potential candidates for St. John's College in Annapolis, a liberal arts institution that promoted the Great Books concept.

Sue Myers had met Rachel on the very day that she'd scored the one-kick decision over Susan Reinert. When Sue saw the way

Bill Bradfield was looking at Rachel she realized she might have more kicking to do.

Bill Bradfield started urging students toward a further education at St. John's, Annapolis, or at the college's sister campus in Santa Fe, New Mexico.

One summer, he and Sue Myers took a trip to Santa Fe so he could enroll in a seminar. Sue had to live in a godawful apartment in the outskirts rather than being close to the school where he spent most of his time. It made her wonder. Then she discovered that Rachel was *also* at the New Mexico campus.

Rachel was a very articulate, seemingly intelligent young woman, as petite as Susan Reinert. She wore no makeup; her clothing was modest; her shoes were flat. Her black hair was slashed down the middle and looked like it was combed with a steam iron. She had good bones and possibly could be attractive but probably never would be.

To Sue, she looked like she belonged on a widow's walk in 19th-century fiction, floating between the gables. Rachel was different and mysterious and Sue Myers feared her more than the others.

This one, she thought, could be a Bill Bradfield "keeper."

Sue was delighted to learn that Rachel had been married at one time. Sue believed that Bill Bradfield could never sustain a relationship with a woman who was not a virgin. Yet the more Sue studied Rachel the more she realized that this young woman looked as virginal as any that prowled the moors in a Gothic novel. And *that's* how she looked: Gothic.

Chris Pappas enthusiastically agreed to join Bill Bradfield in a summer program at St. John's in Annapolis where Rachel would be "helpful" to them. There would be vigorous tutorials, seminars, papers to be written on the Persian and Peloponnesian wars. Chris hoped to emerge more qualified, more confident.

As for his mentor it would be a very busy summer. He now had a whole *bunch* of people to keep apart.

Apparently, Bill Bradfield had talked to Susan Reinert about his fear that some of the folks in his summer seminar might not be up to snuff, morally speaking.

Susan fired off a contemptuous letter early that summer showing that she was aware of his friendship with Rachel:

I think it's a bit hypocritical for you to rave about St. John's lack of moral standards and "bed hopping" when you arranged to have your physical needs met from very early on. I wonder if your visits there are so emotionally difficult because you're unsuccessful in reconciling your own past and present to your idea? Why don't you accept yourself and not preach celibacy to others. Please think about what you can offer me come September.

I want: 1) You to love me. 2) You to be separated from Sue. 3) Us to work through our problems.

> Love,
> Sus

Rachel's name began explicitly surfacing in Susan's other letters that summer:

> You have sent out messages to many women that you were interested in them sexually and that you cared for them in a special way, including former students, Sue, Rachel, me. Sue has certainly borne the brunt of it, hence her misdirected anger at me. I've also felt jealousy, even of Pat, and now Rachel in particular, but always had a feeling of uniqueness to carry me through. Hope it was justified.
>
> Long ago I recognized that I wasn't quite bright enough or disciplined enough for a life of the mind. I opted for a life of service (following my father's footsteps?) yet I am also my mother's daughter. I contemplate human relationships, not philosophy or science. Yes, I know they cast light on each other, but still, does this make us incompatible? It's imperative for us to communicate more with each other. I still think that a serious attempt at therapy would help.

Susan Reinert related to therapist Roslyn Weinberger that Bill Bradfield would get angry at the mere mention of the psychologist's name and ask testily why Susan thought it necessary to talk to "that woman." He never became aware that she was freely talking to that woman about *him*.

••••

That summer, Chris Pappas could not fail to notice that there were lots of nights when Bill Bradfield didn't sleep in his dormitory room, and it was fairly obvious where he spent those nights. Sue Myers must have gotten the vibes long-distance, because one day when she was especially frazzled from trying to keep the

Terra Art store open, she put in a long-distance call to Rachel and simply blurted out her suspicions.

"This is Sue Myers," she said, "and I'm sure you and Bill are pretty much an *item* by now, so I want you to know that I wouldn't mind giving him up. Maybe you wouldn't mind delivering that message."

And then the telephone practically froze to her hand.

"She was *cold*," Sue Myers later remembered. " 'Bitchy' is a word that doesn't even work. She was the original *ice maiden.*"

Rachel said, "I'm afraid you're talking to the wrong party. Mister Bradfield isn't available for messages. I believe he's sailing this weekend. With *Shelly.*"

So Sue Myers stammered something about child molesters and hung up in humiliation, and went back to stewing over things a lot less complex than Bill Bradfield. Things like mid-life crisis and bankruptcy.

Chris Pappas hadn't met Rachel until that summer and often wondered about her relationship with Bill Bradfield.

"I found her to be *very* straitlaced," he said. "She had an underdeveloped sense of humor or none at all, but Bill absolutely appreciated her. He once told me that she was the only woman friend he'd ever had who was able to pull herself up by her own bootstraps so admirably. After a bad marriage she'd gotten her life together. She'd managed to save money and was planning to enter Harvard for graduate study."

When Bill Bradfield talked of Rachel to Chris Pappas, he smiled sadly and said, "She's done a lot better in making something of herself than *I've* ever done."

Chris wasn't in the dormitory very long before he learned that Rachel and Bill Bradfield were very close friends, indeed. He was in his bathroom downstairs one morning when Bill Bradfield came rushing in with his face flushed and his beard frazzled, and his blue eyes aglow with rapture.

He just had to tell someone. It seemed that he and Rachel had had a terrible row and she became furious because of some complimentary things he'd been saying about little Shelly. And when he tried to tell Rachel that he simply saw Shelly as a "perfect human being" she became even angrier. Rachel admitted then that she was hopelessly in love with him and even wanted to have his children. She said that they had so much in common she couldn't imagine why he could even *think* of that child.

And then Bill Bradfield showed young Chris Pappas a look of wonder and said, "I didn't realize just how much I'm *loved* by her!"

Two hours later Chris saw them in the apartment of another former Upper Merion student named Jeff Olsen. Bill Bradfield and Rachel were arm in arm, giggling and chatting. She informed Chris that when Bill Bradfield eventually got his ocean-going sailboat, she was going to have an office on the boat. She'd work while Chris and Bill Bradfield went clamming and fishing and read their Great Books. The ice maiden was tingling. She seemed absolutely girlish.

Susan Reinert made several calls to the dorm that summer and Chris Pappas received them. Bill Bradfield told Chris that he'd made a horrible mistake by offering advice to the troubled woman during the last school year, and now she wouldn't leave him alone. The weekend after Chris took the first call from Susan Reinert, Bill Bradfield made a sudden overnight trip to Baltimore.

And on a balmy summer evening Bill Bradfield felt he had to explain Rachel in light of his views on chastity and celibacy. He confessed to Chris that no matter how much he believed in obedience to God's laws, he could not himself obey at all times.

On that occasion he said, "Because of a weakness in my character, I have an *itch* and I know that no matter how resolute I try to be, that itch will eventually need scratching. That's why I've never formally converted to Catholicism. But I pray that one day I'll be a better man."

About little Shelly, he informed Chris that he'd decided to "send" her to a Catholic college in California. He was very pleased that she was going to convert to Catholicism. He hoped she'd go on to an advanced degree at some Catholic university.

That summer, Bill Bradfield also confessed to Chris Pappas that his life had not turned out as he'd dreamed it in this, his forty-fifth year. He hinted to the young man that perhaps one day he *would* marry Shelly when she was finished with her education, and that he could then develop the character and lifestyle he'd always wanted and couldn't manage thus far.

Bill Bradfield told Chris Pappas that he looked upon him as a younger brother, not just a friend, and that he was confessing things that he'd told no other. He swore that he would *not* be physically intimate with Shelly and that he *did* love the girl whom he saw as something good and real in his life. His relationship with her had inspired him to want to finish a poem he'd begun ten years earlier. It was called "Bloodroot."

It seemed that "Bloodroot" had to do with Maria, a girl he'd once loved in Baltimore. One day when he went to visit her, Maria's parents gave him the terrible news that she'd died suddenly. He had begun the poem in memory of their love, but could never finish it. Now that he'd found this young and fresh and unsullied girl to remind him of the purity of Maria, he was determined to complete the poem.

Bloodroot, the lovely white poppy that grows wild in Pennsylvania, is so vulnerable that it dies at the mere touch of a human being, according to folklore. Apparently, he was implying that he would never "touch" Shelly in that sense.

During that summer Bill Bradfield and Chris had occasion to spend two days on a rented sailboat with two visitors, Jenny and Shelly. Chris Pappas overheard Bill Bradfield telling Shelly about the "Bloodroot" inspiration, and at first Chris thought he must be mistaken. *This* time Bill Bradfield said that Maria had been in an iron lung and he told how he had held her hand as she expired. And before his relationship with Bill Bradfield had gone much further, Chris heard it yet a third time, with a *different* ending.

It was the same when Bill Bradfield told him of traveling to Cuba at the behest of the Central Intelligence Agency. In Chris's version, Bill Bradfield was ordered to count ships for the CIA. During that mission he was forced to creep up and kill a Cuban guard during an intelligence-gathering mission. He killed the Cuban with a knife.

So Chris got a knife killing and Vince Valaitis a garroting. Sue Myers secretly did not believe that he'd even been there at all. She heard that Fran Bradfield had accused Bill of running off to New Orleans for two weeks with Tom, their homosexual lodger. And Sue wondered if it was in a New Orleans brothel that he'd "resisted" all those hussies.

Bill Bradfield once said something about Shelly that Chris Pappas would never forget.

"That girl is my ticket to *heaven*," he said.

Chris Pappas also spent considerable time that summer hearing that Susan Reinert was the "second-worst teacher at Upper Merion." He was never sure who was number one.

"I don't know *why* she bothers me like this," Bill Bradfield told Chris. "I'm just a casual friend. I wish she'd find somebody else for advice and money loans. Sure, I pity her, the poor neurotic creature, but it's too *much* being her friend!"

During the middle of August, Bill Bradfield received a letter from Susan Reinert at St. John's. As was his custom, he couldn't bear to part with it and so tried to hide it away when he got home, but as was *her* custom Sue Myers dug in every nook until she found evidence that he'd been juggling Rachel and Susan Reinert and even little Shelly.

The letter was postmarked August 13, 1978.

Sunday morning

Dear Bill,

Hi honey. I have been uncomfortable since yesterday's phone call, so this is an attempt to straighten it out. First, you said some very nice things. Thank you. My missing you is what I'm most aware of. It's awful. That was why I called you Friday night. Chris was very congenial on the phone, although I'm sure he was wondering why I would be calling you.

He did say you've been working very hard on your papers, but he said a couple of things that made me wonder if you'd been seeing Rachel. When I admitted jealousy yesterday you said it was good. I assume you meant it was good that I care. I HATE it, a waste of time and energy. So do I have any reason to be jealous? If I do, I might as well know. I don't mind that she's typing your paper if she wants to. It's nice that she could help.

Karen and Michael had a great time while I was visiting you. Everyone was complimentary about what a pleasure they were. That really made me feel good. I'm glad I went. I also got to know Rachel better.

Glad you went to a party. We have a tendency to give fun the lowest priority. Hope that, overall, the summer has been worth the agony.

I know you miss me, but I fear that in your loneliness you might turn to someone else who's there. I've never understood the dynamics of our relationship anyhow. When I went to Pat's to pick up Karen and Michael I discovered that Sue Myers had shown some people a very nasty reaction at the mention of my name. I wish Sue would leave Upper Merion or that you would finally leave her. I don't know what more I can do. I do not want to go back to that same scene. This summer has been great without it, which explains my present mood. But I still have lots of feelings and worries I don't like. I'd like to talk to you.

Am taking Karen and Michael to a baseball game with Parents Without Partners, so must close. Write or call. Thanks for the previous phone calls. They help. I love you.

Sus

From everything Roslyn Weinberger was told, Susan Reinert's sexual needs were about normal for a single woman of thirty-six years with a proper upbringing.

"She was interested in sex," the therapist said, "but only when she was emotionally involved with the person. I could never picture her going to a singles bar to pick someone up."

To Pat Schnure, who would probably become Susan Reinert's best friend, she confessed that the only thing she had learned sexually from Bill Bradfield was that physical sex could be acceptable during menstruation. There was never an indication from Susan Reinert or any other woman that Bill Bradfield was some sort of stud. Rather, there were indications he was more of a snuggler and cuddler than a sexual athlete.

It was also his custom to tell each of his close friends about his former friend Tom, the gay lodger in his first "common-law" marriage. He always assured his pals that he'd *never* succumbed to gay overtures, but, clearly, Tom meant something in his life.

••••

Saturday night is still the best time to take a girl to the movies in a place like Tredyffrin Township. And really, there isn't a whole lot else to do on steamy August nights except to catch a movie or have a few slices of pizza. And what with the cinema in the Gateway Shopping Center being so crowded on the evening of August 19, 1978, a young couple decided on the pizzeria.

The moon was low and the young people were sitting on the curb near the Central Penn Bank munching when their attention was diverted by a brown Ford Granada that pulled slowly into the parking lot and stopped next to a Chevrolet van, probably belonging to somebody in the cinema. A man got out of the Ford and walked toward the van and peered inside.

The young couple suddenly forgot all about pizzas and movies. In the available light they could see that the tall man was wearing a cowllike hood over his entire face and head. And it looked like he was carrying something in each hand—*guns.*

The couple didn't run away or even walk away. As the young man later put it, they "sort of crawled away."

By the time the couple got to a phone and the Tredyffrin Township police had arrived at the shopping center, the hooded gunman had gone. The young man told the police that he didn't think the gunman had spotted them, and the police concluded that perhaps he'd been planning to break into the van but changed his mind.

While the young people were still giving their report to the cop, a car pulled into the far end of the parking lot and began cruising slowly in their direction.

"I think *that's* the car!" the young man yelled and the driver turned abruptly and drove away.

A few minutes later, a sergeant and lieutenant from the township police were the first to spot a brown Ford Granada that resembled the one described on the radio broadcast.

The Ford was driving erratically, heading south in a northbound traffic lane. The cops went after it and pulled the car over at the Route 202 on-ramp at Valley Forge Road.

The driver was a tall middle-aged man. He got out and waited as the policemen approached with flashlights, one on each side of the car.

The cops weren't yet certain they had the right suspect and the sergeant asked for a driver's license.

"It's in the car," the driver answered calmly. He turned toward the open door and reached down toward the front seat.

Then, every cop's recurring nightmare. The sergeant heard the lieutenant yell something at him. The lieutenant from his side of the car saw it in the flashlight beam: a .22 Ruger.

"Drop it!" the lieutenant screamed.

A memory in fragments. A finger slid inside the trigger guard. The gun began rising up. The lieutenant could not shoot.

"Drop it now!" he screamed.

A microsecond. Finger pads turned white against blue steel. Then the man said something out of character for a gunman.

He said, "Oh, my goodness!"

He dropped the Ruger and was not shot to death.

The lieutenant later said, "I couldn't fire even after the first command. I was carrying a hot load in my gun and my sergeant was *right* behind the guy. I was scared I'd blast through him and blow away my partner. That guy was very lucky."

The township police found some unusual items in the car of the lucky guy. There was a black leather pouch on the front seat containing four loaded handguns. There was a sleeve of a football jersey fashioned into a hood mask. There was a bolt cutter and other tools that the police assumed were to be used to break into the car in the parking lot.

There was, strangely enough, an oil filter with two bullet holes in the top. Then the cops noticed that the Ruger's front sight had been filed off and on the barrel of the pistol was a cylinder of rubber, the kind used to insulate a screwdriver against electrical shock. With the front sight gone and the rubber cylinder acting as a gasket sleeve, the barrel of the weapon fit perfectly into the oil filter. The gunman had devised an effective silencer.

There were things in the car that at a later time would be of great interest to other police during the investigation of a crime of far greater importance. There was a syringe in that car, and another syringe in the gunman's pocket. A lab report showed the syringe was loaded with ethchlorvynol, also called Placidyl, a tranquilizing drug that, taken orally, can induce sleep. A blood-stream injection can produce unconsciousness within a minute.

The gunman told the cops that he was merely carrying guns to "scare some kids" who'd been bothering him. He said that the drug-loaded syringe belonged to his son-in-law who was an addict. What the son-in-law was doing with such a massive dose was not clear. It was one of the most bizarre aspects of this incident that was not explained.

There was an ordinary plastic trash bag in the backseat of the car and more bags in the trunk. There was a blue plaid jacket in the car with rolls of strapping tape in the pockets. There was a pair of gloves.

The Tredyffrin Township police were the first to receive a piece of news that would occupy the local newspapers for months to come. Their hooded gunman was Dr. Jay C. Smith, the fifty-year-old principal of Upper Merion Senior High School in nearby King of Prussia.

Of course, the police station was humming that night. Yet the cops weren't even beginning to sense the imminent revelations in the secret life of the local educator.

It was near midnight when the arresting officer was walking past Dr. Jay Smith in the booking office. He overheard a remark that the prisoner whispered into the telephone.

Jay Smith said to his listener, ". . . even *before* the bailbonds-man. Get over to the house and take everything out. Including the files!"

••••

The blue metal sign at the township limit reads: NAMED FOR FREDERICK THE GREAT, KING OF PRUSSIA. Jay Smith lived in King of Prussia, only a few minutes from Upper Merion Senior High School. It was well past midnight when township police started acting upon information received from the arresting officers.

At 1:00 A.M. a detective was staked out at the residence of Jay Smith on Valley Forge Road. The cops couldn't imagine who would arrive at the house of the principal to "get everything out." And what would "everything" consist of?

At 2:00 A.M. a car entered the Smith driveway. The driver of the car held four university degrees. He was short and slight and looked as threatening as Woody Allen. In fact, he looked very much like a school librarian, which is what he'd been until the recent Philadelphia layoffs. The librarian had been a close friend of Jay Smith's for many years.

The cops hid by a line of trees and watched the librarian carrying boxes from the basement of the Smith home. Among the items he carried to his Plymouth were some file boxes containing two packets of marijuana weighing a total of 818 grams. The cops pounced on the unsuspecting librarian who said that he was only doing what his friend Jay Smith had asked, and the authorities later decided not to charge him with any crime. But the marijuana in the box allowed them to get the local magistrate out of bed and swear out a search warrant.

At seven o'clock that morning the secret basement apartment of Jay Smith was full of cops. They found an additional 580 grams of marijuana and some vials of contraband pills and capsules, but the drugs were eventually of minimal interest to the police. Far more intriguing were other things that caused many excited calls to other police stations around The Main Line.

Another search warrant was served the next day, a warrant that covered a search more far-reaching than anticipated. The superintendent of schools was asked to come to the Jay Smith home where he identified office machines and other equipment stolen from the Upper Merion school district, as well as reproductions of famous paintings snatched off the walls in the district office. And also something that made absolutely no sense to the cops: Dr. Jay Smith had apparently stolen four gallons of nitric acid from the school. For what?

Then there were the things that had nothing to do with the school. They found two silver badges and uniforms, the kind worn by Brink's security guards. In Jay Smith's desk they found a bogus identification card fashioned from a U.S. Army identification card. In fact, there was a whole packet of stolen army I.D. cards. The bogus Brink's card bore the photo of Jay Smith with the name "Carl S. Williams" beneath it.

The charges against the school principal were piling up when the police found yet another uniform, that of an officer of the U.S. Army Reserve. This uniform wasn't a phony. A call verified that the educator was retired from the 79th Army Reserve Command, and that Colonel Smith had in fact carpooled to army reserve meetings with his commanding general. The general was shocked. He'd always spoken highly of his intelligent colonel. The general was John Eisenhower, son of the thirty-fourth president of the United States.

The cops in the basement that day hauled off a lot of evidence and photographed the rest. The bottles of drugs contained Valium, Librium and Placidyl, but the cops were puzzling over everything *else*. They found five more oil-filter silencers along with a pair of latex gloves. The basement walls were pocked with bullet holes, no doubt from target practice with the silenced guns. Along with the stolen military I.D. cards, they found a pile of blue combs bearing the name of his army reserve unit.

They learned that one of Jay Smith's guns appeared to have been bought by and registered to the assistant principal at Upper Merion, except that when they contracted the man he informed them he had *never* bought a gun. He told the cops that his wallet and identification had been stolen from his desk in the past year.

It appeared that Jay Smith had swiped everything from Upper Merion but the swimming pool, when he wasn't busy terrorizing Sears stores as a bogus courier.

There were lots of other unusual things in the basement, his library for instance. Dr. Jay Smith had books with titles like *The Canine Tongue, Her Bestial Dreams, Her Four-legged Lover, The Bestial Erotics* and *Animal Fever.*

There were plenty of swinger publications, both straight and gay. There were classified ads from "modern" couples willing to exchange information with pen pals. And finally, there was a significant quantity of chains and several locks. The cops photographed the chains and figured that Dr. Jay was a *world class* party animal.

This was reinforced when Stephanie Smith gave her divorce lawyer a dildo described on a later police report as "pink, regular size" and another described as "extra large, black, with manual crank, squirts water."

And what, the boys in the station house wanted to know, would General Eisenhower think of *those* little weapons?

7

Mr. Hyde

For most of his life, Jay Smith had not been all that unattractive. He was six foot two, customarily weighed less than two hundred pounds and carried himself erectly, as befit a military man. He had a good speaking voice and an impressive command of language. But during the months preceding his arrest, a physical change had taken place and it was well documented by news photographs when the educator was in jail trying to raise bail money and facing felony charges leveled by the district attorneys of three counties. There was the Sears theft at the St. Davids store, the attempted theft at the Neshaminy Mall Sears store, the incident of car prowling with loaded guns at the Gateway Shopping Center, the theft of property from the Upper Merion school district, and the possession of contraband drugs. Enough charges to keep Dr. Jay C. Smith in courtrooms for some time to come.

The photographic story was remarkable. He had a high forehead so if there had been additional hair loss it was not noticeable, but he'd gotten heavy and soft and bent, and his face had undergone a coarsening. The Tartar eyes had grown more hooded. The flesh around those eyes collapsed and the sagging lids became reptilian. His heavy dark brows, which always had a tendency to lift cynically, now arched diabolically. Never refined, his wide mouth seemed more fleshy and sagged at the lips from the pull of swollen jowls. And with the added weight and gros-sening, his weak knobby chin receded noticeably within the folds of his neck.

Now the educator did not merely look dissolute, but extraordi-narily *sinister*. Not a face likely to instill confidence in a jury.

••••

Because of the Quaker influence, the sign at the edge of town reads: WEST CHESTER WELCOMES THEE.

"I could have been president of the United States but I lost the election for mayor of West Chester" is the way John J. O'Brien sized up his brief foray into local politics.

John O'Brien enjoyed trial work, especially criminal law, but thus far his triumphs had been limited to cases such as one in-volving a hobo who took upon himself the duty of picking up lit-ter in the public park near a lovers' lane. The litter mostly included discarded underwear and lawyer O'Brien got a kick out of successfully proving that the hobo was an environmentalist, not a voyeur.

A man given to self-deprecating humor, O'Brien was surprised and excited when his divorce client, Mrs. Stephanie Smith, asked him to defend her husband, Dr. Jay Smith, who he knew stood charged with a series of highly publicized crimes.

John O'Brien tilted his round Irish face and his dark brows gave him a pixieish look, when he recalled the request.

"I'm just a small-town lawyer," O'Brien reminisced, settled in his front-yard rocking chair. The wooden sign suspended over the door of his Victorian office in a residential neighborhood of West Chester said: JOHN J. O'BRIEN, ATTORNEY AT LAW. And below it the word NOTARY had been added, proving that it wasn't all that easy for a small-town lawyer to make a buck.

"Like everyone else," the lawyer recalled, "when I first met Stephanie Smith I couldn't believe she was the wife of a school principal. But she was a decent soul, and I really liked her. She was the kind who always gave you a hug and kiss when coming or going, whether you wanted it or not."

It seemed that the principal could not get an impartial trial anywhere in the Philadelphia area what with the newspaper cov-erage of his scandalous secret life. O'Brien wanted at least to win a venue change for the most serious offense, the theft from the St. Davids Sears store, but venue changes were time-consuming.

Stephanie Smith was by then trying to keep her spirits up while her cancer advanced to more critical stages. She still wore her hair teased and sprayed but she'd changed the color to a less garish shade of auburn. And the dying woman even got plastic surgery on her hooked nose during what she knew would be her last year on earth. Possibly the attention of the press was welcomed by Jay Smith's suffering wife who was in and out of the hospital during short periods of remission.

In the first week of the Jay Smith scandal, she held a press interview and said to reporters, "Hon, you can live with a man for twenty-seven years and not know him. Why, Jay didn't even let me know he was in jail 'til thirty-six hours after the arrest. I was *shocked*! I hadn't seen Jay since Saturday and thought he'd went to army reserves or something. He always would come and go without telling me nothing. It wasn't unusual not to see him for *days* at a time."

Then Stephanie told reporters how she'd met young Jay Smith when he was a student teacher at Chester High School and how, like Jay, she was from a poor local family and how, after they married in 1951, she helped to support him during his university years, and waited and worked while he was overseas in Korea as an army officer.

And despite what lawyer O'Brien advised, during every interview Stephanie gave, there would be lots of potentially damaging tidbits about his "eccentric" ways. She gave reporters what they wanted, but she made it known that she admired her husband.

"He's such a thinker," Stephanie Smith said in another interview. "He never talked much around the house but he'd go down to his den and speak into his tape recorder. Hon, he has a wonderful speaking voice! But he always said I didn't own him and I shouldn't get involved in his life, and he wanted his privacy. I was always taught that the man is the master of the house and you just *accept* what he wants."

Stephanie Smith also let it be known that her husband frequently commented that "the devil will rule the earth."

The cops said, so what else is new? But the opinion was entered in a public report as a matter of routine.

General John Eisenhower also gave a statement concerning his former colonel: "I think of him often. He was clever and loquacious. He had a terrific sardonic sense of humor. His only eccentricity was his penchant for being a loner. I remember once hinting that we might get together socially for a beer, but he said that the way he lived he had no friends and *wanted* no friends. I didn't take offense because I knew he was a busy man and perhaps didn't have time for such things. He was a free thinker, versed in the classics. He did not join his fellow officers in the mess or at parties."

The press blitzed Upper Merion, but at first all they could get were some vague statements to the effect that Dr. Jay Smith was a lone wolf who never talked about anything but his work and never mixed socially with colleagues. Despite his years at Upper Merion, some faculty members could not even say for certain if the Smiths had children.

As the fall term was about to begin, Jay Smith was arranging to get out of jail and was composing a few press releases of his own. First, he denied *any* criminal activity whatsoever, stating that it was preposterous to think he was the bogus courier. Secondly, he theorized that part of his problem was caused by the Upper Merion school administrators who were "out to get him" and inflaming the media.

Some observers might note that from the beginning of his troubles and down through the years, Dr. Jay Smith, on those rare occasions when he would speak, was *always* more concerned with allegations of sexual perversion than by the very serious felony charges leveled against him.

As to the other public agencies "out to get him," he had this to say: "The police find a collection of special books that I keep for research. But because they deal with such subjects as sex, homosexuality and bestiality, the police seem preoccupied with them. They see the books on homosexuality and they say, 'Ah ha! Smith's a homosexual.' So they ask my wife and she sets them straight and they scratch *that* one from their list."

He assured his public that he was planning to publish a book entitled *How to Prevent Homosexuality in Your Children.*

As to the canine books, he admitted that he was interested in exploring the possibility of training animals as sexual surrogates and that he planned to launch a mail order firm to distribute his findings.

So naturally, all the cops made up gags about Jay Smith's coming SPCA journal called *Loving Your Pet*. And Jay Smith's version of a Ralph Nader–style blockbuster called *Consumer's Guide to Dildos*.

But of course the cops couldn't care less if Jay Smith was bisexual or trisexual or king of the collies. They *were* interested in the strange little matter of the syringe with the massive dose of drugs, his alibi being that it belonged to his son-in-law Eddie Hunsberger.

Well, where *was* Edward Hunsberger? And where was his wife, Stephanie, daughter of Jay Smith? They represented Jay Smith's potential alibi for *all* the drugs found in the basement.

When the cops tried to find the Hunsbergers, they discovered that Eddie and Stephanie had failed to keep an appointment at a methadone clinic back in February. The clinic employees told them that several attempts to contact the recovering addicts at the Smith home had produced no leads, so the counselors feared drug relapse.

One clinic counselor told police that during her last telephonic inquiry into the whereabouts of her clients Edward and Stephanie Hunsberger, she'd managed to reach Dr. Jay Smith himself who told her that the young couple would not need further monitoring.

"I've gotten them a Placidyl and some *real* good pot," he told the startled counselor. "They're going to de-tox *themselves*."

When she recovered from *that* revelation and told Dr. Smith she didn't think that was a good idea, he surprised her further by saying, "Thank you for the help you've given Stephanie and Eddie. And by the way, I have access to good pot that I got in Trenton. If *you're* ever interested."

When Jay Smith got arrested, he was found to be carrying the social security card of his daughter, Stephanie Hunsberger. And the police discovered that somebody had been forging the name of Edward Hunsberger and Stephanie on several welfare checks that had been sent to the Smith home for six months *after* the young couple was last seen. The cops didn't bother trying to prove forgery against Jay Smith because there were enough charges to investigate, but they were really starting to wonder about the Hunsbergers' disappearance.

The detectives had a theory about the night of his arrest. The local owner of a large supermarket chain owned a van exactly like the one Jay Smith was peeking into. The police wondered if the school principal had been plotting a kidnap.

More than one cop expressed exactly the same sentiment as they tried to piece together a profile of the elusive and mysterious principal of Upper Merion. "For a long time," a cop said, "that guy was a loose cannon, careening all *over* the place."

Shortly after his arrest, while he was in the Chester County Farms Prison trying to arrange bail, he received a letter of sympathy and support from a colleague. And that colleague received a speedy reply from the beleaguered educator. The reply was written in August, 1978, and mailed from the prison farm. The letter from Jay Smith to William Bradfield began:

> Dear Bill,
> Please cut out the Dr. Smith stuff. Jay or Jack is what friends call me. I prefer "Jack." I count you as a friend. . . .

In that letter Jay Smith asked for three books: *Moby Dick, Ivanhoe* and Warriner's *Grammar*. He said that he intended to begin teaching other prisoners if he couldn't get a bail reduction to gain his freedom.

And while Bill Bradfield and Jay Smith were busy writing letters, Susan Reinert was busy writing a letter *about* him. It was sent to her therapist and was dated September 3rd.

> Dear Ros,
> Our former principal, Dr. Smith, has been arrested on robbery charges. The papers have been full of bizarre stories so I'm sure the opening of school will be "interesting." I always thought he was strange but not criminal.
> I have seen Bill. Nothing much different. I still love him. He now says he loves me but there are no more plans for our seeing each other than there have ever been. I have gotten a little more interested in dating others again. Will see what happens.
>
> Love,
> Susan

The diary notes of Susan Reinert indicate that she was groping for new determination to change the direction of her hopeless affair with William Bradfield.

In a sad piece of self-analysis she wrote: "Rejection, low self-worth, constant battle. He would rather live with someone who wants to kill me than to live with me."

◆◆◆

By the time school opened, the police noted that all of the crimes for which Jay Smith was charged had occurred on Saturdays when an educator is free. Then they discovered from Dorothy Hunsberger that she had last seen her son Eddie and Jay Smith's daughter Stephanie on a *Saturday* in February. And it didn't take long for local journalists to discover that when Edward and Stephanie Hunsberger had disappeared, all of their possessions were left behind in the Jay Smith home. They had vanished from the earth with only the clothes on their backs.

Naturally, it didn't take long for a reporter to write: "Dr. Smith or Mr. Hyde?"

◆◆◆

Vince Valaitis was sorry that Bill Bradfield just wasn't around much in the fall of 1978. And when he was, he seemed to have lost much of his need for Vince's humor. Some of it Vince attributed to the failing shop in Montgomery Mall.

Vince and Sue spent lots of time discussing their merchandise, wondering if they should expand into other facets of arts and craft, since the jewelry and pottery and wall hangings weren't moving at all. There were times when, during his shift at the store, Vince Valaitis would take in only five or ten dollars. Yet Bill Bradfield claimed that the store could not be abandoned as a failure. And to all of little faith, he said there *might* be a possibility of opening yet *another* store in Philadelphia, and a *third* in Exton Mall. Far from giving up, Bill Bradfield believed that they might one day control franchise rights for southeastern Pennsylvania.

The corporation treasurer Vince Valaitis and the corporation secretary Sue Myers would nod their heads and agree with the corporation president, and Sue Myers would whisper privately that if Bill Bradfield's father had operated Western Electric like this, Pennsylvania would still be reading by candlelight.

Sue rued the day she'd ever helped hatch this get-rich scheme. She hoped that Bill Bradfield would decide to compete with his old man in some other way. And Vince, she figured, better resign himself to the fact that his 5 percent of the business would turn out to be one clay pot and a beaded headband.

Vince was still drawing a manager's salary so he had no complaints. What Vince missed were the good old times when his friends would invite him up to dinner and he'd have a great meal and go home supremely content from an evening of interesting stimulating talk.

Once when Sue Myers had gone to bed, Bill Bradfield took Vince into his confidence and admitted that in the past he'd been guilty of "womanizing."

Bill Bradfield implied that he would probably remain celibate to the end of his life, and that the absence of sexual pressure was perhaps the best part of his relationship with Sue Myers. He told Vince that the only true love he'd ever experienced had never been sullied. It involved a girl in Annapolis, who, in *this* version, did not do her dying like Ali MacGraw in *Love Story*. This one kicked the bucket in grand style like Merle Oberon in *Wuthering Heights*. He'd been there at her bedside when she passed on to a better world.

From the very beginning of the 1978 fall term, Bill Bradfield was on the move. Sue Myers had to take time off from school to devote herself to the failing store and was so exhausted she hardly had strength to interrogate him when he'd stay out all night. He looked so tired and his beard was so long and ragged that students said you could toss popcorn at him and it'd stick.

Gone were the days when Vince would watch the man he considered the most brilliant and best-educated teacher he'd ever known playing cutesy-pie with Sue Myers. When Bill Bradfield would try to charm her with his imaginary ostrich named "Elliot Emu."

He would trot out his feathered pal and in his Elliot Emu voice say, "Are you mad at me?"

And she'd giggle and say, "No, I'm not mad at you. How could I be mad at Elliot Emu!"

When he *was* home, Bill Bradfield would spend an entire evening doing what he liked best, watching television shows like *Laverne & Shirley* or *Mork & Mindy*. Like Sue Myers, Vince Valaitis had never seen Bill Bradfield reading even one of his five thousand books.

Vince was aware of teachers at Upper Merion who took every opportunity to say that, far from being Upper Merion's intellectual leader, Bill Bradfield was a fraud. One English teacher, a relative of writer Lionel Trilling, frequently ridiculed him and called him "Busy Whiskers." Another, a former military man like Jay Smith, openly resented the entire independent study program ramrodded by Bill Bradfield and referred to him as "a bearded despot with a good two-line opening on any subject, but nothing more."

This teacher complained of what was being done in Bill Bradfield's independent study program, and claimed that high grades were automatic while disciplinary matters were ignored.

Still another English teacher, whose husband did in fact know something about Eastern religions, became interested in hearing Bill Bradfield at a party discussing the impact of Confucius on all of Eastern and Western religion.

So the husband put aside his martini and Swedish meatballs and posed a few complex and scholarly questions to Bill Bradfield who instantly looked about as relaxed as a safecracker.

Bill Bradfield stopped talking and scuttled away as if he'd found a maggot in his meatball.

From then on that teacher's husband was of the opinion that Bill Bradfield's Confucian epigrams came from the Hong Kong Noodle Company, and Bill Bradfield avoided that man like a vampire avoids sunburn.

Vince Valaitis knew about those dissenters, but he did not, *could* not believe that Bill Bradfield was anything less than a brilliant, splendidly educated teaching professional. He longed for the conversations, but nowadays his friend was as busy as a piranha.

In October, he told Vince and Sue Myers that he had to make an urgent trip to Annapolis because during the summer Chris Pappas had damaged a sailboat they'd hired. The boat owner was demanding that he personally see to the repair of the mast. The damage took place during a storm, he said, when he and Chris were sailing with "friends," who of course were Shelly and her pal.

He said that he'd also discovered that their mutual Annapolis friend Rachel had a blue Volkswagen Beetle for sale and he thought he ought to buy it.

He knew very well that Sue Myers was busier than a Gulag gravedigger and could not accompany him on a weekend to Annapolis.

After he'd gone, Sue told Vince that she believed he was going there to be with Rachel.

Vince tried to assure her that she was wrong to fear the ice maiden.

"Bill has *no* romantic interest in anyone," he said. And then diplomatically added what he knew to be false: "except *you.*"

And true to her fashion, Sue nodded wearily and showed no emotion of any kind, keeping it all bottled and buried.

But she said to the young teacher, "You don't know the half of it. I'm in a lot better position to understand Bill Bradfield and I tell you that he and that woman Rachel are strangely compatible. I think there's a relationship developing with *this* one and I don't know what it means."

••••

As to Susan Reinert, well, it appeared that she was through being emotionally manhandled. When Bill Bradfield didn't keep a dinner date at her home, Susan Reinert showed up at Upper Merion the next day with a plastic bag full of leftovers and instructed a student to deliver it to Mr. Bradfield with a message saying, "This is the dinner you *failed* to get last night."

Vince got wind of it and decided to become a peacekeeper since things around Upper Merion were straightening themselves out under Jay Smith's replacement, and intradepartment feuds weren't needed. He took Susan Reinert aside at school and tried to inform her that Bill Bradfield might merely be signaling his desire to withdraw from his role as adviser to the world of Upper Merion, and that their friend had outside business worries with the art store, and perhaps receiving a pile of leftovers could get on somebody's nerves.

Vince knew he had to be very careful when talking to Susan

Reinert. Once, he'd tried to help by quietly informing her that to think of Bill Bradfield in romantic terms was futile because, confidentially, Bill Bradfield *lived* with Sue Myers.

Vince got verbally slammed by the former wrestler for that one. Bill Bradfield told him he had a big mouth and he was giving Susan Reinert information about his private life that was none of her business, and *any* information would only encourage "that pathetic mousy woman" to sit next to him at faculty meetings. And that unless she was ignored she might *never* stop writing those notes with the disgusting sexual imagery that had caused Sue Myers to pop her cork in the first place.

Still, Vince was a helpful and compassionate soul and eager to please everyone, *especially* Bill Bradfield, and he had it in his head that he should gently admonish Susan Reinert about having students deliver bags of garbage to a guy she was deluded into thinking cared for her romantically.

He was in the process of trying to explain all this when she said to him, "Vince, I understand how close you are to Bill and to Sue Myers, but I need to know, will you *remain* my friend?"

And the young teacher answered, "Of course. Why wouldn't I?"

"Because Sue *hates* me so much."

"She doesn't hate you. That's just not so," he said.

"She means to see that I'm harmed," Susan Reinert said, and the tiny woman showed some real fear behind those oversized glasses.

"That's silly," Vince said. "Just plain silly."

"And she means harm to my *children*!" Susan Reinert said. "And I have that on the best of authority."

What could Vince Valaitis do about *that* announcement? Now he was convinced that Bill Bradfield was not exaggerating when he said that Susan Reinert was more than neurotic, that she was absolutely crazy these days, and that Vince simply should avoid her.

As usual, Bill Bradfield found out about Vince's good intentions and the next time they were alone Vince got it again. And by now, Vince was really worried about his friend because Bill Bradfield was so intense that when he did come home he'd treat an episode of *Love Boat* like a bomb squad documentary as he lay motionless before the tube.

Bill Bradfield flatly *ordered* Vince Valaitis to stay completely away from the "demented" woman. And to underscore the depths to which Susan Reinert had sunk, not just psychologically but morally, Bill Bradfield offered the young teacher and Sue Myers a most shocking and irresistible piece of news from an "unimpeachable source."

Susan Reinert, he told them, was secretly dating none other than old Mr. Hyde himself.

"Jay Smith?" Vince Valaitis said. "I can't believe it!"

"I can believe it," Sue Myers smirked. She could always believe *anything* about her hated rival.

"It's absolutely true!" Bill Bradfield said. "And soon I'll be able to tell you how I know."

And as was his way, Bill Bradfield, when relating a story, no matter how incredible it seemed, always tossed in a little detail, like the alligator shoes.

"I can tell you this," Bill Bradfield said. "They even have pet names for each other. Jay Smith calls her Tweetie Bird. Can you imagine? *Tweetie Bird?*"

And while Sue Myers rolled her eyes in revulsion, Vince Valaitis gaped in wonder.

How *could* she do it? There were all sorts of rumors about Jay Smith's daughter's disappearance and that he'd done drugs with her, and rumors of incest, even that he had a mail order business selling penis stiffeners. To Vince Valaitis Jay Smith was evil incarnate.

The young teacher wondered if he'd *ever* understand the intricacies of sexual attraction. Tweetie Bird. Why, it was almost as revolting as Elliot Emu.

8

Death and Dream

In the fall of 1978 William Bradfield was about as placid as a riptide, and the riptide formed an enveloping whirlpool. It all began with a death and a dream.

The death was that of Susan Reinert's widowed mother who passed away unexpectedly in October, leaving each of her children $34,000 in cash and half an interest in western Pennsylvania timberland. Susan was also bequeathed her mother's wedding ring valued at $1,500.

Her brother Pat Gallagher became executor of Susan's estate and her children Karen and Michael were named as her beneficiaries. The timberland was left to appreciate, but for the moment, Susan Reinert had more cash than she'd ever had to manage before.

The dream involved Bill Bradfield, who awakened one morning sounding like Martin Luther King. He announced: "I had a dream!"

And poor overworked Sue Myers wondered if it was a wet one because they hadn't had sex for well over a year.

"What dream?" she asked.

"It came to me in a dream," he told her. "It's about Doctor Smith. He's innocent of the Sears robbery! I've been thinking about it and now I'm certain. He couldn't have committed the theft because he was with me that very day last August. I saw him on that Saturday at the shore in Ocean City. So if he didn't do *that* robbery, he could hardly be guilty of the other one since both crimes obviously involved the same man!"

"You never mentioned seeing him in Ocean City," Sue Myers said.

"It didn't seem important at the time. Now I'm sure of it. I don't know what to do about it, though. I need to think it over."

And then he was dressed and out the door and Sue Myers went off to work and figured she probably wouldn't see him for another couple of days what with this new crusade to save Jay Smith.

Bill Bradfield now became even busier and more elusive. And he began having *nightmares*. On the nights that he was at home he frequently awakened her by crying out in his sleep. Sometimes he wept without waking. She thought he was going crazy.

Even Bill Bradfield's beard had gone wild and tangled and shapeless. He truly began to resemble the man his faculty detractors had always compared him to. Bill Bradfield was so tormented and tense and exhausted he looked like Grigori Rasputin underwater.

Finally he let Vince in on the greatest secret yet: that he alone had the power to free Jay C. Smith.

Bill Bradfield, driving his father's Cadillac, was taking Vince home from the art store after they'd built some Christmas displays to stimulate business.

Bill Bradfield affected his I-know-the-secret-of-the-Bermuda-Triangle voice and said, "I've learned something and I don't know *what* to do about it."

"What?"

"About Doctor Smith. He's a hit man for the Mafia."

"Bill," Vince Valaitis said. "Bill, that is *the* nuttiest . . ."

"Listen to me," Bill Bradfield said. "I tell you it's true! He's killed people. Lots of people. And that's not all. He's going to kill others. People we know."

"People we know. Sure."

"People like Susan Reinert."

"Susan Reinert! Doctor Smith is going to *kill* Susan Reinert? And I suppose he told you why."

"He says she knows too much about his trash."

"What trash?"

"The trash at school. You know the rumors about the disappearance of his daughter and Eddie Hunsberger. Vince, he's been . . . well, I think he's chopped up some bodies and put them in the trash cans around school!"

"It's insane," Vince said, as calmly as possible.

"Is it? What do you think he was doing with the nitric acid he stole from the school? And how about those homemade silencers the police found? You know Doctor Smith well enough, don't you? *You* named him the prince of darkness."

"He makes things up, Bill," Vince said reasonably. "Jay Smith always tries to shock."

"He's been having an affair with her, Vince. He told me all about it."

And Vince Valaitis now had a dozen images ricocheting in his skull: of Norman the janitor sniffing at those unspeakable bundles in the school Dumpster, and of Jay Smith himself, standing in a cloud of steam from a broken pipe, calling "Tweeeeetie Bird!" in a ghostly voice. Vince made a concession. "Well, maybe *part* of it could be true."

"We can't go to the police, Vince. You have to swear to keep this a secret."

"But we've *got* to go to the police!" Vince Valaitis cried.

"We have no proof," Bill Bradfield informed him. "Not a shred of proof. They'd laugh at us. They wouldn't believe us. And then we'd be in grave danger."

"We," Vince said. *"We?"*

"The man's diabolical. He'd come for us. He'd come in the *night.* He'd come for our parents. Or his Mafia friends would. He'd be relentless."

And by now it was a good thing Vince was *not* driving because he had one hand on his rosary and the other on his scapular. This was no monster movie. This wasn't something from Hitchcock or Rod Serling. For the first time in his life he wasn't shivery in a fun sort of way at talk of the macabre. This was *real.* For the first time in his life young Vince Valaitis was face to face with Dread and Terror.

"What are we . . . *you* going to do, Bill?"

"I think I can control him," Bill Bradfield said. "He's rather demented but not completely insane. I think I can convince him not to harm anyone. Then when I get sufficient evidence I can go to the authorities."

"Oh my," Vince Valaitis said. "Oh my, oh my, oh my."

"There're *others* in danger."

"What others?"

"He's so paranoid he wants revenge on everyone who's wronged him. People who didn't support him when he got arrested for the crimes he says he didn't do. He's talked about killing Bill Scutta."

"My God, Bill's a dear friend!" Vince cried. "We've *got* to do something!"

"And the superintendent. And a local policeman that he says is trying to frame him, and . . ."

Vince didn't *have* to ask the next question because his eyeballs were pressing up against the lenses of his eyeglasses and he was so cotton-mouthed he looked like a cat eating bubble gum, and Bill Bradfield anticipated the Big Question and said, "No, he didn't mention *you*."

"Oh my," Vince said.

"Yet."

"Oh *my!*"

Vince Valaitis didn't believe it *all*, but one thing for sure, he was convinced that if he was to breathe a word of this he might very well end up scattered around King of Prussia in enough pieces to offend *lots* of custodians like Norman the janitor.

••••

When Bill Bradfield told Sue Myers about his clandestine meeting with Dr. Jay Smith, the educator's motives for murder had changed some.

When she asked why Jay Smith would want to kill Susan Reinert he told her that he didn't know why, but offered the same warning about not telling the police.

"I can handle Doctor Smith for the time being," he said to her. "You've wondered who I've been seeing these past weeks. You probably thought I was being unfaithful all those nights that I've been away. Well, now you know. I've been with Doctor Smith."

"I don't like this," she said.

"Trust me," he urged her. "Just once more. Be *obedient.*"

••••

Sue Myers was *tired.* The jobs of teaching and retailing and hearing about Jay Smith were way too much for her. But as far as Jay Smith was concerned, there was at least a silver lining. Since Bill Bradfield was gone four or five nights a week and often slept away from home, it was better to imagine him humoring a madman like the former principal than it was to think of him in bed with Susan Reinert, or Rachel, or somebody new.

Sue Myers wanted out of all this, but knew she hadn't the will or the strength. Sue Myers felt fossilized. Where Bill Bradfield would eventually lead her she couldn't say, but she'd been tagging along for fifteen years and knew she'd have to follow a while longer.

Sue also had an uneasy feeling that she might be asked to contribute a little something to the alibi defense of the accused. And she was.

It happened after a meeting that Bill Bradfield said he'd attended with Jay Smith's brother and his lawyer. Bill Bradfield wanted Sue to remember that he had once encouraged their friend and teaching colleague Fred Wattenmaker to make a bet with another teacher, who claimed Bill Bradfield would never make good on a promise to visit Fred at his summer home in Ocean City, New Jersey.

Sue vaguely remembered the bet. Then Bill Bradfield asked her if she remembered that he had in fact made an August visit to the shore, but that Fred wasn't home. And she said yes, she remembered his saying that.

And then he reminded her that the visit had been on a Saturday, hadn't it? And she said yes, it had probably been on a weekend.

But when he asked her if she remembered that it had been the weekend just prior to a Labor Day sale that she'd scheduled at the store, she said no, she was certain it had been the Saturday *before* that one.

He dropped it and never asked what *else* she might remember.

◆◆◆◆

Sue Myers had been given the job of locating the three books requested by Jay Smith at the prison farm. But with the help of relatives, he'd put up bail and became a free man long before she'd managed to get the books he'd wanted.

One evening, Bill Bradfield informed her that they were going to the home of Dr. Smith on Valley Forge Road in King of Prussia to deliver the books personally, even though Jay Smith no longer needed them. That didn't thrill her, and she didn't get out of the car when Bill Bradfield presented himself at the door of Jay Smith, books in hand. Sue Myers was very happy that her former principal didn't come out to the car to say hello.

While they were driving home, Bill Bradfield said, "Damn, I think Doctor Smith's innocent. I can't believe the things he's being accused of. I think he needs good legal help and lots of advice."

But regardless of what Bill Bradfield thought about Jay Smith's innocence, Sue believed that Bill Bradfield had better not seek *this* advisory position. *Nobody* was going to control Dr. Jay C. Smith.

◆◆◆◆

Whatever Jay Smith was doing in the fall of 1978 wasn't being shared with a coterie of friends. He was no Bill Bradfield. His wife was living at home when not in the hospital, yet she hardly saw him. If he and Bill Bradfield were spending all those evenings together, there were no witnesses.

Stephanie Smith was still writing her own little diary entries about her two-timing husband, which may have helped take her mind off her cancer. She was preoccupied with the woman he'd been seeing for some time.

Stephanie Smith wrote in her diary, "All women like to hear that love bit. After he uses her he'll tell her to go fuck herself and he'll find another sweet woman to get what he wants from her. I'm jealous!"

Jay Smith seemed desperate to get his wife out of his house for good. He made a strange request of his former secretary.

It had been a bad year for Ida Micucci. Her husband had died, and she had broken her hip and was at home trying to cope with it all when she received a telephone call from Jay Smith that had to be as crazy as any communication she'd ever received when he was still her boss.

Jay Smith merely said, "Ida, I'm apologizing for not calling you when your husband died, but would you do me a favor and let Stephanie *live* with you?"

Just like that.

She replied no, she didn't think she wanted any roommates at this time.

And he thanked her politely and hung up.

9

Magnet

There was always a lot of talk about the "magnetic" personality of William Bradfield, or the "magnetic field" around the man. Well, in the fall of 1978 those magnetic filings—his chums and protégés and secret lovers—weren't all lining up according to positive and negative influences.

Susan Reinert was doing something that no woman had *ever* done to Bill Bradfield. She was giving ultimatums. It could have been that she felt more independent now that she had a modest inheritance. It could have been that, as she reported to her therapist, she'd finally had "more than enough."

According to Roslyn Weinberger, when Susan gave Bill Bradfield an ultimatum he got very angry. Then he calmed down and pointed out that if he walked out on Sue Myers it might prove fatal.

"She's hysterical, unstable, and God only knows what she might do," he argued.

But this time Susan Reinert wasn't buying. She said, "Sorry, that won't work. Not anymore."

And she told the psychologist that now she was able to withstand the litany of excuses, rationalizations and arguments that in the past had always confused her and resulted in an agreement to be patient and let one of his schemes cook a bit longer.

This time she said, "No way. Good-bye, then."

And she *meant* it. And he *knew* it.

He humbly suggested that if he could have just a *little* more time he might "ease Vince Valaitis into a relationship with Sue Myers," thereby allowing for less trauma when he left home.

She managed a little derisive laughter over this one since it would be about as probable as "easing" Jay Smith into holy orders. And at last it appeared that Bill Bradfield was going to cave in. He told her that he was indeed moving out of Sue's apartment and into his parents' home as a show of good faith. He outlined some major plans, and for the remainder of the school year, he said, he would simply have to extricate himself from his financial arrangements with Sue Myers and make ready for a new life.

Susan Reinert told Roslyn Weinberger and Pat Schnure the hot news that could not be announced until Sue Myers was completely out of the picture: she was marrying Bill Bradfield in the coming summer of 1979.

Susan Reinert's old friend Sharon Lee got married in December and Susan Reinert went to the wedding. The wedding was at Sharon's parents' house near the shore. The weather wasn't very cold and the morning after her wedding Sharon and Susan took a stroll along the beach. Susan Reinert told her friend that she and Bill Bradfield were being married in the coming summer, and that they intended to take her children to England with them.

The secret had to be kept from the children, Susan said, because she didn't want to put them in the position of having to lie to their father. She feared that her ex-husband Ken might suspect that they were going to *live* in Europe and try to stop her from taking the kids. Susan Reinert had picked up some *very* secret ways.

••••

Sue Myers suddenly found herself in need of an attorney. In one of his more bizarre moments Bill Bradfield told her that he was going to present her with a "cohabitation agreement" that she must sign and that she should "trust" him. And now Sue tried to decipher the scheme *behind* the scheme.

Having lived with Bill Bradfield for five years and having been his lover for fifteen, she immediately started thinking about the famous palimony case in California involving actor Lee Marvin. The theory behind the cohabitation agreement was that if two people parted by mutual consent, with a full disclosure of each partner's assets, the agreement couldn't be overturned at a later time should one party have a change of heart and want a bigger share.

Why did Bill Bradfield and she suddenly need *this* in their life? she asked.

Well, it seemed that he feared that Susan Reinert had gone and named *him* as beneficiary on a small insurance policy, and if Jay Smith were *actually* to kill her, Bill Bradfield might become the subject of enormous scandal because of that silly insurance policy.

"I want to protect *you* from scandal," he told Sue Myers.

"And how will signing an agreement protect *me*?" she wanted to know.

Because, he said, he might be drawn into a sticky civil lawsuit involving the Reinert heirs, and Sue Myers as his live-in companion might be subject to a piece of the liability as though she were his wife. This way, she'd escape the whole mess, attorney fees and all.

"And *would* you stand to inherit insurance money?" Sue Myers asked Bill Bradfield. "If something happened to Susan Reinert?"

"Out of the question," he said. "I've simply got to convince that neurotic that gestures like this are futile. She'll go to any lengths to draw me into her snare. I simply *despise* the woman."

And *that*, Sue Myers believed utterly. She was convinced that he truly despised Susan Reinert. And she would never change that opinion. So Sue Myers made herself an appointment with an attorney and never told Bill Bradfield about it. The lawyer told her that the whole thing sounded absurd and that she should not be talked into signing such an agreement under any circumstances.

When she talked to an outsider about such things, they all *did* seem insane. She wondered if she needed a psychiatrist rather than a lawyer.

Bill Bradfield also told her to get out of town for Thanksgiving because Jay Smith often "killed on holidays," and he might be unable to control the former principal. Sue Myers started to object, but thought it less stressful to humor him. Sue Myers was beginning to feel that she was watching this on television. She couldn't walk away without seeing how it would end.

In one of her many search-and-explore missions, Sue found what she called his "jogging diary." Bill Bradfield, the world's foremost keeper of notes, enjoyed jotting down his ideas and brainstorms when he returned from his morning jog. He probably thought that at least these were safe from prying eyes. But she was able to get a fast peek at the jogging diary one morning when he was in the shower.

His diary entry confirmed to her that maybe for once he *was* telling the truth, and that even if he'd been sleeping with Susan Reinert in the past, he was now simply trying to elude her clutches.

The entry read: "I'd like to kill Susan Reinert."

If Sue Myers feared that Bill Bradfield might be seeing Susan Reinert on Thanksgiving weekend, she needn't have. At a later time she learned that he'd traveled to Boston over that holiday. And, as it turned out, she had someone else to worry about. Bill Bradfield was visiting Rachel who had left Annapolis and moved on to Harvard for graduate study.

After the Thanksgiving weekend had ended and Jay Smith had not knocked off Susan Reinert or anyone else, Bill Bradfield took credit for keeping Jay Smith "under control." The word "control" surfaced frequently in conversations with Bill Bradfield.

Sue Myers began seeing a sex therapist in Bryn Mawr to learn if she could ever hope to experience sexual desire again—assuming that she survived whatever was to happen, his mental breakdown or hers.

She wondered if there *could* be sex after William Bradfield.

♦♦♦♦

During December, Susan Reinert contacted the USAA insurance company and tried very hard to secure a life insurance for half a million dollars, naming a "friend" as beneficiary. The name of the friend was William S. Bradfield, Jr.

The insurance company denied her application on the grounds that such a large policy would overinsure her life.

During the same week Susan Reinert wrote a letter to the man that Bill Bradfield claimed was trying to murder her for walking out on a clandestine affair. It was a straightforward business letter:

Dear Dr. Smith:

I am applying for an exchange teaching position in England under the Fulbright-Hays program for 1979–80 and could use a letter of reference from you.

I hope you are doing all right, especially considering your present circumstances. If I can be of any aid, please let me know.

Jay Smith responded immediately:

Susan,

I have some familiarity with the Fulbright programs and would be happy to fill out a reference for you. While teaching at Rider College in Lawrenceville, New Jersey, last year, I was on a review committee re Fulbrights.

Send whatever data you have and I will write a reference geared toward the requirements.

Hope you and your children are in good health.

Jay Smith

And that was all. It was a letter from one colleague to another. He didn't even call her Tweetie Bird.

••••

Bill Bradfield held a critical meeting with Vince Valaitis at school. It was so intense it was subdued. Bill Bradfield's soft husky voice could hardly be heard at times.

"I need to tell you something. I need advice," he said.

"I'm listening."

Bill Bradfield took a date book from his pocket and thumbed through the pages. "I'm troubled," he said. "I don't know what to do. You see, I was *with* Doctor Smith at the shore on Saturday, August twenty-seventh, of last year."

"I don't see what . . ."

"That's when the Sears store in St. Davids got robbed. So Doctor Smith's been truthful all along. It *was* a case of mistaken identity. So it was probably the lookalike, whoever he is, who did the *other* one too!"

And Vince started pondering because in the newspaper they

said that the police found all kinds of evidence like security guards' uniforms and badges and I.D. cards and guns.

"But maybe he *did* do the other robbery. After all there was other evidence."

"I'm only concerned with the St. Davids case," Bill Bradfield said. "Whatever else he did or didn't do isn't my business. All I know is he didn't do *that* one."

"What about the stuff the police found in the house? What about all that?"

"It's very possible he's telling the truth that Edward and Stephanie Hunsberger are not only responsible for all the contraband, but the robberies too. They may've had a partner who resembled Doctor Smith."

It didn't take a lawyer to conclude that if Jay Smith could show he didn't do the first one, he'd have a very good chance of beating the second case, and if the evidence in the basement could be suppressed due to search and seizure laws, Jay Smith might get his life back to abnormal, free once more to save children from homosexuality and prove to the American Kennel Club that it owed a debt to America's women.

Vince Valaitis got confused thinking about it. All he could say was "I don't know, Bill. I've never encountered anything like this."

"Of course not," Bill Bradfield said. "Nor have I. But damn it, I have an obligation as a citizen to come forward when I can save an innocent man who's being harassed by the police. They're twisting the evidence and forcing witnesses to identify the wrong man!"

"Jay C. Smith is . . ."

"Innocent of this. Whatever *else* he is. He's innocent of this crime, Vince. And I fear it's my duty to help him no matter what I feel about the man personally."

••••

Chris Pappas hardly knew Susan Reinert other than to say hello when he was substituting for regular teachers at Upper Merion. Of course, there had been those telephone calls from her last summer when she'd called Bill Bradfield at St. John's. And he'd guessed that Bill Bradfield had gone to Baltimore to see

Susan after one of those telephone calls, but Chris accepted Bill Bradfield's explanation that she was simply a pitiful friend and that he wanted out of his advisory role.

In that he hardly knew her, Chris wasn't as shocked as Vince Valaitis to hear from Bill Bradfield that she was the secret lover of Jay Smith, and that Jay Smith was very angry that she'd jilted him and wanted *revenge*.

It was a lot more shocking to hear that Jay Smith was a "screened hit man" for the Mafia—which meant that he was screened off from knowing who the contractor really was and vice versa. Bill Bradfield told Chris that ads were taken in the classified section to let a killer know all he needed to know, and that was how Jay Smith did business. Jay Smith had told Bill Bradfield about a vendetta against several of the people involved in his legal problems, and against school officials as well.

Now Chris Pappas was warned that he must *not* go to the police or Bill Bradfield was a dead man. And besides there wasn't a shred of evidence.

While Chris spent a few days digesting the news that Jay Smith was a Mafia hit man and wondered why his friend had *ever* offered to be Jay Smith's character witness, Bill Bradfield came to him with an even more bewildering secret. He'd had a dream and worked out a date in 1977 and now he wasn't just a potential character witness, he was an *alibi* witness. Jay Smith had been with him in Ocean City on the very day that the Sears store was victimized.

It was put to the introspective, insecure, worrisome, thoughtful young fellow almost like a philosophical proposition. What would he do if he knew that a truly wicked man was innocent in a specific instance of a wicked crime even though he was by his own admission guilty of scores of *more* wicked crimes? Did Bill Bradfield have a duty to the rule of law, or would society be served better by letting Jay Smith get wrongly convicted?

Chris worked on it for a while, but it was clear to him that Bill Bradfield had the distasteful duty of stepping forward and protecting the integrity of the system. He had no choice but to be an alibi witness for Jay Smith.

Bill Bradfield reluctantly agreed.

◆◆◆◆

English teacher Fred Wattenmaker thought a lot of his colleague Susan Reinert. He once described her as "sensitive, sincere and caring." He thought she was a wonderful mother.

He got to know her children when she chaperoned some students on a Puerto Rican field trip supervised by Fred Wattenmaker. He told people that Karen and Michael were the type of children he would want if he ever had his own. During the past spring, Susan and her children had visited Fred Wattenmaker at his vacation home in Ocean City. A few weeks later, Bill Bradfield and Sue Myers also accepted an invitation and stayed for a few days. It was the only time that Bill Bradfield had been there except for a day in August, 1977, when Fred Wattenmaker found a note on his door saying, "Tell McKinley you won the bet. I was here but you weren't."

Fred Wattenmaker forgot all about that incident until the fall of 1978, after the entire school was overwhelmed by the arrest of Jay Smith and the scandal surrounding his secret life.

Fred Wattenmaker was surprised when Bill Bradfield approached him at school and said, "Believe me, Fred, I've questioned Doctor Smith for hours and hours and there's no way he did any of the things he's been accused of doing."

And Fred Wattenmaker didn't think too much about that odd little aside except that Bill Bradfield approached him again a month later and said, "I've covered everything with Jay Smith and he's innocent. I'm sure of it except that we can't *cover* the theft at the Sears store in St. Davids."

Fred Wattenmaker thought it was awfully decent of old Bill Bradfield to be trying to help his former principal, but he did seem to be getting rather obsessive about it.

And then in November, Bill Bradfield talked about it yet another time. He asked Fred Wattenmaker to step outside his classroom and he said, "You won't believe this, but I know where Doctor Smith was when he was supposed to have robbed Sears!"

"That's fantastic!" said Fred Wattenmaker. "And where was he?"

"We were visiting you in Ocean City!" Bill Bradfield announced. "Remember the note? Well, Doctor Smith was *with* me. It was the Saturday before Labor Day."

Fred Wattenmaker said, "But I was there with a house full of people over Labor Day weekend. You must've come a week earlier."

"I forget the date, but anyway, it coincides with the Sears theft."

"I'll look for the note," Fred offered. "That might help."

"That's not important," Bill Bradfield said. "There was no date on the note. It's *not* important."

••••

By the Christmas holidays another former student was privy to the worst-kept secret in Bill Bradfield's life: that Susan Reinert was the mistress of Jay Smith who was threatening to kill her because "she knows too much." This time he informed a former pupil of his who was presently a student at St. John's College on the New Mexico campus.

The young man was home for the holidays when Bill Bradfield told him. It was pretty much as it had been told to Vince Valaitis, Chris Pappas and Sue Myers, but there were variations.

This time Bill Bradfield said that Susan Reinert, if she wasn't killed by Jay Smith, would no doubt be done away with by somebody she picked up because "she frequents dangerous bars and dates black men."

"Sometimes," he told his former pupil, "she seems to have a death wish."

And Bill Bradfield added that though he was nothing more than a friend who'd tried to help with financial and emotional problems, she had, alas, gone bonkers over him and included him in her will naming him guardian of her children in the event of her death.

Bill Bradfield also mentioned that Susan Reinert had, in her pathetic attempts to ensnare him, made him *beneficiary* on some insurance policies.

The young man reacted as everyone else had upon hearing all the business about Jay Smith murdering Susan Reinert. He said that the police must be notified, and Bill Bradfield responded as he always had by saying, no, that wouldn't help at this time.

But Bill Bradfield assured the young man that he would do something. He said he *might* take Susan to England in the summer to "diffuse" the situation.

It all sounded as loony to the young guy as it did to everyone else, so, like everyone else, he decided not to tell Susan Reinert that a loose cannon out there named Jay C. Smith was threatening her life. Anyway, Bill Bradfield's secret seemed to have all the exclusivity of the Democratic National Convention.

••••

There was some strange business involving typewriters that added to the overall confusion of Sue Myers. In their apartment was a red IBM Selectric that Bill Bradfield had bought for her birthday back in 1975, during much happier times. The typewriter had cost $350 and when they went to pick it up in downtown Philly he made her close her eyes while he brought it to the car. That was back in a time when Elliot Emu was still alive. Now, old Elliot was nearly as dead as her libido.

In any case, the IBM was a perfectly good typewriter and they didn't need another. So she didn't know what to make of a machine that she found in their attic. It was there along with a tape recorder that she'd never seen before, and when she examined the typewriter she almost cried.

There was a foreign student at Upper Merion, a handicapped boy who had very little speech or motor control. He was twenty-one years old, but Sue always thought of him as a little child.

To say "Hi, Miss Myers" took him thirty seconds of enormous effort. Sue admired the lad enormously.

The school district supplied the student with a special typewriter mounted on a typing stand that he could manage. The machine typed extra-large letters of one size. When the lad's parents thought he needed more individual attention he was transferred across the hall to the class of Bill Bradfield, along with his machine.

The boy had a great sense of humor and there wasn't a kid at Upper Merion who was ever less than kind to him. He did everything he was told to do and did it about as well as he could, which was about first-grade level. The teachers gave him straight A's and because of his straight A's he would always be at the aca-

demic awards banquets and would always receive a standing ova-
tion.

A terrible thing had happened after the last spring term. The
typewriter had been stolen from school. There was no mistaking
the machine Sue found in the attic, and she speculated that the
tape recorder also belonged to Upper Merion.

She was as furious as she could get, and confronted Bill Bradfield who at first seemed a bit vague. But then he said that he'd
bought the typewriter from Jay Smith for $75, and was going to
give it to her as a Christmas present to type little merchandise
signs for the art store. He said that he didn't know the machines
were stolen.

Sue Myers said the typewriter had been bought by the school
for the handicapped boy and that Bill Bradfield knew it and this
was too much and he must be absolutely insane to be buying stolen machines from Jay Smith. And then Sue Myers demanded
that Bill Bradfield take the typewriter back to the school.

"They'll think I stole it," he said.

"*Sneak* it back in the school," she said, and then she started
crying.

From that day on, she was absolutely certain that Bill Bradfield
was meeting with Jay Smith. The typewriter proved it. Soon the
machines disappeared from the attic, and Bill Bradfield swore
he'd returned them, but the special stand for the typewriter was
later found by Vince Valaitis in the basement.

Sue didn't know why in the name of heaven Bill wanted *another*
typewriter in the first place. She thought a whole lot about mental illness in those days.

♦♦♦♦

Bill Bradfield suddenly wanted to get out of town during the
Christmas holidays, the precise time at which he felt Jay Smith
went around massacring half the population.

To Sue Myers it made about as much sense as everything else
he said. She didn't question it much. She was just glad to be away
from school and the art store and the cold damp weather. She
looked forward to heading south. She might even get a suntan.

Vince Valaitis, who was also asked to go along on the trip to
Florida, thought that his friend had just about reached his limit

because of what was happening with Jay Smith. He was pleased to tag along.

They rented a camper from another teacher and hit the road. But if Sue Myers thought she was going to spend a Christmas vacation without hearing about Jay Smith she was dead wrong.

They weren't five miles out of Philadelphia before Bill Bradfield said, "If Doctor Smith's true to form and kills on holidays, there's nothing I can do about it if I'm in another state, right?"

"You've done all you can do," Vince Valaitis reassured him, while Sue Myers might as well have been stone deaf.

And that was about the best way to deal with it. At the mention of Jay Smith or Susan Reinert, she would let the hum of the engine obliterate human speech. In self-defense she'd make herself immune to voices.

Vince Valaitis was still partly ascribing the talk of murder to a symptom of Jay Smith's mental disorder. He continued to reassure Bill Bradfield that Jay Smith loved to shock people, and that Bill should try to forget about it, at least during the holidays.

But Bill Bradfield started telling some things that Vince hadn't heard. For example, he said that Jay Smith claimed to have "hit" *more* than a few people.

And when Vince asked how many, Bill Bradfield without blinking those brooding blue eyes said, "Two hundred and fifty."

That did it. Vince Valaitis hoped there'd be lots of room in the funny place for Jay Smith *and* Bill Bradfield. Maybe they could go to St. Elizabeth's together and share Ezra Pound's old padded cell.

Whether or not Jay Smith had killed his own daughter and son-in-law, it seemed obvious to Vince that the only guy with two hundred personal hits was Count Dracula.

The more outrageous claims that Jay Smith made (always according to Bill Bradfield) the more Vince was discouraged from telling Susan Reinert or police authorities for fear of looking silly.

••••

The itinerary included Charleston, Atlanta, Orlando, St. Augustine. They got as far as Charleston when the specter of Jay Smith once again hopped aboard the camper. They had gone to a store to buy a sleeping bag when Vince called Bill Bradfield's attention to the gun display, and *that* brought up maybe having to *shoot* Jay Smith, and the next thing Sue knew Bill Bradfield decided he had to buy a handgun.

Sue got furious at Vince and at Bill Bradfield and at Jay Smith and at Susan Reinert and at Bill Bradfield's parents for buying him that toy truck, because as far as she was concerned all this was mostly an attempt to get the new piano his sister got and the attention that went with it instead of that lousy stinking goddamn toy truck!

Bill Bradfield bought something else in Atlanta without specifying why. He bought a pair of gloves.

••••

In a St. Augustine hardware store he made another try at buying a .22 handgun, but he was told he had to be a Florida resident and got turned down. Pretty soon Vince was informed that a gun might not do much good anyway if it came to a showdown with the prince of darkness. Due to his years of army training, Jay Smith could kill with *any* ordinary household utensil, according to Bill Bradfield.

Despite himself, Vince started to believe again. He envisioned nightmare chases by a potato peeler and a curling iron.

Vince Valaitis went to mass in Orlando and Bill Bradfield accompanied him. When they got to St. Augustine, Vince went to mass again. Bill Bradfield went to a Quaker meeting *and* to the Catholic mass. Sue said that that made him a Quack-lik.

While in a Catholic church with Vince, Bill Bradfield lit a candle and said, "I pray that no evil will befall Susan Reinert."

That sort of talk terrified Vince Valaitis, because when you started bringing the Church into this business it had to be true or else sacrilegious. And the fear of God was by far the dominant fear in his life.

Vince and Bill Bradfield had occasion to stay up one night talking. Just when Vince thought he'd heard every possible bit of Jay Smith gossip, Bill Bradfield, with his secret-sharer voice, said, "Vince, Jay Smith told me something *else*. I can't vouch for its authenticity. I can only repeat what the man said. Jay Smith knows how Jimmy Hoffa was killed. He was chopped into pieces and dissolved in *acid*."

And Vince saw in his mind's eye several big bottles of nitric acid that Jay Smith had stolen from Upper Merion. And if you took *parts* of Jay Smith's lunatic talk and joined it to demonstrable events in his weird life, and if you thought about his daughter Stephanie and Eddie Hunberger . . .

"Jay Smith knows how to make human beings absolutely *disappear*," Bill Bradfield said, his last words on the subject during that holiday trip.

Vince's nightmares now included ghastly parcels dropped into school Dumpsters to offend and bedevil poor old Norman the janitor.

••••

After they got home, Bill Bradfield managed to see little Shelly during the end of the holidays when she was back from college in California. Shelly was by now pushing nineteen and she told Chris Pappas that Bill Bradfield had promised she only had to wait until graduation when they would be married in a "cathedral in France." He was going to be financially secure by then and they were going to buy an oceangoing sailboat. The rest of it was open-ended.

According to Shelly's later statements, she and her intended sometimes went to motels in King of Prussia, but the girl always denied that there was sexual intercourse during the few hours they would spend there. Snuggling and hugging and kissing were implied in Shelly's statements.

When this devout girl, a Catholic convert through the efforts of Bill Bradfield, later denied sex with Bill Bradfield few witnesses believed her. But the more that became known of Bill Bradfield's romantic techniques, the more it was thought to be true. The motel trysts may have been a job for Elliot Emu.

Once when Sue Myers was working at the store, he took Shelly to their apartment. Shelly told her girlfriend that during this visit Bill Bradfield had said, "Someday all this will all be yours."

As might be expected, Bill Bradfield also told Shelly that Jay Smith was on the loose and threatening to kill Susan Reinert. This time he said that the reason was because Jay Smith had an idea that she was somehow going to interfere with the alibi testimony that Bill Bradfield felt obliged to offer in Jay Smith's upcoming trial. He told Shelly that Jay Smith had admitted that he'd killed a couple of people in King of Prussia, probably prostitutes. But Bill Bradfield still had the moral obligation to testify.

He told Shelly how frightened he was for Susan Reinert, but that he didn't dare go to the police because Jay Smith's contacts were everywhere in the police service. Bill Bradfield had to resort to protecting Susan Reinert on his own. He said that he circled the streets around Susan's home late at night and often rang her on the phone only to hang up in relief when she answered. He *prayed* for her.

Of course Shelly promised not to breathe a word, and before she returned to college in February they went to motels a couple more times and played with the invisible ostrich or whatever they did.

10

Disciples

The associates of William Bradfield had certain traits in common: they were either especially impressionable, riddled with self-doubts, fearful of the future, or all three. Intimate experience with the opposite sex had been very limited or nonexistent in their lives. None had spent a significant period of life outside a classroom. Sue Myers, Vince Valaitis, Chris Pappas, Shelly, and Susan Reinert were decent trusting people. They were also more vulnerable than bloodroot.

The only one who was in *some* ways different was Rachel, now off at Harvard pursuing a graduate degree, and learning how to look even more like Charlotte Brontë. Her love letters to Bill Bradfield, always mailed to Upper Merion Senior High School, are penned in the tiny precise formal script taught in British boarding schools, though she hailed from the American West.

Dear William:
   I thought about you all day yesterday & (so far) all day today. Knowing you wouldn't, but hoping to have you call up. Vaguely nervous with your people so close. I imagine what a confrontation would hold. All nonsense, of course, but inner dialogues haunting me all day. Have been in foul mood upon foul mood. You said something about my new-found interest in political matters. It isn't. That is, the interest has always been there. The feeling of responsibility. But my notions of what seems sane don't coincide

117

with anyone's—well, maybe yours, and that's why I talk to you about things and the frustrations of never being able to get the kind of information I want. I keep wanting to have you here to say—"That's why!"

Perhaps you weren't even here this weekend? That would be strange. You've been locked up in my head these days. I miss you horribly. CSEPAHC? Center for the Study of Ezra Pound and His Contemporaries. (see clipping) Stung. Paralyzed. What can be said which will do justice to such a thing??? It's beyond me. At Yale, yet. They should be ashamed.

I sat here gazing for a minute at the Pound picture. Not thinking about it really, or you. But having my head—the whole pan of my mind, my senses—feeling all the parts of your world coming to me through these black and white dots. Because I am so inextricably bound to you and you to the something that is, was, Ezra Pound. My nerves work differently. My heart and breathing speed up whenever I bump against one of the objects of your world. I cherish them all and no one can tamper with them in the least because what's there that could be tampered with isn't in the object but in the relation. And there for as long as I hold up my end, it is safe.

I have the control over things at last. The frustrations of not determining my world can ease. And there is peace and calm and quiet. The writing of these letters is an exercise in indulging myself—holding up of my end and revelling in the control and ownership. Generating rewards—exquisite ones—for myself. To end the letters becomes almost impossible. The stopping of the motion and the empty space and the thoughts that continue in my head but cannot go to you bring again the frustration that signals my entry back into the setting of things beyond my control. There is nothing else left to me but to make do with whatever it is that must be done to keep us together. Don't worry, William. Sometimes I feel as if I surely must be getting wise.

Love me. Think of me. Something MUST be done to get around all the intricacies. I need your hugs.

Those who knew about Rachel were puzzled by the nature of her love affair with Bill Bradfield, Sue Myers in particular. Their relationship seemed as intricate as a DNA blueprint.

The letters that Rachel posted to Bill Bradfield at the school deal mostly with ethereal matters and a conviction that a unique notion of "sanity" is theirs. Sue decided that despite Rachel's earlier marriage she was the icy Gothic maiden he'd always needed and if you took her picture it would come out sepia.

But in her Ezra Pound letter Rachel had mentioned "control"

three times and hugs once, so if he controled her three fourths of the time and hugged her for the remainder she might be quite obedient and happy. Probably, Rachel was more like Sue Myers and all the others than Sue cared to admit.

••••

All of the Bill Bradfield cohorts led pretty ordinary lives on a day-to-day basis, lives revolving around school and books and papers, until Bill Bradfield, tireless as a laser beam, scorched them with the latest from Jay Smith.

Bill Bradfield was like an *auteur* film director who writes the scenario while he shoots the movie, and ends up with a plot so convoluted that he has to withdraw for a few days to let the players wait and wonder while he conceptualizes the *next* scene.

All in all, their lives were as sinuous and intertwined as an Argentine tango, but nobody was certain who was doing the choreography. *Was* this a Jay Smith production? Or a Bill Bradfield dance *choreographed* by Jay Smith?

••••

Victims of confidence schemes, especially those that later appear childishly transparent, often report that in retrospect it seems dreamlike, but when it happened it was real, logical, even exciting.

Chris Pappas was in many ways the most vulnerable of all. This reflective young man who felt that he'd gained such confidence and insight through his close friendship with Bill Bradfield confided that he'd been disappointed when the Vietnam War ended. He'd thought that perhaps the battlefield would give him a chance to take up a challenge involving personal courage and determination. He'd always wondered how useful his intellectual and academic background might be in something as real as war. He wondered if the "epiphany" he'd felt as a student of philosophy would sustain him.

Well, he was about to get his chance at "combat." The next months represented the most intense and vivid time of his life. He described himself as living with his antenna humming. He said he was *electric*. The high voltage was switched on by Bill Bradfield.

One memorable evening in the apartment when Chris and Bill

Bradfield were alone because Sue Myers was off at the art store, the older man decided to stage a demonstration. He prefaced it by announcing that since Vince Valaitis was too excitable and timid to be of assistance during these terrible days, it was falling on young Chris's sturdy shoulders to help him save the life of Susan Reinert. Testifying for Jay Smith in his upcoming trial was hardly discussed anymore. Bill Bradfield's mission in life was stopping a killer who had as yet done nothing that could be proved.

Bill Bradfield excused himself and went to the bedroom and got into costume. When he returned, he wore a knitted woolen cap and his favorite blue ski parka with large cargo pockets.

"I've been forced to enter into a teacher-disciple relationship with Doctor Smith," Bill Bradfield said, "to get the evidence that'll put an end to him."

With that he pulled the cap down over his face and revealed it to be a ski mask. Then he took objects from each pocket. He had chains in one, tape in another, plastic bags in a third and a pair of exercise gloves in the fourth. Suddenly he wrapped the chain around Chris's wrists and padlocked the links together.

He wasn't all that graceful about it, but he hadn't had that much rehearsal time. It made the point. Young Chris was then unshackled and listened to the lecture that went with the demonstration.

"You have to practice," Bill Bradfield said, "until you know without thinking *which* pocket contains each item. The tape's for the eyes and mouth of Doctor Smith's victims. The plastic bags go over the victim's head to either suffocate or stop the flow should the victim begin bleeding from the mouth or nose. He *never* uses surgical gloves because fingerprints can be lifted from the rubber."

Chris Pappas was informed that Jay Smith had given these instruments of murder to Bill Bradfield because he feared that with his trial coming up, the police might find some other pretext to search his home.

Chris agreed with his leader that the items were likely to be found in any household and in themselves didn't constitute proper evidence that could be taken to the authorities. Bill Bradfield had decided to hold them until such time as he could accumulate enough circumstantial evidence to make a case against his former boss. However, with the Jay Smith trial approaching he was afraid the police might get upset about his being an alibi witness. They might decide to search Bill Bradfield's apartment. And how could he explain his difficult mission to plodding policemen?

So he wondered if Chris could take the stuff home for a while? And Chris agreed that he'd do *anything* to stop the menace of Jay Smith.

Then Bill Bradfield asked Chris if he'd mind hiding a few other things. One was a big typewriter that Jay Smith had stolen from Upper Merion, and a tape recorder as well, and a film-strip projector that Jay Smith had stolen from Rider College. For all Bill Bradfield cared, Chris could throw this stuff away because it wouldn't go toward proving much. They were after a killer. They needed *killer*-type evidence.

Chris Pappas made an astute observation that night. He said, "Bill, whenever you talk about Jay Smith I notice you always refer to him as *Doctor* Smith. What do you call him when the two of you're alone?"

And Bill Bradfield thought for a second and said, "*Doctor* Smith." Then he quickly added, "I have to *appear* subordinate. But I won't relinquish control, don't worry."

Bill Bradfield then went on to give a dissertation on the M.O. of Jay Smith who didn't want to be known as an "assassin." He preferred "terrorist."

Jay Smith, he said, theorized that it was far better to terrorize the survivors of a hit than merely to dispose of a victim. He "disappeared" people, left no trace of a victim. The person would vanish from the earth, and that was far more terrifying than an ordinary dead body could ever be. Besides, dead bodies could result in some forensic evidence that might lead back to the hit man.

"You make them disappear," Jay Smith had supposedly said, "and you get a public reaction. You have a *social impact*."

Bill Bradfield said that Jay Smith carried two guns. One was the "menace" gun and the other a .22 caliber pistol equipped with a silencer.

"The menace gun has to *look* like a gun," Bill Bradfield told his enthralled young friend. "You scare them into obedience with the big gun." And then Bill Bradfield showed Chris his Jay Smith impression pointing an imaginary big gun.

"You talk, you die!" Bill Bradfield said, pointing his finger. "You move, you die!"

And after he was through with the imaginary big gun he brought out his imaginary .22 caliber pistol with a silencer and said, "This gun of course doesn't even look like a gun. While the victim's watching the menace gun you pop him with the little silenced twenty-two."

And then things got pretty technical because Bill Bradfield pointed out that Jay Smith divided the sound of a gun into three parts: the mechanism of the gun, the explosion of the powder, and the sound of the bullet's flight.

Bill Bradfield knew that Chris Pappas was very clever with his hands and enjoyed tinkering perhaps more than he enjoyed academics, and he said, "You can use an oil filter with an internal diameter of one inch to make a silencer. You never know when *we* might need a silencer against him. It could come to that, Chris. Let's not kid ourselves."

Supercharged though he was, Chris Pappas hadn't bargained on shooting somebody, even somebody as thoroughly shootable as Jay Smith.

He said, "Are you sure we can't go to the authorities with all this? I mean, even if he's connected with the Upper Merion police, we might try . . ."

"It's no use," Bill Bradfield said. "It's hopeless. I didn't want to alarm you, and I don't *dare* tell Vince what I'm going to tell you because he'd go to pieces on me. You see, Jay Smith is connected with the State Department and with *several* police agencies. He's paid some police officials to protect him. I didn't believe it at first, but he proved it to me."

"Proved it?"

"His contacts told him all about my trip to Cuba, *all* of it. He knows that I posed as a journalist and that I was working through the CIA and that I got shot at and shot back."

"I thought you *stabbed* a guard there. I didn't know you shot anybody."

"That too. He knows all of it. I was shocked to learn what the man's found out in the short time since I agreed to be his alibi witness. He knows the number of my post office box. He knows where my parents live. And for all I know he may know where my friends live and where their parents live! He has fantastic access to public agencies. I can't go to the police until he can be locked up for good. And even then I'll be uncertain *which* agency to contact."

"It's a nightmare," Chris Pappas agreed.

Then Bill Bradfield took a pamphlet out of his pocket and said, "Jay Smith gave me this monograph on silencers. He trusts me as much as he's capable of trusting anyone. Do you think you could use it and *build* a silencer for us?"

This was the kind of challenge that Chris, the handyman, got stoked about: to use his mechanical skill and ingenuity on such a strange and valuable mission. "I'll play with it," he said.

Bill Bradfield *lavished* praise on his young protégé. "I believe you could make *anything* with those good hands," he said.

Bill Bradfield was not clever with his hands and not mechanical, as his last act of the night demonstrated. The strapping tape was very sticky and when he tried to show his disciple how Jay Smith could whip out his tape and wrap up a victim's mouth, Bill Bradfield got the tape all stuck to itself, and pretty soon the performer was dancing around in his ski mask getting grouchy because he was wrapped up in his own tape and the stuff was even getting stuck to his beard and Chris thought he was going to have to take him to a barber.

The final thing he said to Chris that night was that Jay Smith wore a *hairnet* during his killings so as not to leave hair and fiber evidence. That was a Bill Bradfield touch. The little details: alligator shoes, hairnets.

On the drive home Chris Pappas was humming like a tuning fork. He didn't realize something that Vince Valaitis, the horror buff, would have noticed right away. The last male killer to wear a hairnet was Anthony Perkins in *Psycho*, and look what happened to *him*.

••••

In January, 1979, Susan Reinert phoned her brother Pat Gallagher who lived near Pittsburgh. She wanted to let him in on a terrific business deal. It appeared that her friend Bill Bradfield knew of an "agent" who had found a reputable party willing to offer 12 percent interest for a substantial short-term investment. She informed her older brother that she was going to invest $25,000 and Bill Bradfield was coming up with $12,000 and asked if Pat cared to kick in $13,000 because a tidy $50,000 would guarantee the favorable rate.

Pat Gallagher had never met Bill Bradfield face to face, but during visits with Susan he'd heard enough from his sister's friends that he didn't *want* to meet him. He believed Bill Bradfield to be a "womanizer" and wished his sister would end the long relationship. He declined the investment opportunity.

••••

About the same time, Susan Reinert decided that she needed a far larger insurance policy on her life. She made another inquiry into "term" insurance, the cheapest kind of life insurance. There was no cash value, no dividends. It just paid a beneficiary in the event of death.

She wanted her children to be beneficiaries of a term policy, but an insurance agent discouraged her by saying it would be better to name an adult who would be an administrator or trustee for the children. She named William S. Bradfield, Jr., as beneficiary. She asked the agent to inquire if New York Life would insure her life for $250,000. The home office was queried, but agreed to issue only a $100,000 policy.

Susan Reinert was disappointed and explained to her insurance agent that she was marrying her beneficiary William Bradfield, and that he was quite well off, owning a farm in Downingtown and a retail business in Montgomery Mall. She told the insurance agent that she hoped to get a teaching position in England and felt she needed a lot of insurance before leaving the country.

There were some negotiations with the home office about the $100,000 policy, and it was agreed that she could purchase an additional $150,000 of life insurance. The children were listed as contingent beneficiaries in the event the original beneficiary also died. Susan Reinert then said that she was satisfied that she could go to England with peace of mind.

But in February, Susan Reinert made another attempt to purchase a policy with the USAA insurance company. This time she reduced the amount of requested coverage to $250,000, but with a $200,000 accidental-death rider. This time in her application she listed beneficiary William S. Bradfield, Jr., as "intended husband."

It was a one-year term life policy with no residual cash value, and would pay only if Susan Reinert died within a year. The $200,000 accidental-death clause *did* cover murder.

••••

Things were speeding up. Sue Myers was surprised in February to be handed a written cohabitation agreement. It was all typed up and ready for her signature, and seemed designed to prevent either of them from suing the other for palimony. It specifically cited the Lee Marvin lawsuit in California.

As part of the cohabitation agreement Bill Bradfield listed his assets, current and future, as required by law. Without full disclosure the agreement could be nullified. On the disclosure list was "beneficiary on mother's policy, $250,000." As well as an undescribed "insurance policy, $500,000."

Another item read, "inheritance expected in future, $500,000," with no further description of that inheritance.

Once again, Bill Bradfield told Sue that the agreement was for *her* protection and that she should trust him. Once again, her hummingbird eyes darted all over the place and she said she'd think it over. And he whirled off in his dervish frenzy on some errand.

She got herself to the telephone and made another urgent appointment with her lawyer, deciding that Bill Bradfield had more financial secrets than the Teamsters' Union.

••••

Also in February, Muriel Bradfield got an important visit from Bill Bradfield that eventually led Sue Myers to the discovery that not only was Muriel his legal wife, but that Fran, Muriel's predecessor, had *also* been his legal wife.

It had taken Sue *fifteen* years to find out that her lover was a married man. Muriel had married Bill Bradfield in a civil ceremony before a Virginia justice of the peace in 1963. They'd lived as man and wife for three years.

During his visit, Bill Bradfield told Muriel that he was going to need a fast divorce. He assured her that she could remain in his house and he offered to send her on a paid vacation to the Republic of Haiti for the quickie. He explained that his art store in Montgomery Mall was in dire trouble and that there might be some liens and encumbrances cropping up very soon. He convinced Muriel that, as his legal wife, she might find herself in the middle of a lawsuit that was not of her doing. In short, he wanted to *protect* her from harm.

To Sue, Bill Bradfield explained the need for the divorce by saying something about civil marriages in Virginia not being *exactly* legal in Pennsylvania, so that's why he'd never considered himself married. But now that Jay Smith was on the rampage and might get Bill Bradfield's name in the newspapers, he didn't want the publicity to stigmatize his wife Muriel, who wouldn't be quite as stigmatized if she was divorced from him.

Sue Myers didn't think the explanation made any more sense than Ezra Pound's translation of Confucius, but what the hell difference did *any* of it make at this point? She knew she was sticking around till the final curtain; she just prayed that the props wouldn't come crashing down on her head.

Sue Myers would later say that nothing really meant much to her as far as Jay Smith and Susan Reinert were concerned. Bill Bradfield had been crying wolf so long that she'd just humor him and go about her business, because she had the whole thing figured out: he was in the midst of a world-class, monster-size, life-threatening, mid-life crisis. She figured that the hunt for Jay Smith was an interlude. Bill Bradfield, at the age of forty-five, was a middle-aged Tom Sawyer run amok, but from all that she'd read on the subject there was every reason to hope he'd pull out of it in a year or so.

Meanwhile she was enduring her *own* mid-life agony. The sex therapist assured Sue that the libido couldn't atrophy like a broken leg, so she could hold out hope for resuscitation. She felt like dialing 911.

••••

One chilly day in February, the branch manager of Continental Bank in King of Prussia was informed by a teller that a customer *insisted* on withdrawing $25,000 in cash from her savings account, which showed a balance of just over $30,000.

To bankers, large cash withdrawals often signify confidence schemes, so the manager's policy was to question customers to make sure they weren't being flimflammed.

The manager was a very large fellow, a bit younger than the little lady in the big coat. He introduced himself and told her he simply could not understand her demand.

"Mrs. Reinert, there's no *need* for cash," he said. "In a legitimate investment there's no purpose served by handing over cash."

"It's my money. I'm not a child. I want cash," she said.

"Why not accept a cashier's check?" the manager said. "It's every bit as negotiable as cash."

"I need cash for this transaction."

"How about a wire transfer? The money could be moved from our bank to the credit of your person in *his* bank."

"No, that's not acceptable," Susan Reinert said. "Are you going to give me the money or not?"

Her high-pitched voice was getting a bit screechy, so the manager said, "Mrs. Reinert, let's continue this in the conference room."

When he got her to a private place he said, "Let me do you a service. I can call the person you're investing with. I can ask a few questions on your behalf. This pressure you're under to provide cash is *not* reasonable."

"I'm not under pressure," she said, "but I don't want to reveal the investment information. I can tell you that it's for a very high percentage of return."

"I haven't heard of anyone offering more than nine percent," the banker said.

"It's for much more than that," Susan Reinert countered. "And I don't want you to call anyone for me."

"All right, then," the bank manager said. "How about a compromise? Take your person a cash deposit of, say, fifteen hundred dollars. Ask your person why the balance couldn't be provided in a more conventional way. That's fair, isn't it? I'll make you a withdrawal ticket for fifteen hundred dollars in cash."

The banker would later say that there was a little-known legal banking perogative that allowed his refusal to release cash if he was certain there was something amiss. He had never done it before and doubted that he would ever again.

Susan Reinert took the $1,500 and left the bank. On February 21st, she telephonically transferred $11,500 from her savings account to her checking account. A few days later she transferred another $5,000. She then opened a new account at the American Bank in King of Prussia and transferred all her money there. On March 13th, she wrote a check for $10,000 in cash. On April 11th, she wrote another for $5,000 in cash.

The money was given to her in $50 and $100 bills. In all, she made six cash withdrawals bringing the total amount withdrawn to $25,000. Thus, she eventually succeeded in getting all of the "investment capital" in cash.

••••

There was at least the promise of spring in the air when Bill Bradfield drove to Chris Pappas's home one afternoon. He was wearing his blue parka with the big pockets that were capable of holding all sorts of Jay Smith death devices. He indicated that Chris might be named custodian of the chamber of horrors, and that it included acid.

"Acid?" young Chris Pappas said that day. "*What* acid?"

"He says he uses it to destroy parts of his dismembered victims," Bill Bradfield said blithely. "I may have to hide it for him."

And then Bill Bradfield added, "He also tortures living people with it. He uses an eyedropper full of acid to elicit cooperation. He drops it onto the victim's skin and wipes it off with a damp cloth after they start to talk."

Chris Pappas's recollections of the events of that time always remained exceedingly vivid. His total recall impressed many outside observers. It was as though his memories were etched by that very acid.

"I'll hide it out back under your boat," he told Bill Bradfield. "How long do I have to store it?"

"Just like everything else, Chris," Bill Bradfield told him. "Until we deal with this man. I have to pretend to be his disciple. If he says store it, I store it. If he wants it back, I have to obey."

And then Chris Pappas asked questions about young Stephanie and her husband Eddie because any talk of dismembered bodies and acid would lead to the grisly speculation that was keeping everyone guessing.

"He's not *that* confident about me," Bill Bradfield said. "If he were, if he'd tell me anything I could prove regarding their disappearance, we'd have all we need to have him locked up."

"We've got to keep trying," Chris said.

"I can tell you this," Bill Bradfield said. "He's talked about using truth serum on victims. And you know that Stephanie and her husband had access to methadone and other drugs. There's a drug connection somehow, but I can't quite put it together. One minute he talks about taking over the drug operation in Chester County and the next minute he's preaching an antidrug sermon. The man's demented."

"Do you really believe all of it?" Chris said. "I mean about cutting people up and acid and all that?"

"He places newspaper on a carpet when he kills his victims. The bloody newspaper's wrapped in foil and then the whole thing's wrapped in plastic trash bags. Then the bodies're taken to a landfill above the Vince Lombardi service area on the New Jersey Turnpike."

"Maybe *some* of it's true," Chris said.

"He uses out-of-town newspapers for the bodies. In case they're ever found."

And there it was. A Bill Bradfield detail: the alligator shoes, the hairnet, the out-of-town newspapers.

"I guess it has to be true," Chris Pappas said. "I guess what he tells you *has* to be true."

"We can doubt some of the details," Bill Bradfield said. "Because the man uses marijuana. I find that shocking in light of his daughter's drug problems."

While Bill Bradfield was shocked about pot smoking, but not so shocked about chopping and dissolving human beings, Chris Pappas got a brainstorm.

He said, "Maybe I should conduct a reconnaissance on Doctor Smith's house! After all, you're exhausted. You can't do all this alone."

Bill Bradfield said, "We might try that, Chris. I'd never let anyone else take such a risk, and certainly not Vince Valaitis. But I think you have what it takes to pull it off. Only don't ever try to follow him. He's very alert for tails."

"I could just take down license numbers and descriptions of any cars that visit him," Chris offered. "When we *do* go to the cops we might need all that."

"I can tell you this: his actual number of mob hits, and I'm relatively sure of it, numbers between twenty and thirty. And he's sent away for banana clips because he's going to rob an armored truck eventually. He's got a rifle that he's altering to fire full-on automatic."

And that led Bill Bradfield to an inquiry as to whether his handyman had made any progress with the armament, so Chris took Bill Bradfield out to the back of the Pappas property where his father raised flowers.

Bill Bradfield had a .357 Colt magnum, a gun he said he'd had for some time, and wanted Chris to tinker with it and oil it and make it ready in case something big happened. He'd also brought along a .30 caliber rifle and a bag of bullets.

With the rifle Bill Bradfield brought a story that was *so* tortuous that at a later time several outsiders dismantled and inspected it, saying it was like a homemade eggbeater held together with Krazy Glue.

It seemed that the .30 caliber rifle had its barrel cut down and the stock removed. It was a Jay Smith killing instrument, of course. Chris was asked to alter the illegal weapon even *more*. And the reason was only acceptable to performers in a play within a play within a labyrinth.

It seemed that the sawed-off rifle might actually belong to Bill Bradfield. Yes. It seemed that he had once *owned* a similar .30 caliber rifle and kept it in his parents' farmhouse. He made the mistake of mentioning this to Dr. Smith, and of course, given Jay Smith's demonic powers he very soon turned up with this rifle in this altered condition. Bill Bradfield immediately suspected that Jay Smith had drifted into his parents' home in Chester County and spirited the gun away, disguising it in *this* fashion to torment Bill Bradfield by revealing just how omniscient and omnipresent he could be.

And yes indeed, the Bradfield .30 caliber rifle *had* mysteriously disappeared from his parents' home, so this might be the very gun! But he couldn't tell because it was cut down, and disguised.

And what did he want Chris to do with the gun? That was easy. As easy as an elephant's pedicure. He wanted Chris to grind the serial numbers off the weapon so that if Jay Smith recalled the weapon from his bogus disciple, Bill Bradfield, and if Bill Bradfield couldn't stop Jay Smith from using the weapon to kill someone, like Susan Reinert for instance, and if the murder weapon should happen to fall into police hands, it could *not* be traced back to Bill Bradfield who *might* in fact be the registered owner of the rifle in the first place!

It was just that simple. *If* you're more Byzantine than Constantinople.

And Chris said something like "Makes sense to me!" And started up the old grinding wheel.

While the handyman was grinding away at the serial number, he inadvertently damaged the barrel of the rifle. Chris later learned that Dr. Smith thought it was a lousy grinding job and that it screwed up the weapon.

Chris expected Bill Bradfield to be pleased that he'd ruined a Jay Smith death weapon, but Bill Bradfield didn't seem too happy about it.

✦✦✦✦

Chris Pappas made up for the lousy grinding job by calling Bill Bradfield over to the house a few days later to see what he'd managed to accomplish in the ordnance department.

The young man had a small .22 caliber handgun of his own, and he'd tinkered and experimented with some pieces of pipe and steel wool and screen and anything else that would act as a baffle. It was like constructing a miniature car muffler.

This time he could show off a little, even as Bill Bradfield perused the monograph he'd given Chris to work with. When Bill Bradfield read the monograph, his fingers slid over the pages at incredible speed so that Chris, always a painfully slow reader, continued to marvel at the older man's many skills. But Chris showed him some skill of his own that day and addressed all the problems in the pamphlet on silencers that Bill Bradfield had loaned him.

As Jay Smith had purportedly explained it, the gun mechanism was noisy and had to be coated with a rubberized material. The second noise in a gun shot was caused by the explosion of the powder. The third noise Jay Smith defined was the sound of the traveling projectile. He added that he used .22 caliber short ammo.

The methodical, reflective, pondering handyman had gotten some specifications at a gun store that listed muzzle velocities, and he'd computed that there's only one bullet that travels below the speed of sound: a .22 caliber short. Therefore, the tiny piece of technical information relayed to him by Bill Bradfield, that the traveling projectile makes a *sound,* seemed absolute proof to Chris that Bill Bradfield was spending a great deal of time with a fire-arms expert, a military man like Jay Smith.

"Bill Bradfield knew nothing about guns or machinery. He couldn't even drive a nail," Chris Pappas later said. "If ever I needed convincing that did it."

"Vince has gotten freaky on me," Bill Bradfield informed him. "He's taking tranquilizers to sleep. He's no help whatsoever. As far as weapons, I've told him that Doctor Smith's given me his guns and that you're subtly altering them so they won't be able to be fired. He's satisfied with that. He isn't able to cope with much more these days. He's not . . . shall I say *man* enough to under-stand that one day I may have no choice, no choice at all."

"You may have to . . ."

"That's right," Bill Bradfield nodded grimly. "I may have to *kill* him."

Chris started throwing off high voltage over *this* one, and he asked, "Have you given any thought to logistics? How'll you do it? Do you have a plan?"

Asking Bill Bradfield if he had a plan was like asking Dwight Eisenhower if he'd given any thought to the June 6th channel crossing. The "plan" involved more props. There was an old car seat on the Pappas property. Bill Bradfield and Chris walked over to it and rehearsed. He told Chris to sit down on the left, as though he were Jay Smith driving.

"Pretend that I have this little silenced pistol in a plastic bag," he said, lifting Chris's .22 pistol. "Doctor Smith likes to do his talking in the car while we drive around, so that our conversations can't be monitored. Now, I'll wait until the appropriate moment, maybe when he stops at a stop sign, and then I'll pull my pistol from the plastic bag and pow!"

With that, Bill Bradfield popped a few rounds at a tree, and they were hardly audible. Chris had done a great job with the homemade silencer.

"I've just shot Doctor Smith in the head!" Bill Bradfield cried, and then became appropriately grave.

Chris became *more* grave with the last news of the day. "*Your* parents' lives may depend on *our* silence," Bill Bradfield said. "If he finds out how much you know, he'll kill my parents and yours."

Bill Bradfield put the gun in his pretend bag and practiced a quick draw. Then he put a target on a tree at about the height of Jay Smith's head. He drew and fired. He shot up a lot of ammo. He even tried shooting from the hip. He only stopped when he nearly blew his balls off with a superquick draw.

11

Ambergris

It was time for a break in the action. A Bill Bradfield former student who attended St. John's College in Santa Fe, New Mexico, was about to be married there.

Chris asked Bill Bradfield if he was going to the wedding but Bill Bradfield declined, one of the reasons being his suspicion that the young chap hadn't heeded his advice to stay pure and chaste until marriage.

But in that Bill Bradfield was as predictable as a Tijuana dog race, he called Chris a few days later to say that he'd changed his mind and *was* coming along so that he "could do a favor for Doctor Smith."

••••

The wedding in Santa Fe was happy and the young couple was handsome and Chris wondered what Jay Smith could want done in New Mexico. He found out the day after the wedding when Bill Bradfield said that they were going to take a little drive from Santa Fe to Taos.

The Jay Smith "favor" had to do with the fact that cops were starting to pressure Dr. Jay about certain welfare checks that had been cashed around The Main Line, checks issued to his missing son-in-law, Eddie Hunsberger, and bearing Eddie's forged signature. Jay Smith figured he had enough to worry about with his upcoming court trials so he asked his alibi witness, Bill Bradfield, to plant a seed or two in the arid soil of New Mexico.

Jay Smith supposedly told Bill Bradfield that there was a Spanish-speaking couple in a Taos commune with whom Stephanie and Eddie had stayed for a period of time. Jay Smith wanted to establish the time-frame when Stephanie and Eddie had been with the couple, a time that hopefully would be close to the period in which the stolen Hunsberger checks were being forged and cashed by person(s) unknown. That way, Jay Smith could tell the cops to get off his back because his daughter and son-in-law were alive and well, and maybe they'd stop implying that Jay Smith was the kind of guy who would murder his own daughter.

Off they drove from Santa Fe to Taos, not to visit the Spanish-speaking couple, but to phone the couple to *arrange* a visit. Chris Pappas didn't ask why they hadn't called the couple from Santa Fe before driving clear to Taos. He didn't have time for such things. He was too busy trying to understand why they were trying to prove that Jay Smith *wasn't* murderous enough to have killed his daughter when for the past several weeks they'd been glowing white-hot with the certain knowledge that Jay Smith was as deadly as plutonium in your drinking water.

After they got to Taos, Bill Bradfield made a private call from a pay phone outside a restaurant and informed Chris that the mission was accomplished. No further action was necessary. Back they drove to Santa Fe. Chris assumed by what Bill Bradfield told him that the Spanish-speaking couple had alibied Jay Smith by verifying that the Hunsbergers had been with them during the time in question. But Chris assumed incorrectly.

◆◆◆◆

When they got back to Pennsylvania Chris received an urgent message from Bill Bradfield that their Taos trip had been *another* devious plot by Jay Smith to *use* and humiliate him. Jay Smith had just confessed to Bill Bradfield that he had in fact forged and cashed the Hunsberger checks. And according to Bill Bradfield, Jay Smith *hinted* that he *had* killed and disposed of Stephanie and Eddie Hunsberger.

What Bill Bradfield *didn't* tell Chris Pappas was that on the

very day that they were in Taos, a friend from work of Jay
Smith's wife had accepted an urgent collect call at the dry
cleaner's on behalf of Stephanie Smith who was back in the hospital for cancer treatment.

The friend talked to the Taos operator and then to the caller
who said, "Hi! This is Eddie Hunsberger. Everything's okay with
my wife and me. Please pass on the message to Mrs. Smith."

She had never talked to Edward Hunsberger before, but was
delighted to relay the good news that he was alive and well in
Taos, New Mexico.

▸▸▸▸

Chris was called off his surveillance activities. Bill Bradfield decided that for now Jay Smith was probably not a great threat to
Susan Reinert because he was too busy slaughtering prostitutes.

The prostitutes were also known as "remotes," because they
were remotely connected with the Jay Smith investigation. Bill
Bradfield claimed that the "remotes" had made the mistake of
smoking dope with Jay Smith, thus spoiling his defense that the
drugs found in the Smith home belonged to Eddie and Stephanie
Hunsberger. Dr. Jay was determined that the remotes should
never appear as character witnesses against him in his upcoming
trial. They had to go.

Sure enough, the next day in the papers there was a double
murder-suicide in King of Prussia (which had been announced on
the radio the day before) and Bill Bradfield pointed out to Chris
that Jay Smith had done in the poor remotes and made it look
like a family affair.

Chris was shown a legal document by Bill Bradfield who
seemed almost as distressed by it as he'd been when he got the
news that Jay Smith smoked pot. Susan Reinert had listed him as
a beneficiary on a will and had made him the guardian of her
children in the event of her death.

So now, in addition to his moral obligation to provide an alibi
for the Sears theft for a guy who'd probably "disappeared" his
own daughter and son-in-law, and to protect Jay Smith's secret
mistress from being disappeared, Bill Bradfield had *his* life complicated by this damn will!

There was only one consolation. "This will is *not* a final version," he said. Bill Bradfield thought he still had a chance of getting her to drop her mad scheme of "obligating him" in her affairs. He had to persuade her to change the will, so that *if* she met a terrible fate the police wouldn't think he was connected with her.

But Bill Bradfield had another worry: he knew of a *second* guy who wanted to kill Susan Reinert.

She'd been dating a black man from Carlisle named Alex, Bill Bradfield said. Alex was into kinky sex in a big way: he liked Susan Reinert to tie him up and beat him. And he wanted her to urinate on him, as did some other boyfriends she dated.

Chris was repulsed by the news of all those golden showers, and while he was wondering if Susan Reinert was worth the hazardous duty on her behalf, Bill Bradfield said that the reason she'd confessed this to him was that she was making a last futile attempt to persuade him to marry her and take her away from the degradation.

◆◆◆◆

From time to time even the most ardent disciple needs an offer of proof. Chris's need came when Bill Bradfield told him about the "double-screen contact system" he and Jay Smith had devised to eliminate unwanted calls and to protect themselves from each other in the event that one of them was cooperating with authorities. It appeared that the dog distrusted the pony, and vice versa.

The double-screen phone system was designed so that if the calling party wanted to phone the other he'd let it ring three times, then hang up and call again. He'd let it ring once, then hang up and call again and let it ring three times.

If the other party was at home, he'd then take the phone off the hook so that when the caller tried to call a *fourth* time he'd get a busy signal and know that it was okay to put *phase two* into operation.

Phase two went like this: each man had a list of fifteen pay phones, with a numerical designation beside each number. The phones were all located within twenty minutes from home. They had each selected their own fifteen public phones and then exchanged lists. The caller would wait twenty minutes and start with the first phone number on his list. He'd continue calling until a phone was answered by his partner.

There was a *third* phase that might be used in the event of a perceived threat. It went like this: Bill Bradfield might reach Jay Smith on phone number five. But Dr. Jay might decide that he didn't like the looks of a lady in a red bandana loitering nearby, so he'd pick up phone number five and quickly say, "Go to number seven."

Then Bill Bradfield would wait ten minutes and call number seven on his list.

Bill Bradfield explained that Jay Smith admitted to having a favorite phone. It was one of the public phones in the Sheraton Hotel in King of Prussia. The phone booths were surrounded by mirrors so that Dr. Jay could sit in the booth and watch for dolls in red bandanas or guys with green carnations, or whatever.

While they were relaxing with a cold snack from the kitchen Chris made the mistake of asking if there might be a *simpler* way to accomplish their phone calls, because these two had done everything but square the telephone digits. Bill Bradfield looked at Chris like he'd found a strange pubic hair in his face soap.

He reluctantly decided to demonstrate to Chris how brilliantly it worked. Bill Bradfield looked as though he was doing one of his methodically devised seating charts at school, as though he *enjoyed* the control he was exercising over Dr. Jay by sending him scurrying around his neighborhood.

By and by, Bill Bradfield said, "Hello," and beckoned Chris to the phone.

Bill Bradfield held the phone to Chris's ear and there was no mistaking his former principal's carefully enunciated speech. But before Chris could make much sense of the conversation Bill Bradfield took the receiver and by gesture indicated that he would conduct the rest of the conversation in private.

Nevertheless, just witnessing the double-screen telephone system in action, and hearing Dr. Jay Smith's own voice after all this time, brought on a huge power surge. Chris was *never* more convinced. He now believed *every* word that Bill Bradfield had ever uttered.

◆◆◆◆

One night in April, Bill Bradfield took Vince Valaitis to the movies to see *The Deer Hunter*. But after leaving the cinema he didn't want to talk about the movie. He wanted to talk about his troubles.

"Susan Reinert's named me in her will as executor for her children," Bill Bradfield said calmly.

"She what?"

"I know," he said. "I know. The woman'll do anything to entrap me."

"It's hard to believe."

"Now what's going to happen to *me* if she gets killed by Doctor Smith? Or by one of those weird guys she's dating? Do you know, Vince, I've been in her home maybe two times in my life, and one of those was to help install an air conditioner."

"The whole thing is just so bizarre!" Vince said.

"When I was installing that air conditioner I made the mistake of lying down on the sofa to rest a minute. Do you know what happened?"

"I can't imagine," said Vince, but he *could* imagine.

"She tried to make advances. The woman's sex-starved. I had to practically insult her. I've done about all I can do."

"All anyone can do," Vince agreed.

"I've even managed to get my hands on Jay Smith's guns. I'm going to make them unworkable and then give them back to him."

"Susan Reinert's volunteered to be transferred to the junior high, from what I hear," Vince said. He didn't like talking about guns.

"You have to pity her," Bill Bradfield said. "She's a rotten teacher."

"I pity her," his young pal agreed.

"By the way, you've worked so hard at the store for us, I'd like to give you five hundred dollars."

Vince thought he was joking. "Five hundred dollars? Where'd you get five hundred dollars?"

"Not from the store, of course," Bill Bradfield said. "From my personal fortune, which has diminished considerably. Still, I'd like you to have it."

"You're too generous, Bill," Vince Valaitis said. "Too generous with *all* your friends. Thanks, but I won't be needing any more than my salary, for as long as it lasts."

"Well, keep it in mind."

"You're too generous."

Bill Bradfield didn't disagree.

••••

Vince had paid a lot of money in his life to get scared, that was one way to look at it. Nowadays, Bill Bradfield provided more fright than a dozen horror films, but Vince didn't like it a bit.

One night, Bill Bradfield, who seldom drank and had never been known to use any kind of drug, came puffing into Vince's apartment. He was overwrought and exhausted. He looked more crazed than the Ancient Mariner.

He sat down and said, "I don't know how much longer I can go on. Jay Smith just put a *gun* to my head! I dared to doubt one of his stories about killing for hire, and he whipped out a roll of reinforcing tape and before I could move he'd taped my wrists and put a gun to my head!"

"Oh my, oh my, oh my," Vince Valaitis said. "Oh my."

"I'm afraid I'm losing my health," Bill Bradfield said. "I need your help, Vince. I need it tonight."

"Sure, Bill. Anything," Vince said.

"I need you to come with me to Jay Smith's house."

"Oh my."

An hour later, still unable to believe he was wide awake on a cold spring night in King of Prussia, Pennsylvania, U.S.A., and not in some galaxy far away, Vince Valaitis found himself driving his Camaro to a house on Valley Forge Road. A house with a basement apartment where unspeakable things occurred. A house that maybe looked like Anthony Perkins's horrible house right next to the Bates Motel where he . . .

"Pull over and park!" Bill Bradfield told him suddenly.

Vince parked and cut his engine.

"Take the bulb out of the dome light!" Bill Bradfield ordered, and Vince's hands were so sweaty he could hardly manage.

"Now continue driving. We're almost there!" Bill Bradfield whispered, while Vince tried not to hyperventilate.

The house on Valley Forge Road was quiet. There was a light burning, perhaps two lights. Vince parked and cut his headlights. Bill Bradfield got out quietly and left the door open.

It was a secluded street with an orchard across the road. There obviously wasn't much traffic here at any time. The garage that led to the mysterious basement apartment could not be seen from the street.

Vince could see Bill Bradfield blowing steam in the moonlight as he crept up the driveway toward the back of the house in a tangle of shadows.

A blood-freezing scream would not have surprised the young teacher, but after a moment Bill Bradfield came skulking back to the Camaro, jumped in, and said, "I've got it!"

"Got what?" Vince asked, afraid to know.

"My key. He had a key belonging to me. Let's get *out* of here!"

••••

Vince didn't see Bill Bradfield all that much. He kept *trying* to lead a dull ordinary schoolteacher's life.

Vince was in his apartment one night taping a horror movie when Bill Bradfield barged in. It was almost midnight. He had something in the trunk of his car to show Vince, and Vince hoped it wasn't a body belonging to Jay Smith.

"What's *that*?" Vince Valaitis asked when Bill Bradfield opened the trunk.

"It's a gun."

"It looks like an oil can," Vince said, peering closer in the darkness. "It *is* an oil can. It's not a gun."

The driveway beside the apartment house in Phoenixville was next to the woods that marked a wildlife preserve. Bill Bradfield walked toward a row of trees and pointed his oil can. Vince heard it pop five times.

"I once saw Doctor Smith fire one into the ground in broad daylight. Right outside a restaurant."

"Is that a *silencer*?"

"I may have to use it on Doctor Smith," Bill Bradfield nodded.

"Put that away!" Vince cried. "Put that away!"

But Bill Bradfield grinned and whirled and sped away on some other madcap adventure and Vince returned to movie horror.

••••

Vince Valaitis was finally upset enough to talk it over with his father. The blue-collar mechanic from South Philly listened to the story about all the nutty school teachers and shook his head and said, "Son, it all sounds crazy!"

And Vince was relieved. Just as Sue Myers had felt relieved when her lawyer said it sounded preposterous. He slept a little better that night. It was *too* crazy to think about. Jay Smith was just tormenting a decent man like Bill Bradfield for the perverse pleasure of it. Vince prayed that his friend would abandon this folly.

••••

Most people have a general understanding that a sociopath's personality disorder means that he has little or no conscience, no capacity for guilt. Some call it an underdeveloped superego. And some people understand that a sociopath would rather manipulate and control than go to heaven. Actually, to many sociopaths, manipulation and control *is* heaven.

A lesser-known symptom of sociopathy involves an obsession to always raise the stakes. A sociopath needs greater and greater risks.

Bill Bradfield may have had a demonstrable reason for spreading Jay Smith terror among certain of his friends. But among others the bizarre gossip provided nothing but more risk to the teller. Or perhaps it provided titillation. The larger a daredevil's audience the greater his personal reward.

Or perhaps it was simply assumed that if enough people hear a rumor it *becomes* true.

Another English teacher was told by Bill Bradfield about being a reluctant alibi witness for Jay Smith with the usual explanation given. He was also told, during a secret conversation in the English office at Upper Merion, that Bill Bradfield might be mentioned in a will or insurance policy belonging to Susan Reinert. And that Bill Bradfield had learned that Susan Reinert was seeing a "kinky" person who used human feces in his disgusting sexual rituals.

By playing around with people like that, Susan Reinert might get herself killed, he said. But she wouldn't listen to anyone's advice, Bill Bradfield told the astonished teacher.

◆◆◆◆

In May, 1979, Susan Reinert went to an attorney and had him draft a new will. In the event of her death, her brother Pat Gallagher would no longer be her executor, and her children would no longer be her beneficiaries. The *sole* beneficiary, executor and trustee of her estate would be her "future husband," William S. Bradfield, Jr.

◆◆◆◆

It was getting hard to talk to Sue Myers these days. Vince would drop in from time to time when he was bored or tired from correcting papers. Once he tried to bring up The Subject.

"Where's Bill?"

"I don't know."

"Do you think he's with Doctor Smith?"

"I don't want to know. I don't want to know *anything*."

"Did Bill tell you that he and Chris went to a commune in New Mexico and found someone who actually saw the Hunsbergers?"

"No."

"Don't you and Bill talk anymore?"

"Hardly."

"Do you ever see Rachel?"

"I never see her. I don't know if he does."

"I hear she's going to Harvard."

"That's *real* nice. Especially on Memorial Day. I'll bet she has *lots* of family graves to decorate. In Salem, Massachusetts."

◆◆◆◆

And that's how the conversations would go. Sue Myers knew too much and she was too tired. Her bones were tired. Even her *hair* was tired. Bill Bradfield made her feel older than coal.

What could she do? When she fell in love with the guy sixteen years earlier, she'd been a twenty-three-year-old college graduate, who, the statistics claimed, had a fifty-fifty chance of getting married and having children. *Now* what?

••••

Toward the end of April, Bill Bradfield asked Chris Pappas to come over to the apartment and help with a little spring cleaning. So Chris put on an old shirt and jeans and looked forward to some good wholesome sweat. But something in the back of his mind told him that a Bill Bradfield housekeeping chore might not be like anyone else's.

They weren't up in the attic for more than five minutes before he learned he was right.

Bill Bradfield said it casually as he was dragging a box of books out of the attic. "I've got some things in the trunk of my car, Chris."

"What things?"

"Cash. Thousands."

"Of dollars?"

"Yeah. And some acid."

"Acid?"

"A very large bottle of hydrochloric acid. Doctor Smith gave it to me and told me to hide it. He uses it to dissolve the fingertips of his victims. And their facial features."

"Their facial features?"

"And their teeth, of course. Teeth can be identified."

It wasn't an extraordinary conversation. Not in the spring of 1979. Not among Bill Bradfield's friends.

Chris wanted it slowly, so he could reflect. "Okay, Bill, Doctor Smith gave you *acid* and told you to hide it for him?"

"Precisely."

"And he gave you thousands of dollars?"

"No. The money's mine."

"Where did *you* get thousands of dollars?"

Then Bill Bradfield asked, "Can you keep a secret?"

But Chris wasn't into irony, not at the time, so he just said, "Of course I can."

Bill Bradfield said, "I wouldn't want Sue to know. This is money that has nothing to do with her or the store. I've been saving for years. I sold property sometime back and this is what I've ended up with."

"Why's it in the trunk of the car, Bill?"

"I withdrew it from the Elverson City Bank, and I tell you I'm lucky I did it. Do you know they'd only let me withdraw five thousand at a time? That's how nervous the banks are. That's how uncertain the whole economy is. A bank's the worst place in the world to keep your money. I've been saving to buy a new boat."

"But Bill, the banks pay interest on your money!"

"I think they're all going under. I want this money accessible. I'm thinking of putting it in a safety deposit box."

Chris had to sit down and start working on it by the numbers.

"Bill, if you've got a lot of money in the trunk *with* a bottle of acid, that isn't wise. Is it?"

"Doctor Smith stole the acid from Upper Merion, by the way."

"So if you have this acid and this money, don't you think you better get that money *out* before an accident destroys it?"

"Good thinking," Bill Bradfield said. "Let's go get it."

The bottle of acid was in the trunk all right, and so was the money. There were several envelopes full of money. Some of them were in a gym bag. Some of them were concealed in piles of clothes and in the toolbox. They gathered up the envelopes and took them into the apartment.

Chris noted that the bills were fifties and hundreds. The numbers were consecutive and the money looked as though it had been packaged in batches of $1,000.

Chris counted the money and it totaled $28,500. Bill Bradfield stuffed it in three envelopes and said he was going to hide it in the top drawer of a black filing cabinet in the apartment.

"Bill," Chris said. "The United States *insures* bank savings, you know. I mean if a bank should fail."

"Unwise," Bill Bradfield said. "Unwise at this time."

Chris didn't have time to argue. There was yet another job, and this one took some talking, even for Chris, even at this juncture of the secret mission. They had to obliterate fingerprints.

"*Why* would we need to wipe our fingerprints off the money, Bill?" Chris asked, after being given a handkerchief.

"Very simple, Chris," Bill Bradfield replied.

Chris got gooseflesh whenever Bill Bradfield said, "Very simple."

"It all goes back to Jay Smith. If he should kill Susan Reinert, you know how terrible it would be for *me*. I'm this fool who's tried to help her and what do *I* get for it? I get my name on her will as some sort of insurance beneficiary. Well, when the authorities come talking to me and find *my* money, they're going to be looking for a scapegoat. As you know, Susan Reinert inherited an estate from her mother. And if she inherited an estate I assume she got some money. So, the police will see my name as her beneficiary and start searching my things and probably take fingerprints or something on any money they find. So really, the reason we're wiping down all this money is to protect *you*. I wouldn't want *your* fingerprints on *my* money."

Chris was fuzzier than a boll weevil so he decided to shut up. And there they sat all afternoon on a day that was perfect for spring cleaning but even better for money wiping. The student and teacher, mentor and disciple, the director and his grip, getting all the props ready for opening night. They chatted and wiped each bill carefully.

Of course the handyman was given the task of taking the acid to a safe place on the Pappas property and storing it until Jay Smith should make a demand for its return. He said he'd store it under the small boat belonging to Bill Bradfield. The boat he was making shipshape for the skipper.

Another English teacher might notice that it was like the scene in *Moby Dick* where Ishmael and Queequeg are kneading the ambergris, and it's all so intoxicating: the smell of ambergris and the silkiness of it as it slides between the fingers. And once in awhile the whalers accidentally squeeze each other's hands and that served to strengthen the male bonding.

So they wiped and wiped and wiped the day away, smelling the long green as it slid through their fingers. It was not an unpleasant way to spend a spring afternoon.

••••

Sue Myers couldn't avoid talking with Vince Valaitis about the frantic coming and going of Bill Bradfield. But when Vince started babbling about something new in the life of Jay Smith,

Sue Myers would give him a blank stare, and her darting brown eyes would get as placid as mud and she'd just tune him *out*. Simple as that. Sue Myers had honed her ability to turn deaf as a snail. But she could still sneak and peek with the very best of them.

Her lawyer had told her to advise William Bradfield what he could do with the cohabitation agreement, and he said that the whole business sounded nuts. But Sue had started keeping a lookout for anything that might be lying around the house, because there were surprises written on that cohabitation agreement. One, of course, was the reference under "assets of William S. Bradfield, Jr." that consisted of very large insurance policies in his favor with the name of the insured person unlisted. The other was an asset of $20,000 that he supposedly had in the bank.

Now, Sue Myers didn't know anything about a pile of money in some bank. In fact, she'd been forced to raid a savings account that *he* knew nothing about in order to pump some life into the art store. She'd depleted the secret account and figured that they now stood to lose $80,000. On one memorable day the store took in 84 *cents* worth of business. Sue Myers was starting to foresee a future as an indebted old maid, saving grocery coupons.

She also started wondering why he was suddenly locking the filing cabinets. At first she thought he might be keeping Jay Smith paraphernalia in there: tape, or rope, or chain, or other nonsense that in his mid-life fantasy had become instruments of torture and death. Now she wasn't so sure about *anything*.

As usual, she waited until he was sleeping and then she lifted his key ring and opened the cabinet drawer. And lo, he had some hideout money! A *lot* of hideout money. In fact, he had a two-inch stack of crisp U.S. currency. On top was a picture of Benjamin Franklin.

Two weeks later she repeated the exercise and *this* time she found a will. She later claimed that she'd only read the first page and seen that the beneficiary was William S. Bradfield, Jr. But the beneficiary's name was on the *third* page of the will, so no matter what she said, Sue Myers had taken a closer look at the will than she would ever admit. Without a doubt, she knew that there was some very funny business going on between Bill Bradfield and the woman she hated, Susan Reinert.

Sue Myers always said she didn't want to know too much about his business, but the fact is, she already did know quite a bit more than she wanted to know.

••••

Bill Bradfield may have sensed that the will or the envelope full of money in the file drawer had been disturbed. In any case, Chris Pappas got a call to report for duty. Bill Bradfield had changed his mind, which wasn't shocking.

His newest plan involved a safety deposit box. Bill Bradfield told Chris that he'd decided that the money should no longer be kept in a file cabinet in his apartment, but should be tucked away in a safety deposit box.

Bill Bradfield said, "If something does happen, and if the police start making inquiries at local banks, I hope they don't discover *my* name on a safety deposit box."

And Chris found himself staring into those brooding, poet's eyes, and the pondering bard was twisting his whiskers and trying to figure a way to handle all this when Chris said, "I'll go and rent a safety deposit box in *my* name, Bill."

What an idea! Bill Bradfield told him.

••••

Did Chris Pappas get a chance to walk into a bank and rent a safety deposit box like anybody else? Not a chance. Bill Bradfield wanted little Shelly to have access to the box.

That afternoon Chris Pappas went to the Southeast National Bank in West Chester and signed a contract for a safety deposit box. He signed the signature card and took additional cards for Bill Bradfield and Shelly.

A friend of Shelly's had been planning to visit her in California so Chris asked her to deliver the signature card. And, naturally, Shelly blabbed all about the weird goings-on between Jay Smith and Susan Reinert to her pal.

Chris Pappas borrowed $1,300 of the money to buy his brother's 1973 Datsun, which was about to be traded in on a new car.

So by now there were several teachers and former students and parents and at least one lawyer and maybe Norman the janitor who'd heard that Susan Reinert might be in jeopardy.

One might think that somebody would just *accidentally* slip and say something like "Morning, Susan. Nice to see Jay Smith didn't cut your throat over the weekend."

Yet the fact is that nobody at any time so much as hinted to Susan Reinert or to any of her close friends that Bill Bradfield had been saying for months that Jay Smith or "Alex" wanted her dead.

And if a Gothic tale needs an element of the bizarre, many outsiders would later say that *this* was probably the most bizarre and incredible thing of all.

12

Witness

The day had finally arrived: William Bradfield was subpoenaed to give his alibi testimony for Dr. Jay C. Smith in Dauphin County on the 30th of May. John J. O'Brien was attorney for the defendant, and deputy district attorney Jackson M. Stewart, Jr., represented the commonwealth.

Because of pretrial publicity, O'Brien had been successful in gaining a change of venue for this, the most serious crime, the 1977 theft at the Sears store in St. Davids. The trial was held in Harrisburg.

But John O'Brien's attempt to discredit the eyewitness testimony failed. There was something about Jay Smith. Although he was now wearing his hair longer and had sprouted a mustache, although he wore eyeglasses instead of contacts during the trial, although his hair was black while the bogus courier had had some gray in his hair, none of the witnesses showed the slightest hesitation when it came to identifying him.

This, even despite the substantial weight gain that had turned his features gross as he awaited trial. The puff and sag of jowls, the enlarged pouches under the hooded eyes, and now a stoop in a former military officer who had always stood tall and erect did indeed make him look different from two years earlier.

Still eyewitnesses, more often than not, would say, "I'm one hundred percent sure."

Such certainty is rare in criminal cases, especially with so many eyewitnesses who had had such a brief look at the bogus messenger. But as one of them said from the witness box, "There was something about his face. It's not an ordinary face."

Positive identification by the witnesses was probably explained by the wife of the defense lawyer who said that she had *feared* her husband's client when she was pregnant with their first child.

"Those eyes," she said. "There was so much depravity in them."

She'd had an unreasonable eerie feeling that her pregnancy could be threatened by whatever essences surrounded him. She also felt that he literally changed *size* from one meeting to the next. To be sure, there *was* something different about Dr. Jay C. Smith.

Stephanie Smith was now in an advanced stage of stomach and liver cancer. During the months awaiting trial she'd been unable to discern which produced the most misery, the rampant cancer or the futile chemotherapy. The scandal and attention of the press might have been a welcome respite.

Only two months from death, she, who had labored for her husband for twenty-eight years, served him one last time.

The desperately ill wife of Jay Smith took the stand as an alibi witness to her husband's whereabouts when the crime occurred.

"August was a very busy month," she began. "The summer school was ending, see, and then he had to pick teachers, like I said. And with this basketball, see, they had to have a basketball coach at that time."

And so it went. Her husband could not have committed the crime, she finally got around to saying, because she and Jay were in Ocean City that day in August, 1977, when someone posing as an armed courier victimized the St. Davids store. She testified that with them in Ocean City had been her eldest daughter, Stephanie Hunsberger, and young Stephanie's husband, Edward.

Stephanie Smith told the Harrisburg jury that Jay had dropped them at the pier in Ocean City to go off for a few hours to contact an "educational consultant."

When it was his turn, the assistant district attorney pursued a line of questioning that had to do with the missing Hunsberger couple.

"Your husband's lawyer asked you several questions about a phone conversation you had with your daughter sometime around Mother's Day which was two or three weeks ago," he began.

"Yes?"

"At that time you knew your husband was coming up for trial, didn't you?"

"Yes."

"Did you think to ask your daughter whether they would come back here about that Ocean City alibi?"

"Well, it was more of a Mother's Day conversation," Stephanie Smith said. "I didn't want to go into details about this trial. It was more *sentimental*. That was a sentimental phone call."

"Sometime after that phone call were you trying to get in touch with her?"

"Like, we couldn't find her."

"Are you stating to the jury that you have no idea where she is?"

"Well, see, she said she was calling up from California. She was making telephone calls from different places. Say, from L.A. to Oregon. See, they *travel* a lot."

Stephanie Smith was then asked if her husband had mentioned meeting anyone in Ocean City on the day of the crime, and she responded, "When we came back and we were driving back he mentioned that he bumped into a Mr. Bradview. My daughter said he was a teacher of hers . . . Mr. *Bradfield*," she quickly added.

And when asked about the most damaging physical evidence, a bogus identification card found in their basement apartment, Stephanie Smith said, "Oh *that* thing. My daughter's husband was reading a book on Brink's. They read a lot. So we just humored him. He brought out this card. I said, 'What are you doing?' He said, 'I'm making an I.D. card.' I said, 'I.D. card? It looks like a Walt Disney thing, that blue paper around that. It's not an I.D. card. You'd never get away with anything with that!' "

"Was he trying to get *away* with something?" the prosecutor asked.

And then Stephanie Smith offered one of her many non sequiturs: "He was trying to invent some patent on something."

There was no need to badger her. The dying woman spoke her piece for her man: "I'm sorry they had to go to all that trouble, the D.A.'s people. See, Ed *made* that card. It was a joke, hon."

But the disappearance of Edward Hunsberger was no joke, not to a sixty-year-old woman in the courtroom, who would attend *every* trial of Jay C. Smith. Dorothy Hunsberger waited for something. For anything. *Any* news of her son, Edward, and his wife, Stephanie.

••••

Bill Bradfield apparently presumed that his style of testimony was dignified and professional, but many courtroom observers thought his delivery was flat and lifeless and rigid. The journalistic references to "cold blue eyes," which were inaccurate, came as a result of his courtroom demeanor.

He wasn't sworn. Being a Quaker he "affirmed" to tell the truth. After giving his name and being asked what he taught at Upper Merion, the English teacher replied, "English, Latin and Greek."

Then Bill Bradfield gave an account of how on August 27, 1977, he'd had occasion to be in Ocean City to visit fellow teacher Fred Wattenmaker, and how he happened to run into Dr. Smith at the entrance to a restaurant at 12:25 in the afternoon. And he said that Dr. Smith decided to accompany him to visit Fred, and how Fred wasn't home and he left a note. They went back to the restaurant and ate lunch and said good-bye at 3:00 P.M., which of course would have made it impossible for Jay Smith to be impersonating a courier at the Sears store back on The Main Line.

Bill Bradfield, who admitted to the jury that he had no head for dates, was nevertheless positive about this one because it was the Saturday before Labor Day and he'd been opening his Terra Art store in Montgomery Mall.

When asked by Jay Smith's attorney to describe his relationship with Dr. Smith, he said to the jury, "I've been a leader of the teacher's association of Upper Merion. I've been a student advocate and a student adviser. That put me working with Doctor Smith for twelve years, under constant conflicts with him. After Doctor Smith was arrested, it occurred to me I ought to testify to this. The date didn't mean anything to me at first and then I proceeded to think. It occurred to me that that was the day we went to see my friend. And then I proceeded to think whether I wanted to get involved in all this. For a number of days I was tortured over that. Doctor Smith meant nothing to me, nor I to him. I decided that, like it or not, I had no choice."

Lawyer O'Brien asked, "Have you ever socialized with Doctor Smith?"

And Bill Bradfield replied, "Never."

Then Bill Bradfield gave a great deal of testimony regarding a mustache that Jay Smith had had in August of 1977 at Ocean City (the courier was clean-shaven) and how his hair never had any gray in it (as the bogus courier's did), and how Jay Smith's mustache then had been the same as it was *this* day in court. And since no one else had ever seen Jay Smith with a mustache until this very day in court, Bill Bradfield went on to say that they had joked about his growing a summer mustache on that August day.

When it was the prosecutor's turn to cross-examine, there was a great deal of testimony as to how Bill Bradfield got around to remembering the date that he'd seen Jay Smith at the shore, but he didn't tell his "I had a dream" experience.

He had to repeat it all again, about how he'd been driving along in the Cadillac, and how he stopped at a restaurant because he hadn't eaten all day. And there was Dr. Smith, and they talked, and decided to visit Fred because Dr. Smith "suggested we not eat."

"*That's* why you didn't eat?" the prosecutor asked.

"That's correct," Bill Bradfield testified.

"Not to be facetious," the prosecutor said, "Doctor Smith's judgment *overprivileged* you?"

And there he was, Bill Bradfield, in front of twelve good men and true, and a courtroom full of people, and members of the press, and a few teacher witnesses who knew him. He was being asked publicly if Dr. Jay C. Smith could *overrule* Bill Bradfield's hunger pangs with a mere suggestion.

Bill Bradfield lost his professional demeanor. He got *mad*. He said, "It wasn't a judgment of privilege!" And he started stammering. "That didn't . . . the present interest was . . ."

The prosecutor tried to speak but got cut short by Bill Bradfield who said, "I don't think that is relevant at all! I don't think it was a judgment of privilege!"

"Just answer the questions," the judge advised. "Just answer the questions."

Bill Bradfield eventually testified to driving around lost with Jay Smith as his helpmate. (The prosecutor asked if Dr. Smith was his "co-pilot." It was droll, rather the opposite of having God as your co-pilot.) And they drove around and around until they found a man working in his garden. His name turned out to be Rudy. And they were directed to Fred's and knocked and left a note and departed.

"Can you identify Rudy here in the courtroom?" the prosecutor asked.

"I don't know," Bill Bradfield replied.

"Would you know Rudy if you saw him?"

"I don't know that I would."

Then the prosecutor said, "Isn't it a fact, Mr. Bradfield, that you didn't meet Rudy until 1978? And never saw him in the summer of 1977? Isn't that a fact?"

"I saw Rudy with Doctor Smith on August the 27th of 1977!" Bill Bradfield said. "Mr. Wattenmaker told me that Rudy said two tall men in a red Cadillac came looking for directions."

"So if Rudy said he *didn't* meet you until 1978, that would be inaccurate?"

"That's correct," Bill Bradfield testified.

And then Bill Bradfield added a little detail that made it as vivid as alligator shoes. He said that when they returned to the restaurant Dr. Jay Smith had stuck him with the check. He looked toward the jury, but no one smiled.

Fred Wattenmaker's neighbor Rudy was called as a witness by the commonwealth and testified that he *had* seen Bill Bradfield at the shore. But it was *last* year. He denied that he'd seen William Bradfield or Jay Smith or anybody else in 1977.

"I'm in my seventies," Rudy testified. "But I still have a good working mind."

••••

After less than two hours of deliberation the jury returned with a verdict of guilty in the theft at the Sears store in St. Davids.

That wasn't the worst of it, not for Bill Bradfield. The jury foreman was interviewed by the press as to the alibi testimony of William S. Bradfield, Jr., and the juror said, "We sure didn't believe *that* teacher!"

The juror's comment was in all the newspapers the next day.

Sue Myers said that Bill Bradfield was furious. It wasn't so much that Jay Smith had been convicted. It was that the jury hadn't believed him. He was depressed for days.

••••

William Bradfield was too busy in June to remain depressed for long. He had arrangements to make with Shelly and Rachel who were both finishing their college semesters.

His unique relationship with each of the women in his life is best described by the women in question, and *can* be because of his reluctance to discard any proof of their love and devotion.

Whereas Susan Reinert's letters often contain references to sexual love and her need for more of it than he was willing to give, and Rachel's letters are loaded with obscure sentiments as to philosophical and psychological need, Shelly's letters are written by a nineteen-year-old girl in love with religion and books and love itself:

Dear Mentor,

In reference to your letter of the fifth, this from Sonnet 25: "Then happy I that love and am belov'd . . ."

I thank you for the Kenner reference list. What is my library going to look like when I've finished the book? My husband may have to cut my chocolate chip allowance to give me more book money. I haven't gone any farther in *The Pound Era* than the first chapter, but I've read that twice. Maybe when I get to the last chapter I'll understand his English even if I don't know what he's referring to.

I knew some of the terms you wanted me to look up from Greek, and I'm pretty sure I understand the others. You'll just have to see me in person to quiz me, won't you? (Heh heh. Devilish laugh. I'm so devious.) When we're bound for Greece, I'll get up every morning and declaim from "The Seafarer" or "The Wanderer."

I was reading a book by C.S. Lewis the other day and it captures perfectly a certain type of happiness. What I'm building up to is that if your letters or visits or love makes me cry, it also makes me feel like having a great deal of buttered toast.

Love always

Chastity until their inevitable marriage is also on the girl's mind, even as passion awakens.

Dearest Love,

I've been to see the monsignor about your annulments. He says there should be no problem about Fran since she married outside the Catholic Church. The problem comes up with Muriel. The Church considers a civil marriage between two Protestants valid, so we have to know if you were validly married according to civil law.

On to more pleasant topics. I love you madly, passionately, eternally, and infinitely. There, I've been wanting to get that off my chest. Seriously, I miss you so terribly. Do you know what I've been doing? Whenever I come into my room, if there's no one there, I kiss my pillow and pretend it's you. I can't believe how silly I am.

I tell myself I will not be ruled by my passions, that it's silly to think I'm not strong enough to get through college without you, but I'm lying through my teeth. I want you, heart's-all-beloved-my-own, and I need you to be with me. I don't see how I can survive days, let alone years.

Will anyone ever recognize the quality of our love? I think not, but somehow I don't care.

I'm enclosing St. Joseph's prayer for you to replace the copy I gave you. You are my dearest darling.

Always and all ways yours,

Shelly's letters also reflect her concerns about his holy war, namely to protect his colleague Susan Reinert from the evil Dr. Smith.

Sweetheart,

Your letter came yesterday. I was so happy to get it that I almost kissed it right there in the dining hall.

I'm so sorry that school is troublesome and that Dr. Smith is such a worry to you. As for that teacher, my claws start unsheathing when I think of her. Please be careful, William. We have a long time still to go and if you should get hurt before you are mine in everyone's eyes I don't know what I would do. It's hard enough to be circumspect as it is. Won't it be nice when I can be at your back as you fight your battles?

••••

In May, Susan Reinert had to see her friend Pat Schnure on a matter of urgency. She was agitated to the point of tears.

"I've heard that Sue Myers is *also* going to England this summer!" Susan confided.

"What's that mean?"

"I don't know! But that's not the worst part. I can hardly believe Bill did it!"

"What?"

"The testimony at the Jay Smith trial. He *lied*. You see, I was *with* him at the shore when he says he saw Jay Smith. He never mentioned seeing Jay Smith at that time. He would've mentioned it to me. We were together almost constantly."

"What do you make of it? Why would he lie for Jay Smith?"

"I don't know, but he did."

"It doesn't make sense. Did you accuse him of it?"

"Of course. He's outraged. He says that I don't remember. He says I'm confused. He's furious that I don't believe him."

"Are you going to overlook it or what?"

"Overlook it? I don't know. I could live with a certain amount of dishonesty from Bill, I suppose. I know about all the romantic entanglements and so forth. But lying under oath? Perjury? I don't know if I can *live* with it."

••••

The only person *ever* to see William Bradfield with Jay Smith outside of school was a teacher at Upper Merion, a friend of Susan Reinert, who spotted them at a diner on The Main Line.

"I was going in and they were coming out together," the teacher told Susan. "They stood in the parking lot and talked for a little while before getting into their cars and leaving."

"*That* explains why Bill was late for our date," Susan told her friend.

Susan Reinert was troubled by that incident and saw fit to discuss it again with her friend, in that Bill Bradfield had adamantly denied meeting Jay Smith at a diner or anywhere else.

"Why?" Susan wondered. "He says he was with Jay Smith at the shore when he wasn't. And he says he wasn't with him at the diner when he was!"

Susan Reinert was *troubled*. And she obviously had a serious talk with Bill Bradfield about his involvement with Jay Smith, because later, when a friend of hers was speculating about the Bradfield testimony and whether or not Jay Smith really *had* murdered and disposed of his daughter and her husband, Susan Reinert's friend asked her point-blank if Bill Bradfield knew *anything* about the missing couple.

Susan smiled cryptically and said, "Officially or unofficially? I *can* say this: Stephanie Hunsberger's alive. I'm not at liberty to say more than that."

And she didn't say more than that, and her friend didn't learn what little secrets Bill Bradfield was sharing with *her*. Clearly, it wasn't the *other* secret. The secret that she might be murdered by Jay C. Smith.

••••

There were bits and pieces of Bill Bradfield's biggest secret, that Jay Smith was going to kill Susan Reinert, that one friend would get and another wouldn't. There was one little detail that was shared only with Chris Pappas.

Bill Bradfield said that Jay Smith was *extremely* angry with Susan Reinert for having jilted him. According to Bill Bradfield, Jay Smith called her a "social climber," and he was going to deal with the social climber in his own way. He was going to beat her severely before he murdered her.

••••

All the insurance coverage that Susan Reinert had purchased in the last few months, along with a small policy she'd already had, along with the accidental death rider meant that if she was

to die accidentally or be murdered within a year, her "future husband" stood to inherit $730,000.

   The last policy came just in time. She'd asked for *two* copies because her "executor" wanted one, but the company refused. The
agent delivered one copy of the policy to the Ardmore home of
Susan Reinert on June 20, 1979. She said that she expected to be
leaving the country in a matter of days.

13

Bloodroot

For a few weeks Susan Reinert had been concerned about a lump in her breast, but by May 25th she received the good news in writing: "Ultrasonic breast exam showed only some shadowing behind nipple of left breast. No evidence of any lump or mass in either breast. The single calcification is of no consequence except that it might represent the area of shadowing seen on the ultrasound exam."

Bill Bradfield told Vince Valaitis that Susan Reinert might die from cancer if Jay Smith didn't get her first.

On May 31st she called to tell her therapist, Roslyn Weinberger, about Bill Bradfield's testimony in the Jay Smith trial. She called again a week later to say that she believed he'd perjured himself because he was sure that Jay Smith was an innocent man, and that he rationalized his perjury because he was seeking a "higher justice."

She said, "I'm not finished with this. I *must* know the truth. We've made a date to talk about it and I'll have to be satisfied."

When asked if she still intended to go to England with Bill Bradfield, Susan Reinert said, "If I do, I may live with him for a while to be sure I can trust him before we marry."

Susan Reinert told Roslyn Weinberger that despite her re-

161

peated requests he refused to talk to the psychologist and resented Susan's need to do so.

"There's still an open invitation," her therapist told Susan Reinert.

Susan made some notes about the coming trip to Europe. Her jumble of thoughts included worries about notifications to his ex-wives and to his children, as well as her own notifications:

> What and when to tell about leaving? David and Muriel, parents, brother, Ken, Fran, Sue, friends. How long expect to stay in Europe. Leave together or separately? Jobs? What to do about medical coverage, bank accounts, safe deposit, charge account, mailing address, change of support—Ken, resigning, storage, clothes, books, records, furniture, bicycles. Marriage: When? Where? By whom? Technicalities? Divorce decree, blood tests, license, witnesses, ring(s). Announcements: Karen and Michael, Ken and Reinerts, friends.

Pathetically, at the bottom of her notations she wrote: "When can I meet family?"

••••

Throughout the late spring, at least three of the neighbors of Susan Reinert began seeing a faded blue VW Beetle parked on their street. By early summer the car was being seen there late at night and was still there in the morning when they went out for their newspapers.

None of the neighbors had ever talked to Bill Bradfield, but all had seen the man with a beard coming and going. Only one had learned his name. The neighbors had often said that Susan Reinert was an ideal mother and a fine quiet neighbor. They were a bit surprised that her gentleman friend was apparently being allowed to sleep over.

In early June, something unusual happened at Susan Reinert's home. Her neighbor Donna Formwalt was standing on her front porch on a very warm afternoon and saw Susan Reinert's friend leaving her house in a hurry.

"He wasn't running," she later said. "But you could tell he was determined to leave."

As he got to the yard, Susan Reinert came out the front door, crying.

"Bill!" she called, but then she saw Donna Formwalt and went back inside.

The event approximately coincided with Susan Reinert's call to her therapist claiming that she was going to demand satisfaction regarding his perjury on behalf of Dr. Jay C. Smith.

On the 15th of June, a more unusual event occurred at the quiet and peaceful Reinert home in Ardmore. It was just days after Michael's tenth birthday, and he had a baseball game to play that afternoon. His grandparents John and Florence Reinert drove twenty miles from Phoenixville to watch their grandson play, but they had only remembered the game at the last moment and didn't call before coming. When they arrived, the house looked empty. The windows were closed even though it was a warm evening.

They spotted Michael and Karen playing in the yard next door, but instead of running to the car for hugs and kisses, both children looked apprehensive. They ran straight home across their neighbor's yard.

Florence Reinert called to Michael and asked if he had a baseball game and he only said yes and went inside.

The elder Reinerts walked to the porch and waited. After a minute or two, Michael came out with his baseball uniform on and Susan Reinert followed, but quickly shut the door behind her.

She didn't invite them in and didn't make small talk and the Reinerts didn't know what to think.

"We'll walk to the game," Florence Reinert said to her former daughter-in-law. "Aren't you coming with us?"

"I'll be over later," Susan said, and went back in the house.

Florence and John Reinert took Karen and Karen's friend Lee Ann, and went to watch Michael play. Halfway through the game Karen and Lee Ann got bored and decided to buy some water ice and go home for a few minutes.

"We'll be right back," Karen told her grandparents, but when they didn't return John Reinert decided to check on them.

Donna Formwalt was at home when the girls came back from the game that evening. They were carrying cups of water ice, and Lee Ann asked her mother if she could have the water ice before dinner. She was told to put it in the freezer until later.

Karen decided to run next door and put hers in the freezer too, but she found the front door locked. Donna Formwalt saw Karen climbing in the window by the back porch.

A minute later she heard Karen scream and then start to cry.

When John Reinert got to the house, he didn't see the girls so he drove his car back to the ball park. About ten minutes before the game ended Susan and Karen Reinert finally arrived. Karen was visibly upset and so was her mother.

When the game was over the grandparents wanted to take everyone for ice cream but Susan declined and said she and Karen wanted to walk home.

Michael decided to ride with his grandparents so they waited and drove him home. When they got to the corner of his street they saw a seedy-looking VW Beetle with a bearded man behind the wheel driving away from the house. Then they saw Susan and Karen running toward the car. Susan began talking to the man after he stopped.

The Reinerts dropped off their grandson and drove home to Phoenixville confused and disturbed. They'd never seen Bill Bradfield prior to that day and knew nothing about him. It got them thinking. Earlier in the spring when the Reinerts had their grandchildren over for a weekend, Michael had spotted a van in the parking lot of a shopping center and said, "We're gonna get a van like that when we go to Europe with Bill."

And when his grandmother said, "Who's Bill?" her grandson would only say, "My mother's friend."

Susan Reinert's secrets were obviously taking a toll on her children. She'd started telling her therapist that she was fretting over having let her relationship with Bill Bradfield get to the stage where they were sleeping together under the same roof with the kids, and turning *them* into secret sharers.

••••

Some say that the land around Downingtown is so lovely it can break your heart, and that it's impossible to drive through the rolling countryside near the frontier of Amish country without at least a minor attack of nostalgia. It's what a city dweller longs for when urban life gets unbearable, this postcard-pretty landscape.

Fields of corn and alfalfa envelop those twisted country roads, and past each winding turn is a traveler's delight: an eighteenth-century inn turned restaurant, restored with reverence for history, or a cedar and stone farmhouse snugged within a cleavage of hills patched by wild lavender, or one of Chester County's historic covered bridges. Haystacks are scattered about the farmland, eccentric-looking haystacks molded like enormous loaves of bread.

Pat Schnure, the best friend and colleague of Susan Reinert, lived with her husband Biv and daughter Molly near Downingtown. They were tenants on a large piece of land just off Pennypacker Road. A grand white barn on the property had been turned into a meetinghouse, and the Pennypackers had developed part of the parcel into a tennis and swim club.

The Schnures occupied a "springhouse," so called because a century ago there had been water below the house that sustained the people who worked this land. A fine elm still stood beside the house, as well as an ancient hollow maple that fascinated children but had to be watched because of the tendency of old maples to shudder and die without warning.

Susan Reinert loved the old springhouse with the rounded Chester County curve to the walls, and the inimitable patina on wood dating from the American Revolution. The doorways were so low that Biv had to duck through them. It was a warm, cozy, enduring retreat.

In June of 1979, Karen Reinert was eleven years old and Michael was just ten. Visiting the Schnures on Pennypacker Road was always a fun event, especially for Michael.

"A real boy" is how Biv described Michael. "I'll never forget how thrilled he got when he hooked a small trout in the pond. A real boy."

The Schnures had one child, brown-eyed Molly, not yet two. When Molly was born, Biv Schnure had received a telephone call from Bill Bradfield.

"He recited poetry by way of congratulations," Biv recalled. "I think it was from Ezra Pound. I didn't know what the devil he was talking about."

When Molly was a baby, Susan Reinert had given Pat a white youth blanket that used to belong to Karen. Molly wouldn't part with it even when it went gray with age.

Karen later gave Molly a baby doll in a blue dress. It was a very old doll made of real rubber and Molly called the doll Karen. The doll's eyes were blue, but the real Karen had the kind of eyes that went from dove-gray to olive-green depending upon the light and the color of her clothes.

Michael's hair was dark blond, but Karen's was changing color. It was chestnut now, with streaks of butterscotch. She was an especially photogenic child with an instinct for the camera. Her poses could range from tomboy to coquette depending on the photographic moment.

Karen was a moody little girl, squeamish about insects and field mice and other critters she might encounter around the springhouse, but she enjoyed playing with Molly and loved to mother the tot. She said she couldn't wait for Molly to get old enough to play school. Karen, of course, wanted to be the teacher like her own mother whom she obviously idolized.

Pat Schnure recalled how Susan sometimes brought Karen and Michael to faculty meetings where they'd sit in the back of the room and quietly draw pictures. They actually enjoyed the company of adults, and Susan probably brought them to show off a bit. She was extremely proud of those children.

In that they spent so much time with their mother they were accustomed to adult games. When they stayed with Pat and Biv as houseguests, Karen and Pat would challenge Michael and Biv to a game of bridge. The losers washed dishes and the winners went to Downingtown to buy ice cream.

Usually they came for day visits but sometimes the children and their mother stayed at the springhouse when the Schnures were out of town. Twice during the preceding weeks they'd stayed overnight with Pat and Biv while their mother was occupied.

It was left unsaid with whom she'd be occupied. The children were ordered by their mother never to discuss the man who would one day be their stepfather, but sometimes Pat couldn't resist trying to draw out a kernel of gossip.

"I'd ask something about Bill Bradfield and the kids'd just look at each other," Pat Schnure explained. "And I'd say, 'Oh, come on. It's *okay*!'"

The children never mentioned Bill Bradfield when they visited their father, nor to the Reinert grandparents, but Pat Schnure, well, she was their mother's friend.

"I like him okay," Michael told Pat. "He's teaching me how to wrestle."

But Karen said, "I think he's kind of weird. I make him pancakes for breakfast and he says it's great. Michael makes him a sandwich and he says that's great. It's *all* great. I mean, nobody eats a sandwich with pancakes. Shouldn't someone tell the truth and say he doesn't *want* a sandwich with pancakes? Sometimes I don't think he's an honest person."

There was a large pond by the country road and it attracted squadrons of Canadian geese, some of whom stayed year-round. Karen thought they were beautiful, so large and sleek with heads and wing tips like sapphire. These wild honkers were mostly unmolested and didn't panic at the approach of humans. They'd swivel their ebony heads for a wary look, but fly only when commanded by their leader. But *when* they flew there was a roar of wings like a hundred heavy banners snapping in the bright brittle air.

The children found the honkers exciting. It was fun to watch their precision flight in exact formation. It was thrilling when a young honker would get rebellious and break from the squadron for no better reason than to shatter the silence on the pond with a rifle crack of wings. Simply to cry out and *fly*. Any child could understand the impulse.

But on the ground, that was another story. Karen would just as soon sit on the grass a safe distance away and watch her braver brother try to tempt the honkers with food.

Karen was even more wary of garter snakes and frogs, but as a result of her exposure to country life there near Downingtown she wrote some whimsical verse. Beneath the picture of a golden Egyptian slave bracelet that she'd clipped from a magazine, the sixth-grader wrote:

> Oh, snake, you're so gold.
> I wonder if you're ever cold,
> Scaly or slimy.
> Please don't climb me!

Her poem to a Downingtown bullfrog revealed more about her own contemplative nature:

Froggy, Froggy
Why are you so green?
I wonder. And dream.

They were very easy children to manage and the Schnures hated to see them go home. When Susan Reinert would arrive for the kids she and Pat took strolls together. As the end of term approached it was just about impossible to discuss anything but the impending wedding.

Susan Reinert told her friend that she hoped that a query she'd sent regarding a teaching position in England would be favorably received. She smiled when she told Pat that she'd included Jay Smith's letter of recommendation, trusting that his notoriety hadn't spread clear across the Atlantic.

They speculated that anything he'd stolen was long spent on lawyers, and paying for his wife's illness. And that he was reportedly living on welfare and food stamps while facing a prison term. But on such a night it wasn't easy to talk about a man who, as Susan Reinert reported, had always "made her skin crawl" when he so much as entered the same room at school.

It was far more pleasant to talk about the wonders to be seen in Europe, while American crickets sang cheerily by the pond in the maidenhead fern. At night it was spectacularly beautiful out there with tree shadows like black satin, and buttery light shining from the barn and the springhouse. Shadows on the moon were only made by the coming and going of migratory birds.

And beautiful wild flowers like bloodroot grew wherever they chose in this fertile country, but were too delicate to survive the touch of a single human being, or so said folklore, and William Bradfield.

14

Summer Storm

Woman? Oh, woman is a consummate rage,
but dead, or asleep, she pleases.
Take her. She has two excellent seasons.
—EZRA POUND

On the day in June that Susan Reinert's last insurance policy was being readied for delivery to her home in Ardmore, Bill Bradfield took a drive to Cape May, New Jersey, to book rooms for himself and three companions for the coming weekend. He drove to the shore by way of downtown Philadelphia where he made a stop at the kind of hotel where guests hope that night screams are only coming from overly theatrical hookers.

It was later learned that the Harvard graduate student had been staying in that hotel for a *month*. Rachel's room was registered to "Mr. and Mrs. William Bradfield." One would think that with nearly $30,000 in cash lying around, Bill Bradfield might have booked a better hotel.

But it could have been that the old hotel had its own ghost or a body entombed in a wall, or something else to pique a Gothic taste and compensate for an occasional flea or cockroach. In any case, she accompanied him on the drive to the shore that summer day. Bill Bradfield booked two rooms at the Heirloom Apartments and returned home by way of downtown Philly to deposit Rachel back on the mean streets until further notice.

When Sue Myers was told that she was going to the shore for the weekend she was happy about it, but wondered why he'd gone to the trouble of driving to the shore to book rooms. Ordinarily they just took pot luck when they got there. Naturally, she suspected shenanigans, figuring maybe he'd gone to the shore and maybe he hadn't. Sue Myers guessed that little Shelly was probably home from college.

••••

It appeared that Susan Reinert was mistaken if she thought Bill Bradfield was going to England that summer. In fact, the only one going to England was Sue Myers who intended to take a course in Shakespeare at Oxford.

Bill Bradfield had *his* summer all set. He and Chris Pappas were enrolled in the summer program at St. John's College in Santa Fe. And Rachel was going along as a helpmate.

The first day of class at St. John's was to be Monday, June 25th. The plan was that Bill Bradfield and Chris would fly down on Friday, June 22nd. Chris Pappas bought himself a plane ticket.

"Why are you going to the shore, Bill?" Chris found himself asking a few days before their scheduled flight to Sante Fe.

"I need the recreation before starting classes at St. John's," Bill Bradfield said. "A weekend at the shore might do *you* some good too."

"I want to leave for Santa Fe on Friday and get over my jet lag," Chris argued.

"I *need* you to come to the shore on Friday," Bill Bradfield said. "I have a feeling Doctor Smith's going to finally make his assault on Susan Reinert this weekend. Monday he'll be sentenced on the weapons and drug charges and this'll be his last chance. If it happens I want to be able to account for my whereabouts. I need you to help provide my alibi."

"But Bill," Chris pleaded, "if you want an alibi why not fly with me to Santa Fe on Friday? We'd be two thousand miles away from here!"

"Well," Bill Bradfield said, "well, there's *another* reason I have to be here. Doctor Smith's attorney may call me with orders to report to court on Monday to be a character witness at the sentencing."

That explanation had all the symmetry of melanoma, since seeing Jay Smith get *more* not less jail time had been their professed goal all along. But by now, Chris Pappas was lost in Bill Bradfield's maze. The young Greek just wanted out before a minotaur got him.

"Well, when *can* you leave?"

"I can fly to Santa Fe on Monday night."

"You'll miss the first day of class."

"*We'll* miss it, Chris," he said. "I *need* you to be with me this weekend. In case something happens."

"I guess I can't let you down," Chris Pappas said.

••••

Vince Valaitis and Sue Myers and Bill Bradfield decided to celebrate the end of the school year by seeing the movie *Hair*. After the film, Bill Bradfield asked Vince, "How'd you like to go to the shore next weekend?"

That sounded okay to Vince, but then he thought about the summer job he'd accepted now that Terra Art could no longer afford its treasurer.

He believed he could get the day off so he said, "Fine. Sounds great."

But a couple of days later, Vince started worrying and figured he'd better not ask his new boss for a day off quite so soon. He went up to Bill Bradfield's apartment and found him alone.

Bill Bradfield listened as Vince told him why he wouldn't be coming on Friday.

When he was all through Bill Bradfield stared at him and those eyes started throwing off arctic blue sparks, and he said, "You *have* to go. Plans've been made."

That stunned the young teacher. He'd done a whole lot of things for Bill Bradfield and listened to a whole lot of very strange stories, but this was too much. He *had* to go?

And Vince started stammering and repeating his good reason for not wanting to go, but Bill Bradfield said, "I'm afraid that Jay Smith is going to harm Susan Reinert this weekend. I want to be at the shore and I want my closest friends to be in a position to protect me. You're going."

And Vince Valaitis, a twenty-eight-year-old college graduate, like Chris Pappas, a twenty-nine-year-old college graduate, said, "Okay."

And that was that.

••••

Probably the busiest day in William Bradfield's life was June 22, 1979. Early that morning Chris Pappas received telephone instructions to go to the safety deposit box to withdraw enough to buy Bill Bradfield a round-trip plane ticket to New Mexico and also provide him with some walk-around money for a few weeks.

Chris drove to the bank and used his key to open the box. He counted the money and took about $1,100 from the total. He put $500 of it in an envelope and dropped it off with Sue Myers since Bill Bradfield wasn't at home. But when Chris was on his way to his own house he spotted his friend's car in Valley Forge Park and flagged him down. They stopped and had a talk.

Bill Bradfield said that he'd been delayed by a meeting with Jay Smith. Chris filled him in on what he'd done and was instructed to buy them tickets for the Monday night flight to Albuquerque.

Bill Bradfield said, "We'll pick you up at home sometime tonight. Be ready."

And off he drove, as relentless as decay.

••••

Friday afternoon was reserved for Shelly business. Bill Bradfield picked her up at 3:30 P.M. and they drove straight to a motel on Route 30. According to Shelly there was lots of hugging and kissing, but as always, it went no further.

Then he filled her in on what had been happening and what her duties were for the next days. Shelly heard all about Dr. Smith's chains and weapons and silencers. Bill Bradfield told her how Dr. Smith had fired a gun outside a restaurant in King of Prussia in broad daylight to demonstrate the silencer. And he told her how exhausted he was from his mission of trying to get the goods on Dr. Smith to protect everyone on the hit list.

Then he told her something that *nobody* had heard before this. He said that even poor old Sue Myers was on the hit list!

He told Shelly that he patrolled Susan Reinert's neighborhood more than the local cops, and Shelly agreed that he looked totally pooped. The wild tangle of his beard seemed to reflect the anarchy he was trying to set straight.

After all the murder talk was concluded, they got down to the real business. Shelly was informed that she had to go to his bank and do a little transaction. But first he showed her a pile of money and some envelopes, and he counted $4,000 in cash. She was told that she was going to withdraw some *more* money, a lot of it.

They were in the motel for about three hours before they checked out and drove to West Chester. Bill Bradfield went to the wrong bank because he'd never been to the safety deposit box. Then he grumbled about how he had to do everything, and went to a telephone and called Chris Pappas to get the name of the right bank. And that meant that Chris now knew that Bill Bradfield was doing some *more* money business, and apparently he didn't want Chris to know about it.

Finally, at 7:30 P.M. they parked outside the Southeast National Bank. Bill Bradfield told Shelly that this bank contained money he'd saved for many years, and that if Dr. Smith really did kill Susan Reinert in the next few days, well, his assets might be frozen because of his name being in her silly old will. He wanted her to go in there and with her access card draw out all the money and bring it to the car.

When she asked why he had so much money in a safety deposit box instead of an interest-bearing account he said it had to do with a tax shelter. And since Shelly was into great books and religious dogma rather than investment banking, she didn't question it further. She withdrew the money and after she got back to the car they counted it.

Shelly's next job was to take the money to her home in Wayne and stash it where her parents wouldn't find it. He told Shelly that due to his being in a state of utter exhaustion he was going to the shore for the weekend with troublesome old Sue Myers to recuperate before summer school. He said that Vince and Chris were coming along, and that he just *had* to get away somewhere so that in case Dr. Smith did his foul deed he'd be far enough away not to get blamed because of that distressing will.

And so forth.

The last bit of teaching that Bill Bradfield ever tried on Shelly involved a crash course in code and cipher. He gave her a copy of Ezra Pound's book on Confucius. On pages 12 and 13 he'd numbered each line. The letter beside the number indicated a letter in a cipher and code he'd worked out.

He told her that all future correspondence between them might have to be coded and decoded by Confucius. It might become extremely urgent that Shelly master this system, he said, but he knew she could do it.

But she saw right off that the code was harder than the Hope Diamond. Shelly wanted to kiss pillows, not study cryptography. That afternoon it might have occurred to little Shelly that marriage to Bill Bradfield wouldn't be all chocolate chips and snuggle hugs.

••••

It seems fairly certain that Elliot Emu passed away at about 5:00 P.M. in the motel on the afternoon of June 22nd. That was the last time that Bill Bradfield was jolly enough to whip out Elliot Emu and let him preen and gawk and stretch his limber neck. From that day on, Bill Bradfield would never again be carefree enough for his imaginary ostrich.

••••

Colleagues of William Bradfield and Jay Smith frequently said that the two educators "marched to a different drummer," or "danced to a different tune." But Bill Bradfield could only dance a *pas de deux;* he was never a solo performer. Jay Smith seldom danced in tandem. Jay Smith was a dissonant soloist, dancing his own peculiar lonely jig to his own peculiar off-key melody, maybe played on the kazoo.

••••

After Chris bought the plane tickets he went home and packed and had dinner. He then went to visit his friend Jenny. They were watching television at 8:30 when a car pulled up in front of

Jenny's house. Chris looked out, seeing it was Bill Bradfield's blue VW Beetle dropping Shelly. When Shelly came in the house she said that she had to talk to Jenny alone.

After they returned to the living room, Shelly said they had to go out on some business. Chris knew better than to question any of Bill Bradfield's other pals about "business" so he said okay and went home and finished watching the show.

None of Bill Bradfield's friends saw him for nearly three hours.

The show Chris watched was *I, Claudius,* a tale of duplicity, greed and murder.

••••

On Friday afternoon, Florence Reinert had the opportunity to speak on the phone with her former daughter-in-law. Susan intended to take the children with her to Allentown the next morning to a Parents Without Partners workshop. Since gasoline was still being rationed she wanted John Reinert's opinion as to whether her Plymouth Horizon could go there and back on a tank of gas.

John Reinert told her it would, as long as they didn't take any side trips.

Then Susan discussed plans for Michael to be baptized on Wednesday at the Washington Memorial Chapel in Valley Forge. She was a Unitarian, but said that she was happy to please the Reinerts by having the boy christened in the Episcopal faith.

On Monday Susan intended to deliver Michael to his grandparents where he would stay most of the week while Karen visited her father and went to a gymnastics camp. Susan then planned to take both children to a music fair at Valley Forge, and conduct a weekend garage sale with her neighbor the following Saturday.

She was going to be very busy, she said.

That evening Michael was to play in a father-son softball game with the cub scouts. The game was being played at a church about half a mile from Susan Reinert's home. Ken Reinert arrived at the church with his second wife Lynn just before Susan showed up with Karen and Michael.

Michael was wearing his Philadelphia Phillies baseball shirt with the pinstripes and the big red *P* on it. Ken didn't get a chance to talk to Susan or Karen because Susan seemed in a hurry and drove off as soon as Michael jumped out of the car.

The game had lasted only a few innings when unexpected thunder sent everyone scurrying inside the church hall where the regular cub scout meeting was to be held.

Ken and Lynn sat in the back while the pack leaders tried to control thirty noisy kids. Suddenly Ken looked toward the doorway and his former wife was standing there. She was still dressed in a white knit blouse with multicolored stripes and blue jeans.

Ken was supposed to deliver Michael home after the game and wondered if something was wrong, but before he could ask she signaled to Michael who ran to the back of the church hall and they walked out together. Michael did not return.

Ken and his wife Lynn couldn't figure this one out, so they left for home at about 8:30 P.M. Fifteen minutes later there was a sudden cloudburst and Ken Reinert was standing on his front porch when the phone rang.

It was Michael. He told his father that he was sorry for leaving without an explanation, but that he had to get home to "scrub his floor" because they were going away.

His dad couldn't figure *that* one either because Michael had never scrubbed a floor in his life.

He said to his son, "Michael, where're you going?"

Michael called to his mother and said, "Mom, Dad wants to know where I'm going."

And Ken heard his ex-wife say, "Well, why don't you tell him you're going bowling with PWP."

It was very strange these days for *all* the Reinerts. The children had become uncommunicative and evasive when it came to their mother's business.

••••

That evening the president of the regional council of Parents Without Partners received a call from Susan Reinert who said, "Something's come up. Something personal and I don't want to talk about it. Could you have someone cover for me at the Saturday workshop in Allentown?"

••••

At 9:00 P.M. that Friday night, June 22, 1979, a curious thing happened. An ice-laden cloudburst produced a summer hailstorm over portions of the Main Line communities. There were huge chunks of hail pelting the streets of Ardmore.

Mary Gove, Susan Reinert's next-door neighbor, had a granddaughter Beth Ann who was sixteen years old. Sometimes Beth Ann would babysit with Karen and Michael when she was visiting her grandmother. Beth Ann and Karen and Michael all ran out to the street and tried to pick up as many hailstones as they could before they melted. Then they decided to count hailstones and see which porch was going to collect the biggest ones before the storm ended.

Susan Reinert came hurrying out of the house to call the children inside at about 9:30 P.M.

Mary Gove was surprised to hear two car doors slam a moment later, and then to hear Susan's Plymouth Horizon pulling out of the driveway and heading toward Belmont Avenue.

Mary Gove said to her granddaughter, "Oh, I *hope* she's not going to drive in the rain!"

But then she looked out again and the cloudburst had stopped. She was relieved.

There was much talk of the eerie battering of The Main Line by the summer hailstorm. It was a very unnatural night, everyone said.

••••

Vince got off from his summer job at 5:30 P.M. that Friday, and came home to shower and pack. He was invited to dinner by Sue Myers and they were joined at eight o'clock by Bill Bradfield's son Martin and his girlfriend Donna, who had returned from Europe one week earlier.

They had dinner and chatted and waited for Bill Bradfield, and finally Vince invited everyone downstairs to watch a movie on his VCR.

Sue Myers got sleepy before the movie reached the scary part and decided that this was another Bill Bradfield no-show, so she excused herself and went to bed. She wasn't as mad as she might have been because he'd recently given her five $100 bills for her birthday. She didn't even *want* to know where he got it.

At 11:15, Martin and Donna were about to go home when there was a knock at Vince's door. Donna opened the door for Bill Bradfield.

He was wearing the blue parka with all the big pockets though it was hot and muggy after that unseasonable storm.

Donna said, "Hi! How ya doing?"

Bill Bradfield looked past her and didn't answer. He seemed distracted. He asked, "Where's Sue?"

"Upstairs taking a nap," Vince said. "We'd given up on you."

"Get some gas for the car," Bill Bradfield said to Vince. "Let's get it packed. Let's *go*."

When he got upstairs and wakened Sue Myers he seemed even *more* agitated. He came back down and hardly spoke to his son. He kept telling Vince to hurry up. He actually snapped his fingers at him while Vince poured cans of rationed gasoline into the Volkswagen.

It was after midnight when Sue and Vince and Bill Bradfield drove to Chris's house to pick him up. When Sue Myers asked where he'd been all evening he said that he'd gone to visit his ex-wife Muriel to say good-bye before leaving for summer school, but that she wasn't home. He said he'd waited around for a few hours but finally gave up and left her a note.

Chris drove to Cape May and Sue Myers sat next to him. Vince Valaitis and Bill Bradfield were jammed in the back and the trunk was stuffed with their weekend bags. As they approached the Walt Whitman Toll Plaza, Vince peered at his dozing friend in his Whitmanesque whiskers. He looked as old as the poet.

Bill Bradfield was exhausted. His head kept flopping like a giant puppet's. Suddenly, at the toll plaza he jerked upright and slapped his hand on the front seat and said, "I'm afraid this is it! I'm afraid this is the weekend Doctor Smith could kill Susan Reinert!"

Then Bill Bradfield said, "I *tried* to protect her! I followed him toward her house! I circled her house fourteen times! I lost him in the hailstorm!"

Vince, ever the supportive friend, said, "You don't *know* that, Bill. You don't know that he's going to do her any harm."

But Bill Bradfield said, "It's in God's hands."

Sue Myers would always maintain that she did not hear *any-*

thing while driving the car that night. Sue Myers was as deaf as an oyster.

They reached Cape May, New Jersey, at 3:30 A.M. and went to a restaurant for a snack. They arrived at the Heirloom Apartments at 5:00 A.M., but something had gone wrong. One of their rooms was occupied and locked. The other was unoccupied but locked. They sat in the corridor and grumbled and dozed until 7:00 A.M. when the proprietor found them.

She told Bill Bradfield that she'd thought he'd wanted to book the rooms for the *next* weekend. She apologized and quickly arranged for a room for Bill Bradfield and Sue, and another for Chris and Vince.

She was so distressed that she left her keys behind in Chris and Vince's room. When Chris Pappas found them and brought them to her later that day, she said, "You've saved my life!"

"No, you've saved *ours*," Chris Pappas said.

Vince Valaitis decided to complete his weekly obligation by going to mass on Saturday night instead of Sunday. Bill Bradfield said that he was coming along.

When they got to the church, Bill Bradfield said, "I want to pray for Susan Reinert and you should too."

When they got back from mass, Vince Valaitis stayed in his room but the others went to see *Who Is Killing the Great Chefs of Europe?*

Bill Bradfield saved the ticket stubs.

They went back to their rooms and read to each other from a book by Woody Allen, but nobody laughed much. They drank ouzo and wine that weekend but no one was in a party mood.

On Sunday morning, Vince had to go to mass *again* because Bill Bradfield demanded it.

"We've *got* to pray for Susan Reinert!" Bill Bradfield said.

Susan Reinert got a lot of Bill Bradfield prayers that weekend. He even lit a candle.

"This is to keep evil from her," he said.

••••

The proprietor permitted the guests to make a couple of phone calls in her office on Monday morning, and when Bill Bradfield paid their bill it was with a check that had *everyone's* name on it.

He wasn't satisfied that the check could serve as a receipt; he wanted a written receipt. And he asked the woman to write on the receipt that it was paid in full for three nights, not two.

"Please include *Friday* on the receipt," he insisted.

The proprietor thought it must be for tax purposes or an expense account, and obliged.

Vince got scolded once by Bill Bradfield for failing to get a receipt for some hamburgers.

Bill Bradfield informed Chris that he probably *wouldn't* have to testify on Monday afternoon after all, so they weren't going to have to rush back.

Chris wasn't surprised. These days the former philosophy student expected exactly the opposite of what his faltering logic told him was objective reality.

Before leaving the shore, Bill Bradfield took Chris outside to the VW and said that he had to dispose of some letters that might be "dangerous" to him in case something had happened to Susan Reinert.

"Look at this," he said to Chris, showing him a pile of letters that he'd crammed into the storage space of the Volkswagen.

Chris read a couple of the letters and Bill Bradfield said, "*See* how she is? Nothing but sex on her mind."

But Chris hadn't seen any sexual references at all, and he said so.

Bill Bradfield snatched the letters out of Chris's hand and said, "How about *this!*"

But when Chris read it he didn't see anything extraordinary except a few "I miss you and love you" lines.

Bill Bradfield got angry and said, "Damn, I can't find any of her *filthy* letters. You should see some of the disgusting letters she's written."

Then he added, "I better throw these away anyway. People could get the wrong idea about my relationship with that woman."

So Chris just nodded patiently and watched Bill Bradfield speed through all the letters, and when he'd finished he stacked them in the well behind the backseat with other printed matter.

Later that morning, Vince noticed that the VW looked like a dried-up birdbath. He borrowed a bucket and some soap from the proprietor and volunteered to wash the Beetle. When he was cleaning out the inside of the car he saw a stack of letters and picked them up just as Bill Bradfield was coming outside.

"What do you want me to do with these?" Vince asked.

"Leave them. I'll take care of them," Bill Bradfield said.

Still later that morning, Chris walked down the beach to take a look at the corpse of an old ship protruding from the water. Bill Bradfield spent his last hours lying on the sand, flat on his back with his arms outstretched in a crucifixion pose. Vince thought it was the most depressing day of his life.

The drive back was very subdued until they were nearly home. Bill Bradfield said that he wanted to dispose of some "trash" in the back of the Volkswagen. He needed a trash Dumpster.

Chris drove behind an apartment building near his house and got out. He took the bundle of letters from Bill Bradfield and walked to the Dumpster. Like a Bradfield-trained man, he lifted the first layer of trash rather than just throw the letters on top where the wind could blow them into the window of a police station.

••••

After they'd dropped Chris Pappas and were traveling home by way of Valley Forge Park, Bill Bradfield suddenly said he had to make a call to Chris because he'd forgotten to ask if Chris owned some of the books that would be required reading that summer.

He stopped near the chapel where Michael Reinert was to have been baptized and went to a public phone. He made a long telephone call then got back in the car.

Chris Pappas later said that he'd *not* received a telephone call from Bill Bradfield.

••••

When they got home, Bill Bradfield made yet another call. This time, he told Sue Myers that he was calling Jay Smith's lawyer.

When he was finished with the call, he hung up and told Sue, "Well, Jay Smith was sentenced to jail! Susan Reinert is out of harm's way!"

He looked happy. He smiled.

As far as Sue Myers and Vince knew, he was planning to drive the Volkswagen to Sante Fe. Chris had never told them any different. Each of the friends had little secrets to keep from the others.

Vince was glad *this* weekend was over what with two trips to mass to pray for potential murder victims. He was hoping he hadn't jeopardized his summer job by taking the day off.

He hadn't even gotten his toothbrush put away before Bill Bradfield came exploding through the door.

"I just called Doctor Smith's lawyer!" he announced. "They sentenced him to prison!"

And then Bill Bradfield walked over to a chair in Vince's living room and sat down. And began to *cry*.

At last he arose and came to Vince and hugged him and thanked his young friend for standing by him during all the difficult months.

Vince would never forget the next words out of Bill Bradfield's mouth. With tears streaming, he said, "Thank God he's in jail! I saved that fucking woman's life!"

Bill Bradfield then drove straight to Chris Pappas's house and gave *him* the good news.

••••

By 6:00 P.M. Vince and Sue had helped Bill Bradfield get all of his things packed into the Volkswagen. Vince carried Sue's red IBM Selectric typewriter, which he insisted he'd need in Santa Fe. And Vince was more than happy to say good-bye to his friend. He even packed a thermos of coffee for the first leg of the drive. To keep him awake.

••••

That Monday evening Chris asked Shelly and her friend Jenny to drive him to the airport. Bill Bradfield was delivered by Rachel who had just learned to her very great surprise that he was *not* traveling by car with her. He was flying with Chris and *she* was driving the car to Sante Fe alone.

Like all of his pals, Rachel accepted the drastic change without complaint, and said that it seemed reasonable to her. She didn't even mind when Shelly gave him a kissy-face bon voyage.

When the big bird took off, Bill Bradfield seemed to relax. He bought a round of drinks, and he and Chris toasted each other. Due to their fine work, Jay Smith had been unable to murder anyone.

As Chris put it, "We were very pleased. The bad guy was behind bars."

♦♦♦

The Host Inn near Harrisburg is about a two-hour drive from the home of Susan Reinert in Ardmore. The Three Mile Island nuclear power station is near the hotel, and two men from South Carolina who had business at Three Mile Island happened to be driving into the hotel parking lot at 7:00 P.M. Sunday evening.

The two men spotted an orange Plymouth Horizon in the parking lot with its hatchback partially open. One of the men could see something white inside that he thought was a laundry bag. They entered the hotel but forgot to notify the desk that someone had left the hatchback open.

♦♦♦

At 2:00 A.M. Monday morning, a Swatara Township policeman was on routine patrol in the Host Inn parking lot. He too spotted the Plymouth Horizon with the hatchback open. He didn't get out of his patrol car, but he did make a radio check and found the car to be registered to Susan G. Reinert of Ardmore. He went into the hotel and found that there was no registered guest with that name. He then got a radio call to handle a fatal traffic accident and took off.

♦♦♦

At 5:20 A.M., the Dauphin County police and fire radio dispatcher received a call from a man who identified himself as "Larry Brown." The caller said there was a sick woman in a car at the Host Inn parking lot.

The same Swatara Township cop got the assignment and this time he *did* open the hatchback of the Plymouth Horizon.

She was so slight that her pale naked body could nearly be contained by the luggage well. The man from Three Mile Island had obviously seen her right hip. Susan Reinert had left the world the way she'd entered, in the fetal position.

15

Starship

"Look at them little bastards," he said with a grin that was always lopsided.

Joe VanNort referred to a litter of strawberries huddling against the shale at his weekend retreat near Scranton. He was proud of his new strawberries, and proud of all he'd accomplished in two years. Almost single-handed, he'd cleared a road and built a log house in his twenty-nine acres of wilderness.

His labor was truly amazing in that many years earlier he'd broken his back during an African safari. A Land Rover had overturned leaving him writhing in the bush for four days. He'd refused surgery and body casts and traction and demanded to be sent home after promising incredulous doctors that he'd heal the "natural way." And he did. His only concession to the fractured vertebrae was sitting in straight-backed chairs whenever possible.

The interior walls of the log house were covered with skins and heads from that safari: lion, gazelle, and a mammoth Cape buffalo that had charged him. The ebony horns measured fifty-eight and a half inches from tip to tip, close to the world record at the time. His only regret was that he'd never gotten his leopard, and when he looked in the mirror at his fifty-five-year-old gray-white head he knew it was too late.

One thing that could really aggravate Joe VanNort when he

was weekending in the mountains was the sound of whining engines down in the valley—the swarm of mud bikers. The summer brought them like the gypsy moths that ate his trees.

A biker engine made his spiky black eyebrows arch and he'd need his twentieth Marlboro of the day, or his sixtieth if it was late afternoon. Mud bikers in summer, snowmobiles in winter, horsemen all the time. Goddamn neighbors. Goddamn *people.*

"Them sons a bitches!" he liked to yell at all the world's trespassers.

"*Which* ones, Joe?" his wife would retort from inside the log house.

Betty VanNort was an administrative assistant to the director of the Pennsylvania State Police. She'd been with the "staties" for twenty years, and felt like a cop herself. Joe VanNort, a lifelong bachelor, had proposed to her four years earlier after a courtship that had lasted a decade. She was a domestic dynamo who could clean and cook while chatting with any state trooper who came from the police barracks in Harrisburg to haul logs or clear land or just to see what had been accomplished on the mountain by those two compulsive workers.

Betty always said that Joe shouldn't let people get to him because folks were naturally curious about the middle-aged weekenders on top of the mountain in the log house. Her voice was deep and foggy and disappeared into a rasp when she laughed at Joe.

"Wait'll the lookie-loos come *next* Christmas," Joe VanNort told her. "I'll throw the assholes in jail, is what!"

He was complaining about the rubberneckers who came all winter long to look at the Santa Claus and reindeer and lighted owls he'd attached to the pitched roof of his log house. To keep people out he'd chained the rut-pocked, spine-jarring path leading down to the country lane in the lowlands. And he'd also dropped a few trees across the path that led up to his neighbor in the north.

One "trespasser" almost wrecked the furniture. Joe VanNort and a chipmunk practically demolished the interior, one trying to escape with his life, the other trying to let him do it. In the end Joe accidentally coldcocked the chipmunk and couldn't revive it.

That wouldn't happen anymore because of a remarkable cat. It had been a wounded mangy bag of bones that he'd found limping three-legged in the snow. The amazing thing about the cat was that it loved bread.

Joe VanNort would step out behind his cabin and say, "Here, Snooker. Come Snookie, baby," and throw bread or cookies or a doughnut to the half-wild creature and it would crouch and pounce and devour that meal like a state trooper at a truck stop.

He had one project left before he'd be satisfied with the house he'd built. He wanted a Madonna, with a pool of water at her feet. He had the spot picked but he couldn't decide what the pool around her should look like. He didn't want it round or oval or kidney-shaped like some goddamn Hollywood swimming pool. It had to look natural, and had to be fed by a little waterfall. He was going to light her with a spotlight so she could be seen at night. He was a devout Catholic and this project was so important to him he was uncertain how to begin.

Despite the strawberry patch and a Madonna and the cat named Snookie, Joe VanNort was not a sentimental man, certainly not as far as people were concerned. Nearly thirty years of policing people was right there in the lopsided cynical grin that passed for a smile.

It was a three-hour drive from the state police barracks in Harrisburg. Sergeant Joe VanNort hoped someday to get a transfer to Dunmore Barracks so he could live in his log house all the time. Instead, the telephone call about a lonely little corpse at the Host Inn took him away from the log house and even away from Betty.

The aftermath of that phone call would age and consume Sergeant Joe VanNort. He often felt that his next hunt would never end, that it would last the rest of his life.

••••

The partner of Joe VanNort was a thirty-two-year-old trooper named John J. Holtz who had joined the Pennsylvania State Police in 1968 and who had been working for VanNort as a criminal investigator out of Troop H in Harrisburg since 1975. Joe VanNort had always said that Jack Holtz had the makings of a top-notch "crime man." Jack Holtz enjoyed working "crime," but many investigations were time consuming and the hours were bad.

A lot of the older troopers said that Jack Holtz reminded them of Joe VanNort when Joe was young. Although he never admitted it, VanNort probably agreed, and maybe that's why he picked Holtz to be his partner and protégé.

They had a lot in common, really. Neither was a talker, but Holtz was much quieter and very shy. VanNort got to the point without subtlety when he had something to say. They both liked hunting in the Pennsylvania mountains, although Jack Holtz was happy just to be in the woods, whether he bagged a pheasant or not. He never cared about trophies.

When it came to homicide investigation each had a perfectionist streak that would keep him awake worrying about details. During a stressful investigation the older man chain-smoked Marlboros, lighting each one with the butt of the last. The younger dipped snuff and called himself a "country boy" because of his admittedly disgusting habit. Holtz used to make other investigators queasy with his gum load of snuff and the paper cup or Coke bottle or tin can he used for a spittoon.

The quality they shared that was most telling as far as their professional life was concerned was evident in their faces: Joe VanNort with that cynical lopsided grin, Jack Holtz with his aviator eyeglasses attached so snugly to his face that the metal rims cut into his cheeks when he smiled. And that wasn't too often, not in public during a homicide investigation. Even more than Joe VanNort, Jack Holtz took his job *very* seriously, and was obsessively self-controlled. Those glasses weren't *about* to fall off or even slip down.

Jack Holtz arrived at the Host Inn two hours after the body was discovered. The first thing he noted was that the 1978 Plymouth Horizon was parked in the third row, just a few spaces east of the main entrance. And what with somebody leaving the hatchback open, somebody who was probably the suspicious telephone caller named "Larry Brown," it was apparent that the killer had done everything but light flares to call attention to the body. And that *never* happened in ordinary homicides.

Before and after the corpse that used to be Susan Reinert was removed to Osteopathic General Hospital in Harrisburg, Holtz took a close look at it. There were abrasions and bruises on both forearms. There was dried blood in the mouth and nose.

There were discolored bruises around the right eye. There were abrasions behind both knees, behind the neck, and on the ankle. There were bruises on the buttocks and between the shoulder blades.

Jack Holtz learned from the cops at the scene that the registered owner of the car was Susan G. Reinert of Ardmore, but no one knew if she was this victim. There was no clothing, no purse, no keys.

Dew covered the car uniformly and Holtz could clearly see the swipes across the roof by the driver's door, obviously intended to wipe any fingerprints from that side of the car. Looking closer he saw that everything around the driver's side of the car had been wiped. And instead of just wiping down the rearview mirror, the suspect had removed it. Jack Holtz doubted that they'd get any relevant latent prints.

There wasn't much in the car that seemed particularly helpful. There was a pamphlet from the First Presbyterian Church of Ardmore. There was a deck of playing cards, and some soft-drink containers and hamburger wrappers and a cub scout pamphlet.

They found some notes, a road map, a hairbrush, some candy wrappers, a matchbook from a Carlisle motel and a girl's barrette. There were three stuffed animals: a lion, a duck and a monkey.

There were a couple of items that seemed *not* to belong in a car with stuffed animals and church pamphlets: there was a rubber dildo under the front seat. And beneath the body in the trunk was a brand-new blue comb and on it was inscribed in white: 79th USARCOM, along with an insignia of the cross of Lorraine.

Also beneath the victim was a green plastic trash bag.

••••

While Susan Reinert's body was being taken to the hospital for the autopsy, Jay Smith was only ten minutes away in the Dauphin County Courthouse in Harrisburg for sentencing on weapons and drug and stolen-property charges.

Jay Smith was twenty minutes late that morning and apologized to the judge. He was impassive as he stood to accept the sentence of the court. He got two to five years in the state correctional institution at Dallas, Pennsylvania.

When the judge had finished, Dr. Jay C. Smith simply flipped his car keys to his lawyer, John O'Brien, and said, "My car's in the lot."

And that was that. Jay Smith was taken from the courtroom to begin serving his sentence and to await court dates for the other criminal matters.

Jay Smith didn't appear to notice the gray-haired couple in the courtroom who never missed a day when he was scheduled to appear—the couple still searching for a clue to the whereabouts of their missing son, Edward, and his wife, Stephanie Smith Hunsberger.

◆◆◆◆

The county had a new coroner who refused Joe VanNort's request for an experienced forensic pathologist. The doctor who did the autopsy took samples of pubic and head hair, both pulled and cut. He took scrapings of the nails and vaginal swabs and blood samples.

When the pathologist put the ultraviolet light on Susan Reinert's dark brown hair, some half-dozen tiny red fibers not visible to the naked eye "lit up like a Christmas tree," in his words. And he found a blue fiber in the hair of her temple and another blue fiber behind a knee. The pathologist found a white sticky substance, probably from adhesive tape, stuck to her mouth, hair, and around her nose.

A corporal from Troop H took fingerprints, and using silver nitrate, rolled an index card on her back. He found some ridge detail on the flesh of Susan Reinert but it wasn't promising. It was a double-loop whorl pattern, but unfortunately, the pathologist had the same pattern on his right thumb.

The deceased was found to measure five feet two inches in height and to weigh just one hundred pounds. There was an absence of rigor. There was post-mortem lividity producing bluish discoloration where the blood had obeyed the law of gravity. There was fixed lividity on the front and the back so that the pathologist reckoned she'd lain about eight hours on each side after death.

Since rigidity from rigor mortis lasts about twenty-four hours, the secondary flacidity found in the body of Susan Reinert, plus the lividity and other objective signs, allowed the pathologist to make a ballpark guess that she'd died late Saturday evening or early Sunday morning.

The abrasions on the back looked to the doctor like marks from the links of a chain. He checked her entire body for any sign of an intravenous injection, but could find no needle mark, though a single needle mark could easily be lost in the many contusions on that body.

When Jack Holtz asked the pathologist if he could take a guess as to cause of death the doctor said, "Asphyxiation." Which wasn't super-helpful in that he could *see* that she'd stopped breathing. And that she hadn't been shot, stabbed, slugged, and probably hadn't been strangled. But that's all Holtz got until the lab reports came back to tell them whether something other than smothering had caused the shutdown in respiratory functions.

By Monday evening the state police investigators had contacted neighbors and friends of Susan Reinert and were reasonably sure by their description of her that the body in the morgue was Susan G. Reinert of Ardmore. Through information from her friends they'd called Ken Reinert and asked him to come to Harrisburg to make a positive identification.

····

To Joe VanNort, any husband, even an ex-husband, is *always* a prime suspect. Ken Reinert reacted pretty much as one would expect after receiving the shocking news. He was saddened, confused, disbelieving, apprehensive. After he identified the body of his ex-wife, Jack Holtz took him out for some coffee. He was in the company of the state police for two hours answering questions and trying to adjust to the shock of violent death.

Suddenly, he looked at the investigators and had a thought. He wondered if the kids were with the neighbors or Pat Schnure or . . .

"Who's taking care of the kids?" Ken Reinert asked.

And an investigator said, "*What* kids?"

····

Ken Reinert called his parents to learn if his children were with them. He found they were not. When he informed his parents that Susan was dead, he was astonished to discover that he *couldn't* tell the truth. He told his parents that she'd been killed in a car accident.

Joe VanNort later heard about it and moved Ken Reinert up a notch on his suspect list. Why would he lie about it? the old cop wondered. But Joe VanNort had been a bachelor nearly all his life, and was childless. He didn't understand how it would be for a father to utter a certain word when his own children were missing. It was impossible for Ken Reinert even to *think* the word at that time. Finally he had to.

He called his parents back and said, "I'm sorry. I just couldn't say it. Susan. She was *murdered.*"

••••

When Ken got home that night his wife Lynn was waiting. They'd called everyone they could think to call and still hadn't located his children.

His wife dug through the trash and located two greeting cards that he'd recently received. They were homemade, one from each child. One message said:

> Nobody else may know that you are the world's greatest dad, but I know you are. Happy Father's Day.
>
> > Love,
> > Karen

The other said:

> There is no one better than you for a dad.
>
> > Love,
> > Michael

Without mentioning the cards she put them in a safe place. There was a horrifying possibility that they might become *priceless.*

••••

By Tuesday afternoon Jack Holtz and the crime man designated as evidence officer were on their way to the Reinert home in Ardmore. The evidence officer was Trooper Lou DeSantis. He was a little taller and a little older than Jack Holtz and looked and sounded like a game of stickball in the old Italian neighborhoods of South Philly. He was a city guy and Philadelphia was home, as opposed to VanNort and Holtz, who rated an assignment in Philly right up there with sandhogging and gassing stray cats. Harrisburg was *plenty* big for them.

It was usually Joe VanNort's style, as the sergeant in the criminal investigations unit, to come into a case after the preliminaries were finished and they'd focused on a suspect. He was the best they had at interrogation. But this one involved missing kids. He was in on the legwork from the start.

Before it was over, Jack Holtz would be inside the Reinert home a dozen times. On this first trip it was to try to determine what had caused them to leave the house so abruptly on Friday night, just after the hailstorm. He found that the house was full of cardboard boxes packed with things for the coming garage sale. In the kitchen he found cereal bowls and milk glasses with milk still in them.

He checked the children's rooms. Karen had a Bambi bedspread. She liked books and stuffed animals close to her. Michael had a *Star Wars* bedspread. He preferred his favorite toys nearby, and his baseball mitt.

Both children had neat piles of clothing, enough for a day or two, folded on the foot of their beds. Michael had changed clothes after the game. The cops found his Phillies baseball shirt in the clothes hamper.

Wherever they had gone that night, they couldn't have intended to go far. They obviously planned to return shortly.

Susan Reinert's brother Pat Gallagher had insisted on meeting the police at his sister's home. He sat and waited as the cops searched and took photos and tried to lift latent fingerprints in all the rooms.

Pat Gallagher was distant, cool, and not friendly. He was several years older than his sister. Jack Holtz thought he was there to keep an eye on the silverware. Of course he was a suspect. To Jack Holtz and the man who trained him, *everybody's* a suspect.

••••

Bill Bradfield received lots of notifications about the death of Susan Reinert. An early notification came from a woman teacher with whom he'd been romantically involved in the past.

Another came from little Shelly who informed Chris and Bill

Bradfield of the news, exclaiming, "Guess whose name's in the paper?"

She was obviously not going into mourning.

Sharon Lee, Susan's friend and former colleague at Upper Merion, got the word on Tuesday from another teacher who'd heard a news broadcast. She immediately called Bill Bradfield at St. John's, but was told he was in class. She left her name and number.

He called her at 7:00 P.M. He was whispering. He admitted he was not shocked to hear about Susan Reinert because another teacher had already told him the sad story.

Sharon Lee asked when he had planned to see Susan again and Bill Bradfield said, well, when school started in September.

And *that* stunned Sharon Lee. Then she got mad. Very mad, because she'd been told by Susan all about the trip to England, and the marriage plans.

When she began pointing out a few of those things to Bill Bradfield, he simply said that Susan Reinert had been pursuing him, but he had always told her he wasn't interested.

When Sharon Lee asked if he had *any* idea what Susan was doing in Harrisburg, Bill Bradfield said that he believed she had a friend named Don Jones in the Harrisburg area.

By then, Sharon Lee was having trouble maintaining composure and she said, "All right, Bill, well how about the *children*? Do you have any idea where they might be? Is someone we don't know taking care of them? What do you think?"

And Bill Bradfield said, "Oh yes. How old were the children?"

After Sharon Lee had hung up, she was confused and upset to think that he was trying to deny involvement with Susan Reinert. She was more upset to think that he was pretending not to know anything about the kids.

Sharon Lee had been at Susan Reinert's house once when Bill Bradfield showed up unexpectedly. She saw him making a fuss over Karen who seemed to enjoy all his attention. He had given her an autograph book for her birthday and inscribed a little message in Greek.

She was *most* upset when she belatedly realized that he had spoken of the children in the past tense.

"How old *were* the children?"

194 •••• *Joseph Wambaugh*

••••

They knew about the insurance very quickly. An agent from New York Life called the state police barracks and presented them with a motive when the first news flashes hit the tube.

They also realized that this investigation probably had little or nothing to do with the Harrisburg area, for whatever reason the body was dumped there. Joe VanNort had to bite the bullet and move his team of eight investigators to Belmont Barracks in Philadelphia.

By the end of the first week, he was living in a Holiday Inn near Philly along with Jack Holtz who was stewing over having to raise his eleven-year-old son long-distance. Like Susan Reinert he was a divorced parent with custody of his only child. Fortunately, Holtz's mother only lived a few minutes from his home and could take over temporarily. He figured the investigation would be over before the holidays.

Joe VanNort had a lot of questions for Sue Myers and made an appointment with her for Tuesday night. He said that love and murder go together like Fred and Ginger and figured she'd have something to tell them. They'd already heard about the fight in the faculty lounge.

When the cops got to Phoenixville they found Sue Myers waiting in her apartment with Vince Valaitis whom she'd called home from work. And when Vince saw them he looked as if he'd been caught in the bathtub by Jay Smith with a shampoo bottle full of acid. Wearing his hairnet.

Vince was as blanched as a dead azalea. His ear was glued to the telephone into which Bill Bradfield was saying, "You don't have to talk to the police! You'll get yourself in trouble! Let Sue talk to them! Keep your mouth shut!"

Sue Myers invited Joe VanNort and Jack Holtz to sit and said, "Vince, that phone isn't working very well, why don't you use the one in the bedroom?"

And Vince nodded and tried to mumble a hello to the cops and sidled into the bedroom because he was so terrified he was losing feeling in his limbs.

He talked to Bill Bradfield a bit longer while Sue Myers told the cops the lie she'd been ordered to tell by Bill Bradfield, namely, that they'd left for Cape May at four o'clock Friday afternoon.

When Bill Bradfield said good-bye and Godspeed and hung up, Vince began to discover that lying to the cops was like ski jumping. You can't get hurt as long as you stay in the air. And as one would guess, Vince was out of practice. The last time he'd tried lying to an authority figure was in the fourth grade and a nun rapped him with a ruler for it.

Now he was trembling before Joe VanNort whose ruler would probably turn out to be a leather sap, and Vince was expecting a thump or two across the nose as soon as he told his first whopper.

"We left here at four P.M. on Friday," Vince croaked, and they reacted like he'd just said toxic waste was good for New Jersey tomatoes.

"How well did *you* know Susan Reinert?" Joe VanNort asked, and that gave Vince a chance to start winging it.

He said how they were absolutely wrong to think that any of them would do anything to hurt Susan Reinert. Why, she was a woman who could *easily* get herself killed. She was sex crazy. She made a pass at him at a party one time, he said. She probably went out and made a pass at some bluebeard, Vince assured them.

There was only one problem with Vince's Method acting. He couldn't stare anybody in the eyes. He just couldn't stop looking *up*.

The cops couldn't have known that Vince was looking for The Man Upstairs. But Vince's Man Upstairs didn't resemble the Michelangelo ceiling. In Vince's case, the Big Guy wore a two-toned leotard. Vince wanted nothing less than the starship *Enterprise* to come swooping down on Phoenixville and take him *out* of this earthly nightmare.

When Vince ushered the cops out of the apartment that night, his good-bye face said it all. Vincent Valaitis, two minutes from hyperventilation, was silently screaming: "Beam me up! Beam me up! Beam me uuuuuuuuuuuup!"

16

Snakebites

Chris Pappas was probably never closer to reviving the stomach ulcer he'd had at the age of ten. The summer session at St. John's in Santa Fe was an endurance test. It took every bit of self-discipline and self-delusion to pretend that the glory that was Greece had any relevance.

They were getting clippings from the Philly newspapers. And Chris was no longer electric. His wiring was as tangled as Lebanese politics. It was bad enough when he thought Jay Smith had gone and done it, but somehow it was even worse when Bill Bradfield made an announcement.

"Chris," he said, "I don't think Doctor Smith killed Susan Reinert. It's not his style. I think he was set up by the mob to make it *look* like he did it."

Chris used the word "fuzzy" to describe what he felt when trying to follow Bill Bradfield's logic. After hearing that Jay Smith *hadn't* done it, he was fuzzier than Burlington Mills. Even as he was trying to articulate a logical response, Bill Bradfield had another notion for him.

"Of course," Bill Bradfield conceded, "it *could* have just been Alex, the kinky black guy from Carlisle. I told her a hundred times to stay away from that guy!"

"The mob," Chris Pappas mumbled. "Alex."

"If the police should ever talk to us, we've got to downplay our involvement with Doctor Smith," he warned. "For example, let's say that the police find out that *you* filed the serial numbers off Doctor Smith's rifle, that wouldn't look very good for *you*, would it?"

Chris had only a couple of questions. The first was "Am I in trouble?"

"Trouble? Well, there's potential trouble for us, but not if we're careful," Bill Bradfield said.

"When we first heard about Susan Reinert's death, you said, 'Doctor Smith finally went and did it.' Isn't that what you said?"

"Ah, yes. But that was before I talked to his attorney on the phone. Didn't I tell you? Doctor Smith had an alibi."

Chris felt as if somebody just wrapped his brain in ten yards of angora. He felt fuzzier than the whole peach crop of the whole goddamn state of Georgia.

••••

The living arrangements at St. John's College in Santa Fe were simple but comfortable. They had dormitory accommodations and were all settled by the time Rachel arrived with the Volkswagen Beetle. The ice maiden was pretty well thawed after driving alone across the desert. She and Bill Bradfield went off in private to get intelligence reports on Susan Reinert and do whatever they did together. Chris was never sure what *that* was.

Bill Bradfield and Rachel had two adjoining dorm rooms with two desks in one room and two beds pushed together in the other. In the room with the desks was Sue Myers's red IBM typewriter, which Rachel had brought in the Volkswagen. The typewriter had suddenly gotten very important. Chris Pappas was told for the first time that Bill Bradfield had "lent the machine" to Susan Reinert.

Bill Bradfield informed him that he was afraid that Susan Reinert had used the typewriter to type "certain legal papers." The legal papers had to do with her "financial situation."

That particular statement stuck like a turkey bone in the esophagus. Chris couldn't forget it.

••••

"I was snakebit from the start," Joe VanNort said, referring to his hot new case involving a dead schoolteacher and two missing children.

The first reptile bite was indirectly caused by Three Mile Island. Due to the meltdown scare at the nuclear power station, the Nuclear Regulatory Commission of the U.S. government had placed a hold on all broadcast tapes in the possession of the Dauphin County emergency radio system. Somebody apparently thought there was something to be learned from listening to the panicked citizens who phoned in messages which were recorded as a matter of policy.

The trooper who was sent to pick up the tape containing the voice of "Larry Brown" who had reported the "sick woman" in the Host Inn parking lot was told that he'd need a court order.

He wasn't an old-school homicide investigator like Joe VanNort who would've walked over the guy and snatched the tape. So he went through the delay of getting a court order while Joe VanNort lined up a voiceprint expert in New Jersey.

But because of the NRC edict, there was a shortage of tape. And someone had inadvertently reused the one in question. They'd taped over and obliterated Larry Brown forever.

The second screw-up was the homicide equivalent of a nuclear meltdown.

"They what?" Joe VanNort yelled into the telephone Wednesday afternoon.

It was true. They'd lost the body for good.

The autopsy had been done on Monday, and VanNort was not satisfied. He was trying to arrange for a more experienced forensic pathologist to come in to do a lot more work.

They'd told the funeral home on Tuesday that they did *not* want the body cremated. Susan Reinert's brother had requested cremation, thinking the cops were finished. Somebody didn't get the word. On Wednesday Susan Reinert's body was burned to dust.

So they'd lost their voiceprint. And they'd lost their corpse. Joe VanNort called it snakebite, but the snake was a python and the evidence was being swallowed whole. Before he went home that night, he finished his eightieth Marlboro of the day and asked if anybody had stolen Susan Reinert's car yet.

••••

On Thursday, the news of the Reinert murder and the disappearance of the children was all over the Philadelphia area, along with the information that she was heavily insured. Vince Valaitis had even heard himself described as a "Bradfield intimate."

When his phone rang that evening he thought it was just somebody from the English department, or some nosy old sandbox pal, and he was getting ready to deny again that he'd ever been "intimate" with anybody. Which every close friend of Vince Valaitis knew was surely true.

It was Bill Bradfield on the phone. He had a little summer shoptalk for Vince Valaitis.

He said, "If you speak to the police again you're going to put me in the electric chair."

Vince knew Bill Bradfield was always a great one for exaggeration and resorted to hyperbole to get his way, but the electric chair?

In fact, Vince said, "*What* electric chair?"

And Bill Bradfield, who wasn't keeping too cool these days out in New Mexico, said, "*What* goddamn electric chair do you think?"

"But Bill," Vince said, "you haven't done anything wrong! Jay Smith killed Susan Reinert. You tried your best to prevent it."

Bill Bradfield had a little news flash of his own that Vince hadn't heard.

"Jay Smith didn't do it."

And now Vince had to sit down. If Jay Smith didn't do it, and Bill Bradfield was worrying about having his skull shaved for ten thousand volts, who the hell *did* it?

"Who the hell did it?" Vince asked bleakly. He was afraid to hear that maybe the *real* killer was Ida Micucci.

"I don't know who did it," Bill Bradfield said. "But it's not Doctor Smith's style. I want you to go back to the shore and cover all our steps to verify our whereabouts last weekend."

"Back to the . . . I won't do it!" Vince Valaitis said. "I won't go near the shore! I haven't done anything. You haven't done anything. Maybe we should tell the police what we know."

"No!" Bill Bradfield said. "You mustn't talk to them."

"Then what should I do?" Vince cried.

"I think you should get a lawyer," Bill Bradfield said.

After he hung up, Vince Valaitis searched his video collection for some sci-fi. There had to be a better world than this one. Somewhere in a galaxy far away.

••••

Jeff Olsen was attending summer school at St. John's and living in a professor's apartment with his bride. He had frequent visits from his former teacher who was usually accompanied by Chris or Rachel.

Jeff was twenty-two years old then, a clean-cut, fair-haired lad, who, like Shelly and several others, had followed Bill Bradfield's advice to enroll at St. John's.

Jeff Olsen had met Bill Bradfield when he was a sixteen-year-old student at Upper Merion and they became close friends over the years. He'd been to the apartment of Bill Bradfield and Sue Myers many times, and like all the others, had been told by his teacher that the living arrangement with Sue was purely platonic, and that Jeff should strive for chastity and even celibacy in his own life.

When Jeff Olsen was just eighteen years old, about to begin his college education, Bill Bradfield said to him, "Jeffrey, you're a good man. In fact, you're *such* a good man that if anyone came to me at some point in the future and told me you'd killed eight or nine kids, that wouldn't shake my feeling for you as a quality human being."

Jeff Olsen never forgot that remarkable statement, particularly now that the newspapers were implying terrible things about his former teacher and friend.

The young man had many conversations with Bill Bradfield about the murder of Susan Reinert, particularly since Jeff was one of the madding crowd who'd heard that it *might* occur.

And now that it had, and now that reporters were writing about insurance and a will, Bill Bradfield came to Jeff for reassurance that his friend was not doubting him.

"I don't want the goddamn money," Bill Bradfield told the young man on more than one occasion.

But then he modified that declaration by saying, "But *if* I end up with it I'll put it in trust for the children."

◆◆◆

Joe VanNort was the first to ask the question: "Where's this pond I keep hearin about? This Ezra Pond?"

On July 4th, Joe VanNort and Jack Holtz were on their way to Santa Fe for a talk with Bill Bradfield and Chris Pappas.

The Cape May crowd hadn't given them much, and the cops were considering the possibility that they'd *all* conspired to murder Susan Reinert for insurance in favor of William Bradfield. Since she'd died sometime Saturday or Sunday when they were together, it was certain that if one of them had done it they'd all done it.

The cops touched down in Albuquerque and rented a car to drive to Santa Fe. It was hot and tiring and it wasn't all that easy to find a motel on the 4th of July holiday, particularly since the state cops had Pennsylvania "hotel orders" that were reimbursed by the commonwealth but not honored by all lodging places.

That evening, Jack Holtz was sitting in a bar and looking up at the Rockies for the first time in his life and drinking a Coors. Joe VanNort didn't order a Manhattan as he usually did, but had his second favorite drink, Black Velvet with water back. He smoked a dozen cigarettes while they enjoyed the New Mexico sunset.

They arrived on campus by late morning. To Jack Holtz the college looked like a place where old hippies go to meditate. Their business suits were definitely out of place, at least in the summer session. People were flopping around in go-aheads or sandals, dragging their beads and rawhide behind them.

Joe VanNort and Jack Holtz were accompanied by a New Mexico state policeman just in case anything terrific happened, like Bill Bradfield throwing himself on the floor and confessing to the murder of his girlfriend. The cops were already convinced that Susan Reinert had definitely been his blanket partner.

Through prior arrangements with the school administrators they met Bill Bradfield and Chris Pappas in the school library. Naturally, the cops tried to separate them, but Bill Bradfield refused.

"We'll answer questions together," he told Joe VanNort who said okay and tried to keep it friendly. After commenting on how hot it was and what pretty Indian jewelry everybody was clanging around in he asked Bill Bradfield to tell him a little about his relationship with Susan Reinert.

Bill Bradfield said, "No, we don't wish to talk to you. We both have attorneys and they've advised against it."

"Who's your lawyer?" Joe VanNort asked.

"John Paul Curran of Philadelphia," Bill Bradfield said.

"And who's your attorney, Mister Pappas?" Joe VanNort asked.

"John Paul Curran," Bill Bradfield answered.

So far, Chris Pappas hadn't done anything except sit there with his head on a swivel.

"Have you ever been in Susan Reinert's car?" VanNort asked.

"Yes," Bill Bradfield said.

"No," Chris Pappas said, so they *knew* he could talk.

Bill Bradfield said, "Write your questions down and we'll review them and answer them after our attorneys have gotten a chance to look them over."

The cops trucked on back to the headquarters of the New Mexico state police and typed up twelve questions that they'd just love to have answered. Then they called the college and scheduled another meeting. But not before Joe VanNort had called the office of John Curran in Philadelphia and talked with a law partner who verified that they did represent William S. Bradfield, Jr., but said they didn't represent a person named Christopher Pappas.

VanNort and Holtz arrived back at St. John's at 1:00 P.M. and presented their written questions to the summer scholars.

But Bill Bradfield said, "I'm sorry, we can't answer them at all. I've just talked to my lawyer."

"I've been told that John Curran doesn't represent you," Joe VanNort said to Chris Pappas. "How about you looking over the questions?"

"John Curran represents him *now*," Bill Bradfield said. "And I'm afraid we have to go back to our work. You can mail your questions to our attorney and he'll forward them to us."

Jack Holtz decided to take a shot. "That'd be very time consuming," he said to Bill Bradfield. "We're trying to locate two missing children and we need your help."

"I'd like to help," Bill Bradfield told him, "but my first concern is with my studies."

It was a long flight home. Joe VanNort was no longer so concerned about Ken Reinert or anybody else. He *wanted* Bill Bradfield and his little gang.

◆◆◆

Bill Bradfield had a few duties for Shelly that summer which the teenager performed with varying degrees of proficiency. The duties involved banking, ordnance and cryptology.

Shelly was instructed to take $300 out of her $28,000 secret treasure and put it into the safety deposit box. Bill Bradfield had been stewing over the notion that the cops might somehow find the box, and he thought that an empty safety deposit box might not look kosher.

Then Chris got on the phone and asked Shelly and her girlfriend to go to his house and dismantle the gun with the silencer and dump the pieces in the Schuylkill River.

But then Bill Bradfield threw her a knuckleball. He told the teenager that he feared his mail might get intercepted by the police who would be trying to link him to Dr. Smith. So he would have to write to her in the code they'd discussed.

And Shelly, who'd tried so hard to master Ezra Pound, and Greek, and his Bible studies, and had even become a Catholic for him, said sure she could. But that code was tougher than the Pittsburgh Steelers. Little Shelly failed him.

◆◆◆

Joe VanNort and Jack Holtz were both suspicious, cautious, deliberate crime men. Jack Holtz's caution extended into all phases of his life. He did very little on impulse and didn't like surprises. Perhaps his personality was the wrong kind to mesh with his former wife's. She had a flair for art and always talked of a need for self-expression.

The first time Charlotte left him, he did all of his "hurting and healing," as he put it. But then "Chaz," as he called her, came home. A little later she left for good, seemingly on impulse.

He claimed that when she left the second time it didn't hurt, especially since she didn't try to take Jason away from him. He and his son lived in a little house he'd bought on a twenty-eight-year loan. He'd put a workout room and a weight machine in the basement and decorated the place with lots of ducks and outdoors pictures.

He dated occasionally, but always felt that his job and his son kept him too busy for chasing around. He was thirty-two years old and Jason was nearly eleven so he figured with his mother helping they could go it the rest of the way without a woman in the house.

He could cook Chinese and had decent recipes for shish kebab and chicken cordon bleu, but Jason would rather have a steak than the fancy stuff so Jack Holtz got pretty good on the grill.

Jack Holtz had thick black hair, and behind his aviator glasses were large, heavily lashed dark eyes, the kind they used to call "bedroom eyes." As a result of an incorrect bite alignment his lower jaw looked unusually small and called attention away from the large neck below it and the big chest below that—the neck and chest of a guy who'd pushed some iron around. You had to be around him a bit before you noticed that he was fairly tall and well put together.

That hair of his was the kind you see on the Bryl-Creem ads, full and dense and black. Before he was finished with *this* case it'd be the kind you see on the Grecian Formula ads: steel-gray, all of it.

He was something of a loner and didn't hang around with other cops, but the relationship between Joe VanNort and Jack Holtz worked for them. Jack Holtz was the kind of investigator who wanted to be as good as he could be, but wasn't sure he could be better than that. He worried about not having been to college. He thought he didn't express himself well, especially in court, when in fact he was an excellent witness. He was content to play second banana.

Joe VanNort on the other hand pointed out that the Bill Brad-field gang had a whole bushel of college degrees and not one of them could tell a cat turd from a candy kiss. He wasn't intimidated by sheepskins and mortarboards. He was a confident top banana.

••••

The comb found in the trunk of Susan Reinert's car got worked during July. Information arrived in bits and pieces. A call to the War College in Carlisle identified the acronym, 79th USARCOM. A call from a cop in the King of Prussia area gave them a lead on a former principal named Dr. Jay C. Smith who'd taught at the same school where Susan Reinert had worked. Another call to the 79th U.S. Army Reserve Command brought the news that Jay C. Smith had been a colonel in the command prior to his retirement. Then they learned that Jay Smith had gone to prison on Monday, June 25th, from a Harrisburg coutroom.

When the comb and the Jay Smith connection was explained to Joe VanNort, he wasn't impressed.

"It's too obvious," he said. "This Jay C. Smith is in a whole pack of trouble and a comb from his army outfit ends up under the body. Too obvious. Sounds like something our pal Bradfield might dream up to throw suspicion on his old nut-case principal."

Joe VanNort stuck with that notion for several months.

••••

While Bill Bradfield and Chris were winding up their summer studies Joe VanNort and Jack Holtz made another trip to St. John's. Only this time they made a prearranged visit to a New Mexico judge and had a court order when they arrived, an order requiring Bill Bradfield and Chris Pappas to submit to finger-printing so that their prints could be compared to unidentified lifts taken in the Reinert home and car.

Bill Bradfield didn't like any of it, particularly the ride to the state police headquarters where he was mugged and printed like a thug. And he *really* didn't like being driven in a separate car from Chris Pappas. And Chris didn't like being photographed, because the mug shot had nothing to do with fingerprint comparison.

When Bill Bradfield next called home he told Vince Valaitis that Joe VanNort was an extremely "unintelligent" man, and that as far as VanNort's partner was concerned, he'd like to have thrown Holtz into the school fountain.

He was incensed with Holtz because when he was trying to explain to the cretinous cop about the Great Books Program at St. John's, and how demanding it was, and how he resented being subjected to police harassment, Jack Holtz had said, "The Bible's a great book. I don't read it myself, but I know it says in there, thou shalt not kill."

Bill Bradfield asked only one question the whole time he was with the cops during their second visit to Santa Fe.

He asked, "How long do the state police stay on a murder case?"

When the cops had made their second appointment at St. John's a college staff member informed Chris Pappas they were coming, and Chris told his mentor who ordered him to get the IBM typewriter out of Bill Bradfield's room and into his own.

After the cops went home, Bill Bradfield visited the Olsens after class and brought a small metal strongbox with him.

"I've got some papers in here," he told Jeff Olsen. "They're not really important, but the police might find them and manipulate them to try to manufacture some evidence. Could you hold this box for me?"

"Sure," Jeff Olsen said. "I'll lock it in the trunk of my car."

"And I'd like you to keep a typewriter for me," Bill Bradfield said. "It was used to write some letters to Susan Reinert. They were nothing of course, but you know the cops."

"Just leave it in this apartment," Jeff Olsen said. "Put it right there on the dining room table."

Naturally, Chris got the assignment of lugging the heavy typewriter to the Olsen apartment. These days he was all muscle and faith.

Later, Bill Bradfield, accompanied by Rachel, came again to the apartment of Jeff Olsen, with another important request. He wanted to use the fireplace. Bill Bradfield was carrying a wastebasket filled with documents of one sort or another.

"These're just school papers and things belonging to Susan Reinert," Bill Bradfield explained. "I don't know why I save everything. It's mostly stuff from her students."

Young Olsen told him to fire away and Bill Bradfield fed the papers into the fireplace and burned them and stirred up the ashes.

Then he said, "Jeffrey, if the police should come here or contact you at any time, you don't have to cooperate with them. They'll try to trick you. But don't tell them that I warned you of that because then they'll twist what you say and try to make *me* look as though I'm obstructing their investigation."

And the student nodded and said, "Gotcha."

"I simply trusted Bill Bradfield completely. I believed he was not guilty," Jeff Olsen reported at a later time.

••••

"I need a favor," Bill Bradfield said to Chris as they were preparing for departure from Santa Fe. "Could you switch typing elements for me? You have a machine just like it, and I'm sure the typing balls are interchangeable."

But now for the first time Chris was thinking about saving his own skin. He was starting to get some very funny feelings about the whole business.

He said, "Bill, why don't you just throw the typing ball away if it bothers you?"

The answer was pure Bradfield. "I'm afraid to," he said. "You never know when you might need something and if you throw it away it's gone for good. I'd feel so much better if *you* kept it. You know how to remove them, don't you?"

"After we get home I'll see what I can do," Chris Pappas said.

But the handyman realized it didn't take a Wernher von Braun to replace typing balls. Chris had started worrying a whole lot when Bill Bradfield first said that he'd loaned the typewriter to Susan Reinert. And it goosed Chris a bit when he heard about a $25,000 "money receipt."

He'd read a news report that Susan Reinert had been unable to remove her $25,000 in large increments, and had to withdraw it in smaller increments. He started thinking about Bill Bradfield claiming that *his* life savings of $28,000 had to be removed in increments of $5,000.

Chris Pappas felt like a cripple who didn't *want* to walk, but some hairy gorilla in a white smock kept dumping his wheelchair and forcing those baby steps.

He was beginning to put Bill Bradfield's stories under a bright light for a little third degree. And the answers were not in English, Latin or Greek. Bill Bradfield just *might* have had a little something to do with misappropriating the $25,000 investment of Susan Reinert.

As to Bill Bradfield having something to do with the *murder* of Susan Reinert and the disappearance of her children, Chris Pappas wasn't ready to deal with *that* one yet. He was protected by deductive reasoning. To Chris Pappas it was a simple syllogism. If Bill Bradfield revered Thomas Aquinas, then he could never be a truly bad man. At worst he could be a flawed good man. A flawed good man might be tempted to misappropriate a sum of money that he intended to repay, but only a truly evil man could do the *other* thing.

It can be theorized that Chris Pappas suffered a bit of added torment over the whole business of the "flawed good man" and the "misappropriation" of money. It is not precisely clear whether he actually informed Bill Bradfield that he was taking $1,300 out of the safety deposit box to buy his brother's trade-in car.

Flawed good men. The concentric circles around William Bradfield were full of them, and Chris Pappas was beginning to indulge some uncomfortable ideas. He absolutely refused to give Bill Bradfield his own typing ball. The typeface style on Bill Bradfield's typewriter was Gothic, of course.

••••

The commandant of the Pennsylvania state troopers, a recent appointee of Governor Thornburgh, was a former special agent of the FBI from the Pittsburgh office. The governor had served western Pennsylvania for several years as a U.S. attorney so they knew each other pretty well.

Ken Reinert had been calling his congressman and the U.S. attorney trying to persuade somebody to bring the FBI into the case. He didn't have faith in Joe VanNort and his state troopers. So whether it was pressure from the congressman or from Senator Schweiker or Governor Thornburgh, the FBI agreed to enter the Reinert case on the pretext that the children were possibly kidnap victims being held in some other state for a future ransom demand. Farfetched, but it satisfied federal requirements for the time being.

••••

Joe VanNort treated the news that the feds were coming as if the Reds were coming. He had a little talk with his team of five cops telling them what to expect.

"Okay, we *gotta* cooperate with them," he said. "But they ain't never goin in the Reinert house unless there's a trooper with them. Got that? And if anybody tries to push you around, you come to me and tell me right now! Remember, they know nothin about homicide. They're glory boys. They come in and give press conferences, and like that. They got no real field experience. They got no real court experience. No real police experience. They're not cops. They're a bunch of lawyers and bookkeepers. No, they're a bunch a . . . *schoolteachers,* is what they are!"

It was the worst thing Joe VanNort could think of to describe a special agent of the FBI.

••••

Civilians have seldom understood the real danger inherent in police work. It has never been particularly hazardous to the body, not since Sir Robert Peel first organized his corps of bobbies. This line of work has *always* been a threat to the spirit.

That summer it was dramatized. It was a night like other nights since the investigation had started: frustrating, fruitless, maddening. And now they were awaiting the arrival of eighteen special agents to form a joint task force.

There they sat long after they should have gone home: Joe VanNort, Jack Holtz and a few other troopers. No one remembers who started it, but it was a night when the spirit of a cop could burst loose and show itself without the badge and veneer of cynicism. That scarred-up cop spirit can turn as panicky as a colt in a barn fire.

One of the troopers had a bad thought, just a little jock-itch of a thought, but within five minutes it was like a raging syphilis epidemic.

The trooper said, "Do you know something? Our photos of the corpse aren't all that recognizable. I mean, she was beat up pretty bad. I mean, a person who knew her could look at our photos and *think* it was Susan Reinert. But what if it was somebody else?"

Everybody laughed.

But then Jack Holtz said, "You know, that mortician who cremated her said he was a little mixed up by what her brother told him to do. What if Pat Gallagher told him to burn the body, and after it was done tried to convince the mortician that he misunderstood the instructions?"

"You mean what if Pat Gallagher is on it with . . ."

"Bill Bradfield!"

"And Ken Reinert is . . ."

"Also in on it! He identified the wrong corpse on purpose!"

"And Susan Reinert is . . ."

"In England with her kids waiting for her boyfriend to inherit seven hundred and thirty G's!"

"And the body we have is . . ."

"Maybe some poor hooker that could pass for Susan Reinert in morgue photos!"

"And then Bradfield . . ."

"Gives Gallagher and Ken Reinert their quiet money and goes off to England and meets his new family and they buy a boat and go sailing off to . . ."

"The Greek islands or the Aegean Sea or some canal in Venice where Ezra Pound mighta flushed his freaking toilet one time!"

Well, there it was. The homicide investigator's nightmare. All the cops were sitting around stunned. And Joe VanNort's cynical blackjack mouth was hanging open, about to lose his eighty-first Marlboro of the day.

Jack Holtz was beating his snuff to death and spitting juice into a Coke bottle at a rate of forty globs per minute. He was also pressing the nose piece on his glasses, which is a laugh because he was so cautious and controlled you could heave him off a cliff in Acapulco and he'd come up with his Timex and those glasses digging into his cheeks like surgical implants.

Every cop in the room had a nightmare vision of eighteen FBI agents strutting in long enough to have lunch. Then in forty-eight hours they'd load the real Susan Reinert and her kids on a London Concorde heading for JFK and a press conference where Joe VanNort and Jack Holtz and all the others wouldn't be heard over the thunder of cackles, snorts and guffaws. The horror of it all was professional *humiliation.*

A telephone call was made. The latent-prints specialist verified that the fingerprints on the corpse matched the lifts found all over the bedroom and bathroom of Susan G. Reinert of Ardmore.

The cops all looked at each other with shit-I-knew-it-all-the-time grins.

And that's how a cop's mind works.

17

Dr. Jekyll

As FBI agents go, the state cops could have done far worse. In the first place, the special agent in charge, Don Redden, was almost as young as Jack Holtz, and younger than several of the agents he was supervising. And he wasn't one of those FBI agents whose secondary mission in life is to look preppier than George Bush.

Don Redden was more of a Harrisburg kind of guy. In fact, he'd worked in the Harrisburg office and knew Jack Holtz. He was a Kentuckian and sounded like chicken-fried-steak, and looked as though he'd be right at home dipping snuff with Holtz or tramping around on VanNort's mountain with a twelve gauge.

But it was tough for Special Agent Don Redden or any of them to get chummy with Joe VanNort. Every other day he was having a faceoff with somebody.

Once he grabbed three feds and said, "I hear somebody in this group was reinterviewin witnesses and said the staties done a piss-poor job!"

And of course the agents denied it, and maybe they hadn't said it, but Joe VanNort went to Don Redden and said, "We're gettin it together here. I want everybody to know who's in charge of this investigation. Me. That's who's in charge."

Don Redden knew Joe VanNort was a daddy cop from the old school and he understood the resentment and jealousy that goes

212

with these cases, and he didn't say too much when VanNort braced his agents with embarrassing questions.

"Any a you people *ever* investigated a murder?" Joe VanNort challenged. "I mean, even *one* little murder?"

Of course VanNort knew that the FBI rarely had the opportunity, but he even accused the "goddamn schoolteachers" of never having seen a dead body in all their lives.

You had to be careful with Joe VanNort because you couldn't be certain *which* group of goddamn schoolteachers he was talking about. Bill Bradfield, et al., or the feds.

When any of the special agents wanted to go to the Reinert house, VanNort demanded that a trooper be present. When the agents wanted to bring Ken Reinert or Pat Gallagher into the house for any reason, Joe VanNort would get so hot he could set off sprinklers because those two still hadn't been officially cleared as far as he was concerned.

The feds weren't around a week before he turned to Jack Holtz and said, "When this case is over I ain't never workin with the FBI again. No matter *who* orders me."

The FBI agents immediately liked the blue comb lead and the other Jay Smith connections. Despite Joe VanNort, they began working in that direction.

As far as VanNort was concerned, Bill Bradfield was a hugger-mugger, acting alone. The kind that picks on plain or homely women, turns on the charm and gives them some cuddles while he picks their purses.

There was something else that Joe VanNort maintained from his first encounter with Bill Bradfield and from everything he'd learned.

"I can get that guy," he promised, "because he's got a mouth he can't control. And he'll *never* be able to control it. He'll talk his way right into the joint."

••••

While Stephanie Smith lay dying of cancer, a former co-worker at the dry clearner's released Stephanie's diary to a local newspaper. And it was full of lurid fact and fantasy.

The newspaper accounts in August were enough in themselves to keep a task force busy.

One headline said: SEX RING LINKED TO MURDER. SWINGER'S GROUP PROBED.

> State police have uncovered explosive new evidence in the Susan Reinert murder case linking the Upper Merion teacher to a bizarre sex ring. Officials have categorically refused to disclose any details publicly about the group. But sources said yesterday that Mrs. Reinert's knowledge of the love cult may have been a motive in the slaying.
>
> The individuals contacted by reporters have said that as many as 20 to 30 men and women regularly paticipated in "swinging sessions" that included homosexual and sado-masochistic acts. However, it could not be determined whether Mrs. Reinert actually participated in any of the orgies.
>
> One police source said that Mrs. Reinert may have been killed because she was about to expose the existence of the group and its members, most of whom are "professionals."

A Sunday edition of a Philadelphia paper printed an interesting story that caught Jay Smith's attention in his cell at Dallas prison.

The headline read: SATAN CULT DEATH?

> Teacher may have been sexually assaulted, tortured, before she was slain, probers say. The murderers of Upper Merion High School teacher Susan Reinert may have been members or associates of a Satan worship cult, investigators have told reporters. Mrs. Reinert may have been stripped, tortured and sexually assaulted as she lay on a makeshift sacrifice altar during a black Mass devil worship ceremony on the weekend of her murder last June. Federal and state investigators have found evidence of the existence of the cult in the Upper Merion area.
>
> Cult members were described by one investigator as "intellectual professionals." They did not balk at using animals in sex exhibition and encounters, the investigators said. Investigators said they were not sure if Susan Reinert was actually a member of the cult or whether she attended the black Mass rituals and other ceremonies out of curiosity, but they said they were certain Mrs. Reinert knew about the cult and the identity of many of its members.
>
> Satanism or devil worship is as old as Christianity itself. Its members traditionally dress in dark hooded robes and gather at a narrow altar to witness Satan, usually a cult ringleader in Satan garb, perform a sexual sacrifice on an unclothed maiden. Literature about the cult attests that in modern times the ceremony has included the use of sexual stimulation devices. Satan performs sado-masochistic acts on his victim who is tied up and heavily

drugged while other cult members hold lighted candles and chant ancient prayers of Satanic worship.

Some of Smith's papers, letters, and diaries that were made public last week in a copyrighted story in a Montgomery County newspaper, indicated that Smith engaged in sexual activities while wearing such costumes as military fatigues and a Satan outfit.

With school soon to resume, Upper Merion Township was taking a lot of shots.

A front-page headline read: THE ABC'S OF A SCHOOL GONE BAD.

At least four teachers are currently under investigation for criminal offenses according to a police source. And as many as a dozen more are suspected of involvement with, or knowledge of, a love cult.

There were pictures on the front page of the harried school-board president and the school superintendent facing an irate mob of parents who wanted William Bradfield and his intimates fired.

A Philadelphia paper ran a picture of a furious mother brandishing a microphone at a school board meeting. The headline said: SEX, DRUGS, TROUBLE, UPPER MERION HIGH.

Angry parents were asking politicians to probe the entire school district, according to an article with a headline that said, LIFE IN THE SUBURBS IS SUDDENLY SCANDALOUS.

And while tabloids were calling Upper Merion THE SCHOOL FOR SCANDAL, the new administration was trying to assure everyone that a breakdown in discipline under Dr. Jay C. Smith was being greatly exaggerated.

"It's a real bitch!" one administrator was quoted as saying. "They don't teach you how to handle *these* things in graduate school."

The yearbook of Upper Merion Senior High School had been dedicated to the new principal and was printed just before the term ended. The dedication said:

In becoming principal, you took on a school that was certainly in need of direction. You turned it around and sent it on the right course.

The billboard at the city limit said: UPPER MERION TOWNSHIP IS A GOOD PLACE TO LIVE, WORK AND WORSHIP.

But one night a vandal painted a huge scarlet notice on the side of the school.

It said: THE DEVIL'S WORKSHOP.

····

"All because a one little rubber dick!" Joe VanNort griped.

He figured that the dildo found in the car, and Stephanie's diary detailing Jay Smith's exotic sex practices, were having a squirrel cage effect on his task force. The FBI agents were diving into the Satanism gossip on the theory that the children were being held by a devil cult. Joe VanNort figured they weren't going to stop till they found Rosemary's baby.

And every time he turned around there was an indication that one of his *own* men was blabbing to a certain woman reporter. He was being diverted from the Reinert case by one of his guys with a big mouth and an erection. He despised all reporters and they felt the same about him.

Joe VanNort said, "I don't give a shit if Jay Smith wore the skin of a bare-ass oh-rang-itang, we ain't chasin no devils except that bearded son of a bitch with *my* birthday."

To his great chagrin, Joe VanNort had discovered that he and Bill Bradfield were born on the same month and day. He was hoping to send Bill Bradfield a card next year, care of state prison.

Despite what he said, Joe VanNort got dragged into one cult raid out in the country. Acting on a tip that Satanists were holding two young kids in a vacant house, the cops broke in, but there were no demons. There *was* a semidevilish pentagram painted on the floor.

····

Stephanie Smith finally succumbed to her cancer and was buried on August 12th at the Immaculate Heart of Mary Cemetery in Linwood. Jay Smith was permitted to attend the funeral while escorted by a state prison guard.

Though William Bradfield was mentioned more frequently, Jay Smith was more intriguing to the journalists. There were many feature articles.

AN EDUCATOR NAMED JAY C. SMITH WAS A MYSTERY TO HIS WIFE TOO.

JAY C. SMITH, EDUCATOR AND MAN OF SECRETS.
EVEN WIFE COULD NOT BE SURE.

The FBI was fascinated by the sexual flavor of the case. They used the Stephanie Smith diary like a Michelin guidebook to perdition. Special agents were all over the sex shops in Times Square following tips that Susan Reinert had been murdered by a snuff-film killer.

They went after a lead that Jay Smith had killed a pair of Dobermans that were found months earlier with their sex organs mutilated. They checked out the story that a black hooker found dead in Valley Forge was a Jay Smith victim. They perused a story that Jay Smith wanted to open his own massage parlor, and at least that one was true.

The FBI followed up rumors that he frequented Plato's Retreat in New York. They worked on a letter Stephanie had filched, a letter from a man who had sent Dr. Jay a nude pinup of himself. They even looked into the alleged Jay Smith mail order scheme for penis enlargers.

Then the FBI got a call from a federal inmate in Kentucky who said that when he was in prison in Trenton, New Jersey, William Bradfield had come to him looking for a hit man. The FBI pursued the lead extensively all across the country until they found the reported hit man. It came to nothing more than the butchered dogs, the snuff films, the dead hooker and all the rest.

Joe VanNort just showed the frustrated agents his lopsided grin and said, "Welcome to homicide, boys!"

The FBI also worked hard on the car of Susan Reinert. Debris jammed under the bumper was analyzed and found to be slag. They explored the possibility that the Reinert children had been taken to a place where the car was backed into a slag heap. But the car still contained half a tank of gas, and since Susan Reinert had filled it Friday afternoon, it wasn't likely that it had gone anywhere but straight to Harrisburg. Unless the killer was willing to stop at a filling station with one body or three in the luggage compartment.

It was a time-consuming exercise. There's a *lot* of slag in Pennsylvania and the FBI saw more that year than U.S. Steel.

◆◆◆◆

The fourth estate was losing confidence. A news headline said: A PERFECT CRIME? TRAIL RUNNING COLD IN REINERT MURDER CASE.

A U.S. attorney for Pennsylvania's eastern district was quoted as saying, "There's a rule of thumb among homicide detectives that if no significant clues to the murder are uncovered within the first forty-eight hours of the slaying, the investigation proceeds proportionately downhill."

When he could no longer avoid them, Joe VanNort told reporters that he'd worked homicides that were solved in three days and others that took eighteen months.

When he was asked by a reporter about the fate of the Reinert children he characteristically got his syntax tangled and said, "My guess is as good as yours."

That brought the seers into the news. One described a seance where she'd "seen" the shallow grave of the children.

Ken Reinert saved *all* the stories.

"I cried a lot during those times," Ken Reinert later said, "but the only time I cried from happiness was when the FBI entered the case. It was the first time I felt involved and not powerless. I'd done as much as I could through my congressman and the U.S. attorney to make it happen."

He tried to talk to Joe VanNort on the Monday that the FBI arrived. Ken Reinert wanted to tell the old cop that he'd helped bring in the feds, thinking VanNort would be glad. But he couldn't say what he wanted to say because he began weeping.

Ken Reinert believed that Joe VanNort was hardened to murder. He eventually directed all inquiries to Special Agent Matt Mullin who was working his first murder case and seemed to care about what Ken Reinert was feeling.

"For the first time I understand what the families of MIA's experience," Ken Reinert told him. "Not knowing is the most terrible thing you can imagine."

••••

Lawmen were disturbing the peace of the residents of Woodcrest Avenue in Ardmore. The neighborhood went gray with guys in cheap suits.

"It's like an invasion," one complained. "They use up all the parking on the street and they swoop in at all hours."

The task force found a statement of Susan Reinert's savings from Continental Bank that showed deposits of $30,000 in December, 1978. Some of her later withdrawals and notations caught their interest:

```
2/15/79   1500 B cash
2/20/79   1500 B cash
2/21/79   10,000 T. check Am
3/2/79    5000 B cash
```

There were several cash withdrawals, adding up to $25,500.

A bank statement from American Bank showed total deposits of $15,000 in late February and early March, followed by checks for cash in amounts of $10,000 and $5,000.

There seemed to be money shuffled from one bank to another and a lot of cash transactions that would need to be explained, particularly after another financial document was found.

It was a typed form entitled "credit memo." It was dated February 24, 1979, and reflected that Susan Jane Gallagher Reinert owned 25 percent of a $100,000 certificate that drew 12 percent interest plus or minus, and would pay in six months.

The salesman of the certificate was E. S. Perritt, Jr., and the person who had approved the transaction was M. E. McEvey. The entire transaction had been handled by Bache and Company.

The cops weren't terribly shocked to discover from a phone call that Bache and Company had no employees named Perritt or McEvey, and had never heard of Susan Reinert.

On her calendar diary were the following entries:

```
22 Feb    $3500, money—ring to courier
 1 May    Sailing test
20 May    Bradfield in Harrisburg, Smith trial
31 May    Smith trial over—guilty
 4 June   B left angry
13 June   Sick, depressed, lawyer cancelled
14 June   Last day of school. Maybe last day to see Sue Myers.
          Freeze. Wonder what's going on.
18 June   Call
23 June   P.W.P. moderator's workshop. Reservations G. W.
          Motor Lodge
```

One of the most puzzling notations was the "ring to courier." After the telephone records of everyone connected with the Reinert case were subpoenaed, it was discovered that on February 22nd a telephone call had been made to St. John's College in Santa Fe from Susan Reinert's phone. They learned it had been made in the morning, when Susan Reinert was at her doctor's office for a breast examination.

She didn't make the call, so whoever did might have had something to do with the $3,500 and a "ring to courier."

The cops found a teaching application addressed to the Department of Health, Education and Welfare, Washington, D.C. In the "personality" box was the following:

Mrs. Reinert is a strong minded individual who maintains a becoming professional posture even in the most trying circumstances (confrontations, discipline, etc.).

I lived abroad myself as a civilian and as an Army colonel. I have known Mrs. Reinert for eight years. I have no reservations in recommending her to you. I can state securely that she will be a plus factor to your program. She is a person you can depend on to fulfill her commitments and who will be a teacher that exemplifies the best aspects of American Education.

Jay C. Smith

(Principal of Upper Merion Senior High School 1966 to 1978. Promoted to district director, special services.)

There was another reference to HEW along with Jay Smith's:

Mrs. Reinert is an extremely able and sensitive person who holds very high standards of integrity for herself. She would, it seems to me, be an ideal representative of this country. I recommend her to you without reservation.

William S. Bradfield, Jr.
(Teacher of advanced placement
English, Latin and Greek.)

There was a sad letter written by Susan Reinert to Bertha Perez of the USAA insurance company:

For clarification, please tell me what is covered under accidental death. For example, if I fall of the back of a sailboat, or if I am shot, are those considered accidents? (Not that I'm planning on either of those situations!!)

Two months later, an insurance agent wrote:

> The applicant wanted it known that the reason she applied for insurance was to protect her children. She is going to England, taking her two children with her on a teacher exchange program. She will spend one year in England starting in July or August. Eventually, Mr. B. will visit her and they will be married in England.

Susan Reinert was not granted the fellowship for which she was recommended by Jay Smith and William Bradfield. A brief letter arrived in April saying that the number of qualified candidates greatly exceeded the number of positions available.

She didn't have even that little triumph.

••••

Some of the FBI agents who waded through every scrap of paper in the Reinert house reported being charmed by the photos of the children, especially Karen's.

"That kid was a photographer's dream," one special agent said. "She was meant to be a great-looking woman."

And they noticed that they'd *all* begun talking about the children in the past tense.

It is unknown if any of the agents read an astonishing document written by Michael Reinert a month before his tenth birthday and subsequent disappearance. It was a story for his fifth-grade English class:

> One day I took a trip on a rocket into space. I was headed for the moon. But instead, because I was hit with a falling star I came to be on a weird planet.
>
> I couldn't see a soul in sight. All of a sudden, I saw ten people that looked alike. One of them went behind me. One of them went to one side. One went to the other side. One went to the front. Then they put me into a cage. They threw me into a ditch with a bunch of worms. Then came Mr. Hyde (Dr. Jeckyl) to kill me. Then I just remembered that I had a duplication gun. So I shot myself with it and they didn't know which one was the real me. That is how I got away. I was glad when I repaired my rocket ship so that I could leave the weird planet. The press wanted me to tell them about my trip. I said, "No way!" Nobody knew why I wouldn't tell them, but I'll tell you. I never wanted to remember it again.

Any cop or FBI agent would have found it chilling. Michael Reinert had perhaps written a prophetic story. Michael had perhaps identified his abductor.

••••

The children were being sighted all over the eastern half of the country from communes to gypsy camps. Then the old rumor surfaced that Eddie and Stephanie Hunsberger were somehow involved in Jay Smith's life of crime.

There was a newspaper headline in September that posed a question: ARE REINERT CHILDREN WITH SMITH'S DAUGHTER?

One of the cops had a very cynical and grim answer to that one. He said, "You bet they are."

By then, most of them believed that the children *were* in a ditch. With a bunch of worms.

18

Buses and Bombs

The Reinert task force installed their own phones and had their own stenographers at the state police barracks. Each day the teams of agents and state cops were assigned leads to pursue. Agent Don Redden had to report to the special agent in charge of the Philadelphia office at least every other day.

The FBI referred to the massive joint investigation as SUMUR, for Susan Murder. The code name allowed for quicker communication and better information storage. It was rare that an FBI criminal case was important enough to get a code name.

Don Redden pointed out to the state cops that the designation SUMUR gave their investigation the status of a major government case.

Joe VanNort said it sounded like typical FBI bullshit, but it was hokey enough that Bill Bradfield might like it.

◆◆◆◆

It took three months for the cause of death to be finally established. The toxicology examination of Susan Reinert's blood and tissue samples revealed about 1.1 micrograms morphine per milliliter of blood—about ten times the normal medical dose and enough to kill even a junkie pretty fast. The concentration was so high she'd just stopped breathing, hence, asphyxiation. She'd also been given a mild barbiturate sedative, probably to quiet her.

The Carlisle motel matchbook found in Susan Reinert's car didn't help. She'd stayed at that motel with another woman teacher some months before her death. But the task force learned that on that occasion she'd driven into Harrisburg to meet Bill Bradfield at Harry's, a popular watering hole in a seedy neighborhood. Bill Bradfield liked seedy neighborhoods.

A friend and associate from Parents Without Partners told the state police that Susan Reinert and Bill Bradfield had planned to go to her mother's former home in Ridgway, Pennsylvania, to "attend to some legal matter," and that they were taking the children. The cops wondered if the reference to "lawyer" in the June diary entry may have referred to this.

One week before her death, Susan called that friend and told the woman that she was never going to marry Bill Bradfield because he kept canceling appointments with attorneys about "certain legal questions."

But then she called back five days before her death and said that everything had been "smoothed out."

Then Susan Reinert said something puzzling. She said that she and her friend could have no more contact. The reason given was that it was "getting too close to the time that Sue Myers might do something."

Susan would not explain further. She was *very* secretive toward the end.

••••

The state cops had talked to every neighbor and friend of Susan Reinert who had come to their attention and the feds were duplicating the effort. Just after they came into the case the FBI interviewed sixteen-year-old Elizabeth Ann Brook, the granddaughter of Susan Reinert's next-door neighbor, Mary Gove. Beth Ann described the eerie hailstorm and the clothing that they'd all been wearing when she last saw them. It didn't seem like a significant interview at the time.

◆◆◆◆

Before going back to college in California, Shelly returned Bill Bradfield's money and accompanied him to a storage locker on Route 202 near West Chester.

He told Shelly that he had to store the red IBM typewriter as well as some other dangerous things. The typewriter, he said, had been used by Dr. Smith and Mrs. Reinert to type some things that could get him in trouble. Shelly learned that the assignment to rent the storage was given to Chris Pappas.

Before returning to college, Shelly told the FBI and state cops that she'd been with Bill Bradfield on Friday, June 22nd, taking a stroll around Haverford College, his old alma mater.

During a later interview she amended the time she'd been with Bill Bradfield to cover the period when they were withdrawing money from the safety deposit box, and perhaps saying farewell to an ostrich.

Shelly's girlfriend talked to the cops and then flew to Austria to visit relatives, but the FBI had INTERPOL chase her down to ask her a few more questions.

Sue Myers, Chris Pappas and Bill Bradfield took private polygraph exams for $125 each and were found to be absolutely truthful. Chris took another for the FBI and was found to be deceptive.

He later admitted that during the "truthful" exam he'd been lying worse than Stalin at Yalta.

◆◆◆◆

Living in a Philadelphia motel and going home to Harrisburg only on weekends was probably hardest on Jack Holtz because of his son. Jason was the same age as Karen Reinert and he knew that a boy that age needed his old man. Jack Holtz called his parents almost every night to reassure his son that the case couldn't last much longer.

When he and Joe VanNort were sitting in their rooms at night watching TV, it was obvious that VanNort worried about Holtz being away from his son. Joe VanNort frequently needed reassurance from his young partner that working for him hadn't been the primary cause of Jack's marriage rupture.

Jack Holtz never forgot how shaken Joe had been when he first admitted that Chaz had left home for good. They were on a flight to Alabama during a tough investigation. You'd think Jack Holtz had just announced he was going to Morocco for a sex change.

"It's workin crime, ain't it?" Joe VanNort had said. "Did that wreck your marriage, workin crime with me?"

Holtz tried to reassure the old cop by saying, "It's for the best. She's gone and it's over."

But Joe was stricken with Catholic guilt and he actually *hushed* Jack Holtz and said, "Don't tell nobody!"

Holtz looked around and said, "Joe, who can I tell? I don't know anybody on this airplane!"

It was during the long nights in those motel rooms in Philadelphia, drinking and watching the frequent flame of Joe's cigarettes flowering in the gloom, that Jack Holtz wished hard for a break in the case, while Joe VanNort prayed for one.

••••

Wishes and prayers were about to be answered by a Clark Kent–ish young English teacher who'd been carrying twice his weight in guilt and fear for two months. The heavy load was dumped on him at the memorial service for Susan Reinert.

It was a Unitarian service and was held in the evening in a chapel in Malvern. Ken Reinert was there, and Pat Gallagher, and all of Susan Reinert's friends, and her psychologist, and most of her colleagues.

Pat Schnure was crying her eyes out and saying to everyone within earshot, "Make a note of who's *not* here!"

She was of course referring to the Bradfield retinue, but one of them *was* there. Vince Valaitis was praying harder in that Unitarian chapel than he'd ever prayed in a Catholic cathedral. With the stories in the news about the Bradfield Bunch he figured that everyone thought they were a pack of killers. He felt that therapist Roslyn Weinberger was *glaring* at him.

It was a sad little ceremony with various people saying a few things about Susan Reinert as a teacher and mother and friend. When it was over, Vince tried to tough it out by holding his head up and saying hello to everybody, but he felt his colleagues trying to avoid him. For the very first time in his life he saw people staring at him with fear in their eyes.

Vince had been the only one giving press releases. To one reporter he said, "We're not part of any sort of cult. Bill Bradfield doesn't want anyone's money. He doesn't care about things of this world. He cares about a *better* world. And as for me, I'm not some kind of killer! Why, I'm a God-fearing person. How many twenty-eight-year-olds do you know who carry rosary beads?"

Vince had informed his colleague Bill Scutta that he wished he could join a seminary and become a priest. Preferably a Trappist monastery in Tibet.

••••

One night, Vince went for a drive to sort things out. He drove through Valley Forge Park and admired the flora, and tried to think good things about Susan Reinert, and said some prayers for her and her children. Somehow he just couldn't go home. All he could do was drive and think and pray.

Then a funny thing happened. The sky was no longer where it was supposed to be. Something *else* was up there in its place: a bunch of titanic inkblots. It was only a storm taking shape, but not to Vince. And what did the inkblots contain? Nothing much. Only hairnets full of trapped leering *demons*.

The next time Vince looked at the swirling inkblots he saw cowled shrouded figures chanting in Latin as they made ready for a black mass. And Vince took a leap into full-scale *panic*.

When Vince later told the story of that night, he used the word "Gothic." The National Weather Service verified that it had not been a Vince Valaitis Gothic hallucination. The sky *did* go black. The Rorschach test in heaven *was* split by shards of lightning. The thunder rattled the trees in Valley Forge and the rain cascaded down.

To Vince Valaitis there was absolutely no question. God Himself was speaking.

His message was something like "Okay, you little putz, you want Gothic? I'll *give* you Gothic."

Vince found himself skidding, sliding, careening, through the rain, hell-bent, as it were, for destruction. Then in the midst of it all, between the jagged flashes and the torrent of black water, he saw before him a miracle: Vince had driven on automatic pilot to God's house.

He skidded to a stop in front of Mother of Divine Providence Church in King of Prussia. He jumped out of the car, but he was paralyzed. Vince Valaitis stood ankle-deep in puddles of dark water and verdant slime and watched his suit shrink. He pulled his necktie loose so he could breathe, and felt his shoes turn spongy. He forced those few sloshing steps to salvation.

But there were bat shapes in the night, and a fist of iron in his belly was making him retch. And if this church had even one lousy little gargoyle on the roof, Vince knew he'd bolt and run screaming in front of a truck if he could find one.

He rang the bell at the rectory and waited with the blades of rain slashing his face, hearing those terrifying Latin chants growing fainter in the distance.

When the priest opened the door that night he saw a half-drowned young fellow flashing a demented gerbil grin and doing deep breathing exercises to help ward off levitation.

Here's what Vince heard inside his head: "I am a rational human being. I need fear no evil. I am in control. I shall begin at the beginning in a calm businesslike manner."

Here's what the priest heard outside Vince's head: "FATHER, I KNOW WHO KILLED SUSAN REINERT!"

The priest feared for the stained glass. Pigeons flew from the belfrey.

Soon, Vince Valaitis found himself sitting in the rectory bawling his heart out with a priest who was trying to figure out if he should hear this kid's confession or have him blow in a bag. And finally Vince started to talk. He was interrupted by sobs from time to time, but did he *talk*. He told about acid and hairnets and jigsaws and bloody bags of trash and silencers and Jimmy Hoffa and 250 hits and devil suits and dildos.

Pretty soon the priest was wondering if he should call the chancery office to see if they had an exorcist hot line, because he had himself a dilly!

Vince couldn't shut up. He segued right into Brink's guards and chains and locks and strapping tape and golden showers and feces fiestas and humping hound dogs. He even got into Jay

Smith's mail-order penis stiffeners, but that was gilding the lily because by now this priest had heard so much that a dick splint couldn't shock him.

When Vince came up for air, the padre became the first person to tell Vince Valaitis that he'd better tell his friend Bill Bradfield to call the cops.

Three little words. Heeded earlier they could've saved a lot of people an eternity of pain: call the cops.

◆◆◆◆

Jack Holtz and an FBI special agent, Carlin "Call Me Chick" Sabinson, got the assignment to meet and interview Vince Valaitis. Chick Sabinson was nothing like the sterotypical law school prep. To start with, there hadn't ever been many FBI agents called Chick. And he didn't even look like an agent. He was a smallish, ethnic-looking guy. You figured he'd spent his life eating deli food, but you weren't sure which deli.

Don Redden said he'd once spotted Chick Sabinson sitting at his work table writing a task force report with both hands. One hand held the pencil and the other made identical sweeping strokes of penmanship *without* a pencil. So there was a bit of the artist in Chick Sabinson, and it showed in his interrogation technique.

Jack Holtz, the ever-shy second banana, let Chick Sabinson do the talking when they were sitting face to face with pale and trembling Vincent Valaitis who was puffing away on a cigarette, even though he'd never smoked in his life.

Chick Sabinson had a voice something like W. C. Fields, and after advising Vince of his constitutional rights, he got around to the business at hand. "Vince," he said, "can you see that we're not the kind of people Bill Bradfield said we are?"

"Yes, sir," Vince said, getting green around the gills from his own smoke.

"Call me Chick."

"Yes sir, Chick," Vince said obligingly. He was one sick gerbil.

"Vince," Chick Sabinson continued, "I'd like you to use your imagination. I'd like you to imagine that the government is a bus."

Vince stopped puffing and said, "Bus. Yes, Chick."

"Imagine that the bus makes a certain number of stops as it rolls down the street, Vince."

Vince imagined a red, white and blue bus chugging right along. A streetcar named Desire. A bus named *Salvation.*

"But Vince," Chick said, and now there was a note of caution in his voice, "if a person doesn't have the right fare and if the peson isn't there at the bus stop when the driver says 'All aboarrrrrrd!' what's gonna happen?"

"They'll miss the bus, Chick," Vince said, and he almost wept. Because he *was* on time. He'd pay any fare they wanted!

"And the bus never returns, Vince. Never never never."

Chick reached over and clutched Vince's arm because tears were welling in the teacher's eyes.

And apparently he had no idea how anxious Vince was to get *on* the bus because he kept drawing word pictures. With both hands.

"Let me put it another way," Chick Sabinson said. "The government is a bomb shelter. And when the war starts and the bombs begin to fall, the doors will open to let a certain number of people in. But only the early birds. And only if they come *when* they're invited. Do you understand what I'm saying, Vince?"

Did he ever! That time Chick Sabinson accidentally picked the right metaphor. While Chick was talking bomb shelters, Vince Valaitis was seeing trekkie space wars. The clash by night involved megatons. Nukes mushroomed. Firestorms raged. People got vaporized in their beds!

And there was Vince, three feet from the shelter door, a steaming little bespectacled radioactive lump. Wrapped in rosary beads.

Vince let out a wail. "Do I need a lawyer? Have I done anything wrong?"

Chick Sabinson said, "Tell us what you know about Jay Smith."

That did it. Vince started crying. Between sobs he said, "He's murdered all kinds of people! I think my life's in danger! I don't want to be murdered. I only want to teach English!"

And while Vince was sniffling Chick Sabinson got up and came over and put his arm around him and said, "There there, Vince. It's all right. You're *ours,* now."

It was wonderful belonging to somebody. Again, Vince Valaitis started talking and couldn't stop. He could hardly believe he was sitting there so happy with the FBI, and even with Jack Holtz who Bill Bradfield had said was a dyed-in-the-wool Fascist. It all felt so good he just *kept* talking.

Chick Sabinson and Jack Holtz almost got writer's cramp. Before they were finished with this young man in the months ahead, the FBI reckoned that Vincent gave them nearly a hundred hours of his time.

Vince had only one real fear after that. When they saw the Mary Hume tombstone in his living room, they might accuse him of bumping off old Mary.

····

On September 3, the FBI was called and informed that Bill Bradfield wanted to "set the record straight." He and Sue Myers and Vince Valaitis agreed to meet with the agents at a Howard Johnson's restaurant in King of Prussia. Bill Bradfield didn't know that Vince had already been setting the record a whole lot straighter than he'd ever dreamed.

They met with Chick Sabinson. Bill Bradfield told the special agent that he was just a friend of Susan Reinert's and was shocked by the insurance and the will. And what he really wanted to do was to put up a reward for the return of the children, but he'd been advised by counsel not to do so.

Bill Bradfield offered the opinion that if the children were alive there was obviously someone else involved with Jay Smith. Bill Bradfield said that he was now starting to conclude that Dr. Jay was probably the actual killer of Susan Reinert.

He was relieved that Chick Sabinson was an educated man as opposed to Joe VanNort and his sidekick Jack Holtz. He said that while he was at St. John's he'd been studying the contribution of Ptolemy to Western thought, but couldn't explain it to the cops who thought he was taking a math class.

Chick Sabinson did not tell him about the government bus or the bomb shelter. Bill Bradfield admitted nothing. They parted amicably.

····

During one of his secret FBI meetings Vince told the lawmen about a typed letter that Bill Bradfield had once received at school.

It said, "Please come and meet me." It was signed "Deirdre Paxton."

When Bill Bradfield showed Vince the letter he'd smiled and said, "That's from Doctor Smith."

He'd borrowed Vince's car and left the campus for forty-five minutes.

Vince also gave the FBI a list of telephone numbers from the Jay Smith–Bill Bradfield square-root-of-the-last-digit-of-Alexander-Graham-Bell's-birth-date telephone system.

Bill Bradfield had left the list with Vince Valaitis for safekeeping. Bill Bradfield left trails of evidence scattered through his forest like a bearded Hansel, fearful of being lost.

••••

Vince was a mess when it was time to go with Bill Bradfield to meet attorney John Curran for a strategy discussion. Vince had no intention of discussing strategy. Vince belonged to Chick Sabinson and the FBI. Vince was on the bus. Vince was in the bomb shelter. He was a nervous wreck trying to bring himself to confess this to Bill Bradfield and convince him to do likewise. But at the slightest hint of going to the law Bill Bradfield would start *screaming* about Fascists.

Vince agreed to drive Bill Bradfield to Ocean City for the meeting. He must have been exceptionally quiet during the drive because Bill Bradfield apparently sensed something.

When they were almost at the restaurant, he said quietly to Vince, "You talked to them, didn't you?"

"Yes," Vince sighed. "I've been talking to the FBI and you should too. Bill, they're nice people. We've got nothing to hide. We should tell them all about Jay Smith."

"Who else have you told?" Bill Bradfield asked, even more quietly.

Vince saw that the blood had drained from his friend's face like a sink full of dishwater.

"I've told Bill Scutta and my parents."

"You've killed Scutta," Bill Bradfield informed him. "You've killed your parents."

Vince knew of course that Bill Bradfield was alluding to the Jay Smith legion who'd knocked off everyone from Jimmy Hoffa to hookers from Philly, and he cried, "You *have* to trust them, Bill! You have to talk!"

"Stop the car," Bill Bradfield commanded, and when Vince did, he got out on the sidewalk and said, "Are you coming to talk to Curran?"

"No, I'm not," Vince said.

"You've betrayed me," Bill Bradfield said, slamming the door. "You've broken your solemn oath. You've *killed* me."

Bill Bradfield arrived at the restaurant meeting in such an agitated state that he was twisting and torturing his beard. He greeted John Curran who was already talking with Chris Pappas and Sue Myers, and he asked Curran to excuse them for a moment, saying he needed an urgent private talk with his friends.

After John Curran took a walk, Bill Bradfield informed Chris and Sue that Vince had talked to the FBI. But Chris and Sue weren't quite sure what that meant, and they seemed a bit relieved because though maintaining silence about Jay Smith might save them from a mob hit, they were looking more and more like killers themselves.

Bill Bradfield was obviously trying to talk away his panic before Curran arrived. He jabbered something about selling everything he owned and going to England or someplace else in Europe. Then he added that *of course* he'd give all his money to Sue Myers before leaving.

Sue Myers thought, sure, and he'd invite her to join him in England. About the same time Wallis Simpson got invited for tea and scones with the Queen Mum.

Bill Bradfield said that he, an innocent man who'd done nothing except try to protect Susan Reinert, might end up with a load of dirt in his face because of that sniveling little son of a bitch, Vince Valaitis.

Chris said, "Bill, they wouldn't electrocute an innocent man."

But Bill Bradfield told him testily that he wasn't worried about being smoked by the authorities. He was afraid of being snuffed by Jay Smith because of Vince's big mouth.

Chris Pappas was getting all mixed up again, and he said in frustration, "Jay Smith's in prison. So maybe we should tell the cops *our* side of all this."

Ah, but Jay Smith's minions were *everywhere,* Bill Bradfield reminded him. And Vince Valaitis might have just signed his own death warrant. And they'd better be very careful or their names would be on a murder contract right along with his. They were not yet free from Jay Smith danger.

By the time Bill Bradfield was through twiddling his beard, it looked like Medusa's hairdo.

••••

After Vince Valaitis had talked, and all of Bill Bradfield's friends knew about it, Trooper Lou DeSantis and Special Agent Matt Mullin got the assignment to travel to California to interview Shelly again. It was the first time that her Catholic college had ever had the law arrive to chat with a student about murder.

After being taken to a private room and advised of her constitutional rights, Shelly told the lawmen that she was willing to talk, but she might need some sort of immunity.

The lawmen were licking their chops because little Shelly was showing a brow like a pile of linguini, and they thought they had something going. But then she told them what had her so worried. When Bill Bradfield and Chris were at summer school, she and her pal Jenny had been driving Chris's car all over the place without a proper registration or driver's license.

The lawmen couldn't believe it. *They* were talking about a murdered woman and two missing children and *she* was worrying about a traffic ticket. The Bradfield bunch made them yearn for cattle prods and ice baths. Anything to wake them up.

Shelly told them her version of the weekend as she and Bill Bradfield had rehearsed it, replete with all the lies. The lies kept getting tangled as to where she and Bill Bradfield had been on Friday, June 22nd. She now said they *may* have been walking around Haverford College. As to the time he dropped her at her pal's, she changed it from 7:00 P.M. to 8:45 P.M.

As to Bill Bradfield's obvious perjury at the Jay Smith trial,

Shelly finally conceded that he could have made an honest mistake because he was bad about dates.

Then the cops told her a few things to test her response. They talked about some of Bill Bradfield's amorous affairs, but Shelly said she didn't believe for a minute that there'd been anything at all between Susan Reinert and Bill Bradfield. Ditto with Rachel even after they pointed out that she'd been registered in the Philly hotel for one month prior to the murder under the name of Mrs. William Bradfield.

Shelly looked pretty smug when she heard that because Bill Bradfield had explained to her that Rachel was afraid of the seedy neighborhood and wanted any potential rapists in the hotel lobby to think she had a man in the room. Besides, Bill Bradfield had told her that he'd been celibate for five years. Rachel was *just* a friend and it was a pretty sad thing that in 1979 people couldn't accept friendship between the sexes that didn't involve something sordid. She informed the investigators that Chris and her girl-friend had that kind of relationship.

But they pointed out to Shelly that they'd seen the phone records of the hotel and learned that at 5:35 A.M. on June 1st, Bill Bradfield had made a call from that hotel to Upper Merion High School to say that he wouldn't be able to make it to class.

Shelly was stopped by that one, but finally she said, "Okay, maybe he spent the night with Rachel. But it was probably for a good reason. Don't you understand that people can spend the night together without thinking of sex? He was just exhausted."

Then she tried to tell them how he taught English and Latin to her. And how he tutored students in Greek and even taught Bible studies on his own time.

The lawmen at this time didn't know about all the money storage and the rest of it. Nor did they know that Bill Bradfield and Shelly were going to get married in a French cathedral and de-claim from "The Wanderer" as they followed the trail of the My-cenaeans and their thousand black ships.

Matt Mullin had some compassion for the young woman, but Joe VanNort did not.

After they returned, Joe VanNort said, "The FBI maybe wants to pay her tuition to Notre Dame. I wanna see her graduate through a correspondence course. In state prison."

••••

The federal grand jury happened to be in session in Philadelphia. The Reinert task force used the powers of this grand jury to subpoena phone records, credit card information and bank records, to go deeper into the affairs of William Bradfield and his friends. And of Jay C. Smith, as well.

Vince Valaitis couldn't *wait* to talk publicly about the terrible dilemma that he and his friends found themselves in. Prior to volunteering his testimony to the grand jury, Vince talked to reporters again.

"Bill Bradfield refuses to be interviewed," Vince told them, "because he fears no one will believe him. And because he has a higher moral motivation. He doesn't care about this world at all. He cares about his soul and *another* world. I've prayed a rosary with Bill and he wants to become a Catholic. I see Bill in an entirely different way than you do."

He told the grand jury his strange story and then he volunteered what he thought might set the record straight for all of them:

"In the news it says 'this clique of teachers.' It sounds like we're some kind of insidious group. This is something that evolved slowly. I can't even believe I'm sitting here saying all I've said to you.

"There's nothing insidious about our group. We're good people. We're friendly. We love each other. I feel that people in our school district think we consider ourselves superior. They're saying that because Bill Bradfield is such an aggressive man, such a brilliant man, such an overpowering man, that we all believe in everything he does. That's not true."

When Vince was through talking that day, one of the grand jurors said, "Explain to me, to all of us, why in the world didn't you at some time go to Mrs. Reinert and *warn* her?"

And by now Vince knew he'd spend the rest of his life being asked that question. And by now he knew that even when the words were not being uttered, the eyes were asking it.

Flattened and humiliated, after an interminable pause, Vince said, "I . . . just did not . . . *deal* with it."

It was as good an answer as any of them would give. And it would never get any better.

••••

When it was time to pay his lawyer a little installment, did Bill Bradfield just send a check or money order or even walk in and plop some cash on John Curran's desk? Of course not, since a straightforward move like that might cause him to limit his cast which already had more players than *Nicholas Nickleby.*

He didn't want his lawyer to know that he had the pile of money that Shelly had been hiding. He told Chris to ask his father if he'd take the cash and buy money orders for several thousand dollars and give the money orders to Bill Bradfield. He wanted his lawyer to think he was broke and having to borrow.

And Bill Bradfield told Chris what he'd like to do about the Judas who had caused all this misery for them.

He said, "I'd like to blow Vince's brains out!"

He said that he was thinking about planting a story with Jay Smith that Vince Valaitis had hired a private eye to uncover things about Jay Smith. That way Dr. Jay wouldn't think that Bill Bradfield had talked to anyone about all the Jay Smith shenanigans, and he might be encouraged to have a member of the mob "take out" Vince.

Chris wasn't worrying about Vince at this point. Mostly he was worrying about Chris Pappas. He'd learned a lot from his master in the past several months. Chris saved potential evidence that came his way. After all, Bill Bradfield himself always said that he hated to destroy anything because he never knew when he might need it again.

••••

The superintendent of the Upper Merion school board promised a crowd of 150 parents and citizens that while 3 teachers whose names were not mentioned could not be legally fired, they would be removed from direct contact with students.

Chris went to work at a construction job. Bill Bradfield, Sue Myers and Vince Valaitis were reassigned to nonteaching duties while the school district tried to figure out what to do with them.

They were ordered to report to the deserted Union Avenue School and were given busy work.

The superintendent said privately to Vince, "Boy, if I could get you *out* of this district, I *would!*"

Unfortunately for Vince, he and Bill Bradfield were forced to share the same basement office, the same work table in fact, and there was no real work to do. They'd just report every day and Vince would read the latest newspaper article on the Reinert case and try not to talk about it to his friend, but once in a while he couldn't help himself.

He saw a tidbit that some reporter wrote and asked, "Did you ever have breakfast at Susan Reinert's house?"

"Absolutely not!" Bill Bradfield answered.

"Pat Schnure says that Karen told her you did."

Bill Bradfield threw a desk calendar against the wall, and shouted, "They're all *liars!* The hounds are after a conviction!"

"They're saying a lot about you and Susan Reinert," Vince said. "It can't *all* be lies."

And then Bill Bradfield looked at him with his blue eyes brimming with sadness and disappointment, and he started mixing metaphors:

"Vince, the Book of Job says that sometimes innocent people have to be punished. God never promised you a bed of roses. During court cases there are battles, and after battles there are bodies."

Something happened then that had never happened to Bill Bradfield. A disciple got mad enough to clench a fist.

Vince Valaitis slammed his fist down on the wooden table and said, "I'm not going to be punished for you! I'm not going to jail with you!"

Bill Bradfield got mad too. He grabbed a piece of paper and a pencil and said, "All right, if I'm going to be blamed for murder, I might well as admit it. Here. I'll show you how I did it."

He drew a square with a little line. He said, "I took the children and I gave them to . . ."

But Vince snatched the paper and crumpled it and threw it on the floor saying, "Don't do that! Don't make things up!"

Vince stormed out of the basement office and was allowed to have desk space in another room.

Over the years he was asked many times to think back on that incident, especially as to Bill Bradfield saying, "I gave them to . . ."

At a later time he would swear that Bill Bradfield said "Smith." He would remember that it was "I gave them to Smith."

Years and memories are tricky. Bill Bradfield may or may not have said "Smith." The implication seemed clear, but Vince learned that lawyers worry a great deal about such things.

◆◆◆

Later calls from William Bradfield to Vince Valaitis came at all hours of the night.

The phone would ring and Vince would pick it up sleepily and Bill Bradfield would say, "Why are you deserting me? I *need* you."

Once he cried, "Don't betray me to the Fascists! Look what they did to Jean Seberg! Look what they did to Ezra Pound!"

Another time he called and said, "Vince, it's all a mistake. We didn't do anything. None of us."

But Vince responded, "How about Jay Smith? How about all the things you told me about you and Jay Smith?"

He almost suffered a blown eardrum when Bill Bradfield screamed, "Don't mention names! It's phone-tapping time! The house is bugged! Everything's dangerous! You don't *know* it was Doctor Smith! None of us knows for sure!"

Bill Bradfield wasn't the only one showing a little paranoia. Sue Myers sat weeping in her apartment one day because of her portrayal in the media. She told Vince that she'd had $1,500 worth of work done on her car but the transmission went out immediately. She was frightened.

Vince said, "That's terrible, but it's nothing to be frightened about."

"Don't you see?" Sue whispered. "The transmission could've been sabotaged by the FBI!"

◆◆◆

It was inevitable. A reporter found out about the Mary Hume tombstone in Vince's apartment and speculated that the "cult" might have lit candles on it as they uttered incantations about Susan Reinert.

During those awful days Vince's parents stood by him. His father invited him to move back home, so Vince slipped out of his digs faster than the Shah of Iran.

Even after he'd deserted Bill Bradfield, Vince Valaitis still did not believe that his friend was guilty of anything except foolishness in not revealing what he knew about Jay Smith to the authorities. As far as he was concerned, a good man had become involved with a bad man for a good reason, and was refusing to save himself.

Vince had a theory that Jay Smith himself had placed the comb under Susan Reinert's body, knowing it would implicate him.

"He always loved to shock and torment," Vince told the FBI. "He'd tantalize you by drawing a circle within a circle within a circle."

During one of his many meetings with Vince Valaitis, Chick Sabinson alluded to Jack Holtz offering Vince a drink and said, "I have to apologize. I didn't know he'd try to ply you with liquor. By the way, I'd like to put a radio transmitter on you in case Bradfield says something incriminating. Would you do it?"

"Can't!" Vince said fearfully. "He'd detect it. He's a hugger."

"Mugger," Joe VanNort added when he heard about that one. "Hugger-mugger, just like I said."

19

The Basement

After the FBI started pressing its agents toward the Jay Smith connection, the red fibers found on the body of Susan Reinert took on significance. Particularly after what Vince Valaitis said about the prince of darkness.

Jack Holtz wanted to pursue the Jay Smith connection along with the FBI, but Joe VanNort still wasn't convinced and ordered him to stick with Bill Bradfield and his cronies.

He said Bill Bradfield and Jay Smith were only connected in the same way that pus and phlegm are connected.

The FBI called on Grace Gilmore, the woman who'd bought the house on Valley Forge Road just before Jay Smith was sent to prison. She said yes, there *was* a red carpet in the upstairs portion of the house.

Grace Gilmore told them that she'd closed escrow on the property prior to the weekend of June 22nd, but Jay Smith was allowed to stay in his basement apartment until Monday in that he correctly assumed that he might get sentenced to prison that day.

Grace Gilmore told Special Agent Hess that she'd gone to the shore with her sister on Friday, June 22nd, and didn't return to the house on Valley Forge Road until Sunday afternoon. She didn't get access to the basement until Monday, after Jay Smith was gone for good.

She'd never really seen him the day she returned. While putting away some things in the upstairs part of the house, she heard
a noise from the basement apartment. Then she heard his car
drive away. He always entered and left the basement by way of
the garage entrance, which could not be seen from the street. His
basement was off-limits to anyone.

The FBI also learned that when she'd bought the house there'd
been a beige carpet in the basement. It was long gone now. She
said it had been sopping wet on Monday, June 25th, and she'd
cut it in four places and had it hauled away.

When the feds asked if it looked as though the carpet had been
washed that weekend, she said that's what she'd figured. Naturally, the feds crawled around the trash dump like rubbish rats,
but to no avail.

Next, the FBI contacted the local cops who'd made the original
arrest on Jay Smith back in 1978 when his secret life was revealed.
The cops said they'd noticed at the time that there was a large
remnant of the upstairs *red* carpet stored in that basement. Yet
Grace Gilmore had found no red remnant when she moved in.

The agents started speculating that Susan Reinert may have
been placed on that carpet remnant to await her fate, but they
hadn't any idea where she would've picked up the two blue fibers
found on her body.

••••

Interviews with Jay Smith's younger daughter were not helpful. Sheri was a sad and lonely young woman, whose immediate
family was dead, imprisoned or missing. She was forced to live
with various friends and relatives.

Jay Smith's brothers had known nothing of his secret life, but
were generally supportive and loyal to him. They seemed to feel
that he might be involved in the earlier crimes but certainly was
not a killer.

But a friend of his missing older daughter came forward with
a tidbit. She told the FBI that young Stephanie had said that
Jay Smith once warned her and a boyfriend that they knew too
much about his business and that he was going to shoot them
both and chop them up and pour nitric acid over their bodies. This
because they'd discovered some information about his unusual

sex practices. He just didn't like people bad-mouthing his sex life.

The owner of a massage parlor told the FBI that she'd been solicited by Dr. Jay to go into business. He'd given her $800 seed money to get started and find a location, but he had one caveat: whenever she called him she was to let the phone ring one time and hang up. Then she was to call back immediately and he'd answer.

She told the agents that she felt intimidated by Jay Smith. He seemed too sure of himself. She thought that if she went into business with that guy she might end up like his timid librarian friend over whom he seemed to have abnormal control. He made her so uncomfortable that she gave him back his money.

The FBI also learned that when Jay Smith arrived late for his sentencing on Monday, June 25th, he told the judge he was late because he'd made arrangements for a friend to deliver him to Harrisburg, but the friend had been unable to make it.

The FBI contacted the friend and learned that Jay Smith had placed a call to him earlier in the weekend, not on Monday. And he did not ask for a ride to Harrisburg. He said that Jay Smith had sounded distressed—his voice was unusually high.

The state cops found out that the 79th USARCOM comb was one of thousands given away as a recruiting gimmick. A tiny bit of ridge detail was lifted from the comb. The ridges were similar to two of Jay Smith's fingerprints, but there wasn't enough for a comparison.

Jay Smith's telephone bill showed calls to his attorney's office that weekend: one at 3:50 P.M. on Friday, and another on Sunday at 8:37 P.M. One more call was made to O'Brien's home telephone, also at 8:37 P.M.

At that time, the FBI and state cops knew nothing of the two men from South Carolina working at Three Mile Island who had reported seeing Susan Reinert's car at about 7:00 P.M. Sunday evening. As far as the lawmen knew, the car could have been driven to Harrisburg anytime before late Sunday night when it was first seen by the patrol cop. The times of the telephone calls to Jay Smith's lawyer had no particular significance yet.

••••

It was time to see the prince of darkness face to face.

Joe VanNort and Jack Holtz paid him a visit at the state prison in Dallas, Pennsylvania. But a more significant visit was made by Special Agent Hess of the FBI. Jay Smith told Hess he was willing to cooperate because he had nothing whatever to hide, and he didn't need all this publicity about the Reinert murder when he was busy trying to appeal his conviction.

He'd decided that it had been a mistake not to take the stand in his own behalf during the Sears St. Davids case, but every FBI agent and state cop who ever talked to Jay Smith was inclined to think that his lawyer John O'Brien had been correct in not putting Dr. Jay on the stand. You just got the feeling that this was not a wholesome fellow the second you looked him in the eye.

Jay Smith told Hess that during that last weekend in his house on Valley Forge Road, he'd completed a few chores prior to turning the house over to the new owner, Grace Gilmore. He said that he was supposed to cut the lawn for her on Saturday but hadn't had time. He said that she'd been at the house on Saturday from early morning to late afternoon getting her own things in order, and that she'd returned on Sunday and was there from 9:00 A.M. until noon. He said that she'd walked in on him once and surprised him when he was working in his basement apartment.

Jay Smith told Hess that he drove his 1973 Mercury Capri to the store to buy some groceries for an apartment he had been ready to move into before the judge sent him to prison. He said that his youngest daughter Sheri had been in a couple of times over the weekend, and that Friday, June 22nd, was her birthday.

When Hess asked if they'd spent Friday night celebrating the birthday, Jay Smith admitted that he hadn't bought her a card or a present or even seen her on *that* day, because Friday night he had to visit his dying wife in Bryn Mawr Hospital, a duty he performed twice daily.

Jay Smith said that on Saturday he'd gone to Wayne to pick up a letter from a minister attesting to his sterling character to present in court the following Monday. He claimed that he'd made four or five phone calls having to do with character witnesses.

As to his personal opinion whether William Bradfield was the kind of guy to go around killing people, Jay Smith said that anyone could kill a man or even a woman in a fit of rage, but he didn't think Bill Bradfield could ever kill children. He said he'd only seen Bill Bradfield a couple of times outside of school to discuss his alibi testimony.

As to the other Bill Bradfield cohorts, he said that Sue Myers would do anything Bill Bradfield ordered her to do and that Vince Valaitis was a polite young fellow who was completely under the control of Big Bill. He figured that latent homosexuality was rampant in the clique. No discussion with Jay Smith would be complete without a little sexual innuendo.

He was forever implying that it wasn't so bad being called a thief and murderer, but as far as sex was concerned he was as regular as the next guy. As to the exotic stuff he seemed to agree with Voltaire that if you try it once, you're a philosopher. He ignored the other admonition that if you do it twice you're a pervert.

••••

Joe VanNort could say what he wanted about the FBI, but they were *thorough*. They showed Jay Smith's picture to every doctor, nurse, patient, technician, secretary, janitor, security guard, gift shop worker, cafeteria employee, *anyone* who could feasibly have seen him during the weekend of June 22nd on any of the three shifts at Bryn Mawr Hospital.

Then they started on the volunteer workers. They talked to every candy striper, priest, nun, minister and rabbi. Cataracts and comas provided the only escape from the feds with their photos.

Many said they'd sure remember that face. Some of those on Stephanie's ward knew him, but no one had seen him on the weekend in question. By the time the FBI finished checking out Jay Smith's version of the weekend, they could at least prove that he was lying.

Nobody had seen Jay Smith from Friday until late Sunday afternoon when he drove away from Valley Forge Road.

Jay Smith was down but not out. After his dead wife's friend turned over the "lovecock" letters and all the rest of Stephanie Smith's diary to the press, he launched a $30 million libel suit against a couple of newspapers. He was turning into quite a jailhouse lawyer. Convicts came to him for help with their appeals.

And he fired off a bulletin to his former colleagues at Upper

Merion to brighten their school year. It was as windy and droll as any of his former open-mike interludes. He called it "Letters from State Prison."

Some of his old subordinates said with a shudder that it was almost like having him back.

Copyright, 1979
Jay Smith, K-4891
Drawer-K
Dallas, PA 18612

Friends,

I want to thank all of you who were able to attend any of the trials or who gave me support during them. Such support takes a great deal of grit in the midst of the horrendous publicity I received and am still receiving. I do not expect it to cease, ever. Annually, you can expect a re-doing of the whole scene. It is a pre-school attention getter in doldrum August, and it is good box office. Frankly, I prefer a free press motored by personal profit than a controlled press motored by bureaucratic propaganda; but we need to lance a few warts and get a few of the bad apples out of the free press barrel. I am hoping that the drift to the right that is detrimental to my current situation will be beneficial to my civil trial conflicts. Decreasing some of the press libel immunity might generate the necessary circumspection they should bring to prosecution feedings.

Regarding the persons whose names have been flung at me, viz., William Bradfield, Kenneth Reinert, Susan Reinert, Chris Pappas, Sue Myers, and Vince Valaitis, I can say sans any fear of being gainsaid that I never met or saw any of these people off the school grounds. I would not know Kenneth Reinert if he came up to my cell door.

I have had no romantic involvement with Sue Myers or Susan Reinert or any teacher or any student or any parent in the Upper Merion area school district, in or out of school, since I've lived and worked there. No sexual involvements either.

I never considered William Bradfield an "adversary" as he puts it; and I never had a "secret close relationship" with him as Mr. Anonymous or Mr. Synonymous puts it. I viewed William Bradfield as a superior teacher who had an uncanny influence on the brightest students and on much of the staff. He also had an unusual influence on the powers that be (superintendent's office and the school board). Thus, he could influence the operations of the senior high. I viewed him as someone I had to be alert about, always. The principal's office is not a windless isle in a tranquil academic ocean. It is a turbulent place with many winds blowing. Bradfield was a strong wind. Not friendly. Perhaps hostile. Perhaps.

Susan Reinert was a pleasant, conscientious teacher, always willing to do more than was required of her. I knew nothing of her out of school activities. The same applies to Sue Myers, an excellent teacher and person. I knew nothing of her out-of-school life.

There was no secret meetings with any witnesses or anyone at any time. I met with each of my witnesses. The topics were substantially the same: don't let the police scare you off; tell the truth; keep it succinct. At the direction of my lawyer, I met with William Bradfield. We met openly in a public place.

I was never a member—(echoes of the fifties)—I was never a member of any sex cult or Satan cult. I have never participated in any group sex or abnormal sex. As defined by my interrogators abnormal sex includes homosexuality, anal sex, bestiality, sadomasochism, bondage and discipline, or the use of any accompaniments such as vibrators, dildos, or special clothes. My home has been searched many times, legally and illegally, by police and lord knows who else. They have my permission to display at any place they choose any items they took from my house that relate to sex cults or Satan cults. They can even display my trash.

Not only was I never a member or participant in any cult activities, but in my whole time in Upper Merion I never heard anyone discussing such things. Until "those authoritative sources close to the investigation" initiated the rumors, it was unknown to any in-school or out-of-school dialogue. I am eager to see their proof of this slander on me, and the Township of Upper Merion, and the other professionals reputed by the rumors to be members.

The first letter is a short introduction to what I want to tell you. There is much, much more. I hope that you will give me a chance to give you my views before you slam the cell door on me and throw the key away. You still have not heard of my SECRET LIFE, as one Harrisburg paper put it. But now I want to ask your help.

Please send me any newspaper clippings you have or any ideas you have concerning the following matters: my wife's property. It should all be in the hands of the court. (My wife's will and my will are the same, viz., what we have goes to our two daughters.) Susan Reinert's murder. Especially newspaper items that indicate my involvement. The Satan cult slander: items that include my name are especially important. Drug use or sex orgy articles. Any that name me as a participant.

Embarrassed, I end this letter as a mendicant. No matter what the amount, I ask you to please send me a postal money order or bank money order. Personal checks and cash are verboten. If you

do not wish to think of it as alms for IRS purposes, think of it as an IOU that I will redeem from you in the future. Regardless, no hard feelings; I know you just got back from a huelga.
  Ciao.

Jay

P.S. I am sure there is no Satan cult in Upper Merion even though I am just as sure that Satan is active there as everywhere.

••••

The chains, and much that surfaced in Stephanie's diary, along with Bill Bradfield's use of women, got the FBI wondering about something new: could there be a homosexual bond between Jay Smith and William Bradfield?

Vince Valaitis told them that Bill Bradfield had warned that the FBI might try to find out about his long-ago lodger, Tom. The feds tried to track Tom out on the west coast, but agents in Los Angeles who located his apartment were never able to speak with him directly. Nor could the FBI ever verify that Bill Bradfield had gone to Cuba with or without Tom to kill for Castro.

At about the same time that the Terra Art store was going under, and Bill Bradfield was trying to unload the stock and dissolve the corporation, Sue Myers learned a little something about the elusive Tom. When the publicity hit, Tom sent a letter to Bill Bradfield along with a book of Ezra Pound's poetry.

Bill Bradfield was deeply touched by the gesture from an old friend and read the letter to Sue, but not *all* of it. She noticed an ellipsis in his reading.

When he turned his back she dashed straight for his files and read it for herself. Tom told Bill Bradfield about his new life as a married man, and how content he was. In the context of the letter it was clear that Tom was married to another guy.

And then Tom told Bill Bradfield that despite his conjugal bliss he would always remember Bill Bradfield as the only man he every truly loved.

Sue Myers had one thought when she finished that letter. She later said, "I wondered if he'd been any more faithful to Tom than he had to the *rest* of us."

••••

Ken Reinert's favorite FBI agent, Matt Mullin, was the quintessential FBI prep. He looked as though he could be Big Brother Biff to any of the coeds at Bryn Mawr. He looked like a cousin of The Main Line's most famous daughter, Grace Kelly.

His old man might have pumped gas at Sloan's Super Service, but to Joe VanNort he was Eights-with-coxswain. The agent's clothes had something to do with it. Matt Mullin *always* wore the FBI prep uniform: three-button suit, button-down Oxford shirt, paisley tie okay but only if you're feeling revolutionary, cuffed pants at least two inches over the wingtip brogues, and those well run over at the heels because you're a lawman, after all.

Matt Mullin's strawberry-blond hair had never seen stickum or spray, and he was forever pushing it off his forehead, boyishly. He looked like he'd spent his entire life blushing, or his systolic pressure matched Rod Carew's batting average. His accent even sounded like a Kennedy's. Okay, so he'd gone to college at La Salle in Philly, he was *still* more Ivy League than F. Scott Fitzgerald. When you saw guys that looked like Matt Mullin, you didn't bother trying to spot the bulge under the coat. They had to be FBI.

The FBI's sex research had outdone Masters and Johnson. They'd interviewed several women who the gossips claimed had been intimate with Bill Bradfield. One of them, described unkindly as "another plain-Jane schoolteacher," agreed to meet Matt Mullin to reveal some information of an intimate nature.

He asked the lady in question to meet him at a precise location in the Sears parking lot at St. Davids, and informed the state cops that he wanted a backup unit. After all, the talk was going to be of a sexual nature, and he didn't want the woman to accuse him of anything.

The cops were amused by this to start with, and Jack Holtz and another trooper agreed to provide the backup for Matt Mullin so there could be no accusations of rape in either direction. Before they left for the parking lot, Matt Mullin started telling Jack Holtz how not to be seen, and where to park, and how to behave, implying that the staties didn't know how to conduct a surveillance. That did it.

In the late afternoon, Jack Holtz and his partner were running all over the Sears store trying to find fake noses and glasses. They arrived at the meeting place fifteen minutes early and roared in at fifty miles an hour, sliding up bumper to bumper with the FBI unit. Both state cops then picked up newspaper pages with eye holes cut out and pretended to read.

Matt Mullin told them okay, you've made your point, and now could we please get down to business, but the cops weren't through yet. They wanted to see Matt Mullin's scarlet kisser go into terminal blush.

They went to an observation point and composed a report while the agent interviewed the schoolteacher. The next morning at the regular task force briefing the special agent in charge read a state police report detailing Matt Mullin's surveillance.

> 1703 hours. White female parked car east of SA Mullin's car. Female exited vehicle and entered FBI car.
> 1730. Windows began to fog.
> 1740. Car rocked violently.
> 1750. White Kleenex thrown from car window. Large German Shepherd seen roaming parking lot. Door opened driver's side. German Shepherd entered FBI car.
> 1815 hours. Kleenex obtained by reporting officers. Sent to lab for analysis. Refer lab report.

The information revealed to Matt Mullin by the former lover of Bill Bradfield was noteworthy. Just before Rachel arrived in May at the downtown hotel, Bill Bradfield had persuaded this schoolteacher to meet him at the same hotel for a quickie. He told the teacher that he often thought of their past romance and because he'd been celibate for so long he now needed her "to bring him back to manhood."

This, when he was already juggling Sue Myers, Susan Reinert, Shelly and Rachel. So okay, the agent wanted to know, is this guy a superstud or what? And to his surprise she told him.

Bill Bradfield was a creamy cuddler and a super snuggler, but not worth a nickel when it came right down to the real stuff, ostrich or no ostrich.

It verified what several of the feds were already beginning to suspect: the charismatic womanizing Renaissance man of Upper Merion was, alas, a bum lay.

••••

Bill Bradfield, Chris Pappas and Sue Myers weren't talking at all, but toward the end of the year Jack Holtz and Chick Sabinson took a trip to Boston to talk with Rachel. *That* conversation was about as relevant as the Harvard football program. As to the murder weekend she said she'd been alone looking at architecture in Philly, and that she'd never heard of Jay Smith before the murder. She'd desert Bill Bradfield, they figured, when they started pronouncing their *r*'s in Boston.

♦♦♦♦

Jack Holtz was relieved to get a few days off over the Christmas holidays. He spent them back in Harrisburg with his son, and saw his brother and parents. It was impossible to be with his boy and not think about Karen and Michael Reinert. He'd never thought he'd still be working this case after the New Year, but he assured his family that they'd have to get a break soon.

When they asked if there was any hope that the children were alive, he shrugged.

♦♦♦♦

Ken Reinert had a Christmas of sorts for the sake of his wife and stepdaughter, and the new baby. His parents, John and Florence Reinert, could not bring themselves to celebrate anything.

They all refused to think that the children were not alive. Ken Reinert had recurring nightmares and sleeping disorders. These people were in torment.

♦♦♦♦

About Susan Jane Gallagher Reinert, it could be said that there were mixed feelings that Christmas. The lawmen said that she'd walked into danger with her eyes open, holding a child by each hand. The more that was learned about the $25,000 investment, and especially the $730,000 worth of insurance policies, the angrier the task force became. It would've been hard to find a cop or special agent who spent much time pitying the woman who ended up in the trunk of her car in a Harrisburg parking lot. You would often hear a lawman say, "She got what she deserved."

But every one of them was working hard in the hopes of finding the children dead or alive. The bulletins showing those handsome young faces were heartbreaking.

What they could deduce about Susan Reinert's death was this: she'd been called away from her house suddenly. When she and her children arrived at their rendezvous, they were met by more than one executioner. It took more than one to control a desperate mother and two hysterical children.

The one-hundred-pound woman fought back but was beaten severely, possibly with fists. Her mouth was taped and she was lashed in chain and cinched so tight that the links gouged a trail around her body.

As she lay helpless she may well have seen and heard her children being murdered. She may have seen and heard more than that.

She could not die until such time as a killer could establish an unshakable alibi. It was at least twenty-four hours, perhaps thirty-six, before Susan Reinert was murdered, in order to fix an acceptable time of death.

One could speculate about the night and day and night of unimaginable agony this mother suffered as she came to understand the folly that brought her and Karen and Michael to this. When the lethal injection came, she probably welcomed it.

Task force members in frustration would often say, "That woman's stupidity was a crime."

To call Susan Reinert's pathetic love for a man a "crime" was acceptable cop hyperbole, but no crime deserved *this* punishment. To devise a death as cruel as Susan Reinert's required a supremely Gothic imagination.

20

Rebirth

The New Year was a time for diving and digging. They dove when lakes were not frozen. They dug when the ground thawed.

Desperation was driving the task force to follow leads from tipsters, seers and lunatics in Maryland and New Jersey as well as Pennsylvania. They once went down twenty-five feet in a landfill. There were theories that the children had been put into fresh graves in cemeteries. So even the hallowed ground was searched by the task force.

Acting on tips from a former boyfriend of young Stephanie, the state police divers searched a water-filled limestone quarry in Valley Forge Park. This, because a tipster told them of seeing Jay Smith kill cats by dousing them with nitric acid and driving their bodies toward the park.

They even spent several man-days on a lead from a seer who described in detail where the children had been buried by "two men."

Joe VanNort said, "Well, after thirty years, police work's come down to throwing your hands up in the air to catch vibrations."

Bill Bradfield, Chris Pappas and Sue Myers still weren't talking, and what Vince had given the task force was hearsay on top of hearsay. They hadn't any way of really linking Jay Smith to Bill Bradfield, let alone to the murder of Susan Reinert.

Agent Matt Mullin had secured photos of all the evidence seized in the basement of Jay Smith in August 1978 as well as photos of several things from his secret life that at that time had no evidentiary value to the local cops: the 79th USARCOM combs and the loops of chain and locks that had been draped over a hall tree and coiled on a chair. The FBI was able to determine the lock brand from the photos.

Luckily, it was possible to size the link marks on Susan Reinert's body because the way she'd been photographed in the luggage compartment of her car, the marks could be compared to the print size on a *Time* magazine lying beside her.

Matt Mullin sent blow-up photos of the chains along with the photos of Susan Reinert's wounds to Walter Reed Army Medical Center. Four forensic pathologists were able to determine the link size by comparing them to the known size of the locks.

They couldn't prove anything in a court of law, but those chains that were once in Jay Smith's basement were exactly the size of the chains that had bound Susan Reinert. The FBI said thank you to the local cops, thank you to Walter Reed, and a silent thank you to Henry Luce.

Though he always referred to Matt Mullin as a "social worker" or "schoolteacher," Joe VanNort was impressed with the superprep on this one.

He took his state cops aside privately and said, "Okay, *we're* gonna start takin a close look at Jay C. Smith."

••••

In the spring, a tow truck driver named Kramer received a routine call to tow an abandoned car that had been parked too long at the rear of an apartment building near Valley Forge.

The driver found the car, hooked it up and took it to the tow garage where he opened up the trunk and searched for valuables. What he found was *very* valuable to a squad of lawmen at Belmont Barracks. The car belonged to Sheri, the youngest daughter of Jay C. Smith, and the truck driver recognized her father's name from the publicity.

They got very excited at Belmont Barracks after the truck driver handed over a letter from Jay Smith to his wife, Stephanie.

It was written from Dallas prison one day following his incarceration, one day after Susan Reinert's body was found.

It was a letter *within* a letter. He'd prefaced the long message by informing his wife that his mail was probably read by prison officials.

> Steph,
>
> I hope they are knocking off that cluster near your spine and you are feeling better. I didn't want to burden you with a lot of tasks so don't worry if you can't get to them. When you get well enough, then give these things some attention.
>
> Among things to take care of:
>
> Capri. First, clean it up *thoroughly*. We will try to sell but not give away. I might use it to store books so don't sell it too fast.
>
> Steph, we must *throw away* most of the stuff. Don't *keep* things because they just seem too good to throw away. We will replace at an auction or other place cheaply. I can't stress the importance of this: *Clean out and then clean up.*
>
> Rug. Downstairs rug is full of matchsticks, cigarettes, old strands of marijuana, etc. from Eddie and Steph and their friends. Every time I walk on that rug something new pops out. It MUST go. I'll write more later about disposal.
>
> I love you,
> Jay

The letter within a letter to his dying wife wasn't much by itself, but the task force was even more interested in chains than Jay Smith was. They were trying to forge a chain of circumstantial evidence and when it was long enough they wanted to see how Bill Bradfield and Jay Smith liked being hog-tied by links of steel.

The troopers went to the state prison to take a handwriting exemplar from Jay Smith. He didn't know why they wanted it, but he didn't like the idea. He tried to fake his handwriting. Dr. Jay gave them an exemplar that was so shaky it looked like it was written by Howard Hughes after he was gooned out from watching *Ice Station Zebra* ninety-two times.

••••

Matt Mullin was on a roll. The next lead he developed had to do with the fiber samples found on the body and in the trunk of

Susan Reinert's car. Jack Holtz went to the former home of Jay Smith and got permission from Grace Gilmore to cut samples from her upstairs red carpet.

The fiber samples matched the fibers found in Susan Reinert's hair. The FBI lab reported that they were polyester fibers and that less than 7 percent of America's carpets are polyester. However, hair and fiber analysis is the most subjective of forensic sciences and the task force knew that any defense lawyer could come up with a couple of experts who would say that they couldn't tell for certain if the fibers were from the same dye lot or even if they were polyester. But they *looked* like the same dye lot and they *looked* like polyester.

Matt Mullin and Jack Holtz later went back to the house on Valley Forge Road, this time with lights and brushes and vacuums.

When Grace Gilmore had gotten rid of the beige carpet in the basement she'd decided to leave the carpet pad. The lawmen divided the basement into quadrants, took out their soft little sweeping brushes and started cleaning that pad. They swept and crawled and vacuumed that basement for hours. They had knees like medieval nuns' when they were through with that job.

Poor Grace Gilmore. Instead of a Welcome Wagon hostess she got cops snipping at her carpet. And what did they have to show for a brutal day's work? Four big dust balls. That was it: huge balls of dust and grime and fuzz that she could've handed them right out of her Hoover any day of the week. But they looked happy with their dust balls.

The task force sent the sweepings off to the FBI lab in Washington, and went about their trips to communes where the children were allegedly being held. There were more landfills to excavate and more lakes to drag.

····

One year after the murder of Susan Reinert, and one day before the fifty-second birthday of Jay C. Smith, American justice finally got around to his peccadilloes of 1977.

Jay Smith and his brothers and sisters gave testimony before Judge Warren G. Morgan as to his accomplishments in life. They told how they'd lost their father when they were children and worked very hard to better themselves. They described how Jay Smith had risen through the ranks in the army reserve and very nearly became a general, and detailed how he'd continued his lifelong formal education until he was awarded his doctorate.

The judge had this to say: "The devotion of this family is of course impressive. Touching. And we are saddened that this defendant has brought such discredit upon his family. As I listened attentively to members of his family testify, I had to think that they seem to be talking about a man who is now really two different persons: the brother they grew up with who worked hard to educate himself and this man who has been tried in this courtroom and other courtrooms of the commonwealth.

"It was the duty of this school principal to provide an example of probity to the young minds who were committed to his charge. He has dishonored his profession in a monstrous way. It is rather interesting that we do not sense today in this defendant any real remorse.

"The court sentences the defendant to pay the costs of prosecution and to make restitution to Sears, Roebuck stores in the sum of fifty-three thousand dollars and to undergo imprisonment in a state institution for an indefinite term, the minimum of which shall be three and a half years and the maximum of which shall be seven years. To commence and be computed consecutively to the sentence being served."

It was a stiffer jolt than Jay Smith expected. That came to a term of five and a half to twelve years. He couldn't expect parole until 1986. As a pretty fair jailhouse lawyer, he began doing legal research into the appeal process, but he kept being distracted by another matter. The Reinert task force was coming after him hard. He'd long since stopped sending whimsical bulletins to former colleagues. He was maintaining total silence. Prison officials and other inmates described him as a quiet loner.

••••

Matt Mullin called Jack Holtz one day and said, "I've got bad news and good news."

"Gimme the bad news," Jack Holtz said.

"There wasn't a blue fiber anywhere in the sweepings. We may never know how she picked up the two blue fibers."

"Gimme the good news."

"In quadrant number one they found a hair. It's the same length as the hair taken out of her head at the autopsy. It's a positive match in twenty-one out of a possible twenty-five microscopic characteristics. That's as good as it gets."

"It's not a fingerprint," Jack Holtz said. "But I'll settle for *that!*"

They also found red fibers in the basement which indicated that a piece of the upstairs carpet might've been down there, but then again the fibers could've been tracked down from upstairs on someone's shoes.

Still, it was another link, and it tied in beautifully with the letter from Jay Smith to his wife asking her on her deathbed to throw away that downstairs rug.

Jay Smith was no longer a lonesome silhouette dancing on some distant crag with little hooves. He was being forced down from the hills. He was giving off pungent goat smells, and it smelled better to Jack Holtz than a gumload of snuff.

••••

Sue Myers was almost through doing needlepoint. She'd done needlepoint when they slashed through Europe like General Patton. She'd done needlepoint through Bill Bradfield's sixteen and a half love affairs. She'd done needlepoint when his money and hers went down the drain at the art store. She'd done needlepoint through the months of blather about devils and guns and acid and bodies and hit men and murder. She'd sat there quietly as Madame Defarge at the guillotine and . . . just . . . done . . . needlepoint.

And then he went too far. It happened in the office of his Philadelphia lawyer, John Paul Curran.

Bill Bradfield would talk to a radish if he had to, and Curran was an expansive Irish type who liked to shoot the breeze too, and the meetings with Bill Bradfield got pretty windy. Sue Myers was sitting there, apparently placid, when Bill Bradfield made the devastating mistake of talking personally about Susan Reinert.

He said to Curran, "That woman was the nearest thing to a nymphomaniac that I ever met."

Sue Myers later said, "Stars went off in my head!"

Sue Myers saw more stars than a steer in a slaughterhouse. She saw stars for weeks and weeks after that. The sniggering way he said it. It could've been said like that at an Elks club smoker.

Curran looked at her, and Sue Myers, with her fortieth birthday approaching, had never felt so cheap, so used, so *foolish.*

She'd hated Susan Reinert in life and hated her in death, and never felt much pity for her. In her own words it was an "un-Christian" way to feel, but she was getting close to understanding the core of those feelings.

If there was one thing she had been positive about, it was that Bill Bradfield had *despised* Susan Reinert, though Susan Reinert was certain that he loved her.

Now, for the first time, Sue Myers was beginning to think: "What if he despises Shelly? And Rachel? What if he despises them all? What if he despises *me*?"

It was starting to seem possible. And though she was not willing to admit consciously that he might have conspired to murder two children, she was getting ready to concede that he might have badly wanted Susan Reinert dead. So what about herself?

Sue Myers dropped her needlepoint one day and walked calmly to the telephone and called a locksmith. When he came home, Bill Bradfield couldn't get in his own apartment. Bill Bradfield roared. He sounded like Oedipus with his eyeballs bleeding into his beard, but she *wouldn't* open that door.

Bill Bradfield was without a roof over his head and had to go home and live with his parents, and be reminded that he'd wanted a piano and what did they give him? A goddamn stinking miserable little toy truck.

◆◆◆◆

A most unbelievable break came at the time of Jay Smith's sentencing. William Bradfield tried to probate the estate of Susan Reinert. As soon as he filed for probate, Ken Reinert and Pat Gallagher joined forces and filed to block him.

In the Court of Common Pleas of Delaware County, there's a court division with the Dickensian title of Orphans Court. In that the ex-husband and brother of Susan Reinert had immediately challenged her will, the court appointed a deputy district attorney, John A. Reilly, as administrator of the estate to safeguard the rights of the missing children.

Reilly was a veteran prosecutor with a good reputation, a Civil War buff who'd been around the courts a long time. Joe VanNort and Jack Holtz felt good about him, but he warned them not to get their hopes up.

One of the functions of the court in this estate case was to ascertain the total assets of the estate. There was the missing $25,000 that Susan Reinert had "invested," and there was a matter of a missing diamond ring that her mother had given her. The court would try to determine what happened to them but Bill Bradfield could stop the bus by agreeing to reimburse the estate on his own. That in itself would cure a big part of the estate dispute even without any admission of misappropriation or criminal conduct.

Sort of a *nolo contendere* situation, as the cops understood it. And that would send them back to sweeping cellars and digging in graveyards.

Jack Holtz had hoped that in Orphans Court Bill Bradfield would at least be compelled to make incriminating statements. He'd fantasized that Bill Bradfield would take the stand, but now he feared it was going to turn into a drawn-out estate squabble that would never allow them to compel Bill Bradfield to talk.

At the time, Joe VanNort showed his lopsided grin and said, "I ain't so sure Bill Bradfield's smart in the first place. And in the second place I ain't so sure he could keep his mouth shut if John Curran gagged him with a lawbook. Let's wait and see if we get a break."

They got a break.

The Orphans Court hearing was held at the courthouse in Media, Pennsylvania.

Bill Bradfield showed up in a three-piece blue pinstripe, and on that cool summer day he carried a topcoat over his arm and had all the wisps trimmed from his beard, and had a fresh preppy haircut. To Joe VanNort he looked like an FBI agent with whiskers.

He'd gained some weight from nervous eating, and the cops saw fear in his eyes, or hoped they did. To their amazement and joy, Bill Bradfield not only took the stand, but after "affirming" an oath on the Bible, he denied *everything*.

He had this to say about Susan Reinert:

"She was a sensitive, easily hurt, intelligent young lady, but very troubled. She was troubled about many things in life and would ask my opinion about a lot of things. But she often did the opposite. She dated people I thought she ought not to date. She went to places I thought she ought not to go."

He told the court in response to John Reilly's questions that he'd spent many evenings with his friend Susan Reinert, but he'd never "dated" her.

"The frequency of my contacts with Mrs. Reinert grew with her demands," he told those assembled in Orphans Court. "The term 'date' implies the kind of relationship Mrs. Reinert and I didn't have."

As in the Jay Smith trial, Bill Bradfield's husky, sometimes gravelly voice flattened out when he was testifying. It added to an overall impression of distance that caused reporters to refer to his "cold blue eyes" when actually he'd raced through life with all the fluttery heat of Scarlett O'Hara.

Reilly asked, "Did you ever stay overnight with her?"

Bill Bradfield answered, "Never."

When Reilly asked, "Did she ever discuss an investment with you?" Bill Bradfield answered, "*What* investment?"

"You didn't know she had money in the bank?" Reilly asked.

"No, sir."

"Did Mrs. Reinert give you sums of money for an investment or any other purpose prior to her death?"

"No, sir," Bill Bradfield said. "I would often give money to *her*. To make ends meet. As did Mr. Valaitis."

When Bill Bradfield even took from Vince the credit for buying Michael's cub scout uniform, Jack Holtz's grin got wider than the Delaware.

"Were you aware that she took out insurance policies naming you as beneficiary?"

"No, sir," Bill Bradfield said.

"Were you aware prior to her death that she named you as a beneficiary in her will?"

"No, sir."

As to the Jay Smith trial where he had been an alibi witness, it seemed so unimportant that it almost slipped his mind.

Reilly said to him, "Immediately after leaving Harrisburg on May twenty-ninth of last year, you went to Mrs. Reinert's house, did you not?"

"Could you refresh my memory," Bill Bradfield said. "Why was I in Harrisburg?"

"I can refresh your memory," Reilly said. "But I think you know why you were in Harrisburg."

"No."

"Were you in Harrisburg testifying at the trial of Jay Smith?"

"Yes, I remember," Bill Bradfield said.

The gate wasn't just opened to them, it was blown off the hinges. Reilly could now call *all* of Susan's friends and confidants.

As to the missing ring, Pat Schnure could testify that Susan Reinert was going to have her mother's diamond ring reset and wear it at her wedding in England, and that Susan had said that Bill Bradfield knew a jeweler who could do the job.

The cops could testify that they'd taken the "ring to courier" notation on Susan Reinert's calendar and checked every courier in the Philadelphia area, and that the ring was *gone.*

The cops could bring in all the evidence of the "investment" with Bache and Company and produce company executives to testify that it was bogus.

Susan Reinert's former banker could tell of her extraordinary cash withdrawal. And her brother could tell of her offer to let him in on Bill Bradfield's investment.

The neighbors could tell of his car being there at all hours and even overnight.

Bill Bradfield had made so many demonstrably false statements under oath that the cops at last had enough evidence to consider a prosecution based on the theft of the investment.

••••

About the extraordinary performance in Orphans Court, Sue Myers said, "Because all of his friends believed him utterly, he thought that everyone *else* should believe him utterly."

Jack Holtz said to Joe VanNort, "We were dead, but now we're born again!"

The *Philadelphia Daily News* had this to say in an editorial:

> Putting it gently, Susan Reinert had an impressive amount of life insurance. Spectacular Bid is insured for more. So, presumably, is Streisand. But for a schoolteacher the figure's a bit high.
>
> What Bradfield is suggesting has a charm all its own. Susan Reinert, under the mistaken impression that she was going to marry Bill Bradfield, tiptoes out, purchases three quarters of a million dollars worth of insurance, didn't tell him a thing about it, didn't tell him about her estate, didn't tell him she changed her will, didn't tell him she had made him sole beneficiary of the estate and the insurance. Now if Mr. Bradfield could only put that to music we could all dance down the yellow brick road.

Bill Bradfield called Sue Myers the night that editorial ran. He was weeping. He said, "Why have *you* forsaken me?"

◆◆◆◆

In August, the cops obtained a search warrant from the state of Delaware to search Jay Smith's blue Capri, now in the custody of his brother.

Joe VanNort, Jack Holtz, a Delaware state cop and another trooper went to the home of the assistant attorney general of the state of Delaware to get a warrant drawn up. The next day it was signed by a magistrate and they waited until Jay Smith's brother returned home in the evening to serve it. They'd brought a deputy attorney general with them.

Mr. Smith was clearly embarrassed by the presence of all the cops and protective of his niece, the twenty-three-year-old daughter of Jay who was without a real home. The cops searched through all of the belongings that he was holding for his imprisoned brother.

In a filing cabinet, Joe VanNort found another bogus Brink's identification card with Jay Smith's picture on it. The deputy attorney general didn't think it fell under the scope of the search warrant, and Joe VanNort handed the card to Mr. Smith.

That bothered Jack Holtz. Maybe they couldn't use it in a subsequent court case against Jay Smith, but maybe they *could*. In any event, why give away potential evidence or contraband? They were outside at the time and he spoke to Joe VanNort about it. He knocked on the door and asked for the card back.

But Jay Smith's brother had already burned it on the kitchen stove. He said that all of that theft business had humiliated his family.

Jack Holtz later felt troubled that Joe VanNort had lost that card. In the old days Joe VanNort would never have done something so careless. Jack Holtz didn't say a word to anyone, but he was concerned.

"I hated to think it at the time," he later said. "But I was starting to feel that Joe was losing it."

In the blue Capri they found more red fibers, but all that proved was that he *could* have used the Capri to haul away the carpet remnant they believed had been in the basement on that weekend last year.

The interior of the trunk had been painted with a sticky substance that looked like some sort of rust inhibitor or sealant, and the car had been outside in the weather. The cops were very disappointed with the search.

Then Trooper Dove of the identification unit walked up to Jack Holtz and said, "I found this pin under the right front passenger seat."

It was dusted for prints but they couldn't lift anything from it. Jack Holtz took it in his hand and examined it.

It was just a little lapel tab. A green metal pin with a white *P* on it. At first Jack Holtz thought it might be something they handed out at the ballpark, but it wasn't the right color and the *P* was wrong to be part of the Philadelphia Phillies logo.

He didn't know what it was, but his investigator's intuition told him that it didn't belong in this car. Something about that pin wasn't right.

For two weeks he worked on it in his spare time. The more he looked at the little metal tab, the more he believed it was something a child would keep. He went to the residence of Susan Reinert's neighbor Donna Formwalt and talked to her eight-year-old daughter.

The little girl said, "Karen wore a pin like that. I think she got it on a school trip."

Jack Holtz started devoting more than spare time to it. He found another neighbor who told him that the pin looked like something she'd seen at the Philadelphia Museum of Art.

It was a hopeful cop who arrived at the museum that afternoon in August and climbed the steps made famous in *Rocky*. He talked to the director who verified that the pins had been in use in June of last year, and were given to show that admission was paid. They were handed out by museum guards who used eight different colors on various days.

Jack Holtz went to Karen Reinert's neighborhood school and learned that the fifth- and sixth-grade classes had gone to the museum on a field trip in the spring of 1979. The principal informed Jack Holtz that Karen Reinert had, in fact, attended school on the day of the museum field trip. Then he learned that four boys from her class remembered the pins. They'd been green. Two remembered Karen being along on the trip. One boy had saved his pin and turned it over to the police. It was identical to the one they had.

Their chain was getting longer. Not long enough to bind. But longer.

◆◆◆

The last real duty Chris Pappas ever performed for Bill Bradfield had to do with closing out the safety deposit box. He did an extra-swell job on that mission.

When the bank teller had concluded their business and told him to have a good day, she'd left the signature cards on the counter. Chris Pappas leaned over and snatched three of the four signature cards, so that if the authorities found the box they wouldn't be able to prove that Bill Bradfield had anything to do with the rental.

His mentor was very proud of him.

◆◆◆

Chris Pappas was at Shelly's house when he saw a news report that detailed Bill Bradfield's testimony in Orphans Court. Chris was stunned. Bill Bradfield had lied under oath about *everything*.

An hour later, Bill Bradfield and Chris and Shelly were strolling through Valley Forge Park having a little rehearsal. Bill Bradfield was positive that when the grand jury sat in September, they'd all get a subpoena. He asked Shelly if she'd take a walk and let him talk privately with Chris.

When they were alone Bill Bradfield asked, "How do you feel?"

"Okay. I feel okay."

"Will you stand by me?"

"Haven't I always?"

"Vince deserted me. I think Sue might desert me. You won't, will you?"

"Desert you? No."

"Will you keep your silence about certain things?"

"What things?"

"The money? All the *other* things?"

"I'll try to stay loyal. Greeks're stubborn," Chris Pappas said.

Bill Bradfield didn't look too happy about the evasive reply.

As they walked, Bill Bradfield made notes on a checklist and scratched things off. And Chris was getting sick to his stomach as he realized that Bill Bradfield was not only trying to maintain his allegiance but was letting Chris know how strong and dangerous was this bond between them.

They sat on the grass, on the ground consecrated by the Revolutionary patriots, and Bill Bradfield handed Chris a brief on what to tell the grand jury. It was actually a scenario. The dialogue didn't sparkle, but it made its point:

> Bill told me that this Smith is really a bad person with a bad character. He said, "I wish I hadn't seen him at Ocean City but I did, so I'll have to testify to that because it's true."
>
> Smith talked about getting the police and other people. Wishing, thinking, they ought to be dead, wanting to kill them.
>
> Bill said, "I don't know whether he's serious or not. I sure hope no one kills Susan Reinert."

Bill Bradfield must've thought that was a wee bit self-serving so he crossed out the last line. He also deleted a reference to Jay Smith wanting to kill the cops, possibly figuring it might not play in Peoria.

> That woman has told me she's leaving her children to me and all sorts of crazy stuff. She's sure chasing me. She says she's dating some real weirdos too. I told her she's going to get herself beat up or killed.
>
> If she gets herself killed and leaves me her children, if she pushes her children on me, I'll fight it in court. That's illegal.

But that also seemed a bit over the top for a budding scenarist, so he crossed out the part about her leaving him the children.

That'll sure put me in a horrible mess. I wish she'd leave Upper Merion, leave the area all together.

They both scribbled changes in the script, which continued with lines that Chris was supposed to say when asked for opinions:

Bill seemed pissed off at Mrs. Reinert and concerned about the weekend and vacation.

After that, Bill Bradfield composed a list of likely questions, and answers to same.

Question: Would you say that Mr. Bradfield suspected that Mrs. Reinert would be killed?
Answer: No. He was worried about her, concerned for her. He told me he wished she'd go abroad or something. I think he said he wrote a recommendation for her for a job.
Question: Did Mr. Bradfield say Smith told him of killing her?
Answer: No. Robbing? No. Drugs? No. Kinky sex? No. Illegal firearms? No.
Question: Did Mr. Bradfield ever show you firearms which he said were Smith's?
Answer: No.
Question: Did you and Mr. Bradfield ever plan to kill Smith?
Answer: Kill him? No, of course not.

The second page of the script listed many more questions and the answers were supposed to be obvious to a man of Chris's accomplishments.

Did Mr. Bradfield ever spend the night at Mrs. Reinert's?
Did Mrs. Reinert visit Mr. Bradfield at Annapolis in 1978?
Did Mr. Bradfield ever tell you about Dr. Smith?
Did Mr. Bradfield ever mention Dr. Smith in connection with any murder or robbery?
Were you involved in the making of a silencer?
Did you ever take out a storage bin?
Did you ever take out a safety deposit box?
Did Mr. Bradfield ever show you a large sum of cash money?
Where have you obtained the money you recently spent on lawyers, bail, etc.?
Did you think Mrs. Reinert was going to be killed on the weekend of June 22nd?
Did Mr. Bradfield seem to think so?

Did you know of Mr. Bradfield and Shelly sharing motel rooms?
Did you know of any romantic involvement between Mr. Brad-
field and Shelly?
What is the relationship between Mr. Bradfield and Rachel?
Did Mr. Bradfield order you to go to the shore that weekend?
Did you speak to Mr. Valaitis in reference to Dr. Smith?
Did Mr. Bradfield instruct or influence you?

The last question was almost too much, even for a disciple as
dedicated and earnest as Chris Pappas.

And then Chris wrote some of his answers on the margin of
the scenario. His dialogue wasn't so hot either, but he mollified
his pal.

I'll fight that in court. She's nuts. Delete "pissed off at."

Bill Bradfield warned Chris that the FBI might try to make
something of his past relationship with Tom, the homosexual
lodger, but Chris thought they should be worrying about things
other than homosexual innuendo.

Bill Bradfield said to Chris Pappas, "Sometimes I think I've
been pathological about women. Sometimes I think I've used
them, and that I didn't try very hard for a lasting relationship."

Chris Pappas immediately thought of a book by the daughter
of Ezra Pound who wrote of her father's philandering.

As though he was reading Chris's mind, Bill Bradfield said,
"You know, if I went to jail, abandoned and scorned by all those
I've loved, I'd use the time for study. Maybe I'd even come to
enjoy the solitude."

Chris Pappas thought of Ezra Pound himself, confined first in
jail then in an asylum: disgraced, vilified, abandoned by his
friends.

He didn't want to think that *this* was what it was all about! He
didn't want to go to state prison because William Bradfield
wanted to *be* Ezra Pound!

Chris Pappas's chest felt like a round cage with a pigeon flut-
tering inside. Now the bird was pecking at his guts. He was wel-
coming home the long-gone childhood ulcer.

Chris wanted to *talk* to somebody. At that moment he knew
that he'd eventually be calling the FBI.

••••

When Sue Myers locked out Bill Bradfield, she wouldn't give him anything but his clothes. She even kept the five thousand books. Among the other things she held on to were documents that he thought were safe from her prying eyes.

One warm autumn day Sue Myers invited Chris to come and "look over some things."

Maybe she sensed that Chris was already talking to the FBI or getting ready to do it. She gave him some papers and asked him to take them home to determine if they were "important."

Bill Bradfield had always underestimated Sue Myers. She didn't miss a whole lot. She *knew* what she was giving Chris was meaningful and she probably knew what he'd do with it.

When Chris decided to call the task force it was ten times better than when Vince Valaitis had done it. Chris Pappas *knew* so much more. Chris had been involved in all the activity that was in itself illegal, all the business with weapons and money.

When Chris talked, he implicated Shelly in criminal activity, since she'd kept the money hidden and had disposed of a gun with a silencer. Best of all, Chris and Shelly had both heard a whole *lot* of talk about Jay Smith, and some of it could be corroborated by physical evidence. Chris Pappas started cleaning out his chamber of horrors and his file boxes.

As the relationship between Christopher Pappas and the authorities blossomed, Chris gave them documents he'd received from both Sue Myers and Bill Bradfield.

One of the documents was a note in Bill Bradfield's own hand wherein he made his list of things that had to be addressed in the event of a grand jury probe.

The list included potential witnesses and friends of Susan Reinert, and things to worry about:

Letters stolen. Mail fraud. Fingerprints on money. I was there during insurance man's call. Visits to New York. Calls to New York and from. Visits to Annapolis. Calls to and from Annapolis. Overnight depositions. Sharon Lee. Pat Schnure. Girls. Pamela, Susan, Rachel, Shelly, Cathy. Unorthodox life. Cuba—killing. Bank deposit slips. Names. Handwriting. No partial fingerprints

on car. Shelly and motel. Rachel and room. Calls from Annapolis
and to Annapolis. Sailing course. In Reinert's room constantly.
Reinert's books in my bookcase. Car missing. Depositions. Smith.
FBI. Reinert's people. Vince. Gun. St. Davids. Lured and killed
kids and taped her.

Latent fingerprints are a lot trickier than most people realize.
They're rarely identifiable if a surface is not hard and clean, and
are seldom left at all unless there's an abundance of body secre-
tions, such as sweat and oil, on the fingers. Actually, the task force
was never able to get a single identifiable lift of Bill Bradfield's
fingerprints from Susan Reinert's house.

So it was awfully decent of him to let them know that he'd been
in there "constantly," the feds remarked.

Joe VanNort's grin got as lopsided as a Cuban election and he
said, "Bradfield's even got a big mouth on paper!"

But if the note was another little link in the circumstantial
chain, the *next* document provided them with a foot of case-hard-
ened steel complete with lock and keys.

It was typed yellow lined paper and bore no handwriting at all.
It was inside an envelope with the typed address of William
Bradfield at Upper Merion Senior High School.

It had been written to Bill Bradfield two years earlier at about
the time that he had the dream that he'd met Jay Smith at the
shore while going to Fred Wattenmaker's house.

The letter began:

> In place of VF phones. If contact is necessary, use: 265-9633, or
> 265-9634 or 265-9635.
> These three phones are located inside the Sheraton and are
> available 24 hours. VF phones are not, as park closes after dark.
> Before I leave to go to the phones, if I think I heard the signal, I
> will take my phone off the hook. After an interval a call to my
> home phone will give a busy signal since it's off the hook. This will
> indicate I heard the signal and I am on my way.
> Big problems re last two weeks of August 1977.
> I went to see Fred W. if possible on Saturday, August 27th to kill
> a couple of birds.
> 1. McKinley to discuss some confidential problems re coaching.
> 2. Fred W. to see his new house. I'd promised him this.
> 3. See more of S. Jersey other than shore as lack of such data
> was hurting in job seeking.

When ran into third party, near Crackerbox, decide it was O.K. since all could go to lunch together.

Since McK and W not available took off after lunch with third party.

Possible approach could be: Told Mitch I remember I saw him in D.C.

He said he also remembered incident. Indicated that you (Fred W.) should have remembered it as JCS called FW a couple of times re McKinley appointment. Even told FW that it was to be JCS recommendation.

B: Fred, I think I sensed that JCS may feel you are afraid of Supt. That's why you have a "bad" memory re Smith in D.C.

Stress silence so other side knows nothing.

The cops called this their "little treasure," a letter from Jay Smith to Bill Bradfield scripting an alibi performance, even as to how he should try to flimflam Fred Wattenmaker into "remembering" what had not happened on August 27, 1977.

The letter was unsigned, but the task force didn't care. On the typed envelope were the fingerprints of Chris Pappas, which was to be expected. And a fingerprint of William Bradfield, which thrilled them. And some beautiful huggable fingerprints of Dr. Jay C. Smith.

Bill Bradfield and Jay Smith were getting double billing, even with Joe VanNort. They were an item. They were scripting each other's performances. They were Gable and Lombard, Tracy and Hepburn, Edgar Bergen and Charlie McCarthy.

Joe VanNort now said he wanted to see Jay Smith in the electric chair with Bill Bradfield on his lap.

••••

They wanted to put Chris Pappas in a glass bubble. He was more than valuable. He was the most priceless Greek treasure since Schliemann found a mummy he thought was Agamemnon.

Through the weeks of secret interviews, Chris sat and pleaded with them to understand that even if Bill Bradfield had conspired to perjure himself for Jay Smith, and even if he'd swindled Susan Reinert out of twenty-five big ones, he couldn't have *murdered* anybody.

Chris Pappas told every agent and cop he met that Bill Bradfield had been *sincere* on the airplane when he drank a toast to saving Susan Reinert's life. He tried earnestly to make the cops understand that any man who could discuss Aquinas and *Summa Theologica* couldn't possibly commit murder.

They cherished Chris Pappas so much that they humored him about Bill Bradfield's absence of malice, even when Chris turned over the practice chains and locks that Bill Bradfield had asked him to keep during the rehearsals. They agreed that perhaps Big Bill wasn't a Bluebeard even when Chris gave them the acid and his mentor's magnum pistol.

They humored him even after Chris told them how Bill Bradfield had coached Shelly on her testimony before the grand jury, describing for them Shelly's anguish over swearing to falsehoods on the Bible.

They showed Chris nods of understanding when he assured them that Bill Bradfield would probably set up trust funds for the kids if they could be found alive.

But the humoring had to stop when he told them one last incredible incident that they would *never* have believed if they hadn't become so thoroughly familiar with the Bradfield disciples.

Just before June, 1979, graduation at Upper Merion, Bill Bradfield had come to the Pappas house with urgent news.

"I received a call from Doctor Smith tonight," he'd told Chris. "He said he's going out. I know that means a hit, but I don't know who or where."

"Do you think it's Susan Reinert?"

"I don't know, but I don't think so. He gave me a *hint.*"

"What's the hint?"

"He said, 'I'm getting all dressed up for it. But I won't be going *inside.*' "

"What's it mean?"

"What do you make of it?"

"Getting all dressed up ... The prom! This is prom night!"

"That's silly," Bill Bradfield said. "Who would he kill at the prom?"

Chris went home feeling silly about the prom idea and went to bed. Thirty minutes later the phone rang. It was Bill Bradfield.

He said, "I've got it all figured out. That cop who searched his house. He's working off-duty at the prom tonight. Doctor Smith wants him dead so he can't testify!"

Forty-five minutes later, the capeless crusaders were speeding to Upper Merion in Chris's Datsun. Bill Bradfield was relaxed and cool and chatty. Chris Pappas was so energized he could see everything in detail. Even in the darkened car he could see wisps of gray in Bill Bradfield's coppery beard. He saw oil drops on that goddamn homemade silencer that Bill Bradfield held in his hands. Chris Pappas glowed in the dark.

As if Chris wasn't terrified enough Bill Bradfield calmly rolled down the window and said, "If we're going to kill a human being, we'd better test our weapon."

He fired three shots into the night sky over King of Prussia.

Chris Pappas literally felt his pulse jerking in his neck. It was like some maniac version of a Gidget movie: *Prom Night,* starring Jay C. Smith with a supporting cast of disappeareds and remotes.

They stayed till the last dance but, as usual, Jay Smith danced alone whenever he danced.

Bill Bradfield said, "He must be killing somebody else. Let's go home."

The cops could only sit dumbstruck when Chris told this tale.

One of the troopers couldn't help himself. He looked at Chris like he was something that had materialized at a seance, and said, "Chris, I gotta understand how you felt. When Bradfield had you shinnying up that rope, did you maybe think if you let go you'd fall and vanish forever in a lake of drizzly *bullshit?*"

Chris later said that he wished the police could've tried harder to understand him.

••••

Chris Pappas received two memorable phone calls after Bill Bradfield obviously sensed that Chris was talking to the task force. The first call was angry and contained an implied threat.

Bill Bradfield not only accused his young pal of turning Sue Myers against him, but of having an affair with poor Sue.

He said, "Read the last chapter of the *Odyssey,* Chris! Read it!"

During the long rambling conversation, he repeated it five times.

Finally, Chris said, "You mean the *next* to last chapter. You're talking about when Odysseus comes home and reclaims his woman and his betrayers are killed."

"Don't get snotty!" Bill Bradfield wailed. "Read the last act of *Macbeth*!"

Another call came even later at night. Bill Bradfield was crumbling fast. He wasn't threatening anybody. He was certain now that Chris was talking to the task force and said so.

Chris described Bill Bradfield as speaking in a "quaking grandmother's voice." It sounded like the grandmother was dying. Chris had to press the phone to his ear to make out the feeble little sounds.

"Is . . . is that you, Chris? Is . . . is that my friend? I . . . I don't understand why you're doing this to me, Chris! *Why* does my friend turn against me? They'll trick you, Chris! They'll get to you!"

"Somebody's already gotten to me, Bill," Chris Pappas said. "That somebody's you."

It was the last time in his life that Chris Pappas ever spoke to his friend William Bradfield.

21

Confucius

By February, they were able to secure a search warrant to seize all relevant material described by Chris Pappas as being in the former attic of Bill Bradfield who was now on sabbatical and living with his mother, keeping a *very* low profile out in the country.

Sue Myers had been alone for nearly a year and still hadn't been allowed to return to her Upper Merion classroom. She had no money in the bank and owed legal fees to her attorney and got lots of nutty phone calls from Bill Bradfield accusing her of betraying him. She was taking Librium to keep herself together. It was probably a perfect time for search warrants. She needed a pal.

In fact, when the searchers arrived she was chattier than they'd ever seen her. She and Jack Holtz started talking about his hobby of cooking and Sue thought he was sort of an attractive guy when you got to know him.

Sue helped them search, and along the way thought she might as well tell them a few things she'd never told them. She talked about seeing the stack of $100 bills in the file drawer, and how the date coincided pretty well with Susan Reinert's bogus investment of $25,000. And as long as she was on the subject she added that just before Susan Reinert's murder she'd seen a *will* with Bill Bradfield named as beneficiary.

And Sue Myers said, "Wait'll you see *these* letters. Are they ever sickening!"

The boys got handed some Shelly letters wherein the teenager told him that he'd just *have* to learn to dance before they got married. And then Sue helped them locate some Rachel letters written in that tiny, precise script. For good measure, Sue threw in some Susan Reinert letters that Bill Bradfield had squirreled away.

Sue told them that she wished she'd saved his jogging diary because in it he once wrote that he'd like to *kill* Susan Reinert, but added that at the time she had thought it was overstatement.

Between exchanging recipes with Jack Holtz and getting it all off her chest, she was really starting to like these guys. Sue told them how Bill Bradfield sometimes made rough drafts of important letters, and voilà! they found a lulu of a rough draft. The message was written in cipher and became known to task force members as the "my danger conspiracy" letter.

It was a most pleasant day for all concerned. They had lots of little snippets and treasures to link Bill Bradfield and all his friends in a conspiracy of deceit and perjury. A case against him for stealing Susan Reinert's investment was starting to look awfully good.

So Sue Myers had climbed aboard the government bus, along with Vince Valaitis and Chris Pappas. She had a pretty swell time talking chicken cordon bleu with Jack Holtz. And she grew certain that Joe VanNort's partner, who was seven years younger than she, was a downright flirt.

She used to get mad when Joe VanNort referred to "Bradfield." She'd always say, "It's *Mister* Bradfield." But now she was calling them all by their first names.

Everyone was in such a great mood that Joe VanNort's lopsided grin almost straightened itself out.

••••

The "my danger conspiracy" letter was sent to the FBI for a cryptanalyst to examine and explain in the event they ever got to court. A code generally deals with words or phrases, and a cipher works from individual letters with number substitutes. What the cops had was a mess of numbers separated by commas, with several letters interspersed.

They knew from Chris Pappas that the key to the cipher was to be found in the Confucius translation by Ezra Pound, and Sue obligingly provided that tome. On page 12 there were Bill Bradfield's handwritten numbers beside the lines.

The cops figured this could wow a jury. They'd get the FBI cryptanalyst to do a presentation complete with a quickie course on ciphers, and lots of big blowup charts, and maybe some slides.

It was *only* to wow a jury, because Bill Bradfield had obligingly written the correct letters in the English language right above each cipher on his rough draft. So every searcher could just sit right down and read the deciphered message for himself. It said:

"Does FBI know V has it. Has V removed ball and destroyed or better claim whole thing stolen. Then get rid of it. Did I sell it to you. FBI must not get it. Does FBI know you mailed it."

When the cops got that far they said, wait a minute, the only *V* in the case was Vince Valaitis. But Vince was riding the bus named Salvation and was tickled to death to be aboard.

Then they compared it to the scenario that Bill Bradfield had penned for Chris Pappas. It was in the same barely coherent style. He'd write in the third person and then switch to the second person or even the first. The *V* referred to a "her" so they decided that the *V* was a code within a code, and stood for Rachel. Then it worked as jottings to himself *and* to her on a rough draft of a message to her.

The garbled message continued:

"Can you think up substitution or substitute saying wait and tell V or have her say it's stolen. Immunity improbable. My danger conspiracy."

On the back of the message he'd scribbled "Smith," then scratched it out and written "P of D."

The police and the FBI did not have the authority to tap Bill Bradfield's phones or read his mail. If the message *was* meant for Rachel, Bill Bradfield could have mailed her a postcard and they'd never have known. He could've hired a skywriter to smoke his message over the Harvard campus and they probably wouldn't have heard of it. Or he could've picked up a telephone some evening and called her and told her his fears and said, "Would you please switch typing balls."

He *could've* done that very easily. But if he had, he wouldn't have been Bill Bradfield. And perhaps the disciples wouldn't have remained so steadfast without all the melodrama. Ezra Pound had *also* loved ideograms.

Matt Mullin got the duty of securing a handwriting exemplar from Bill Bradfield, and during the process, he was asked to identify things they'd found written by him in the Reinert residence.

Among these was Karen's autograph book with Mickey and Minnie Mouse on the cover. Bill Bradfield had written on one of the first pages. His entry was dated October 25, 1977.

It said: "To Karen, Lorelei-To-Be." Then there was a good-luck message written in Greek, followed by "From her friend, B. Bradfield."

Part of the exemplar procedure required him to write the names of everyone connected with the case for further comparison.

When he wrote Karen's name he said to Matt Mullin, "Karen was a beautiful, gifted child."

••••

The theory of Susan Reinert being lured away from her home was based on information from her friend at Parents Without Partners. The friend said that Susan had claimed she was going to meet an attorney on Saturday, June 23rd, to "sort out" various legal matters with Bill Bradfield. The cops believed that the night she disappeared, she'd gotten a call from Bill Bradfield saying that they had to meet the attorney that night, and to bring along her will and investment certificate.

This would explain why she'd taken Michael from the cub scout meeting and made him change his baseball shirt, and why she had changed the blouse Ken Reinert had seen on her when she picked up Michael. They were dressing up to meet a lawyer, the cops believed.

If she hadn't made a photocopy of that certificate, the police would never have known it existed. As to the will, there was the copy retained by her attorney, but it seemed possible that someone else had demanded to see it, and that's why it was gone.

They turned Bill Bradfield's alibi for June 22nd into a state trooper drive-a-thon. Various tests were conducted at different hours of the night and day. During the lightest traffic time it took more than one and a half hours to drive from Shelly's pal's house to Susan Reinert's house where Bill Bradfield had allegedly "lost" Jay Smith in the hailstorm, to his ex-wife's home in Chester County where he supposedly hung around alone for an hour or two, either inside or outside, depending on his version of the story.

••••

When the FBI contacted Rachel at Harvard she said that she'd bought the typewriter from Bill Bradfield. She gave them a typed exemplar from the machine and this time did it so willingly that they figured she'd switched typing balls.

They weren't able to match the exemplar with the photocopy of Susan Reinert's investment. The FBI lab could only say that they'd both been typed by an IBM machine with a Gothic typeface.

Sue Myers said she was just pleased as punch to hear that he'd "sold" *her* typewriter to the ice maiden. She wanted to have the lovebirds thrown in jail for theft, but Joe VanNort had to tell her what he'd soon be telling the FBI: "We ain't after typewriter thieves. We're after *murderers.*"

The FBI investigates few criminal violations and does most of its work with the blessing of U.S. attorneys and magistrates. Police investigate a wide variety of criminal activities, involving huge numbers of lawbreakers. They usually don't have the time and opportunity to obtain warrants, and often have to improvise and move along to the next case. The differences in style between the FBI and the state cops was never more evident than when the discussions began as to how they should proceed in the arrest of William Bradfield.

Joe VanNort announced that he was going to arrest Shelly along with Bill Bradfield and charge them both with theft by deception.

"You can't arrest that young girl," Special Agent Matt Mullin said.

"Watch me," he was told.

Joe VanNort's blue-gray eyes were getting squinty at that point and not from his cigarette smoke. There was a confrontation that evening in Belmont Barracks. The old cop and the young agent were getting testy.

"You don't have enough to charge her with," the agent said.

"The hell I don't. She stashed away money for him. She either wiped fingerprints off the money or watched him do it. She lied to us and she lied to the grand jury. She's a *conspirator* in my book."

"I'd like to talk to her one more time before you arrest her," Matt Mullin said.

"You can talk to her *after* I put her in jail," Joe VanNort said. "That's it. Period."

But Matt Mullin figured, that's it, semicolon. He said wryly, "Rachel has Sue Myers' typewriter. Why isn't *she* part of the conspiracy?"

Then Joe VanNort erupted: "Goddamnit, boy, I ain't after no typewriter thief and I ain't after no perjurers! I ain't gonna arrest Rachel or Pappas or Valaitis or Myers because I'm gonna need them *all* one a these days to testify for me when I get Bradfield's ass for murder!"

"It's a malicious arrest," Matt Mullin said. "You're arresting Shelly because she won't cooperate. The U.S. attorney would tell you it's violating her civil rights and violating a federal law."

"I don't need no U.S. attorney to tell me when to take a crap or when to book a suspect," Joe VanNort said.

"Let's agree to talk about it tomorrow," Matt Mullin suggested, and his always flushed face looked like somebody had double-dipped him in Day-Glo.

The next day, Matt Mullin came to the state police barracks with a U.S. attorney who also tried to persuade Joe VanNort not to arrest Shelly.

When the U.S. attorney was all finished, Joe VanNort sucked a fresh cigarette down to a nub and said, "We ain't botherin you with this. It's a state law, not a federal law. I'm goin to the district attorney and I'm gonna file charges. Period. And when we make the arrest, the FBI don't have to be there if it bothers em."

••••

Since the conspiracy to commit theft by deception involved three counties they had to have a lot of meetings with different district attorneys, and finally Deputy D.A. Ed Weitz from Delaware County got the job of prosecuting the case.

The arrest of William Bradfield took place in May, 1981, almost two years after the murder of Susan Reinert, and the FBI did not take part.

The cops preferred to arrest Bill Bradfield when he was out jogging. He was said to be doing three miles a day at that time, trying to control his weight and soaring blood pressure.

Joe VanNort, Jack Holtz and Lou DeSantis had a woman trooper call his mother's home to see if he was at home. The trooper was told he was asleep, and the message was relayed to the waiting cops who drove up the lane to the ancient stone farmhouse where the Bradfields lived. They were met at the door by an old woman: frail, respectable, upper middle class, frightened.

The cops stated their business and Mrs. Bradfield asked them to wait a moment. She returned to the door looking even more frightened and asked to see their identification again. After that, she disappeared and when she returned she let them inside.

Jack Holtz sneered, which is no mean trick with a gumload of snuff, and whispered, "Hiding behind his mother's apron strings, as usual."

Bill Bradfield got dressed quickly and greeted them in the living room with one question: "Are you arresting me for murder?"

"Naw," Joe VanNort said, showing his lopsided grin. "Just for theft by deception and theft by fraudulent conversion."

They could literally see the color return to his face. He was *relieved.*

They drove to the district magistrate's office and he was garrulous. As usual he talked about everything but what they wanted to discuss. He told them how his father used to take him hunting around Chester County and that it was lovely and peaceful living out in the country.

And by the way, he said, he'd like to give them some "concrete evidence" about Susan Reinert's murder, but he couldn't do it because of his lawyer.

The only unpleasant moment came at the magistrate's office when he refused to sign a form stating that the cops had advised him of his constitutional rights. Then he said that he wanted a cash bail-out on the spot.

Jack Holtz glared and said, "Screw him. Let's take him to *jail*."

But Joe VanNort was in a jovial mood. They called John Curran's office and a lawyer said he'd come, and Bill Bradfield's mother said she'd arrange for the bail money. Joe VanNort was enjoying himself.

In fact, he took Bill Bradfield to a deli while they were waiting for the $25,000 bail to be posted, and bought his prisoner a sandwich.

When they'd finished eating and returned to the magistrate's office, Bill Bradfield said to the lawyer, "I want it on the record that these police officers are gentlemen, and have treated me *so* kindly."

Jack Holtz later said it was all he could do to keep from grabbing Bill Bradfield by the throat.

Bill Bradfield asked Joe VanNort, "Are you arresting any of my friends?"

"Yeah, Bill," the old cop said, with a Marlboro between his teeth. "Afraid we gotta bust poor little Shelly."

Bill Bradfield's brooding blue eyes turned exceptionally misty, and he said, "I *wish* you'd let me call her, first. She's such a fragile child."

"I don't see nothin wrong with that, Bill," Joe VanNort said. "I always kinda liked kids myself."

••••

There were a couple of hearings prior to the August trial, hearings in which John Curran challenged the various warrants and the introduction of certain evidence. The testimony in support of the warrants was given mostly by Sergeant Joe VanNort and it was striking to hear.

Joe VanNort was more rambling and disjointed than Ronald Reagan without a script. Joe VanNort had been a cop for nearly thirty-one years and he'd given a whole lot of testimony, and though he wasn't an articulate man he knew how to testify. But in those hearings he sounded like an untrained civilian.

In fact, on the morning they went to the courthouse in Media, Pennsylvania, for the trial of Bill Bradfield, Jack Holtz was driving and Joe was sitting next to him and being very quiet.

When they drove into the lot, Joe looked at Jack Holtz and his blue-gray eyes were as cloudy as the Poconos in autumn. He asked, "Where *are* we?"

Jack Holtz thought he must've dozed off, but Joe was wide awake.

"What're we doin here?" Joe VanNort asked.

Jack Holtz laughed and said, "This is the Bill Bradfield trial. You better wake up."

When they got out of the car and walked inside, Jack kept glancing over at Joe. He didn't look well.

••••

The state police and the district attorney had worked out a deal with Shelly's lawyer. She flew in from California and surrendered herself at the district magistrate's office and the preliminary hearing for the felony charges took place right there. It was very convenient for Shelly.

Both defendants were held to answer for the criminal charges against them and bound over for trial. Shelly was taken by Jack Holtz and Joe VanNort to a women's jail for mug shots and fingerprints, and was released to her parents who posted $10,000 bail.

It wasn't long before Joe VanNort got a telephone call from the district attorney. Shelly had agreed to become a witness against Bill Bradfield if the commonwealth would drop charges against her.

"Of course we will," Joe VanNort said expansively. "Shelly belongs to *us* now. Why she's almost like a daughter to me already."

He said it so loud the FBI director in Washington could've heard. Joe VanNort didn't believe in making life easy on the feds.

••••

The three-day trial in Media was held before Judge Robert A. Wright, with John Paul Curran and his law partner Charles Fitzpatrick for William Bradfield, and Edward J. Weiss appearing for the commonwealth. The small courtroom was jammed with press and gallery.

Both sides were warned that any undue mention of a murder investigation could result in an immediate mistrial, and the whole show would have to be restaged. Bill Bradfield was being charged with theft by deception and theft by failure to make required disposition of funds received. Shelly was granted immunity.

John Curran made a judgment call and decided that Bill Bradfield would not take the stand in his own defense. He'd said too many things in Orphans Court that Ed Weiss could use as a bludgeon. Bill Bradfield later said that he very reluctantly agreed to heed his lawyer's advice.

The bankers testified to Susan Reinert's maneuvers to secure $25,000 in cash, and how she insisted that her investment required it.

The father of Chris Pappas was called and testified to getting $3,000 from Bill Bradfield and purchasing money orders which were returned to Bill Bradfield so that he could pay Curran, the implication to the jury being that Bill Bradfield didn't want the guy defending him to know about all his nice crisp $100 bills. Chris's brother testified to doing the same with another $2,000 worth of $100 bills.

Chris Pappas took the stand and told of seeing $28,500 in the trunk of Bill Bradfield's red Cadillac, and told the bizarre story of wiping down the money in the attic.

All trivia fans from that day forth had a question for the barroom:

> Question: How long does it take to wipe the fingerprints off $28,500 in $100 bills?
> Answer: Thirty-five minutes.

Then Chris testified to hiding the money and later putting it into a safety deposit box in a bank in West Chester.

The defense was badly hurt when the prosecutor asked Chris if Bill Bradfield had told him where he got the money.

Chris said, "He told me that he had a savings account at the Elverson City Bank."

"Did he specifically mention that account?" the prosecutor asked.

"That's correct," Chris said.

"And did he tell you how he'd been withdrawing that money?"

"He did," Chris said. "He told me he'd attempted to withdraw all of it at once and the bank officials gave him a hard time about it. He explained that it was his own money and they were reluctant to let that large a sum go all at once. And he told me that he could only retrieve the money in increments of about five or six thousand at a time."

Of course the jury started to get the idea that Bill Bradfield had merely borrowed Susan Reinert's story of banker problems when he'd explained the money to Chris.

John Curran asked a lot of questions trying to establish that Chris knew his mentor to be a man who owned valuable property, but Chris let the jury know that prior to the spring of 1979 the man of property had not thrown $100 bills around.

Sue Myers took the stand and testified that she'd known Bill Bradfield since 1963 and lived with him since 1973. She said that after she moved in with him, she'd done all the bill paying, and that they didn't have a savings account at Elverson in the amount of $25,000. In fact, she said that Bill Bradfield had had to take a second mortgage on the property his ex-wife occupied, and had to refinance it in a futile effort to save the business. It was dreary testimony for Sue Myers.

"Did you also put money into the business?" the prosecutor asked Sue that first day.

"Yes."

"And what profit did either of you earn from that business?"

"None."

"Zero?"

"Yes."

"I mean at *any* time."

"None."

"What happened to that business?"

"Mister Bradfield sold it."

"And the proceeds from that were what?"

"I don't know."

It was very embarrassing stuff for Sue. The hummingbirds were flying all over the courtroom and sometimes hovering over the heads of friends and colleagues who were looking at each other in disbelief. Because of all the saps and suckers, she'd been with him the longest time. By virtue of seniority she was the sappiest.

Her testimony was wooden and aided by tranquilizers. It was

only as responsive as it had to be. Distance was the best way to deal with utter humiliation. Sue was so distant she couldn't have been reached by Houston Control.

Shelly took the stand and for the first time began telling the truth. She testified that a friend had flown to California to bring a signature card for a safety deposit box. She testified to coming back to California and getting the money out of the box and counting it and stashing it away in her house.

She testified to sending a couple of $100 bills to Bill Bradfield's ex-wife later in the summer when she was instructed to do so. That was relevant because it shot down his defense of having saved the money for years; those particular bills were not in circulation until 1978.

An FBI accountant did a good job of proving that Bill Bradfield did not have that kind of cash potential in any bank account. The judge thought it was prejudicial for the witness to say he was from the FBI. So he didn't, but when his coat fell open the jury saw an accountant who was packing heat.

••••

Bill Bradfield's mother took the stand on the second day. She was a refined old woman who was mortified to be there.

"Good afternoon," Curran said, preparing to ask his first question.

"How do you do," she answered.

"What is your relationship to the defendant?"

"William is my son," she said.

And the jurors' eyes went from his mother to William Bradfield. Questioning eyes asked: How?

She testified to living in a two-hundred-year-old fieldstone home and said that they'd formerly lived on a one-hundred-acre farm in Chester County. She said that she and her husband had built a home for William and one for their daughter.

Curran was trying to show that the money that everyone had been stashing and wiping could have come from Bill Bradfield's mother. She testified that over the years she had written him three checks that totaled $17,000.

The old woman said that her son had been raised in a Christian home, and so she did not approve of his living arrangements.

"But I accepted it," she said, "and in no way did it change my love for my son."

Mrs. Bradfield wasn't fond of Sue Myers and said, "I considered her a very extravagant young woman. She set a very lavish table. Her clothing was quite expensive and I considered her a woman who spent a great deal of money."

The prosecutor had a go at Mrs. Bradfield and brought out that the larger amounts that she'd given to her son over the years were loans which had been repaid, and not gifts that he could have socked away.

✦✦✦✦

Toward the end of the trial there was a conversation held in the judge's chambers among Judge Wright, John Curran, Bill Bradfield and Ed Weiss. It had to do with the judge charging the jury and explaining the defendant's failure to take the stand.

Bill Bradfield was upset that he wasn't going to get a chance to talk.

The judge said to him, "You don't have to take the stand."

"I would *like* to, if I may," Bill Bradfield said.

Curran said, "Bill, are you willing to accept that this is something *we* recommended under the circumstances?"

The defendant said to the judge, "I feel compelled to accept the advice of my attorney. For two years I've *wanted* to tell my story. I wanted very much to in this case."

"Of course we are past that now, Mister Bradfield," the judge informed him. "The evidence is closed and I can't permit you to tell your story now."

"I have to go with my attorney's advice," Bill Bradfield said glumly.

Weiss was a feisty prosecutor and he was getting irritated by Bill Bradfield's claiming that no one had ever given him a chance to speak. He piped up with an observation that got Bill Bradfield steamed.

Weiss said, "Your Honor, I'd like to make a comment in response to Mister Bradfield's remark. I've repeatedly offered to withdraw these charges if he'd come forward and tell *his* story, and he's declined to do so."

"That's not correct!" Bill Bradfield cried.

288 •••• *Joseph Wambaugh*

"Bill, do not participate," John Curran warned. He was always having to tell Bill Bradfield not to participate.

"We are *not* going to get into an argument here," the judge told them all.

Bill Bradfield kept trying to interrupt and John Curran kept shutting him up and finally Bill Bradfield started to cry. He was pretty weepy those days.

••••

When John Curran got to address the jury he talked about Runnymede and the Magna Carta because he was a lawyer who liked big pictures. Then he said that it all came down to guilt by innuendo, guilt by suspicion, guilt by association.

Of Bill Bradfield he said, "You heard about Mister Bradfield. In many ways you may not like him. In many ways you may think he's spoiled. In many ways you may think he lives in that academic area where people do not deal with day-to-day problems that people in the working world have to deal with. Maybe his mother spoiled him by giving him all this money, maybe she spoiled him by building him a house and giving him seventeen thousand dollars in checks and a thousand dollars a year in cash gifts over a period of fifteen years."

About Susan Reinert he said, "Where is the evidence that some theft by deception took place? If Susan Reinert loved Mister Bradfield as the evidence indicated, she would've *given* him the money. She would've given him twenty-five thousand dollars if he'd wanted it. If she loved him. It seems to me that if she were here today, she'd be mortified to see *the man she loved.*"

Pat Schnure and Susan Reinert's friends were groaning like a herd of Herefords after *that* one. Bill Bradfield was starting to sound like Edward VIII when he abdicated.

Then it was Weiss's turn and he waxed poetic from Sir Walter Scott: "Oh, what a tangled web we weave, when first we practice to deceive!"

He talked of Bill Bradfield's dreams of sailing around the world, and of his opening a business that bled him dry, and of how his dreams were gone. And of how he'd succumbed to greed.

••••

When the judge at last charged the jury, he said, "You may have heard evidence which may be construed to show that the defendant took part in what you may consider immoral conduct for which he's not on trial. This evidence must not be construed by you as evidence of his guilt in this case. I call your attention to the fact that this case has nothing whatsoever to do with the death of Susan Reinert or the disappearance of her children. If you in any way let those things enter into your minds or your consideration, you will be violating your oaths that you took as jurors, and will tend to make a mockery of our criminal justice system."

◆◆◆◆

The jury was out less than an hour and when they're that fast, it's bad news for the defendant. When he was found guilty on both theft charges, the courtroom broke into applause.

"All right! Let's have none of that!" the judge warned the cheering gallery.

The prosecutor felt that now Bill Bradfield might have cause to flee the jurisdiction and so asked that the bail be revoked, but the judge compromised and increased it to $75,000. It was guaranteed by his mother.

The best part of the trial for Jack Holtz had occurred right after Chris Pappas testified. Bill Bradfield had gone out to vomit. He said it must have been something he ate.

At a bar in Media that night there was a celebration involving Joe VanNort, Jack Holtz, Lou DeSantis, prosecutor Ed Weiss and Ken Reinert's attorney from Orphans Court. They saw Bill Bradfield on the news, and all the celebrants drank a toast to his *next* trial. Which they hoped would be for murder.

◆◆◆◆

When Vince was eased back into his teaching post he was warned that his job would depend on how people responded to him.

On the first day that he was allowed to teach, he walked up to every teacher in the department and said, "Okay, ask me *any* question you want. Anything!"

When Sue Myers was finally allowed to teach again she developed a posture of answering questions with such a look of exhaustion that people thought she might expire. It discouraged them.

Chris Pappas went to work on another construction job, which may have been what he was always meant to do.

Chris was never really able to believe in his heart and head that Bill Bradfield could have murdered Susan Reinert. As to the children, such a thought was out of the question.

Vince Valaitis could intellectually accept that Bill Bradfield had committed certain misdeeds, but could never accommodate the notion that a loving friend could have committed murder.

Sue Myers would only shrug or nod when she was asked. It was impossible to know if she believed that he'd conspired to kill Susan Reinert. Like the others, she couldn't begin to think that the children would have been in murder plans.

••••

Sue Myers received at least one telephone call a week from Bill Bradfield while he lived quietly in his mother's house. The calls would be about his belongings. Sometimes he'd demand and other times he'd beg her to return them.

"You're holding my books hostage!" he roared during a memorable call.

In one of the strangest calls, he did something he'd never done. He talked about the children. He theorized to Sue Myers that perhaps they'd been "sold." He said that he feared Karen had been bartered into "white slavery."

On still another occasion he demanded that she return *some* of his books. When she refused, he said he'd settle for the return of his old football pictures, but she said nix on the pix.

One night she received *four* calls between the hours of 2:30 and 3:00 A.M. He demanded his marriage certificate to Muriel. She refused. He called again and asked for the divorce papers. Ditto response. He called another time and said he had to have the cowboy suit he'd worn as a tiny tyke, but Sue said, sorry, little wrangler.

The last time he called he sounded like he'd sucked helium. In a quivering grandma voice he said, "You've betrayed me! You've abandoned me! You've wronged me! *Why* won't you meet me for a soda?"

Some might wonder why Sue Myers didn't have her telephone number changed and unlisted. But after seventeen years of lost hopes and shattered dreams, and now poverty—after being unmarried and childless and only now being allowed back in a classroom—would she give up the last pleasure left to her? Bill Bradfield had saved everything but old toenail clippings and she was keeping it *all*.

In the fall, when she got back to Upper Merion, she was able to cut down on the Librium. She started feeling a little better. She began going to a chiropractor. She began getting facials. Sue Myers needed *touching*.

Someone told her that if they ever made a movie about the Reinert murder case maybe Jane Fonda would play her part. That lifted her spirits.

22

Blood Crimson

One of thousands of contacts made by the Reinert task force came by way of a registered letter to Joe VanNort. The writer of the letter was Raymond Martray, an inmate of the state correctional institution at Dallas, who claimed to be a friend of inmate Jay C. Smith.

The writer said that he could not talk at Dallas but if a short transfer could be arranged he'd tell them what was on his mind. He'd sent a similar letter to the FBI, but had gotten no response.

He was transferred for two weeks to the state prison at Pittsburgh and was taken by VanNort and Holtz to the Holiday Inn in Uniontown where they held a short meeting.

Martray was a thirty-seven-year-old ex-cop from Connellsville, Pennsylvania, who was serving a prison sentence for perjury and burglaries, stemming from an arrest by state police while he was still a policeman in Connellsville. He'd been in Dallas prison since 1979 and didn't go around bragging that he'd been a cop, because former lawmen are only a little more popular in the prison yard than child murderers, or "baby killers" as the cons refer to them.

Ex-cops and baby killers pick their friends carefully. Raymond Martray was one of the first inmates that Jay Smith met on the day of his arrival at Dallas. The property room officer asked Martray to show Jay Smith around because he was being put in F Block where Martray also lived.

Martray and Jay Smith had only a nodding acquaintance for about six months because the former educator seemed wary of everyone. Martray was about as tall as Jay Smith, but huskier and much younger. Yet Martray told the cops that he was afraid of the former educator.

Martray said that he'd been asked by Jay Smith to alter a property record to read that his clothes had not been sent to his brother, but were still at Dallas. This, according to Martray, was because Dr. Jay feared that the clothing might contain "forensic evidence" of an unspecified kind, if the cops should search his brother's house and find it.

VanNort and Holtz weren't all that impressed with his information. After all, the Reinert murder had gotten lots of publicity and through his friendship with Jay Smith, Martray would know quite a bit about the investigation. Besides, Martray was serving three and a half to seven years on his perjury conviction and in Pennsylvania a person convicted of perjury can't be a commonwealth witness in another criminal case, so anything he might give them would be tainted.

Before they left him, Martray said that both his perjury and burglary convictions stood a good chance of being reversed on appeal, and if his perjury conviction was overturned, he could then give testimony against the former educator. And the legal counsel who had framed the appeal for Raymond Martray was none other than Jay Smith, jailhouse lawyer.

That had such a nice touch of irony that Joe VanNort gave him their phone number and said to call collect if he got anything good from Dr. Jay. And Martray was transferred back to Dallas.

The second visit with Raymond Martray took place in September after he was transferred to Fayette County Prison where he was housed during his appeal. VanNort and Holtz took Martray to a hotel in Uniontown for a long private conversation. This time it was much more interesting. Martray told the cops that while he was being brought back to Dallas after their meeting in April, he had seized the occasion to be of tremendous service to Jay Smith.

It seems that Dr. Jay had told Martray to watch for an inmate named David Rucker who might shuffle into his life during his prison travels. Jay Smith said Rucker had been an armored-car robber with an M.O. similar to the one he'd been convicted of using, and Jay Smith had not given up hope for a successful appeal on at least one of the Sears convictions.

He described David Rucker to Martray, but he needn't have gone into detail. When Martray got on the prison van that day he was certain that the con sitting behind him was either Wayne Gretzky or David Rucker. The inmate was wearing a hockey helmet.

Rucker had to spend the rest of his life helmeted because he fell down a lot. The reason he fell down was that when the police had captured him he didn't want to go back to jail and had stuck his gun in his mouth and tried to see how many times he could pull the trigger. He managed it once, but botched the job. He had a horseshoe scar on his face and a brain like a milk cow. He just did as he was told and tottered through life. As Martray put it, "He was a very mellow individual."

So David Rucker just sat there like a kindergartner on a school bus and grinned obligingly during a long conversation with Raymond Martray. Another inmate on the bus and a prison guard witnessed the conversation, but did not hear it.

So Martray got to run to Jay Smith with the great news that not only had he met Rucker but a guard had seen him *talking* to Rucker. Jay Smith had suddenly gotten himself another alibi witness. Martray was asked to say that Rucker had confessed to him that he'd been the actual armored-car courier at the Sears store.

Jay Smith really started working hard on Ray Martray's perjury conviction, so that Martray could testify in a court of law. And then, as luck would have it, David Rucker got hit with one too many hockey pucks, as it were, and expired. So he wasn't around to refute the phony confession that he'd never made in the first place.

Well, it wasn't the most promising basis for overturning Dr. Jay's conviction, but jailhouse lawyers have nothing but time. Ray Martray had taken Bill Bradfield's place as Jay Smith's favorite alibi witness.

Jay Smith and Martray became constant buddies that summer.

Jay Smith hired a private investigator named Russell Kolins to take a sworn statement from Martray in the presence of a stenographer. But before that could be done, Jay Smith had to prepare Martray for the interview so that Kolins would believe in him completely, along with the authorities later.

He insisted on giving Martray a "stress test" in case the Kolins affidavit resulted in his being hooked up to a polygraph. He took Martray up into the bleachers in the yard where the cons play ball, and wrapped an electrical cord around Martray's chest and put paper clips on his fingers. He gave him a play-poly right there with Martray answering various test questions about David Rucker and his own friendship with Jay Smith.

Martray said that a young inmate strolling by the bleachers that afternoon spotted them and did a double take, but you see all sorts of weird things in prison yards, and two grown men playing polygraph with paper clips and extension cords probably wasn't all that loony.

The upshot was that Ray Martray had in his possession the make-believe polygraph charts and an envelope containing "stress questions" for Russell Kolins. Martray had something else. He had a very incriminating statement to whet the cops' appetite, but it had taken place in private, and there was no one to corroborate it.

According to Martray, Jay Smith said that Bill Bradfield had asked Dr. Jay to help kill Susan Reinert because she was going to blow the whistle on Bill Bradfield for the perjury at Jay Smith's trial. Moreover, Martray said that he'd asked Jay Smith about the Reinert children and Dr. Jay had volunteered the statement "I took care of it."

And if that wasn't enough, on another occasion, also in private, Jay Smith had gotten upset about something when they were discussing the Reinert case, and blurted, "I killed the fucking bitch."

On Raymond Martray's make-believe polygraph chart with the typed questions was "Did Jay Smith ever tell you he killed Reinert?"

And "Did Jay Smith ever tell you he was a friend of Bradfield?"

Typed charts and questions that anyone could've typed didn't do anything to corroborate Martray, but the ex-cop handed the investigators an envelope on which he'd jotted notes during his meeting with David Rucker.

There was some other writing on that envelope that read, "Sears St. Davids, August 1977," and, on the other side, "Sears, Neshaminy Mall, December 1977."

These were written in the hand of Jay Smith. So far, it was the only thing that tended to corroborate their informant.

••••

On October 1, 1981, Jack Holtz was celebrating his sixth anniversary as an investigator for Joe VanNort. That was also the day that Joe VanNort had to do his shooting qualification on the pistol range.

The old cop failed to qualify that morning. He was irritated, since that meant he had to come back in the afternoon and shoot the pistol range all over again. Joe VanNort, former hunter, former police rodeo rider, was not a guy who wanted to fail on a routine shoot at the state police range. But Joe wasn't his old self and there was no hiding it, not from Jack Holtz nor from Joe's wife Betty, who'd been begging him long-distance to take his vitamin pills since she couldn't be there in that Philly motel watching over him.

Jack Holtz, after the incident at the courthouse when Joe VanNort didn't seem to know where he was, had asked Joe when he'd be taking his next physical exam. Joe had said he'd do it as soon as the goddamn investigation slowed up. He complained of having gout attacks that were causing some pain in his joints.

Now he told Jack to take the car. He'd call after he qualified on the range.

That afternoon, Sergeant Joseph A. VanNort, age fifty-seven, with nearly thirty-two years as a cop, tried *again* on the police pistol range. He took a tool of his trade and did his best to hit the targets but they wouldn't hold still. He showed the world his cynical lopsided grin for the last time. The heart attack hit like a .357 magnum. And just as in the folksong, this old workingman laid down his iron and he died.

Jack Holtz heard on the police radio that a car was being sent to the residence of Betty VanNort in Harrisburg. He raced back to the barracks and got the news. Jack Holtz couldn't keep his glasses welded to his face on *that* afternoon.

He did his weeping in private and then he drove straight to the home of Betty VanNort and tried not to cry again because Joe VanNort wasn't the kind of guy who would want you playing the baby in his house.

The funeral mass was held at a church in Jermyn, Pennsylvania, near the mountains Joe had loved. He was buried in his family cemetery. Jack Holtz was a pallbearer. It was the first time in six years that he'd worn a uniform.

Betty VanNort was provided for by Joe's insurance and pension, but she couldn't bear to go to the cabin anymore. She turned it over to his nephews with the stipulation that they not sell it until her death.

Joe VanNort never got his Madonna with the pool of water at her feet.

◆◆◆◆

When Jack Holtz got back to work he found that it was very different without the top banana. The FBI had already cut its task force participation to just a few full-time agents, and didn't seem to think that a murder indictment against Bill Bradfield was all that probable. Jay Smith seemed totally out of the question. However, they wanted to take over now that Joe VanNort was dead.

But Jack Holtz showed that in a quieter way he could be just as intractable as the man who had trained him. The state police were not surrendering their authority in this case, not even a little of it. He told the feds that *he* was now in charge.

One of the first things he did was to go through all of Joe's personal files. He could have wept again. He found a note that Joe had obviously mislaid back in 1979, a note from a couple of guys in South Carolina who'd been working at Three Mile Island and saw a hatchback open and called the police after they'd read about the case in the papers.

Jack Holtz telephoned the men who established that Susan Reinert's body had been left at the Host Inn as early as seven o'clock on Sunday evening. For the first time it was clear why Jay

Smith had made calls to his attorney's office and residence anxious to establish the time of 8:37 P.M., when he was far from Harrisburg.

Their driving tests showed that it was a ninety-minute drive from the Host Inn in Harrisburg to the house on Valley Forge Road, so Holtz figured that Jay Smith must have narrowly missed being seen by the men from Three Mile Island.

He hated to tell the others, but he had to. He explained how Joe had been losing it for some time and was obviously a very sick man. He wanted to ask Betty if Joe's death had been related to a cerebral hemorrhage, but couldn't bring himself to do it.

He told the remaining FBI agents that they'd never met the old Joe VanNort, the man who made him an investigator, still the best interrogator he'd ever seen. They just hadn't known the *real* Joe VanNort, he assured them.

Jack Holtz was a very lonely top banana.

••••

It was time to reassess. Since there were so many counties involved in the investigation, the attorney general of Pennsylvania opted to assign one of his own prosecutors as the legal coordinator.

Richard L. Guida was a very aggressive, organized, nervously energetic young guy who could've outsmoked Joe VanNort, particularly at trial time. At thirty-four, he was one month older than Jack Holtz but looked five years younger. He was a natural middleweight but would drop down to a welterweight during a trial because he'd forget to eat.

Guida had originally been a prosecutor but had left to try his hand at private practice. He wasn't cut out to be a defense lawyer. There are many trial lawyers who claim they can do each job with equal enthusiasm, but that's something like a macho celebrity who gets caught in a homosexual tryst and says, "Well, I'm bisexual." And the gay tabloids say, "Oh *sure*. Oscar Wilde used *that* old line."

Lawyers can do both jobs, but *not* with the same gusto.

A good prosecutor needs to be about half-Doberman. Rick Guida qualified. He was one of those prosecutors who always look like they may die of heartburn if the defendant tells just *one* more lie. And in a year when half the guys his age in America had a Tom Selleck mustache, it was a good thing he had one, because it helped hide his deadly sneer when a defense witness told a whopper.

Since the FBI presence had been dribbling away for several months, it was decided that another task force should be formed, a little one. Special Agent Matt Mullin stayed on, as did Special Agent Bob Loughney who'd done extensive work on the slag samples taken from Susan Reinert's car, but who had never been able to discover from whence they came. The little task force included another police detective from Montgomery County, and a deputy district attorney to act as special prosecutor. And of course Jack Holtz and Lou DeSantis from the state police.

They worked from a command post in Norristown, with Rick Guida remaining in Harrisburg and coming east when required. But the little task force didn't accomplish much. The momentum was gone. Lots of days they just sat around and shuffled their reports and looked for things that weren't there, things to move Bill Bradfield from the category of convicted thief to a murder indictment.

By December, the FBI decided to hang out the "closed" sign. Matt Mullin and Bob Loughney were the last FBI special agents to leave. The FBI had done more lab work on this criminal investigation than on any other with the exception of the Patricia Hearst case. Jack Holtz was very depressed by the FBI report that said the Reinert murder was unsolvable.

It was a downbeat Christmas for Jack Holtz. Of course he got to go home to his son on weekends. Still, he logged more nights in motel rooms than Willy Loman, and with Joe VanNort gone the nights were lonelier.

Lou DeSantis was from Philly, so he slept at home most of the time. DeSantis had gotten involved with the task force in the first place because he'd been available when the call came to pick up Ken Reinert in Philadelphia and drive him to Harrisburg to identify the body of his ex-wife.

So far, the investigation hadn't brought any hardship for DeSantis, but he wasn't fond of hearing Jack Holtz talk about relocating the task force to Harrisburg, where *he'd* be the one living in motels.

But that's what happened in April. And now it was a mini-task force. It included Jack Holtz, Lou DeSantis and Deputy Attorney General Rick Guida. And that was all there would be until the end. The bunch of bananas was down to three and they were getting overripe. Jack Holtz couldn't even count his gray hairs anymore, but at least he was again living with his son. He celebrated by redecorating. That meant buying another duck.

When asked why he had so many ducks, he looked surprised, as though the answer was obvious: they didn't want flowers.

••••

The move to Harrisburg coincided with another event that would add hundreds of man-hours to the already mammoth investigation. Jay Smith's work had been successful. Raymond Martray got released from prison on $10,000 bail, pending appeal.

While he was free, Martray again contacted Jack Holtz and Lou DeSantis who went to meet him at his father's house. Martray said that Jay Smith wanted him to fake a story that Joe VanNort had offered Martray a deal to frame Jay Smith. He also said that Jay Smith wanted to kill a deputy sheriff and wanted to poison the water supply at Dallas, and all of this had to do with escape plots if he got indicted for murder. Dr. Jay still had the Reinert murder very much on his mind, according to Martray.

Before they'd left the case, the FBI had administered a lie detector test to Raymond Martray. The polygraph operator said he was possibly deceptive. After his release from prison, the cops administered another. He passed on the "key questions." Though Joe VanNort had been a polygraph operator, Jack Holtz seldom used the machine on anyone.

"It's a good tool, *but*," was his opinion of lie detectors.

Jack Holtz decided that if half of what Martray said was accurate it was time to take a stab at the prince of darkness. He and Rick Guida asked Martray if he'd agree to telephone monitoring, and he signed a consent form in the presence of his lawyer.

The state police secured a telephone number and post office box for Raymond Martray and intercepted all letters from Jay Smith. The letters from prison would always specify when Dr. Jay was going to place a phone call, since all outgoing calls had to be made collect. Martray was then to permit his phone call to be taped. There were dozens of such calls received and recorded by the state police during the next three years.

••••

It was clear from the very first recorded telephone conversation that it was mentor and disciple all over again. Ray Martray sounded as eager to please as Chris Pappas and Vince Valaitis had been.

The calls were full of yard talk and legal talk because Jay Smith was busy with petitions of various kinds for other cons, including a mutual friend of theirs named Charles Montione. There were lots of escape talk with Raymond Martray pretending that he'd checked all the places that his mentor had asked him to, including the courthouse in Harrisburg, in case the state cops ever nailed him with an indictment in the Reinert murder.

Most of the conversations were right out of Cagney and Bogart gangster epics. The cops had to endure endless jailhouse fantasies.

"I walked all around the building trying to figure out which way they'd bring you in and out," Martray told him on one of the early calls.

"What you gotta do is go up and down those side steps in the courtrooms," Jay Smith informed him.

"I already did that. I didn't use the elevator at all."

"Right, but if you go all the way down to the basement where they sell the coffee, they bring you in through that side door. The entrance is to the rear."

"Uh huh."

"When they come in there, they're by themselves. Someone could put a gun on them and take their guns away. You could easily get a guy out of there."

"Okay. I'll maybe check that out again the next time I'm down that way."

And then there were the conversations that drove the cops and Rick Guida absolutely bonkers because Jay Smith would say something that *should* be followed by an incriminating remark, but he'd just back off.

Raymond Martray claimed that he'd been taught by his mentor that "self-serving statements" should always be tossed right in the midst of incriminating statements. Just in *case* there were electronic eavesdropping devices around.

For example, in one conversation, Jay Smith said, "My defense is going to be that I had nothing to do with the Reinert murder. They can't prove anything because I *didn't* have anything to do with it."

And Raymond Martray, sounding as frustrated as the cops, asked, "Is there anybody close there, or something?"

"Is anybody what?"

"Anybody *close* to you, or anything there?"

"No."

"Cause I want to . . . you think there's anything on these phones, or what?"

"Oh well, I think that if anything . . . yeah, I think we *always* have to be careful."

"Yeah, okay. I couldn't understand what was going on," Martray said.

All of these contradictions were repeatedly attributed to the "self-serving" explanation. But the cops were starting to imply that maybe Martray had never been told diddly regarding the Reinert murder. And that he was trying to use the cops to influence the court during his appeals.

When Martray once again took the subject from escape directly to the Reinert murder, Jay Smith said, "Remember, I got a *lot* of things going for me. One, the woman who bought my house moved into it on the day that Reinert disappeared, and she was there *with* me, you know what I mean?"

"Uh huh."

"Second, I had my daughter, whose birthday it was, there *with* me. See, we were moving out of the house."

"Uh huh."

Well, that was demonstrably false. Jack Holtz could prove that Grace Gilmore had *not* been with him, nor had his daughter Sheri. So at least Raymond Martray was correct when he said that Jay Smith would make self-serving statements that were downright lies whenever he felt there might be eavesdroppers.

And the cops became convinced that they should keep recording the calls until Jay Smith gave them enough to put him in the electric chair. At least he was talking a lot about escapes if he got indicted for murder. And escape tended to show a consciousness of guilt.

One call introduced Harry Gibson.

"If I mention the name Harry Gibson," Jay Smith said to his bogus disciple, "then we're starting to think about an escape."

"Okay. We don't have to worry about that unless there's an indictment coming."

"Remember, Ray, this place is confused now. It's not like when they had it organized. You could come in to visit with a long pair of pants, and inside a pair of thin pants. So look around for very thin pants and what we would do is change and I'd go out with some visitor."

During one of the more important calls, Jay Smith started fantasizing about his budding literary career. He was going to write a book called *The Valley Forge Murders.*

In that call, he said, "And just suppose I'm lucky and this book gets off? Then we've got money without any kind of problem. A *lot* of money."

"In the same respect," Martray answered, "what happens if they nail you for Reinert? *Then* whadda we do?"

"Well . . ."

"Where am *I* gonna be at?"

"If they convict me?"

"Yeah."

"They'll probably send me to the electric chair."

"No shit!" Martray said. "Look what it does to *me!*"

"It's a problem," Jay Smith said, sympathetically.

"It's a loose end," Martray said. "Just like you said before, get rid of *loose ends.*"

"I think if they were to arrest me for Reinert, the best thing for you to do is to go kill Bradfield and make him *disappear*," Jay Smith said, casually.

"He *would* disappear. That's it. You made the comment. That's it."

"But see . . ."

"You don't have to say any more," said Martray.

But Jay Smith had more to say. "Get him back in your car. Kill him and take his body up into some woods, up in Fayetteville or someplace, but nobody, see, *nobody* should know where his body is but you. When you deal with a body, only *you* should know. You should never let anyone else know. Do you see the advantage to that?"

"Yeah."

And then, just when it looked as though Martray had Dr. Jay on the verge of an all-out admission, the former principal said, "There's nothing that Bradfield could do to hurt me other than lie, and that's it."

Then the talk turned to more mundane matters such as escaping from jail with electric hacksaws.

••••

In July, Jay Smith wanted Ray Martray to drive up to Dallas to pay him a visit. Martray contacted the task force in Harrisburg and agreed to wear a body wire. They videotaped Martray and Jay Smith standing in the prison visiting area. It was nearly 100 degrees outside. Inside the panel truck where the electronics technician and Jack Holtz were hiding it was a lot hotter. They shot the visiting area with a telephoto lens from outside the fence.

It wasn't a great performance by their man. He was overacting from the moment he stepped back inside the walls of Dallas prison. One of the first moves Martray made after the handshakes were over was to playfully give Dr. Jay a little bump with his hip after he'd said something that wasn't particularly funny in the first place.

Cute, Jack Holtz thought. Showing off because he's wearing a body wire.

Then he made Holtz even madder by hopping around Jay Smith like some kind of oversized puppy, nervously talking over the top of *everything* Jay Smith was saying. He was too hyper to let Jay Smith complete a single phrase that afternoon.

Jay Smith just stood there and put his hand up in front of his mouth in case a guard in a tower could read lips with binoculars. And he pretty well said the same things that they'd been hearing on the telephone tapes. The cops were really sick of the bullshit.

The temperature in the van soared up over 140 degrees and the camera lens started sweating and they lost their video for a while.

On that video, Jay Smith looked for all the world like what he'd been trained to be, a schoolteacher. He gave out lots of advice and acted as though he were humoring his boy by talking about some robberies he was going to pull with Martray to make them both rich. And he figured he wouldn't have too much longer to do, what with a good shot at a favorable appeal. He just chatted as little kids scampered around the area while their mommies visited daddies and boyfriends.

Jay Smith was absolutely avuncular through most of it, but since no Jay Smith meeting would be complete without a little sex talk he told Martray about a mutual friend who was starting to disappoint him a whole lot. He'd started using drugs. And as Uncle Jay put it, "He likes to suck black cocks when he's high."

The cops figured they'd sweated off a combined total of twenty-five pounds while Raymond Martray chewed more scenery than Olivier in *Richard III.*

Three months later, Martray got a chance to redeem himself with yet another videotaping. It was a lot cooler for the cops inside the panel truck. Jay Smith was wearing a long-sleeved shirt this time, carrying glasses and a couple of pencils in his shirt pocket. You'd swear he was the pious chaplain making his rounds.

This time Martray's performance, even though he'd been coached by Jack Holtz, went *more* over the top. He was just too anxious.

Martray blurted out that he was going to "take care" of Bill Bradfield, and it was clear that Jay Smith was very wary of this kind of talk.

Jay Smith said, "But I had *nothing* to do with the murder, Ray."

Then Raymond Martray danced around and promised that he'd never let Jay down. He referred to him as a criminal genius, but Jay Smith kept repeating that he had nothing to do with the Reinert murder, and all the while Martray still never let him finish a sentence.

The cops figured they'd better sprinkle Valium on Martray's waffles before they tried this again. He was so breathless Jay Smith might have to give him CPR.

After about a hundred "like you said's" and "like you told me's" that Jay Smith didn't seem to be buying, the older man apparently decided to quiet his disciple down with, what else? A little sex talk. Jay Smith gave Raymond Martray graphic advice on how to please a lady with cunnilingus.

As relevant film making, these two shows ranked with a Sylvester Stallone movie. The mini-task force was *not* thrilled.

••••

Bill Bradfield, still out on bail while appealing his conviction, had lost his job with the school district and been forced to withdraw his claim against the estate of Susan Reinert.

Bill Bradfield now knew that he would not be following the trail of Achilles and Hector and the thousand black ships. He would not be playing the lyre on the bridge of a ketch with some young disciple peeping up his tunic. He'd have to content himself with sailing boats in his mother's bathtub.

But he was hoping to continue to breathe the free air of Chester County.

••••

During a small dinner party at a lawyers' club in Philadelphia just after his conviction, Bill Bradfield said, "The key to my dilemma is to be found in Ezra Pound, two cantos in particular. It's that I've loved my friends *imperfectly.*"

When he was offered the wine list he refused to choose, saying, "I have no palate for wine."

One was reminded that it was Ezra Pound who wrote: "There's no wine like the blood's crimson!"

23

The Decree

They decided in the fall of 1981 to try for a murder indictment against William Bradfield. From October of that year until March of the next, Jack Holtz and Rick Guida had to contend with the aggravation of running back and forth on the turnpike between Harrisburg and Philly to interview witnesses for grand jury testimony.

The grand jury term ran for five months, but each month's session lasted only a few days. Because their case was so complicated they never had enough time, and actually had to present their evidence piecemeal and hope they could finish by March.

In November Bill Bradfield's day arrived. He had to begin serving a four-month jail sentence for the theft of Susan Reinert's money. He was sent to Delaware County Prison but knew he had a good chance of getting out on bail pending his appeal. Cops have long suspected that the law dictionaries of America have omitted the *F*'s, as in "final," "finish," etc.

Jack Holtz made an uncannily accurate prediction. He told Rick Guida that Bill Bradfield would find himself a friend in prison, and he described the friend. He said it would be a big, street-smart black guy, and that Bill Bradfield would *have* to talk about the case sooner or later because he *always* had to tell his troubles to somebody.

Jay Smith had been in prison quite a while before he made any friends at all, but Bill Bradfield was no soloist. He needed friends worse than Mary, Queen of Scots. He started looking around.

It wasn't long before he was playing chess with a twenty-four-year-old black inmate named Proctor Nowell. And it wasn't long before Proctor Nowell stepped between another black con and Bill Bradfield in the role of protector. Nowell later said that Bill Bradfield had promised that when they got out of jail he'd buy an apartment house in Philly and let Nowell manage it.

After a month in jail, Bill Bradfield was successful in getting a release from prison on bail pending his appeal. Jack Holtz figured that a month had been plenty of time for a man as garrulous as Bill Bradfield. Lou DeSantis called Franklin Center, the state police station closest to the prison, and discovered that Bill Bradfield had been friends with two black inmates, one of whom was Nowell.

During the months that the grand jury was hearing portions of their case, Jack Holtz and Lou DeSantis paid a visit to Nowell at the prison.

Nowell was an alcoholic who'd been convicted of robbery and had a history of petty crimes.

Jack Holtz learned that Nowell had kids, and he played on that angle, describing Karen and Michael Reinert to the convict. It was a short interview in which Nowell admitted that Bill Bradfield had told him "things," but said he didn't want to talk about it.

The cops said to call them if he changed his mind, and that was that. Jack Holtz wasn't holding out too much hope, but within two days he got the call.

It was Nowell who, like Raymond Martray, said, "I know stuff, but it scares me." He didn't want to talk to them in prison.

Jack Holtz went to the district attorney's office in Delaware County to see his old friend from Orphans Court, John Reilly, and had Nowell placed on a court list. The convict was brought in with prisoners who'd be attending hearings.

They met in a private room in the court house, and Proctor Nowell told them of conversations with Bill Bradfield. Jack Holtz called Rick Guida and they arranged yet another session with

Nowell who remained constant throughout their questioning.

Proctor Nowell also needed a friend. He was committed to the alcohol rehabilitation program as an alternative to jail, and agreed to appear before the grand jury.

With Nowell as the last link in their circumstantial chain, they decided it was time to arrest Bill Bradfield, this time for three counts of murder. The arrest plan was only a little less complicated than the Falklands invasion, and about as necessary.

The date was April 6th, the time was 5:00 A.M. Bill Bradfield, according to their intelligence reports, was living with Rachel in a guesthouse on his mother's property. Reports from neighbors said that he had a large attack dog, and from Chris Pappas they learned that he had other hunting weapons in the farmhouse.

The arrest team was composed of Jack Holtz, Lou DeSantis, another trooper, and a woman trooper to make the call just as before. Prosecutor Rick Guida went along, and by 5:00 A.M. he'd already smoked half a pack of cigarettes, but after all, it *was* his first arrest.

Before daybreak they started watching the house with a nightscope they'd borrowed for the occasion. It outweighed two bowling balls and through the thing they could see nothing but green haze.

Jack Holtz and the woman trooper went to a neighbor and awakened the household. Not wanting to alarm the folks in rural Chester County unduly, they said they were working a burglary investigation and needed to use the phone.

But the neighbor said, "You shouldn't waste your time with burglars. We have *murderers* around here."

And while the woman trooper called, the neighbor proceeded to tell them all about this fellow Bill Bradfield. He said they should throw *him* in jail instead of some burglar.

Rachel answered the phone and said that Bill Bradfield was in Birdsboro and wouldn't be back until the next day. She seemed used to female callers.

So the whole shooting match was off to a house in Birdsboro where they'd already heard he was spending time with a friend and was selling diet products.

The police code was "We've located the *package*," presumably because they feared the master criminal was tuned in to the police frequency. Actually, Bill Bradfield would probably have approved of this caper.

It was still dark when they arrived. Their quarry was a notoriously bad driver and they spotted a VW Beetle parked half on the sidewalk. It was a quiet neighborhood. They said their code words and synchronized their watches and got all dressed up in their flak vests and jacked rounds into their shotguns.

The chief of police of this little place moseyed by in his car, and wondered what in the hell was going on. The only thing they didn't have were helicopters and a chaplain.

When they knocked at the door and scared the living crap out of the resident, he admitted that he was forming a company to sell diet products with his pal Bill who was in bed sleeping. They pushed by him and crept into the back of the house with enough firepower to knock down the Luftwaffe.

The first thing Jack Holtz saw in the darkness when his pupils dilated was a set of flashing teeth. Canine teeth. Large.

He yelled, "If it moves, *shoot* it!"

And Bill Bradfield, who was awake in bed, thought they were talking about *him*. He went as rigid as Lenin's mummy. He wasn't even breathing as the cops crept toward the flashing teeth. He didn't twitch when Jack Holtz yelled, "Show me your hands!"

Somebody turned on the lights. The "attack" dog was an English setter named Traveler who needed attention and cuddling almost as much as the guy in bed. Traveler was so happy he leaped up on Jack Holtz and started licking his face. Bill Bradfield almost turned blue before someone told him it was okay to inhale.

Jack Holtz got a great deal of joy out of reading the arrest warrant to Bill Bradfield. He read it with verve. He wanted to read it twice. He was crazy about the part where it said conspiracy to commit murder with person or persons unknown.

He finished it when Bill Bradfield was standing and dressed. Big Bill gave his famous stare to Rick Guida who'd been told by an FBI agent that the Bradfield stare had once made him fall back two steps.

The stare practically demolished Guida. He was literally floored. He sat down on the floor and played with Traveler.

When Jack Holtz got Bill Bradfield back to the lockup in Harrisburg and took off the handcuffs, his prisoner, who'd been as silent as fungus, decided to make life hard for him. Bill Bradfield just dropped down on the floor and lay there on his back.

Jack Holtz said, "If you're gonna act like a baby, I'll treat you like one."

But no baby ever got *this* treatment. Holtz reached down and grabbed two handfuls of Bill Bradfield's whiskers and curled him straight up until they were nose to nose.

Bill Bradfield gave Jack Holtz the stare, but Jack Holtz stared back and said, "That bullshit only works on intelligent people."

Jack Holtz had called Betty VanNort earlier to tell her they were going to arrest William Bradfield for murder, and he went to her house at 7:30 A.M. after they had him in custody.

Betty VanNort said that she'd been awake half the night praying for them. They had a cup of tea together.

◆◆◆◆

Bill Bradfield was sent to the state correctional institution at Camp Hill. He was placed in "Mohawk," the administrative custody section for new fish who haven't been placed in the general population yet, or who need special protection. Prisoners in Mohawk are in individual cells and shout messages down the corridor to each other.

According to information relayed to Jack Holtz, Bill Bradfield was trying to sleep when a black convict yelled, "Braaaaadfield, you killed my schoolteacher. Braaaaadfield, you killed those little babies."

◆◆◆◆

Courtroom number four in the Dauphin County Courthouse was far too small to accommodate the spectators and reporters.

Judge Isaac S. Garb was highly respected in Harrisburg, known for keeping a trial moving and for being fair to both sides. He was a very diminutive man and once when Rick Guida said, "Your honor, I need a few minutes. I have just one short witness," the judge replied, "Mister Guida, there aren't any *short* witnesses in this case. There are brief witnesses."

The defense attorney for Bill Bradfield was a nice-looking

young fellow, Guida's age. Joshua Lock was a second-generation Harrisburg lawyer, his father having been a county district attorney.

By his own admission he became "personally involved" almost from his first meetings with Bill Bradfield. It isn't the best idea in the world to become personally involved with clients, and he knew that, but he truly admired Bill Bradfield. Once during a strategy session, apropos of something they were discussing, Bill Bradfield gave him a thumbnail sketch of the study of grammar and linguistics, as well as literary criticism that the lawyer wished he could've put before the jury.

Unlike Guida, Lock believed that Bill Bradfield was highly intelligent, as was the one remaining disciple, Rachel. But Lock found Rachel to be "very very very very very very strange." And that's all he'd say for the record.

There may have been trial lawyers who worked harder for their clients in 1983, but if so, they probably didn't live to tell of it. Lock personally, and without assistance, compiled notebooks bigger than the Philadelphia telephone directory on virtually every important witness for the prosecution. With the most elaborate and precise cross-references to each FBI report, state police report, and every bit of testimony given before state or federal grand juries or during any other proceedings thus far. His idea was to present a dozen different possibilities for the jury as to where to look for killers.

Naturally, one possibility was Dr. Jay C. Smith. Lock viewed him as a depraved maniac, street-smart and complicated, who'd battled his way up in ways that Bill Bradfield never had. As far as Lock was concerned, Jay Smith had proved himself a liar a hundred times over. He hoped to provide other suspects for the jury to consider, and to point out that a circumstantial case could be viewed many ways. His approach was to be intellectual and scholarly.

He'd spent twenty-eight days in the prison visiting room with William Bradfield. He would spend a total of fifteen hundred hours on the defense of his client.

Lock respected Rick Guida, because when other prosecutors were backing away from the notorious circumstantial case, he'd seized the opportunity. He saw Guida as an egocentric, ambitious, aggressive prosecutor, and he was probably right on all counts.

In fact, Guida was too egocentric to analyze the opposition. Josh Lock was obviously a competent lawyer and that was that. Guida didn't spend much time thinking about the other guy's strengths and weaknesses. As far as he and Jack Holtz were concerned, their case could amost rest on the credibility of only one witness. Jack Holtz said that he would be Guida's *best* witness: that was William Bradfield.

••••

Rick Guida's strategy was to put on the weakest first, and that would encompass all of the forensics. Josh Lock was very strong on forensics. By the time Lock got through with the pathologist, it sounded as though Lock could have done the autopsy.

Through his cross-examination the jury learned that lividity becomes irreversible after four to six hours and that one way to determine if the lividity is fixed is to press the flesh and see if it blanches. Josh Lock knew all the terminology and could refer to "hemolysized portions of red blood cells." Lock extracted an admission that the time of death *could* have been Sunday afternoon or evening when Bill Bradfield had been at the beach for a longer time.

Lock got it into the record that there were as many as twenty thousand blue combs disseminated by the army reserve in eastern Pennsylvania, and that there was a fingerprint or two on the outside of the car that didn't belong to anybody in the case. So whether they belonged to "kinky Alex" or somebody else, no one would ever know. He was extending the possibilities from a killing by Jay Smith to persons unknown, not necessarily having anything to do with Jay Smith.

As far as the hair that the prosecution believed came from Susan Reinert's head, he didn't spend time refuting that, but rather he used it by pointing out that the entire root was intact and therefore it had fallen out naturally rather than being pulled out. He had a theory saved for his closing argument.

If the case had been based solely on forensics, the prosecution would never have filed it. The troubles for the defense started when the neighbors of Susan Reinert started taking the stand and talking about Bill Bradfield's car being there at night and in the morning. Lock did a good job of spreading a little confusion as to the days of the week and the times they'd seen the cars.

Susan Reinert's friends testified, and Lock got everyone to say that Bill Bradfield had never admitted that he was romantically involved with Susan Reinert and had certainly never hinted that he intended to marry her.

All of Susan Reinert's financial transactions were described by witnesses, as well as the alibi testimony for Jay Smith, and the missing $25,000, and the huge insurance policies, and the will.

And then came the disciples. The jury started giving those "Are you kidding me?" looks as Vince Valaitis and Chris Pappas and Shelly and Sue Myers started talking about silencers and acid and money wiping and all the rest of it. Everybody on the jury at sometime or other kept hearing one word and that word was "bizarre."

Sue Myers said, in private, that two years after she'd locked out Bill Bradfield, she happened to be cleaning out the bookshelves when she found a large cache of meticulously catalogued packages of hardcore pornography. She said he must have spent *days* cutting out pictures and subdividing photos, and swinger ads and telephone numbers. It was as detailed and methodical as his lesson plans and seating charts. She was shocked by the discovery.

••••

Jack Holtz believed what Proctor Nowell had told him and thought that the jury would too.

When the witness was called, the prosecutor got the criminal record over with in a hurry.

"What particular institution are you in at the present time?" Rick Guida asked.

"The ABRAX program, an alcohol drug program."

"Are you sentenced there as a condition of a criminal charge?"

"Yes, I am."

"What sentence are you currently serving?"

"Eighteen months to five years."

"Are you married?"

"Yes."

"Do you have children?"

"Two."

"Tell us what trouble you've been in."

"When I was sixteen I was incarcerated for aggravated assault. I served four to twenty-three months. I did, like seven months, and I got out. I was arrested for burglary twice but I wasn't convicted. I was charged with receivin stolen goods, possession with intent to deliver, and two gun charges."

"What was the disposition of all your cases? Did you have a trial or plead guilty?"

"I pled guilty."

"Are you an alcoholic?"

"Yes."

"Do you have any outside hobbies?"

"Yes. Amateur boxin. I boxed Golden Gloves. Ten wins and one loss."

"Mister Nowell, can you associate your criminal problems with your drinking problem?"

"That's the only time I would get in trouble was when I had got intoxicated."

"When did you first meet Mister Bradfield?"

"I was sittin in the dayroom on B block and I was playin chess with another inmate. Mister Bradfield walked up to me and asked me when I got time would I teach him how to play the game."

"Did you eventually play chess with him?"

"Yes. It was about one or two days later. I was in my room, me and this guy Stanley. We were sittin on the bed playin chess and William Bradfield walked past the cell. I hollered. I told him, I said, 'Bradfield, I got time to show you how to move the pieces, but, you know, the rest got to come from you mentally.' "

"How many games did you play over the time that you knew him?"

"Approximately twelve times."

"How did he do?"

"He beat me eight out of twelve. I started playin when I was, like twelve years old, and it was, you know, not easy to get beat like that. I took for granted that he already knew how to play."

"Did you have the opportunity to help Mister Bradfield with regard to another inmate?"

"Yes. Me and Bradfield was comin from upstairs. Another inmate asked him somethin. He says somethin about doin somethin to him. I said, 'No, man, you ain't gonna do nothin to him because that's my friend.' He walked on about his business."

"Did you have an occasion to get a letter from your wife and make a comment to him?"

"Well, I received a letter from my wife that day and I read the letter and I got upset, you know, and she's tellin me, like 'I'm tired, baby,' you know? 'I don't think I'm gonna wait this time.' I got angry. I told Bradfield, I said, 'Good a provider as I have been.' I said, 'You know, I'm goddamn gonna kill that . . . that . . . I don't wanna say what I said. 'I'm gonna kill that hussy,' or whatever."

"What did *he* say?"

"He said, 'No, no, no. You don't ever wanna kill anyone. They never get off your ass.' "

"Did you have occasion to speak with Mister Bradfield when he got back from a court proceeding?"

"Well, I was lookin for him because I had some coffee for him. I walked outta my room and he was standin on the tier. He was standin there lookin up to the ceilin with his finger pointed in his head, you know, like real angry and disgusted. And I called him, I said, 'Bradfield, come here.' He came in the room. And I said, 'What's wrong, man?' "

"What did he look like when he was standing out there and what did he look like when he came in your cell in terms of his facial expression?"

"Like, the veins was up in his head, poppin up. Like, he really had a major problem, like real frustrated and real angry. He came on in the cell."

"What did he do when he was in the cell?"

"He was walkin around in the cell lookin up, lookin out the window and stuff. And he said, 'They're fuckin over me, man. They're fuckin over me. They denied my bail reduction.' Then after he said that, he said, 'You know, if I wasn't in a financial bind I wouldn't be here nor would this have had to happen to Susan.' "

"I didn't really know what he was talkin about. He said, 'I was there when they were killed but I didn't kill them.' And I said, 'Damn, Bradfield! The children too?' And he said, 'None of this was meant for the kids, only for Susan. But there couldn't be a stone left unturned. You have to tie up all the loose ends.' "

And *that,* Guida and Holtz noted, was a Jay Smith expression from *way* back. Bill Bradfield had used the same words to Vince and Chris describing what Dr. Jay had told him. And Raymond Martray had used the same words as well when he described conversations with Jay Smith.

"After he made that statement did you speak with him very much anymore?"

"No, I limited my association with him."

"Did any law enforcement officer or deputy attorney general make any promises with regard to testifying in this matter?"

"No, the only thing I was told was, you know, that my judge would be made aware of my cooperation. That's it."

"When the police first came to you and talked to you, did you tell them about this situation?"

"No, I didn't. I told them I didn't know nothin because I really didn't want to get involved in it. You know, the name the people start callin you while you're incarcerated. And man, I was just scared, really."

"Why did you come forward with your story, Mister Nowell?"

"Because they told me to sit down and think about it. They said, 'Okay, we're not gonna pressure you, but think about it. It was two innocent children involved.' I went back to my room and I was just layin there thinkin about it, you know? I finally started thinkin, like, damn, what would happen, you know, if this was *my* kids? Would I want somebody to do this for mine? That's when I got up and I went in my box and got the number and called them."

"Are you telling us the truth today?"

"Yes."

"So help you God?"

"So help me God."

◆◆◆◆

On cross-examination, Josh Lock attacked Nowell's credibility by trying to show that he was seeking favors from the authorities. He dissected the statement "I was there when *they* were killed," because he'd already shown and the prosecution stipulated that

Bill Bradfield could not have been there when Susan Reinert actually stopped breathing.

But Jack Holtz was never prouder of his idea to look for a Bill Bradfield "protector" in the Delaware County prison. He thought that Proctor Nowell had done just fine.

••••

His moment came. Bill Bradfield wore black frame glasses for the trial, and the day he testified he had on his most dignified three-piece blue suit and a subdued striped necktie. His testimony was flat, as unemotional as before. But this time his voice kept fading and the judge had to continually remind him to speak up.

"State your full name, please," Josh Lock said when the direct examination began.

"William S. Bradfield, Jr."

"How old are you?"

"Fifty."

"And can you tell us your educational background, please."

"I graduated from Haverford College in 1955, and have a master's in liberal education from St. John's. I've done other graduate work at various institutions."

When Lock asked him to describe his relationship with Sue Myers, he said, "We had not been living as a real romantic pair for many many years."

"Do you remember when your relationship with Miss Myers ceased to be intimate?"

"Nineteen seventy-three or seventy-four," he said.

Poor old Sue. That was when they'd *first* started living together. She always claimed that the sex hadn't stopped until 1978. No wonder she needed facials and chiropractors.

Of his early relationship with Jay Smith, he said, "He was a very very intelligent man, very intelligent. And he liked to indulge in a kind of intellectual combat. During teachers' meetings he'd come up to you in the hall and begin talking tongue-in-cheek about some item of education. And he'd use very big words and if I'd ask him what the word meant, Doctor Smith would say, 'Mister Bradfield, I don't get paid to teach you vocabulary.' And I would go look it up and there *wasn't* any such word. He'd say it was Hindustani or Old English.

"The most characteristic thing he did in the cafeteria or in the halls was to interlude very elaborately embroidered conceits. A conceit is a kind of extended metaphor in literature. He would, for example, begin by saying to me that the essence of civilization is the foot, and that it's the most important organ of the human body, and massage of the foot is the most important thing that one person can do for another.

"Another time he talked about the central importance of boots, and it turned out that he'd sold cowboy boots at one time. He wasn't serious, but it was a kind of practice of his skill in rhetoric without reference to the substance of the idea.

"And sometimes if I went down to him with a grievance from a student, Doctor Smith would say, 'Mister Bradfield it's really not incumbent on me to speak. Let's go back and discuss it in my office.' We'd go back and close the door and his language changed into a basic kind of street language. And *never* have I heard obscenities come together in quite the way that he would do it."

Bill Bradfield testified that he had never taken Susan Reinert to a movie, show, dance, party, play, concert, or on a boat. He said that he'd done all these things with other women friends such as Rachel, and he admitted to being romantically involved with Shelly.

There was a danger to the defense in all this, because the prosecution might run with it by showing that, yes indeed, he'd treated Susan Reinert differently from all his others. The prosecution's inference could be that there was a "five-year plan" for *this* one, and that the five years had ended abruptly in 1979.

Bill Bradfield gave his own version of the business of trying to protect Susan Reinert from Jay Smith, but it didn't differ considerably with the Chris Pappas version, though he glossed over the wiping of the money, things like that. He said that he was so distraught that he'd begun to look haggard from all that protecting.

Once, he said, he baby-sat for Susan Reinert in his capacity as adviser, and she came home at 4:00 A.M., and he warned her then and there that she was dating some bad folks.

He said that she'd never admitted dating Jay Smith, but that she'd admitted dating a man named Jay, and he'd put two and two together and got goat vibes. He did *not* mention the Tweetie Bird term of endearment.

He admitted to taking Shelly to motels, and claimed never to have had sex with her, and by then the prosecution believed that much, at least.

The direct testimony ended like this:

"Did you kill Mrs. Reinert?"

"No, I did not."

"Did you plan to kill Susan Reinert?"

"No."

"Did you kill either of her children?"

"No."

"Did you plan to do either of those things?"

"No, I did not."

"Are you responsible for the deaths?"

"Absolutely not. I never hurt Mrs. Reinert or her children in any way."

"Are you guilty of these crimes?"

"I am not."

••••

Rick Guida was one of those prosecutors who live for cross-examination, and possibly in his entire career he'd never looked forward more to one.

Since Josh Lock's last question had solicited denials of murder and conspiracy, he began with the next logical question:

"Who *did* kill Mrs. Reinert, Mister Bradfield?"

"I don't know," Bill Bradfield said.

"Now, in 1979 you told a number of people that Jay C. Smith was going to kill her, and you were so afraid that you went to the shore just to have an alibi. Don't you think Jay C. Smith killed Susan Reinert?"

"I don't know who killed Susan Reinert."

"Do you believe that he did, Mister Bradfield?"

"Do you want me to speculate?"

"Sure, just tell us what you think."

"Objection," Josh Lock said.

"Overruled," said the judge.

"He may have," Bill Bradfield answered.

"He *may* have," Guida said, with a double dollop of sarcasm. "Now what about this other person that you identified in the summer of 1979, do you think *he* may have killed Mrs. Reinert?"

"I think he may have."

"What was his name? If you think he killed her I'd like to know how you know that."

"Mrs. Reinert mentioned the name in the winter of 1979, the name Alex. The only details I knew were that Alex was tall, very well spoken, from the Harrisburg area. And one of the others mentioned was Ted or Jay, I don't remember which, but one was extremely well educated. The other three, she said, were into group sex. They were advocates of bondage and discipline, and deviate sexual practices such as urination during the sex act, and oral sex, and such as that."

"Do you think somebody else did it, other than Jay C. Smith?"

"I think somebody else may have, yes."

"Even in spite of all these threats that Jay C. Smith made, is that right?"

"Yes."

"Why do you think that Jay Smith *didn't* do it?"

"Because I found out from the newspapers that her body was found in Harrisburg. That's where she said Alex was from. Secondly, it seemed to involve some kind of sexual misuse. There was a dildo found in the automobile. And thirdly, the thing that made me really wonder about Doctor Smith doing it is that nothing he ever told me indicated that he would kill in this way. There were chain marks on her as it was reported to the press, and in addition to this, under the body was found a comb from his same outfit. That certainly didn't make any sense to me."

"Does it make any sense that Alex, an unnamed person, would come all the way from Harrisburg to get Jay C. Smith's comb to plant in Susan Reinert's car? If Alex killed her and Jay C. Smith wasn't involved, how did Jay C. Smith's comb get in the car unless it was planted there by Alex from Harrisburg?"

"My wonder about it is that if it was in her car it means that Mrs. Reinert and Doctor Smith had been in the car and perhaps he'd lost his comb. Why the comb was *where* it was, I'm not sure."

"It was in the wheelwell storage area. Would it make sense that he might have been in the hidden luggage area where his comb was found?"

"I didn't know where the comb was found."

On the subject of untouchable Sue Myers, Guida asked, "Why did you move in with Sue Myers for six or seven years if you were no longer lovers and not intimate?"

"Sue Myers offered me the first real comfortable home base that I've had since leaving home for college. We had what I thought was a close, warm and comfortable relationship. That was the place where I felt the most at home, in that apartment."

"You were not in love with her?"

"I loved her."

"You were not intimate with her?"

"Correct."

As to the money he'd put into the Terra Art store, he said that Sue Myers didn't like teaching very much and it was a "privilege" to put up $45,000 to help her ease out of the profession and begin as an entrepreneur. As to where he'd gotten the money he said that he'd mortgaged a house for $25,000 and took out a second mortgage for an additional $25,000.

It was all getting down to the stash of $25,000 that everyone was hiding and wiping. He called that his "boat fund" and said that he'd been saving it secretly for years.

"Why didn't you use the boat fund for the art store?" Rick Guida wanted to know.

"Because I wanted to retain it."

"Why didn't you put *that* money into Terra Art? Because you weren't getting any interest on it anyway, and you could've used that instead of paying interest on these loans. Why didn't you do that?"

"Because Sue Myers, for all her good points, was impossible when it came to money."

"Mister Bradfield," Guida interrupted, "money is money, whether it comes from selling land, or borrowing it, or if it comes from your boat fund. It's the same thing. Now, again my question is, why didn't you use the boat fund instead of borrowing at ten or twelve percent?"

"Because the ten or twelve percent interest that I would pay back on the loan would be paid through monies that were controlled by Sue Myers and me. If, on the other hand, I used the boat fund for the business, I never would have seen that money again for my own use."

Guida didn't bother to ask why he didn't put the secret money in an interest-bearing account, but moved along to the alibi testimony. Bill Bradfield said that the court reporter in that case had misquoted him in his testimony.

And then they moved along to the chains and acid that Jay Smith showed Bill Bradfield during the lazy crazy days of summer.

Guida's tone during the cross-examination of Bill Bradfield never varied. His incredulity was blended with only as much sarcasm as he figured the judge would permit. If you could bottle it, it would've been about 80 proof.

"That brings up something interesting," he said. "You saw tape and you saw chains and yet you said you didn't believe Jay C. Smith had anything to do with the death of Susan Reinert. Did you hear the testimony that there was tape residue around her face and chain marks on her back?"

"Yes."

"To this day you have a relationship with Rachel, is that right?"

"Yes."

"You lived with her in 1981 through 1982, isn't that right?"

"Yes."

"Did you hear her testimony that you had a romantic relationship during the summer of 1978?"

"I don't recall."

"If she *did* say it she would have been wrong, is that right?'

"I didn't view our relationship as romantic. My relationship with Rachel has been of a different sort than that which you would accurately characterize as romantic or sexual. It's not what we really had, I would say."

"Over all this time you *never* had any sexual and/or romantic relationship?"

"Well, we have had some sexual incidents. What I'm trying to do is characterize it fairly for you. It was not the essential relationship with Rachel, and never with me, and never had been. It wasn't in the summer of 1978 and it isn't now."

"I believe you've described your relationship with Rachel as artistic and intellectual, is that right?"

"Yes."

"Was it that same with Shelly? Sex was not at the center of her universe either?"

"It was not."

"How did you rekindle the relationship when you spent a four-day weekend with Rachel over Thanksgiving, 1978?"

"It was not a sex holiday, as you're suggesting."

"A romantic holiday then. What happened?"

"We went to see a number of art films in Cambridge. We went to see the glass flowers at Harvard in the exhibit there. We attended a lecture. We went to the museum of art."

"Where did you stay?"

"With Rachel."

"In her bedroom."

"Yes."

"But you wouldn't characterize this weekend as intimate?"

"I don't mean to suggest that the relationship with her or with any of the other people in my life was either orthodox or proper."

"Now speaking of that weekend, what did you do to protect Susan Reinert?"

"Nothing."

"You told this jury that you drove around her house and did many things over that time period when you found out about the threat, even to the point of sending Sue Myers away because Smith would kill on holidays. Why did you take that critical weekend off and go to Massachusetts if Susan Reinert was in such danger?"

"I tried to spend as much time as I could, *do* what I could about the situation with Doctor Smith. I couldn't do so much that I gave up my life. And by Thanksgiving I was alarmed and concerned and afraid. By Christmas I went away again and I was even more alarmed and desperately tired. I couldn't park in front of Susan Reinert's house during the whole holiday weekend without simply moving in. I couldn't do it."

"So you just gave up on the critical weekends and went someplace else so you wouldn't even be anywhere near her house or near Jay C. Smith, is that right?"

"It was more than I could do. I really don't know how I could've done much more and not ended up in the hospital."

"How about calling the police?"

"Looking back, I wish I had done that. I think we *all* wish that."

"Why didn't you go to Susan Reinert and say, 'Jay C. Smith has chains, he has locks, he has guns, he has silencers, he has all these things. And by the way, he's threatening to kill you. You better do something about it.' Did you ever say that to her?"

"No."

"That would've been another way you could've protected her, could it not have been?"

"I don't know that it would've worked, but it could have. I was not sure that there was a relationship between Susan Reinert and Doctor Smith. I could never find out for sure."

"Wouldn't that be all the *more* reason to tell her if this person you *think* she's having a relationship with was going to kill her?"

"Looking back, I think it was."

"But that didn't occur to you at the time?"

"No."

"It occurred to you to tell the police, but you dismissed it, is that right?"

"It occurred to us to speak, but we decided not to do that."

"*We.* You keep saying *we.* Wasn't it *you* that was bringing all this information to Mister Pappas, Miss Myers and Mister Valaitis? *You* were the one that brought all the information back, is that right?"

"Yes."

"*You* were the one that was making decisions. *You* were the leader, weren't you?"

"I was not making the decisions solely. I sought their advice in everything that I did."

"The group was making decisions on the basis of *your* facts, isn't that right?"

"Yes."

"You indicated that you didn't want to tell the police because they were corrupt, is that right?"

"Correct, and involved with Doctor Smith."

"How many police departments did he control?"

"Not just the Upper Merion Township police. He mentioned

that he knew someone with the West Chester police. He mentioned several people in the Philadelphia police. And he mentioned the police in Bucks County."

"In other words, he had connections, so that nothing would happen to him and you'd be in trouble if you told?"

"Nothing would happen to him, but something would happen to *me*."

"In other words, they'd tell him and he'd come and get you, is that right?"

"Yes."

"Did you ever hear of the Pennsylvania State Police, Mister Bradfield?"

"Yes."

"Are they listed in your telephone book at home?"

"Looking back I wish I had gone to them."

"You could've picked up the phone and called the Pennsylvania State Police and said I don't trust the Upper Merion Township police and I'm going to tell you people about these strange goings-on. You could've done that, is that right?"

"Any one of us could have done that."

"*You* could have, couldn't you?"

"We all could have."

"But *you* could have."

"Yes, indeed."

"You didn't did you?"

"None of us did."

"Have you heard of the Federal Bureau of Investigation?"

"Yes."

"Did you call them?"

"No."

"Did Jay C. Smith have contacts in the state police and the Federal Bureau of Investigation?"

"He never indicated that."

As to the character of his relationship with Susan Reinert, William Bradfield said, "In 1976, Sue Myers had already had a confrontation with Susan Reinert and she said to me, 'You're wasting your life on this woman. She's not worth your time.' But I told her that anyone who is interested in literature to the point of teaching it, let alone of trying to write poetry as I was trying to do, should feel that any *other* person who is willing to be open with him in a real and honest way, in a personal way, is someone that anybody who's interested in the arts can't turn his back on."

"I see. So, the relationship with Susan Reinert, if not romantic, was at least artistic? Is that what you're telling us?"

"On my part?"

"Yes."

"I guess *all* of my relationships are."

"Artistic?"

"Yes."

As to the prom night adventure and other Dr. Jay business, the testimony contained even more "we's" and fewer "I's" than the rest of it.

"Why did you need a silencer to protect yourself?"

"Because both Chris and I felt that if Doctor Smith were to threaten me while I was in the car I would have to try to wound him or disable him or kill him. We agreed that I'd call Chris and he'd come immediately and we'd figure out exactly what we were to do. If I'd have tried to defend myself with my .357 magnum it would've alerted half of Chester County."

"When you're talking about protecting yourself from an armed man who threatens you with a weapon, why did you need a silencer?"

"We were concerned not only with Doctor Smith, but with people in the drug world because of his daughter and so forth. And . . ."

"Mister Bradfield, let me interrupt you for just a second. You're telling me about your fears. I'm asking why you needed a silencer."

"Because I wanted to do more than simply disable him. I wanted after that to be able to call Chris, and for Chris and me to decide where we would go and take Doctor Smith."

"Were you planning on murdering him?"

"We talked about it. Chris and I had talked about it."

"If you had a plan to murder him and he threatened you with a weapon, why didn't you just finish him off right there in self-defense and be done with it? Were you going to take him to a hospital? Why did you get a silencer so that no one would come around? Tell me that."

"We didn't *know* what the best plan would be. We were afraid if I had to produce the weapon quickly and tell him not to move, disable him, tie him up or whatever, and call Chris . . . If I produced a weapon, and if he'd come at me and I had to use it, and if it were an unsilenced .357 magnum, and we were anywhere within earshot of people, all options as to what we could do after that would then be closed. People would hear and they would rush to see us."

And so it went. The jury, Jack Holtz noted during all of this, was slack-jawed, and he was hoping they weren't getting fuzzy like Chris Pappas used to get. He was relieved when they hoisted their chins back up onto their faces.

Bill Bradfield testified that he had believed Dr. Jay Smith to be deranged and dangerous, but still, he was morally obligated to testify for him as an alibi witness in the one crime he had *not* committed. All things considered, Bill Bradfield didn't tell it much differently than it was told by Chris Pappas, Vince Valaitis, Sue Myers and Shelly. If the disciples had believed, Bill Bradfield obviously felt that the jury would believe.

As to the neighbors of Susan Reinert seeing his car parked in front of her house at all hours, he said that he would park his car and leave it there to deter Dr. Jay Smith from creepy-crawling her house.

"Did you move your car *occasionally?*" the prosecutor asked.

"During the four- or five-month period I parked my VW quite often in front of Susan Reinert's house."

"Overnight?"

"Yes, for days and nights."

"How did you get home?"

"I took my Cadillac to school."

"But how did you get the Volkswagen to Susan Reinert's house?"

"Susan Reinert would come in with a lady teacher and then she would drive the Cadillac. And I would drive the VW to her house."

"And then you would get in your red Cadillac and go home?"

"Or wherever I was going."

"Then you *must* have told Susan Reinert why you were doing this?"

"Yes, I did."

"Then you *told* her that Jay C. Smith was after her, and you were parking the car in front of her house as a deterrent, is that what you're telling us?"

"No. I told her that parking at my apartment was very crowded, which it was."

"What about the testimony of the neighbors who saw you coming out of the house at seven in the morning? Were they mistaken?"

"No, there were times, particularly on Saturdays, when I would come by very early to see Susan before I went to my eight A.M. Greek class."

"But they saw you doing it during the week."

"They're mistaken."

"That brings me to Mary Gove. Mrs. Gove said that on at least three occasions a week, she would see your car there at times when she would get up at five in the morning, and then when she'd go to work at seven-thirty your car would be gone. Was she mistaken?"

"It could have happened a couple of times."

"Are you saying that there were occasions when you left Susan Reinert's house very late, say around midnight, and came back at five A.M.?"

"There were many times that I stayed late and there were many times that I went over early in the morning. And I think it would be easy for Mrs. Gove to feel that it happened all at once. I was taking a course at Villanova in Greek at eight o'clock in the morning and I would try, when I could, to come before class and sometimes I came early enough to make breakfast."

"You made breakfast for them? You would drive all the way over to Susan Reinert's house early in the morning on Saturday just to have breakfast with the kids?"

"Yes."

"Can you explain your comment to Sharon Lee when she called you on the phone and you said, 'Oh, yes, how old *were* the children?' "

"I knew that Karen and Michael were grade-school children but I didn't know what age. I really didn't know them that well."

"Why did you use the word 'were'? Why did you refer to the

children in the past tense on June twenty-sixth, 1979?"

"The assumption was that something awful had happened to the children."

••••

One clever bit of business that Rick Guida conceived was to subpoena the court reporter and prosecutor who'd been at the Jay Smith trial of May 30, 1979, when Bill Bradfield had been an alibi witness.

Guida staged a reenactment of that testimony. He played the part of Jay Smith's attorney, and on cross-examination he played the part of prosecutor Jackson M. Stewart, Jr.

Stewart himself played the role of William Bradfield and with each of the performers holding a certified copy of the transcript of that proceeding, they reenacted Bill Bradfield's alibi testimony for this jury, just as it had happened then, without editorial comment.

This was a very effective piece of lawyering. The testimony didn't sound any more believable coming from Jackson Stewart's lips than it had from Bill Bradfield's back in 1979. This jury got a very good idea of what that alibi testimony had been all about and what it meant to this trial.

••••

One of the scores of witnesses against William Bradfield was Special Agent Matt Mullin of the FBI. While he was waiting to testify, he walked up to Jack Holtz and said that he'd been wrong with Joe VanNort, and that the arrest of Shelly had helped turn the case around.

Jack Holtz thought that was a decent thing to say and told him so. He said that Joe would've appreciated it.

••••

By far, the saddest testimony in the William Bradfield murder case was given by Ken Reinert and his mother.

Once when Florence and John Reinert were on vacation in Vermont they'd seen a boy who resembled their grandson Michael. They'd tried to follow his school bus. They'd reported it to the FBI.

They were still unable to celebrate Christmas.

When Ken Reinert had first read in the newspapers that a murder charge was being filed, he was as happy as he'd been in four years. Until he saw that *three* murder charges were being filed. He'd called the state police in tears.

He said, "But you can't file three murder charges! Not *three* murder charges!"

Just before that time, in a newspaper interview Ken Reinert had said, "I'm optimistic that the children are still alive. I know there're people in the world who murder children, but I can't really believe that anyone would kill these children. Not *these* children."

It wasn't until the murder trial of 1983 that Ken, Florence and John Reinert were able to describe the children in the past tense. The children were no more. It had been *decreed* by the commonwealth of Pennsylvania.

24

Widgets

By the time the fourteen-day trial was concluding, Rick Guida was up to five packs of cigarettes a day and down fifteen pounds in body weight. But Josh Lock was in worse shape. The case had consumed him and he was near collapse, by his own assessment.

Lock felt that toward the end he was too exhausted to respond quickly enough to Guida, but the court record doesn't support the self-doubt. What *was* very hard to respond to was being offered from the lips of William Bradfield as his explanation for wills and insurance and silencers, and murder schemes against Susan Reinert by Jay Smith.

The most famous criminal defense lawyers in America admit that because of our system of safeguarding the rights of the accused, they don't often get a chance to defend clients who are "innocent" in the sense that the public defines innocence. If they're going to make a living in criminal defense they have to be content with making the best of a client's story and protecting his rights *despite* what they might personally believe.

In law school they're told that they can have a satisfying career doing just that, and on the rare occasions when they believe in their hearts that they do have an innocent criminal client they can permit a bit of personal passion.

332

But the vast majority of lawyers are the products of middle-class American society and grew up on Perry Mason, and they aren't satisfied with the caveats of law school. They *need* to believe in innocence.

The defense had to make a decision whether to call Jay Smith as a witness, but Dr. Jay told Josh Lock that he refused to "proffer." That is, Jay Smith said that he'd testify if subpoenaed, but as to what that testimony would be they'd have to wait and see.

It was too unpredictable and dangerous. Lock did not subpoena the prince of darkness.

The closing arguments took place on October 28th. Josh Lock was first. After his opening remarks he said, "At the beginning of the trial I suggested that you would be presented with a facade, an appearance, an *illusion* of wrongdoing. The question is whether the facade is a real structure or *merely* an illusion."

He began with a summation of his attack on the pathologist, who was not a forensic pathologist in the first place, and used his impressive knowledge of all forensics. He said that the actual anoxia, or oxygen starvation, could not have taken place before Sunday afternoon, when his client had already been at the beach for many hours.

He hit hard on the fact that no one had *ever* seen Bill Bradfield in a romantic moment with the murder victim. He pointed out that there was evidence that Susan Reinert had dated a couple of other people, and she probably had sexual relations with one of them in her home. He suggested that Susan Reinert was a bit schizoid, and had fantasized the unrequited love affair with Bill Bradfield. He said that there was no evidence that Susan Reinert had made adequate preparations to go to Europe so even that could have been her fantasy.

He suggested that not only "Alex," whoever he was, but even Sue Myers could have drawn Susan Reinert from her home that night by calling her and repeating some of the old threats. Sedate Sue was in it again.

He pointed out that a car very similar to Susan Reinert's had been seen parked at Jay Smith's house in the spring of 1979, and it was not too farfetched to think that she *may* have been seeing Dr. Jay on the sly. He didn't dispute the hair on Dr. Jay's floor, but pointed out again that since the root was intact it had not been pulled out but had *fallen* out. And who knew what they were doing down there.

He said that convicts like Proctor Nowell were not to be believed.

He did what he'd planned to do all along: gave the jury other possibilities to explain—and he *had* to use the word—the "bizarre" circumstances surrounding this case.

••••

It was during Rick Guida's closing that Josh Lock decided that Guida, though irritating and egocentric, was the best prosecutor he'd ever seen.

Guida began by telling the jury that the complex part of their job would be in fitting together the facts. He said that the most important tool at their disposal would be common sense. He told them that was what he'd looked for in selecting them, and he came back to it again and again: use your *common sense.*

In jury cases involving circumstantial evidence, prosecutors often use metaphors such as "weight and counterweights." The presumption of innocence weighs a lot; the circumstantial evidence weighs little until you start tossing each little chunk onto the scale. Guida used "pebbles on the pile."

There were the forensics: the comb, the fibers, the hair in Jay Smith's basement, all pebbles onto the pile. The methods of taping and chaining and injecting morphine were more pebbles. There was the insurance that Bill Bradfield didn't want and had never expected, but nevertheless sued for.

There was the filing-off of gun serial numbers, and Guida implied that the gun was to be the murder weapon and that's the *only* sensible reason why Bill Bradfield wanted the numbers removed, but Chris Pappas had botched that job.

The dildo under the seat, he said, was to implicate nonexistent Alex, and tied in nicely with Bill Bradfield deciding three days after the murder that Jay Smith couldn't have done it after all.

Halfway through, he said, "Mister Lock believes that the crime scene does *not* point to the defendant. At the end of this argument, I'm going to show you the circumstances point to no one *else* in the entire world."

All of the business with the cash withdrawals and calling her brother to take part in the "investment," and the missing ring that was to be reset for the wedding, all added pebbles.

Then he got to the money wiping.

"What happened to the bills?" he asked. "What did Chris Pappas tell you? When they were in the attic, Bill Bradfield said they'd better wipe fingerprints off the money. Why? Who wipes fingerprints off money? Is it because Susan Reinert's fingerprints were on the money? Are any of these actions of an innocent man?"

He went to the quickie divorce which he attributed to greed, since Bill Bradfield was about to come into money. He proceeded to the weekend at Cape May where Bill Bradfield had assembled all the players and said that Susan Reinert might die, and just by coincidence she did.

When he went back to the crime scene, he said it was the biggest circumstance of all.

"Bradfield said that two people could have killed Susan Reinert," he said. "Jay C. Smith because she had an affair with him and was interfering with his alibi testimony, or a crazy man named Alex who was having kinky sex with her. Why is this so important? It wouldn't be if Susan Reinert had been the only one killed, but it *is* important because her children were with her and they were *not* found in that car. What were the children worth to this defendant as opposed to the rest of the six billion people in the world? Who benefits from this scenario? Why weren't the *three* of them in the car? Or in the alternative, if you're talking about Smith, why isn't Susan Reinert in the same place with her children who have never been found?

"Whoever did this, whoever helped in the commission of this crime, was savvy enough to make sure that those children's bodies would never be found, but he took the awful chance of driving a dead body all the way to Harrisburg and parking it in a public parking lot, and walked around behind that car and opened the hatch for the world to see the exposed body of Susan Reinert, and then pirouetted and walked away.

"Does Jay C. Smith benefit from that according to the way Bradfield has explained the situation? Of course not. If he'd killed Susan Reinert because she was his mistress or interfering with his alibi, her body would be in the same hole with the children. What if Alex had done it? Would he transport her to the Host Inn and expose her body to the world?

"Do you know why the body was exposed? Because this body is worth to one person in the world seven thousand dollars a pound, and it *had* to be found during the alibi weekend so that he can say to the world, 'I couldn't possibly have done it.'

"No one else benefits from this scenario. No one would have taken this chance unless they did it for Bill Bradfield, because nobody collects on insurance unless they have a body. Perhaps that's the final irony. The big mistake was when he killed the children, because I couldn't make this argument to you if it was Susan Reinert alone.

"But they panicked. The children weren't worth anything. A real measure of irony, a real measure of justice is that the children's lives were perhaps *not* sacrificed in vain because their absence at this scene speaks so loudly of the defendant's guilt that I submit to you it is impossible to ignore. No one else benefits in this terrible chance of exposing the body except the defendant.

"Today is October twenty-eighth, 1983. Five years ago today Susan Reinert's mother died and the plan to kill her began. And today the conspiracy ends and we are going to leave this to you."

••••

Joshua Lock had married late, but had made up for it. He and his wife had one baby after another, beautiful enchanting children. He believed so completely that Bill Bradfield was not a child murderer that he hoped one day to sail with him in the Chesapeake. And he wanted his daughters to meet this teacher who had such a captivating way about him.

Lock thought that the jury would be out for days even though he had great admiration for the methodical way that Rick Guida had presented the complex case. He was told by many reporters in the courtroom that they were not impressed by Guida. He was later told by some of the jurors that they were not impressed. But he was impressed. This was brilliant organization, he said, and as a professional he recognized it even if they didn't.

Throughout the trial, Josh Lock had a constant urge to throw up.

The jury retired to deliberate at 8:22 P.M. Jack Holtz and Lou

ECHOES IN THE DARKNESS **** 337

DeSantis walked across the street to the Holiday Inn in downtown Harrisburg and figured to have a bite before going home. They imagined that the jurors might get started tonight, but they'd probably get sleepy and turn in before ten.

They hadn't even finished a beer when the phone rang. It was the "tipstaff," or court crier, since Pennsylvania is one of the places quaint enough to retain one. Everyone joked that it was a verdict when Jack went to the phone.

The tipstaff said, "Jack, you're not gonna believe it. The jury has a verdict."

They'd been out seventy-five minutes. They said they had the verdict within forty-five, but thought they should wait to make it look more professional.

A verdict that fast in a case that complex meant only one thing and Jack Holtz could hardly keep from yelling when they ran back over to the courthouse.

He was ecstatic to see jurors glaring at the defendant.

They polled the jury. William Bradfield got to hear "Guilty, first degree" thirty-six times. Each juror uttered it in the murders of Susan Reinert and Karen Reinert and Michael Reinert.

The defendant showed all the emotion of serpentine stone.

Jack Holtz found it hard, but waited until everyone was off the elevator on the first floor. Then he and Lou DeSantis and Rick Guida let out a whoop and raced across the river to Catalano's Restaurant. They closed the bar.

Early the next morning Jack Holtz called Betty VanNort.

****

The swift and effective manner in which the trial had been run by Judge Garb impressed the reporters, the defense and the prosecution.

The judge wasn't known to be a proponent of capital punishment. He said that it hadn't been proved that William Bradfield did any of the actual killing, and there was insufficient evidence to show that he had "contracted" with a crime partner to have it done. The judge therefore decided that as a matter of law aggravating circumstances did *not* apply. He took a possible death verdict away from the jury.

It was only left to determine whether Bill Bradfield would receive concurrent sentences for the three murders as the defense wished, or consecutive sentences as the prosecution was now demanding.

••••

At the sentencing of William Bradfield, one witness after another came forward to say that his teaching had made all the difference in decisions toward higher education.

A former student said, "I can't say that I've ever met anyone who is so seriously devoted to the truth as Mister Bradfield, and so serious in acting morally according to that truth. I would not be the same person I am today had I not met Mister Bradfield."

Another former student said, "Beyond all things, he was an example to me. He taught me what was important in my intellectual life. That it was important to consider things and truths and that one should run his life or fulfill his actions according to what truth could be found in his own investigations. He was a *great* teacher in that way."

Josh Lock said in his plea for concurrent sentences, "If I may presume to anticipate some of Mister Guida's comments, I suppose we would probably hear about the heinous nature of this crime. And we would probably also be reminded that Mister Bradfield remains unrepentant and has demonstrated no remorse either by public confession or cooperation with the authorities. I would suggest that that reposes a level of infallibility in jury verdicts that practice demonstrates may not exist.

"I think the fundamental point for sentencing purposes is something else. As has been suggested by Dante there are qualitative differences in evil. There are evil people who commit evil acts. There are people who are not otherwise evil who commit equally evil acts. However, it is not fair to judge those two groups of people in the same way."

Lock produced letters from students who had unmistakably been inspired by William Bradfield.

One young woman in her third year at Harvard wrote: "Mr. Bradfield taught me ancient Greek when I was in tenth grade. After three years of study at Harvard I still think of that class as the most inspiring I have ever had, and of Mr. Bradfield as the most inspiring teacher."

There was one letter after another. In each of them, young people who had gone on to academic success wrote of Bill Bradfield's inspirational talents, and told of how he'd brought out qualities they didn't know they had.

His attorney said, "There *is* a qualitative difference in the type of life this man has led and the type of life so many others have led. The parallels in this case and the book *Crime and Punishment* are striking.

"Your Honor may recall that the protagonist, Raskolnikov, by recourse to his own system of moral and intellectual values, rationalized the murder of an elderly woman of some means so he could promote his education, propagate his ideas to the world, and demonstrate to himself that he was some sort of superhuman individual. Having killed her, however, he came to the realization of the effect that one act had on what had otherwise been an intellectually and morally superior life.

"At one point in his agony, he said, 'Did I murder the old woman? I killed myself, not that old creature. There and then I murdered myself at one blow forever.'

"And indeed that is exactly what has happened in this case, and it's questionable, the death penalty having been resolved, whether any penalty imposed can exceed the type of penalty that Raskolnikov felt, and that Bill Bradfield feels now.

"*Crime and Punishment* is a story of redemption as well. Sonya the prostitute says to him, 'God will send you life again.'

"In the final paragraph of the book, Dostoevsky said, 'He did not even know that the new life would not be his for nothing, that it must be dearly bought and paid for with great and heroic struggles yet to come.'

"Bill Bradfield has demonstrated that he can live a worthwhile life even in prison, that he can renew himself. He can redeem himself. That suggestion is confirmed by everything about his life up to 1979, and is indicated in these letters and in the testimony we have today.

"The Hebrew word, the biblical word for justice is *tzedek*. That same word in Hebrew means *mercy*. Your Honor, any lawyer would be proud if somebody who clerked in his office said, 'I am a lawyer today because of you.' *His* life is replete with examples of just such testaments. Your Honor has the opportunity to distinguish, as Dante distinguished in the *Inferno,* qualities of evil. That can be accomplished in this case by imposing concurrent rather than consecutive sentences upon Mister Bradfield."

For the fifteen hundred hours of work he'd done on behalf of his client, Dauphin County paid Joshua Lock about two dollars an hour. He'd thought of telling them to keep it. He finally took the money to buy an antique writing table for his office.

····

The first words out of Rick Guida's mouth were "It's interesting that Mister Lock quoted *Crime and Punishment.* The passage indicated that the main character felt *remorse.* We don't have that in this case. Mister Bradfield has consistently told this court and jury one of the most ridiculous stories I've ever heard, and it's very interesting that the people who came here today were very much like the people who testified in our case. People who were convinced by Mister Bradfield's words and ignored his actions."

For the first time in this case, Guida began to toy with an idea that so far he'd avoided, not wanting to make the twisted case any more complex, the idea being that the death of the children had been plotted all along.

He said, "We saw a plan that began on October twenty-eighth, 1978, and carried forward to the death of three individuals. It's true when we were dealing strictly with the commonwealth's case it was our theory that the children were a mistake, that they had to be killed because they were witnesses to their mother's murder.

"Even if they *were* an afterthought, at the final moment when Mrs. Reinert showed up with those two children, there was a choice. The defendant had the choice and the choice was to give up the money, the seven hundred and thirty thousand, and to walk away from it and let the children live.

"We have witnesses here today who said Mister Bradfield strove for perfection. He strove for the highest level. Well, he's finally made it: the highest level that he could achieve in the world of evil, he *has* achieved. And I can't think of a crime that calls out more for consecutive terms of life imprisonment."

Judge Garb said, "Do you have anything *you* wish to say, Mister Bradfield?"

Bill Bradfield stood, and said, "I know that you are constrained to act on the verdict of the jury, but I am compelled to say some simple truths. One, I did not kill Mrs. Reinert. I did not kill her children. I was not an accomplice to killing Mrs. Reinert, and was not an accomplice to killing her children. I didn't conspire to kill Mrs. Reinert. I didn't conspire to kill her children. I cannot show remorse for something I didn't do.

"All the courts and all the juries and all the judges in the world can't change those facts that are true, and I can but pray that the children someday will be found alive. That is all I have."

During his sentencing Judge Garb said, "It doesn't matter which theory you may adopt regarding the killing of the children. Whether they happened to be there and therefore were witnesses to the actual act, or whether it was part of the grand design in the first place. But it's somewhat diabolical that the children's bodies have *never* been found.

"I heard you, Mister Bradfield, express the prayer that they be found alive somewhere. I think we would have to be naïve to assume that this is likely to happen. There are good reasons why the bodies of the children are not to be found. It is somewhat an article of faith by investigators that the best clues actually come from the victims. So of course it makes perfectly good sense to deny the investigator the advantage of those sources of evidence.

"Of course with respect to the body of Susan Reinert there were other considerations, because the motivation for murder was the acquisition of her estate. And so as I view it, a word which hasn't been used in describing these events does apply: 'diabolical.' A triple homicide, regardless of where you draw that subtle line regarding the motivation for killing the youngsters.

"Now, what do we have on the other side? Well, we have a great deal of evidence as to what you are. I don't care to deal in caricatures. It doesn't advance the cause to talk in terms of whether you are a charismatic Rasputin or a noncharismatic Rasputin. Perhaps that is a redundancy anyway.

"I also don't know how Dante defined evil. Yes, I suppose there's a difference between an evil person committing an evil act and a nonevil person committing an evil act. I'm not sure which is more egregious. I don't care to characterize you as evil or not evil.

"I guess it must be said that you are some kind of an anomaly to us. You have heard and I have heard what has been said today about you. It is said that your interests were such that they were in other than material things, yet it has been decided that you were willing to take three lives for something in excess of seven hundred thousand dollars and not for any other reason.

"We find that you are a person of unusual quality, highly creative, intelligent, and with more than just a modicum of charm. But I think it is safe to say that you are also extremely destructive. The inflection in and of itself is of a cold and calculating mind, bereft of human sympathy and compassion, that you are bent upon achieving your end at all cost. Now that is what I see.

"It seems to me that you have manifested those qualities which demonstrate that you are an extremely dangerous person by virtue of your actions, and for that reason it seems to me that the sentence that is imposed must be one that affords the community the maximum of protection.

"Therefore, I will impose the following sentence:

"On indictment number 908, that has to do with the conviction of homicide in the first degree of Susan Reinert, it is ordered that you pay the cost of prosecution and that you undergo imprisonment in the state correctional institution for the rest of your life.

"On indictment 908a, having to do with the conviction of homicide in the first degree of Karen Reinert, it is likewise ordered that you undergo imprisonment in the state correctional institution for the rest of your life, that to run consecutively to the sentence imposed on indictment 908.

"On 908b, that being the conviction of criminal homicide in the first degree of Michael Reinert, it is ordered that you undergo imprisonment in the state correctional institution for the rest of your life, that to be served consecutively to the sentence imposed to number 908a."

••••

At the conclusion of sentencing, Jack Holtz saw a woman weeping in the hallway. He recognized her as one of the writers who had been seeking an audience with Bill Bradfield for the purpose of writing a book.

She said, "Isn't it terrible?"

She had the look of a Bradfield woman. They were as interchangeable as widgets.

Jack Holtz turned to Rick Guida and said, "She's the *next* disciple."

Then he went to phone Betty VanNort.

25

The Anniversary

In one of the telephone calls from Jay Smith to Raymond Martray there was a conversation that went far beyond the "self-serving" Jay Smith method. It was a very long conversation about the William Bradfield trial and it raised two possibilities: either Jay Smith was pretty sure that the authorities had tapped the conversation, or Raymond Martray had lied about Jay Smith having told him *anything* incriminating about the Reinert murder.

During the conversation both men were speculating on Bill Bradfield involving Jay Smith in order to save his own skin. Jay Smith said, "The only thing Bradfield could say is 'I called Susan out, drove her up to the house where Smith was, and he gave her a shot of morphine and he killed the kids and then I left.' "

"Puts you right in the middle, doesn't it?" Ray Martray said, and they both had a chuckle over that one.

"With three bodies? Now what the fuck do you do with three bodies? How did I get rid of them? And how did I get her up to Harrisburg by myself and then get myself back with only her car? See what I mean?"

There was some credence to Martray's explanation that Jay Smith injected self-serving statements for the benefit of eavesdroppers because Jay Smith again repeated the alibi for the weekend in question. He again said that he'd taken his daughter Sheri out for a birthday dinner, and been with the new owner of his house on Saturday.

He couldn't have cared if Martray believed that he had an alibi, so for whom was he speaking? And then, interestingly enough, the name of the ice maiden surfaced.

He said to Martray, "In the newspapers the one thing in the whole case that baffles me is this: here's a name to keep in mind, Rachel."

"Yeah, I heard her mentioned many times."

"Yeah. Now, he was shacking up with this woman for the month of May, right before Reinert died. Okay?"

"Uh huh."

"Now, *she* drove Bradfield's car to New Mexico."

"Right."

"And shacked up with him out there. Now, I think that event of her driving Bradfield's car to New Mexico is significant. Another thing the paper said is somewhere on the way out there she called Bradfield, and that's when she learned that Reinert was dead. What if she had those two kids' bodies in that car and dumped them off somewhere? See what I mean?"

"That would be an excellent, you know, summation."

"She sponsored his bail. See, the critical thing is if Reinert leaves her home at nine-thirty Friday night and goes with Bradfield. He shows up two hours later. So he has two hours. He killed her, gave her to Rachel and Rachel then takes her body to Harrisburg and comes back. Bradfield goes down to the shore, okay?"

"Um hum."

"And then Rachel had the two kids and then she takes them to New Mexico when he flies out there." Then Jay Smith added, "See, Ray, the thing is, here's another thing you have to keep in mind. I have a theory that the attorney general must have something *else* on Bradfield. I have a feeling he must have something else up his sleeve that would link Bradfield to the actual night of the murder. The only reason he would have picked on me to blame is that I was an obvious target out of all the bad publicity. So he dreams up the secret love affair with Reinert and the hit man stuff."

"They got the hair and the comb," Ray Martray said.

"But they still got a problem with *why* did Smith do it," said Dr. Jay. "The only thing they can say is, Bradfield was an alibi for him, and then to pay him back, Smith killed the three people."

••••

It was probably that conversation which convinced Jack Holtz and Rick Guida that Raymond Martray was telling more truth than not. Jay Smith had laid out an entire case for any eavesdropper, a case against William Bradfield. But he'd included too much by repeating his own false alibi for that weekend, an alibi that the police could demolish. It was included for *somebody's* benefit, and it couldn't have been Martray's. They started to think that he'd never make any real admissions over the telephone and they were right.

The most interesting thing of all in that particular conversation was to hear Jay Smith ask Martray and any potential eavesdropper to supply a viable motive. Why *did* Jay Smith do it? he'd asked.

Bill Bradfield's claim that Susan Reinert and Jay Smith had been secret lovers was not believed by anyone. The further claim that Jay Smith had somehow feared that Susan Reinert might refute Bill Bradfield's alibi testimony was sometimes acceptable to the task force and sometimes not.

After all, Susan Reinert had told friends that she was with Bill Bradfield "most of the time" during the weekend in question. She'd said that she thought he *would've* told her had he seen Jay Smith. If Jay Smith had any success with an appeal, as he always seemed to think he would, Bill Bradfield could *still* have done the alibi testimony which had never been much good in the first place.

The motive that Guida did not want to introduce in the William Bradfield trial might have placed a big burden on that jury. It was easier all around to proceed with the idea that the children had been a "mistake," as inmate Proctor Nowell had testified. Yet even the judge in his sentencing had implied more than once that the children might *not* have been a mistake.

Given all they had learned about Jay Smith, Guida had other thoughts, not shared by Jack Holtz, that the children had *not* been a mistake at all. By virtue of practicing law, he knew how difficult it would've been for Bill Bradfield to probate that will if the children had been alive.

Two minor children—excluded by their mother in favor of a friend, and this within days of her murder *after* she'd overloaded on insurance—would have put a very great burden on Bill Bradfield's probate attempt. There was every chance that such a will would be set aside in favor of the children, especially since there wasn't even specific language in the will to exclude them.

William Bradfield, and certainly Jay Smith, must have known what a difficult probate that would have been. But then, why not leave the bodies of the children with their mother's? Guida believed that one would have to consider everything they knew so far about Jay Smith and his penchant for making people disappear, and his obsession with forensic clues. It must've been difficult enough to get him to leave *one* body for the lab technicians, let alone three.

Given the way Jay Smith's mind worked, the disappearance of the children was *not* inconsistent with the planning of their deaths from the beginning. The motive was the same as for Bill Bradfield: *his* share of the insurance upon release from prison.

That probability was advanced by the fact that her copy of the policy had disappeared. Guida was reminded that Susan Reinert had asked her insurance agent for an extra copy for her "executor" to keep, but was refused as a matter of company routine. Guida suggested that Jay Smith may have demanded to see that policy with his own eyes before fulfilling his part of the bargain. The "executor" may have actually been the executioner.

Moreover, Bill Bradfield, a world-class grandstand player, could then offer huge rewards from his "inheritance" for information leading to the missing children.

Though Jack Holtz stayed with the simplicity of the panic killing of the children, Guida thought that the conspirators may have ordained the murder of Karen and Michael Reinert right along with their mother from the day the insurance policies were obtained. But this was intricate and very diabolical, and it was far easier for the prosecutor to conclude for the sake of a jury that the children were an afterthought, that they'd been witnesses killed in panic. There was less to prove.

The irony is that it was better for *everyone* concerned if there was always a shadow of a doubt as to what had happened to the children. The absence of little corpses made it more difficult for other inmates to hang the jacket: *baby killer.*

••••

When Holtz and DeSantis met Charles Montione in December, 1983, he was twenty-four years old. He wore Cuban heels and silk shirts and looked like he could've been an extra in Al Pacino's version of *Scarface.* The task force found his name in a letter from Jay Smith to Ray Martray, care of the P.O. box they controlled.

He'd gotten a sentence of six to twenty years for armed robbery and had gotten out in five. He was living in a halfway house when the cops had a secret meeting with him at the Holiday Inn in Scranton.

He was a friend of Martray's, and had been a passing acquaintance of Jay Smith's while Martray was still in prison. Jay Smith helped Montione too with his legal work. Dr. Jay, according to Montione, never turned down any of the cons who needed legal assistance. They started getting close after Martray got out.

One day, Jay Smith had some bad feelings and wanted to talk about them. He told Charlie Montione that someone named Bradfield had just been arrested for the murder of a woman and her two children and was attempting to implicate *him* in the murders. If Bradfield was successful and got Jay Smith in trouble, there'd be an escape with some help from Ray Martray. And hopefully from his pal Charlie, if he was on the outside by then.

According to Montione, Jay Smith had three plans. One entailed Montione and Ray Martray coming to see him on visiting day. They were to enter the canteen where visitors can get cooked food. They were then to do a "DIC," which Montione explained was Jay Smith lingo for "disarm, immobilize and cover."

His second plan was to wait for his court appearance and to escape from the prison at Camp Hill where the transporting officers have to take off their guns to go inside. This plan involved a shoot-out: Charlie and Ray would come in like Bonnie and Clyde and shoot out tires, then take the transporting officers as hostages and kill them later. If Jay was arrested for murder, the officers would be a couple of state police investigators named Holtz and De-Santis, Montione was told.

The third plan involved a breakout from the Dauphin County Courthouse itself, where prisoners are housed in the basement cells while awaiting court.

And Jay Smith thought he should also bump off the deputy warden at Dallas because he figured this guy was telling the cops every move he made. Jay Smith made a lot of gangsterish plans while daydreaming in the yard.

According to Montione, Jay Smith gave him a lecture on murder that sounded a lot like the ones he'd allegedly given to Bill Bradfield. He said that you should use drug injections to overdose your victims. And that it was best to let a body lie around for a couple of days so the blood could coagulate before you started cutting it up and disposing of the parts in different places. He said the small parts fit nicely in drums or buckets and you could weigh the pieces down with chains before dumping them in rivers or lakes.

Montione claimed that Jay Smith had another talk with him at the end of October, telling him that Bill Bradfield had been convicted. He went over an escape plan in more detail. Since it was hunting season the guards were often sent out on the road to watch for trespassers, and so it might be a great time to vanish.

But he was very mad at Bill Bradfield that day and allegedly told Montione that nearly five years had passed and in only two more years Susan Reinert would have been declared legally dead.

According to Montione, Jay Smith said, "We would have been okay." And that Bradfield's greed in making her body appear had caused all these problems.

Furthermore, he was furious that Bill Bradfield was trying to set him up. He said he should have taken care of Bill Bradfield a long time ago. As to the missing children, he said that he wasn't worried about Bill Bradfield making a deal with police because Bradfield didn't know where the bodies were.

And then, Montione claimed that Jay Smith had backpedaled

and began making the same sort of self-serving statements that the task force was so familiar with in his conversations with Martray. Jay Smith later told Montione that he believed that the children's murder had been a "mistake," that they shouldn't have been present. But that sometimes when you're dealing with large sums of money you have to do such things.

"What would you do if there were witnesses?" was how it was put, according to Montione.

Jay Smith offered a theory to Montione that Bill Bradfield had probably had someone call Susan Reinert on the evening she disappeared to say that he'd been in a bad accident and was dying. That way she would probably just drop everything and rush out of the house without leaving a note for anyone.

Montione said that all these theories were too complicated for him, so on one occasion he'd just asked Jay Smith directly if *he'd* killed Susan Reinert and the kids. Dr. Jay didn't answer.

"He only smirked," according to Montione.

Montione said that he'd performed an unusual service for the former educator. He said that Jay Smith wanted him to look through *Playboy* and *Penthouse* and *Hustler* and find him a picture of a naked woman "lying on her side with her knees pulled up and her cunt closed."

He was very particular about it.

So Montione searched lots of back issues that he traded around with other cons, and Jay Smith rejected several.

He kept saying, "No, no, that's *not* it."

Finally Montione came up with the August, 1983, issue of *Penthouse* and Jay Smith looked through it until he got to page 97, and said, "That's it. *That's* the one."

Jack Holtz acquired that issue of *Penthouse.* Other than lying on the wrong side, the model was posed very similarly to Susan Reinert on the day she was found in the luggage compartment.

Holtz recalled the psychological profile he'd been given in 1980 suggesting that the killer might retain something from the crime so that he could *relive* the moment.

After the Bill Bradfield murder trial began getting big write-ups implicating Jay Smith, Montione said that Jay Smith was seen standing naked in his cell staring at the wall. And *screaming.*

Jay Smith was also seen lying in the yard like a dead man with a newspaper over his face. An old con shuffled by, picked up the newspaper and said, "You can't hide under that paper, Jay."

••••

In 1984, they didn't seem to be getting anywhere. They had Montione, but what he had to say wasn't enough. They had Martray, but he was a convicted perjurer. They actually thought about shutting down the operation.

Then they decided they ought to do some more excavation on the basis of what Montione had told them.

In a conversation, Jay Smith had said that a way to dispose of bodies is to find a freshly dug grave and drop the bodies in on top. Jack Holtz started thinking about the call Bill Bradfield had made to *someone* when they'd stopped at the pay phone in Valley Forge Park upon their return from Cape May on June 25, 1979. He checked with local cemeteries and discovered that there had been a man buried on June 23rd near Valley Forge.

On a cool spring day that was just perfect for gravedigging, the cops and Rick Guida and an operator with a backhoe were out there in a cemetery in their digging duds. It was one of the more macabre moments in a thoroughly macabre investigation.

They'd received permission from the next of kin of the deceased, and so they started tearing up the grave site. As the day wore on and they'd exhausted all their Boris Karloff jokes, they were getting tired and cranky because they'd found nothing. Not even the casket.

They dug six feet, seven feet, and finally, at eight feet, they'd used up all the one-liners about discovering a table for eight with chopsticks.

Jack Holtz had to get down there, and with a fancy Japanese probing device they'd acquired for the purpose, he started fishing around for coffins. He found one, all right. They'd missed the actual grave by six inches.

They were *really* cranky by the time they filled in an eight-foot grave and started digging a new one. For Rick Guida it was a five-pack dig. He had to send out for more cigarettes.

When they got down to the casket, they found nothing *but* the casket. Well, they'd gone this far. They started talking about the possibility of Jay Smith having put the bodies in the freshly dug hole the night before the funeral, and having covered them with a small amount of earth. They might be *underneath* the coffin.

So the casket got hooked to chains and raised up by the backhoe. It had been a long day in that graveyard by the time they got the casket out of the grave and swinging around in the crisp spring air. Then the chain slipped, and the coffin shifted, and it was like someone dropped ice cubes down their backs that slipped right into their underwear. It was the *sound* of the resident of that coffin when he did a 360-degree roll.

A couple of cops and a lawyer got cold chills and hot flashes, and queasy tummies. And they were scared that the next of kin might show up while they were tossing the loved one around like Chinese acrobats.

They dropped that guy back in the ground and got the hell out of that graveyard before nightfall.

••••

By December, Ray Martray was sounding desperate enough on the recorded telephone calls to risk alarming Jay Smith by pushing him into an incriminating statement.

He said, "I'll tell you, Jay, I mean you remember what I told you before about Bradfield?"

"Yeah."

"If he's talking, if he's telling them something, bingo!"

"Yeah, but there's nothing he can tell them."

"The finger, I'm telling you the finger is pointing at that man."

"Yeah, but there's nothing he can *say*. I mean, he'll have to make up something and when they check it, it'll be false. See, everything he said about me was false. And I'm certain they know I *wasn't* involved. You know what I mean?"

Frustrated again, Martray turned the conversation to a little escape talk, featuring the code words Harry Gibson.

"You still got the code?" he asked.

"Oh yeah."

"Okay, I didn't know if you remembered it."

"Harry, right?"

"Yeah, how's Harry doing?"

"Good. He really is. I got a letter from him. He's at Arizona State."

"Glad to hear it."

"He's a *barber* out there."

General John Eisenhower was right. His former colonel had a sardonic sense of humor.

••••

Jack Holtz had been able to send his son Jason to visit the boy's mother in Florida that year. And with the investigation slowing to a standstill he'd been able to spend more time with his son. They pumped iron together and went to Penn State football games. He was starting to think that the most significant event of the year was that his hair turned gray.

But then something happened. When it looked as though they might close the store, Raymond Martray was successful in having his perjury conviction overturned.

Jay Smith couldn't have been more delighted. Martray was no longer a convicted perjurer. Martray could now testify for him that David Rucker of the hockey helmet had confessed to the attempted theft at the Sears store at Neshaminy Mall. Jay Smith had already served his time on the St. Davids theft.

The irony was that now Raymond Martray could also testify *against* Jay Smith. Jack Holtz knew that Joe VanNort would have loved that one.

••••

After the New Year, Jay Smith was not only still repeating the Bill Bradfield frameup routine, he was turning author.

In a telephone conversation to Martray, he said, "See, Bradfield said that this woman Reinert was a whore. He said that she was a bad person. He said that she went out with kooks. She was kinky, you know? He said she smelled bad. And then he said these things about *me*.

"They found out the things he said about her weren't true and he robbed her of twenty-five thousand dollars, and now I think they've seen that the things he said about *me* weren't true. I've got a pretty good idea what was on his mind in trying to set me up. This is the kind of thing I hope I'm able to write about in the future."

The cops wondered if he threw that last part in just in case any potential publishers or literary agents were listening. They were getting sick of it. They gave Martray a script for the next call, and said it was now or never.

The last of the recorded telephone conversations came on February 3, 1985. It started out as usual.

Jay Smith said, "Good evening, Mister Martray."

Raymond Martray said, "Good evening, Mister Smith."

But when Jay Smith asked, "How you doing?" Raymond Martray answered, "Well, not so good."

"What's up?"

"We got a few problems."

"Okay."

"Some people came to pay me a visit."

"Who's that?"

"Guess."

"I don't know."

"Holtz and DeSantis."

"Mmm."

"I tried to do like you told me, Jay. I took notes after they left."

"Sure."

"I remembered them from court. That's how I knew who it was."

"Sure."

"I went through the whole routine. Made em show I.D. and all. But they called me by my number. They said, 'Are you P-3933, Raymond Martray, and were you housed with Jay Smith at Dallas?' "

"Right."

"Then they go, 'Did you ever, uh, hear of, uh, the *Reinert* murders?' I said, 'Yeah.' Then he says, 'What did Smith tell you about the Reinert case?' And I said, 'Smith said he didn't have anything to do with it.' "

But Jay Smith didn't sound too worried. He said, "There's not much you can do. I've been through six years of this stuff. I don't expect it'll ever end, you know."

And then after talking about reporting the cops' visit to private investigator Russell Kolins, Raymond Martray followed his script designed to drag Jay Smith into the courtroom by the tail.

He asked, "What if Holtz and DeSantis come back to me?"

Jay Smith paused for a second and said, "Tell them that you want to talk to them openly, but you want a videotape and somebody representing Jay Smith present."

"Okay, what if they ask me to take a lie detector?"

"Well, say you'll *take* a lie detector, but you don't want to take a lie detector unless you consult with someone from the other side."

"Okay, how do I handle it?"

"How do you mean?"

"Well, I mean, you know, we went over that, but . . ."

"It's certainly in order."

And then Raymond Martray said, "Jay, I'm . . . I'm worried about the *big* question. You know, 'Did Smith *tell* you he did it?' "

"What I'll do is this: then I'll have my people tell them that you're *not* taking any lie detector test."

"I gotcha!" said Raymond Martray.

"See, you're *not* going to do anything unless it's consulted with Jay Smith's lawyer."

And that was as close as they were ever to get to an incriminating statement from Dr. Jay C. Smith.

◆◆◆◆

They went over old leads and telephoned old witnesses. Rick Guida worried about Mary Gove, the next-door neighbor of Susan Reinert, and Grace Gilmore, the buyer of Jay Smith's house. He needed them and they weren't getting any younger.

"It's never going to get any better," Rick Guida said in March. "Let's go to the grand jury in June. Let's arrest Jay Smith for murder."

The last irony that Joe VanNort would have liked is that Jack Holtz went to Dallas prison to arrest Jay Smith on June 25, 1985, six years to the day since he'd found the body of Susan Reinert in the Host Inn parking lot and begun his investigation.

"This is an anniversary," he told the former educator when he walked into his cell.

The cell of Dr. Jay C. Smith contained more files than he'd possessed as a school principal. There were shelves full of books and dozens of boxes containing thousands of documents and articles and notes, pertaining not just to his own affairs, but to those of the many other inmates who came to him for legal work.

Their search warrant was based on the statements by Charles Montione, especially in regard to the *Penthouse* magazine of August, 1983, but there was simply too much for Holtz and DeSantis to search.

They hauled all of Jay Smith's files and belongings to the security lieutenant at Dallas prison for safekeeping and transported Jay Smith to Camp Hill where he was housed until his preliminary hearing.

After his arraignment, Holtz and DeSantis were leaving Troop H in Harrisburg with their prisoner when a reporter from a Philadelphia newspaper yelled to Jay Smith, asking if he'd ever heard of Raymond Martray or Charles Montione.

Jay Smith answered that they were inmates, but he'd never spoken to them.

It was just awfully hard for Jay Smith and Bill Bradfield to be truthful, even when it was foolish to lie.

Holtz and DeSantis returned to Dallas prison in July to complete their search.

They seized a letter to Jay Smith's private investigator Russell Kolins, wherein he outlined his alibi on the murder weekend.

He wrote, "I was with my daughter Sheri. Now this is her birthday so she and I went out to dinner that evening for her birthday. She left me at about ten o'clock. The next day, Saturday, Mrs. Gilmore comes again. She's working upstairs. She gives me coffee and then goes down to the lower level. So Saturday I'm there with Grace Gilmore."

It was another link because it totally contradicted what he'd told the FBI in 1979. A written lie is more damaging than a spoken lie that's subject to the ear of the listener.

They found the *Penthouse* magazine during that search and other things which had no admissible evidentiary value, but were interesting. Jay Smith had books dealing with serial killer Ted Bundy. He'd underlined the passage in one book that dealt with a murdered woman who'd been struck in the right eye. Just as Susan Reinert had been.

••••

The preliminary hearing for Jay Smith was held on July 30th. A Philadelphia lawyer named Glenn A. Zeitz appeared for Jay

Smith, and Rick Guida was the prosecutor. The purpose of the hearing was not to establish guilt but to determine if there was sufficient cause to bind over the defendant for trial.

Zeitz had a style that was something like Guida's: argumentative, aggressive and sarcastic. They might have made an interesting match in a later trial, but it was not to be. After Jay Smith was held to answer, and ordered to trial, he accepted counsel appointed and paid by the commonwealth.

Zeitz was paid twice as much by Jay Smith for the preliminary hearing as Josh Lock received from the commonwealth for his fifteen hundred hours of work.

The only change in witness testimony from the Bill Bradfield trial came when Susan Reinert's neighbor said for the first time that she'd seen Jay Smith enter the Reinerts' house on one occasion two years before Susan's death. Mary Gove said that in all the prior years, no one had asked her if she'd ever seen Jay Smith.

Mrs. Gove was pushing seventy and had a cataract. Holtz and Guida weren't convinced that she was correct, or even if it had any significance. Jay Smith *could* have dropped by once when he'd still been a respectable principal. Guida viewed this as one more instance where he could indicate that Jay Smith possibly had lied. In short, his case was not strong and he was ready to accept *any* old pebble for his pile.

As to Martray and Montione, the prosecutor just didn't know how it would go. Martray was forty-one now, and with distinguished gray hair and a business suit he looked more respectable than Montione. But he tended to testify with that vaguely impatient and irritated tone of a cop who'd worked the graveyard shift and wanted to get on with it.

Montione had penitentiary written all over him, and it wasn't easy to say whether he'd be an effective witness in front of a jury.

At one point in the preliminary hearing Martray had told of a moment when he and Jay Smith were coming out of the prison movie theater and Jay Smith "just flipped off" and made his index finger into a hook and told Martray he could take his eye out of his head if he chose to. Martray said that Jay Smith frightened him. But would a *jury* believe that an ex-cop as big and young as Raymond Martray would fear Jay Smith?

They had many doubts about their case. They talked about fifty-fifty odds.

Jay Smith needed several months to confer with the attorney that the court appointed for him. The lawyer, William C. Costopoulos, was well known and successful and couldn't have taken this case for the small amount of money. He did see in it a chance for publicity, and criminal lawyers rank right behind Hollywood actors in their need for *that* commodity. Actually, Jay Smith was lucky to get a lawyer of his stature.

The defense wouldn't be able to go to trial until the following spring, so the three-man task force prepared their case by contacting all the witnesses. Everyone seemed constant, even as to old opinions.

Shelly now held a master's degree from Notre Dame. She was a fetching, articulate young woman. But when she talked to Rick Guida she admitted that she still couldn't believe that Bill Bradfield could commit murder.

Rick Guida said he felt like strangling her to show that it *happens*.

••••

Just prior to going to trial in April of 1986, Jack Holtz was trying to take care of last-minute business in a desperate attempt to bolster a case that wasn't half as strong as the Bill Bradfield case, thanks to Bill Bradfield's need for confidants.

In going through all the old reports one last time, Jack Holtz saw a note that he'd never followed up. A hunter in 1979 had seen two depressions in the ground and didn't report it to the police until the fall of 1985 when the publicity made him realize that it had been near the home of Jay Smith. The ground had been frozen, and now that spring had arrived Jack Holtz donned the digging duds one last time.

They took the hunter to the spot and dug a crater the size of a swimming pool. They found nothing.

••••

The *very* last piece of business that Jack Holtz was able to perform, other than giving testimony, took place a few days before the jury selection was to begin. They needed something more, something to impress a jury that here was just *one* coincidence too many. They needed to lock the links in the circumstantial chain. They needed one more pebble for Rick Guida's rock pile.

Jack Holtz had gone over and over the reports hoping to find some tiny detail he might have forgotten. He was about to quit when it hit him so hard it almost unscrewed his glasses. It was a report that he'd read a dozen times. Karen and Michael had been playing with a teenager on the day they'd disappeared. They were gathering hailstones with the granddaughter of their next-door neighbor, Mary Gove.

The FBI had interviewed Elizabeth Ann Brook in 1979 and she'd given a description of the clothing the children had on that day, but *he'd* never personally talked to her. So no one had ever asked her about a green pin.

He mentioned it to Rick Guida who shrugged and said, "Might as well give her a call. Maybe we can add her to the ones we have who say Karen owned a pin like that."

Jack Holtz called Mary Gove and was put in touch with her granddaughter, now a young woman of twenty-two, living in Delaware County.

He had a telephone conversation with Beth Ann Brook and when he was finished, he said, "Hold the phone. I want you to tell this to Mister Guida."

After Rick Guida finished talking to Beth Ann Brook, Jack Holtz looked at him and said, "I'd *marry* that girl."

Jack Holtz had secured the links. The only question now was whether or not the chain was strong enough to tether a goat, which is, after all a strange and independent creature of mythic power.

26

Performers

Owing to pretrial maneuvering there was certain information the jury would never know. They would never hear tapes in which Jay Smith and Raymond Martray discussed future armed robberies. Nor would they learn about the defendant's alleged scheme to pin the blame for one of the Sears crimes on David Rucker.

They wouldn't know about things that the police had found in his basement back in 1978. Things like silencers and chains.

Most frustrating to Jack Holtz, they wouldn't know about the things in Jay Smith's possession when he was arrested in 1978. Such as tape and a syringe containing a sedative, things that would dovetail right into the murder of Susan Reinert. They would never know about any of these things because they were deemed to be prejudicial.

◆◆◆◆

The private investigator working for William Costopoulos referred to him as a "magician," and he certainly looked the part. The newspaper artists found him easy to sketch. Costopoulos had the muscular good looks of the Greek islanders, tailored to fit his courtroom image. A leonine head and a rugged jaw decorated with a salt-and-pepper Venetian goatee made you think he'd make a great Iago if he could act.

And he could. Costopoulos was a flamboyant trial lawyer who kept his working-class background in his speech. His suits and shoes were unmistakably Italian, and his high-waisted pants were fastened to striped suspenders.

Whenever he'd come into court looking particularly dapper, his private investigator Skip Gochenour would say, "Godamnit, I wish he didn't *always* have to dress like a pimp."

But it worked. A guy like Jack Holtz was larger than he looked. Bill Costopoulos looked larger than he was. It was a matter of theater. He handed out black-and-white glossies to the reporters and everyone seemed to like him.

Courtroom number one in the Dauphin County Courthouse suited the style of Bill Costopoulos. It was a great legal theater of Italian marble and walnut paneling. Art deco sconces lined the walls, and it had a high ceiling with a skylight. A huge gold crest behind the judge's bench bore the coat of arms of the commonwealth.

The judge's bench was massive and could accommodate a tribunal of judges. Beneath the bench of Judge William W. Lipsitt was carved: NO MAN CAN BE DEPRIVED OF HIS LIFE, LIBERTY OR PROPERTY UNLESS BY JUDGMENT OF HIS PEERS OR THE LAW OF THE LAND.

The security, due to all the escape talk, was very heavy. There were always two deputy sheriffs in plainclothes sitting behind Jay Smith, and other officers from the state police or attorney general's office scanned the courtroom.

Across the courtroom from the jury seats was yet another jury box of equal size. In this trial it was used to accommodate the press.

Seeing the 1986 version of Jay C. Smith was a shock. It made one recall what had been said years earlier by the wife of his first attorney: "He seemed to change each time I saw him. He could even change his *size*."

This time the change of size was explainable. He'd lost fifty pounds or more from the time back in 1978 when his secret life was exposed. And this Jay Smith looked ten years *younger* than that one!

He was tall, gaunt, balding, middle aged. He wore black frame glasses and a blue-gray business suit. Other than the blanched prison pallor, he looked to be in excellent physical health for a prison inmate fifty-seven years old.

This didn't look like the sinister prince of darkness with layers of jowls falling into terraced slabs. *This* wasn't an acid rocker dancing alone to a tune played on an electric bass with a hatchet. This Jay Smith was a mild, middle-aged schoolteacher.

He usually sat motionless, moving only to cross his legs or occasionally to write a note, or whisper to his lawyer.

The most notable Jay Smith mannerism was observable when he was touched. If a member of the four-man defense team approached to whisper in his ear, he would *jerk* his face away. If he'd been wearing a hat it would've gone sailing every time.

Jay Smith did not like having the faces of other human beings close to his. He was obsessive about it, and his reaction never varied. It was as though Jay Smith couldn't bear intimacy.

Bill Costopoulos had the same problem that John O'Brien had had back in the Jay Smith theft trial of 1979. Do you put him on the stand? It's hard to win a murder trial when the defendant doesn't testify. Juries want to hear the accused answer for himself. But Jay Smith had relentlessly denied every bit of wrongdoing with which he'd ever been charged. The only infraction he'd ever admitted was that he owned guns that were not properly registered.

As far as Dr. Jay was concerned, he'd been slandered and prejudged from the first because of his research into doggie sex. He *might* even say that on the stand. So the strategy of the defense was to admit to the earlier theft convictions and get on with it. Later the jury could be told that he'd not taken the stand at his theft trial on bad advice and been wrongly convicted as a result.

Guida countered that strategy by bringing in the Sears witnesses and once again reenacting Bill Bradfield's alibi testimony. And since Jay Smith would unquestionably get up there and *still* deny the Sears crimes, Bill Costopoulos didn't dare let his client testify.

••••

The opening remarks of Rick Guida were brief. He told the jury that the case involved the "heinous, brutal murder of a woman and two children." Then he repeated, "Two children."

He said, "This case involves the most massive criminal investigation in the history of Pennsylvania. Though there is only one defendant present, we will actually try *two*. For the first two or three weeks you will hardly hear Mister Smith's name mentioned.

"But we're going to ask you to find the defendant guilty of murder in the first degree, and, if you should do that, to sentence him to *death*.

"Much of the case is circumstantial evidence. The witnesses will take you where you are going. I'm only a guide. At the end, I'll tell you where the witnesses took you. And where you should take *him*."

The opening of Bill Costopoulos informed the jury that there was a deceptive man involved in this case and his name was "William Sidney Bradfield." Costopoulos often used Bill Bradfield's middle name, and always referred to him with scorn.

He said, "Jay Smith was targeted by a man who was very good at deception. He was made a target of exploitation by a man who was a master of exploitation. I refer to none other than William Sidney Bradfield."

He told the jury that they were going to hear from a man named Raymond Martray, whom the prosecution "pulled from the bowels of the prison system."

He said ominously, "I will *deal* with Raymond Martray when he gets up here and it will be *easy*."

Speaking quietly, but appearing to subdue great emotion, Costopoulos said, "The evidence will indicate that these charges should *not* have been brought. The prosecution in October, 1983, had insufficient evidence to try Jay Smith with William Bradfield, and since then have only added Raymond Martray."

Then he allowed a little sarcasm when he said very neatly, "And with *that* I will ask Mister Guida to call his *first* witness . . . for the *second* time."

Costopoulos was the performer, and private investigator Skip Gochenour fed him the lines. They worked as a team at the council table, whereas Guida seldom referred to his legal assistant, or even to Jack Holtz.

Gochenour was a red-bearded ex-cop, built like a Coke machine. He was a savvy investigator who'd worked for Costopoulos on dozens of cases. The private investigator was not reluctant to tell anyone that he believed the Reinert children had been doomed from the moment their mother took out the insurance policies in favor of Bill Bradfield.

He said, "Bill Bradfield had no intention of being a daddy, and couldn't even if he'd wanted to. They already *had* a daddy and the real one would've helped his children break their mother's will. Those kids were sentenced to death from the start."

He and Bill Costopoulos got Rick Guida's attention within the first two days. One of the prosecution witnesses who'd testified several times over the years in regard to the Reinert murder was a former fingerprint expert who was now retired from the state police.

When Bill Costopoulos was cross-examining him on what appeared to be routine matters at the Susan Reinert autopsy, he innocently asked, "By the way, did you look between her toes?"

And when the witness answered that he had, Bill Costopoulos asked, "And did you *find* anything?"

The witness said that he had, there was a little bit of debris that looked like . . . *sand.*

"*Beach* sand?" Bill Costopoulos asked.

"Yes, *beach* sand," the witness said, with emphasis.

When it was Guida's turn on redirect, he didn't ask how the witness knew beach sand from desert sand. Guida's head was stuck to that high ceiling. Guida was *enraged.*

He spent much of that day and the next practically impeaching his own witness who admitted that as a private investigator he'd worked with Skip Gochenour. Guida brought in half of the task force to testify that at *no* time had this former state police corporal ever mentioned to *anybody* that there were any granules of sand between Susan Reinert's toes.

But that was only half of it. Bill Costopoulos implied that a note found in Susan Reinert's car, with "Cape May" in her handwriting, was further evidence that she could have gone to the beach and been murdered by the Bill Bradfield gang in some sandy place, with one of them transporting her to Harrisburg afterward.

Jack Holtz testified that the note had been thoroughly investigated and referred to a turnoff on the way to teacher Fred Wattenmaker's house where Susan Reinert and her children had been houseguests in the spring of 1979.

Bill Costopoulos and Skip Gochenour had disrupted Rick Guida's methodical, orderly approach.

As Bill Costopoulos put it, "We introduced a couple of grains of sand and Rick Guida brought in sand by the truckload before he was finished."

Rick Guida wasn't going to underestimate *these* fellows, he said.

As to that Cape May murder theory, it was never seriously a part of the strategy of Bill Costopoulos. He privately admitted that he couldn't go very far with it because of Vincent Valaitis. The thought was that he could sell Sue Myers and Chris Pappas to the jury as possible murder conspirators, but Vincent Valaitis screwed up everything. How do you sell the jury a homicidal hamster?

The hair and fiber expert from the FBI testified that in the dust ball presented to him by Jack Holtz and Matt Mullin during their search of Jay Smith's basement, he'd found fifty head hairs but only one was identical to Susan Reinert's. He said that it matched in more than twenty characteristics.

As to the rug fibers, he said that less than 7 percent of rugs are made of polyester and that he'd found "lustrous" and "de-lustered" fibers. He said that fibers clinging to human beings are generally lost after four hours. His conclusion was that she'd picked up the fibers just prior to being thrown into the back of her car.

Jay Smith's lawyer did a job on the FBI's hair and fiber expert. Bill Costopoulos asked questions for which this expert didn't have ready answers. He got him to admit that he didn't know there were four kinds of polyester fibers. Without knowing much about hair and fiber evidence, Costopoulos looked as well versed as the FBI expert in this, the most subjective of the forensic sciences.

When he got back to the council stable he whispered to Jay Smith, "How'd I do, teach?"

To which Jay Smith answered dryly, "You get a B-plus in science."

The defense put on its own hair and fiber experts who had far more impressive scientific credentials than the FBI witness, the substance of their testimony being that the hair *could* be Susan Reinert's or any *other* brunette's. And that the fiber was red polyester but no more could be said.

It seemed certain that hair and fiber testimony was not going to convict or acquit Jay Smith.

The days passed slowly as the parade of a hundred witnesses repeated testimony that they'd given in other courtrooms over the years.

There was a marked difference in the style of opposing counsel. Costopoulos was never argumentative and seldom objected. He could be indignant with witnesses, even scornful, but not toward Guida. He always looked at Guida's multiple objections with a faint smile as though he was *trying* to be more than reasonable with the prosecutor.

Rick Guida was constantly drinking water and dying for a cigarette and rolling his eyes in disgust at what he perceived as the indecisiveness of the judge, who obviously hated Guida's many objections.

Judge William Lipsitt was sixty-nine years old and during the course of the trial marveled that Bill Bradfield had had four women going at one time while he himself didn't even have *one* until he got married at the age of fifty-five. Judge Lipsitt wore oversized black frame glasses. His slicked-down hair looked suspiciously black. He walked as though he were on the deck of a rolling ship, listing from side to side. The judge was quaint and gentle, and Rick Guida was annoying him.

The prosecutor constantly asked to come to the sidebar where he and Bill Costopoulos could argue out of the jury's earshot. Guida was so uncertain about the strength of his case that he had a tendency to overtry it.

The way Judge Garb had handled such requests for sidebar discussion was simple. He'd say *no*.

Judge Lipsitt would say something like, "Uh . . . oh . . . well . . . naturally I *try* to avoid the sidebar."

But he couldn't say no. He'd look as though he'd *like* to say, "Oh, fudge!"

When Guida would object, he'd often say, "Yes, I guess it calls for a conclusion, but, oh, I'll overrule the objection."

The odd thing was that a great deal got admitted into the record from both sides, yet the trial moved swiftly. Even with Rick Guida doing more eye rolling than Faye Dunaway in *Mommie Dearest*.

To a jury who wondered what the Bill Bradfield alibi testimony was all about, Rick Guida once more used the clever device of reenacting the testimony at Jay Smith's trial, with the prosecutor of that trial portraying Bill Bradfield while reading from the official transcript.

And he brought in the Sears employees again to identify Jay Smith as the bogus Brink's courier. Suddenly, the jury was getting the idea that this fellow William Bradfield had told a very big lie for Jay Smith. For *some* reason.

◆◆◆◆

When the day arrived, Bill Costopoulos, as promised, did a good job of trying to discredit the testimony of Jay Smith's prison buddy Raymond Martray. Martray admitted under cross-examination that he did *not* tell in earlier interviews that Jay Smith had said he'd killed Susan Reinert.

There were a lot of people in the courtroom including most of the reporters who doubted him when he said now that Jay Smith had blurted, "I killed that fucking bitch."

And yet, three women on the jury jerked their heads in the direction of Jay Smith when Martray said those words. It appeared that at least those three *did* believe Raymond Martray.

Martray said finally that he'd decided to cooperate with the police because he had children of his own.

"People say that I was a bad cop," Martray said. "I wasn't that bad."

Bill Costopoulos implied that Martray had told the cops that Jay Smith used a "Spanish accent" because he'd read a magazine account of the call to police on the night the body was discovered, wherein the reporter had erroneously claimed that the caller had a Spanish accent.

Bill Costopoulos was all over the courtroom in flourishes, and at one point was right up in Martray's face when Guida jumped up and demanded that he be ordered to back away from the witness.

Judge Lipsitt said, "It's his *style*," but ordered Costopoulos to ease off.

Apparently, the judge liked Costopoulos personally, and didn't like Rick Guida.

After that testimony was over, Bill Costopoulos said that it was his best day.

Charles Montione was another story. He came in like an extra from *Miami Vice*, pinkie ring and all. Montine wore a trim goatee similar to the defense lawyer's. He had street-corner good looks and sported a hairdo like the Wolf Man's. He seemed as though he wouldn't be credible.

Montione testified in a soft cellblock voice. He told of Jay Smith escape plans which added to the consciousness of guilt, but then he told the jury about Jay Smith's "smirking" when Montione asked if he'd killed the Reinerts.

He described the remarkable business of Jay Smith wanting a magazine with a model who was posed in a very particular way.

Montione's attitude as a witness was "I don't *want* to be here, but I am, and you can believe me or not."

Most people in that courtroom obviously did. The defense was worried about Montione's apparent credibility.

••••

Jack Holtz testified about a nine-page letter he'd seized when he arrested Jay Smith in 1985. It was a letter to attorney Glenn Zeitz, care of private investigator Russell Kolins. It was dated January 14, 1981.

The letter from Jay Smith outlined his whereabouts on the weekend of June 22, 1979. He informed his attorney that Grace Gilmore, the new owner of the house, had agreed to let him stay until July 1st, and that he was either visiting or telephoning his wife, and visiting or telephoning his lawyer over much of the murder weekend.

As to the night of Susan Reinert's dissappearance, Jay Smith wrote, "On Friday, June 22, sometime in late afternoon Grace Gilmore came. I heard movement upstairs and went to see what was up. I thought it was my daughter Stephanie returning for some clothes. Grace said she cancelled the trip to shore with sister."

It was extraordinary how casually he tossed in the name of his daughter for his new lawyer, since at the time Stephanie and Edward Hunsberger had not been seen for *three* years.

He then described his daughter Sheri coming into the house and said he was uncertain if she'd seen Grace Gilmore. It was Sheri's twenty-second birthday, he wrote, and they went out to supper. They returned and moved some of her things to her new apartment at about 7:00 P.M.

Jay Smith claimed in that letter that Grace Gilmore had returned on Saturday and they had coffee and a talk about what furniture he would leave. He maintained that she went down to the lower level of the house to look at the heater. Then she went back to work upstairs and he remained below in the basement apartment. Jay Smith wrote that Grace Gilmore had left in the afternoon but his daughter returned and stayed until after dark. He wrote that his brother came during the late morning on Sunday to determine what furniture was to be taken.

A letter to his brother that was also seized by Jack Holtz pursuant to his search warrant was simply an attempt to coach the brother on testimony regarding that weekend *if* he ever had to take the stand.

He told his brother that Grace Gilmore had come on Friday and Saturday, but did not mention her presence on Sunday. As to Sunday he wrote, "You came in late morning or early afternoon. You had granddaughter with you. Sher came late in afternoon and left 8:30 or 9:30 P.M."

As to events after that weekend that he hoped his brother could corroborate, Jay Smith wrote:

1) You moved my stuff.
2) Stuff had been kept intact since you got it.
3) I told you to get rid of clothes.
3) Car remains the same except for normal cleanup and maintenance. Many have driven it.

••••

Prior to the first day of testimony, Jack Holtz had admitted to being scared of Bill Costopoulos who had a reputation for being able to rattle police witnesses and make them look foolish. But Jack Holtz wasn't the same fellow he'd been back in 1979 when he was second banana to Joe VanNort—when he was only thirty-two years old and his hair was black.

He still had those glasses screwed to his face, but he evinced a lot of confidence when he took the stand to describe the seizing of the letters in Jay Smith's cell.

He answered all of the questions on cross-examination in an articulate and careful fashion. He'd answer "Yes, sir" and "No, sir" whenever possible, and remained unruffled when the defense lawyer stalked to the witness box to discuss the seizure of a man's personal correspondence.

Bill Costopoulos was very effective in his use of righteous indignation. He had good timing and didn't pull it from the bag of tricks all that often. In fact he had a gift for creating smokescreens even when he had little substance to work with.

But this time he asked one question too many. It was a mistake and he knew it immediately.

As though the letter was irrelevant, he asked Jack Holtz, "Is there anything in this nine-page letter that would be significant to your investigation?"

Holtz was too serious about his job ever to grin openly on the witness stand, but he came close. He said, "It was *all* significant." Then he launched into all the things about the letter that differed from his findings.

He testified that Grace Gilmore had been at the *shore* from Friday until Sunday, and that Jay Smith's daughter had *not* been at the house, and that everyone except comatose patients had been interviewed and Jay Smith was *not* seen visiting his dying wife at the hospital, and he had *not* visited his attorney, and that his brother had *not* been at his house, and in fact nobody had seen Jay Smith's face from Friday afternoon until Grace Gilmore heard his car drive away on Sunday afternoon.

The inescapable conclusion was that the letter showed a *tremendous* consciousness of guilt.

Bill Costopoulos came back to the counsel table and could be heard by the reporters saying, "Aw, shit!"

It was his worst day. He was more careful with Jack Holtz after that.

••••

Guida kept the witnesses streaming in. Grace Gilmore took the stand and directly refuted the Jay Smith letter by saying she *had* gone to the shore and hadn't returned until Sunday afternoon.

Agent Hess of the FBI testified to interviewing Jay Smith shortly after the crime occurred when Jay Smith told it differently, saying he had *not* gone to dinner with Sheri on Friday, June 22nd.

A representative of Bell Telephone testified that Jay Smith had placed five calls to his attorney over that weekend, but there was a gap between 3:43 P.M. Friday and 8:37 P.M. Sunday, which was ninety-seven minutes after the men from Three Mile Island saw Susan Reinert's car in the parking lot.

And Holtz told the jury that the driving time from the Host Inn to the house on Valley Forge Road was ninety minutes.

••••

Bill Costopoulos had an impressive group of lawyers in his law firm. They all resembled him in that they brought a little passion to their work, but as Josh Lock learned, it's okay as long as you don't get *too* emotionally involved with criminal defendants.

During the Jay Smith trial, one of his lawyers was defending another murder case. A defendant was on trial for killing his mother in her bed. Like Jay Smith, this defendant had a sardonic sense of humor. He called it "mattress-cide."

And in the same spirit of punsmanship he'd torched her saying it was an act of "our-son."

The lawyer was working on this one almost as hard as Bill Costopoulos. During the presentation of his case, the punster happened to ask the Costopoulos law clerk to get him a copy of a martial arts book. He said it might come in handy in prison to learn a few self-defense tricks.

The law clerk obliged, and after the punster was convicted of matricide he demonstrated what he'd learned.

Right there in the courtroom he hauled off and threw a kung-fu special from the direction of Pittsburgh and almost coldcocked his ardent young lawyer.

Shortly after that, the members of the press asked the lawyer if he was now selling tickets at scalpers' prices to the execution.

••••

Reporters need controversy. Most felt that Jay Smith would be acquitted. None believed the comb clue. They thought it had been planted by either Bill Bradfield or a disciple.

The mere fact the body had been driven to Harrisburg where Jay Smith was scheduled to be sentenced was evidence to many that he *hadn't* done the driving.

There were also discussions about the movie *Witness* which had taken place there in central Pennsylvania. In the Bill Bradfield trial, Rick Guida had found it patently absurd that Bill Bradfield would feel that there was no one in the police service to whom he could tell the alleged plot by Jay Smith to kill Susan Reinert.

Yet the entire movie *Witness* was built upon just such a decision. The protagonist thought there was a corrupt superior officer in the Philadelphia police, so he lit out for Amish country with his witnesses. *He* never called the FBI. *He* never called the state police. He just handled it himself. Just like Bill Bradfield. And he was a cop. All the critics in America, both fat and skinny, loved the picture and saw nothing absurd about the premise. It was a good thing for Rick Guida, everyone said, that *Witness* had not been released prior to the Bill Bradfield trial.

The most damaging physical evidence wasn't the comb, whether it had been lost by Jay Smith or planted by Bill Bradfield or a Bradfield disciple, or even, as some thought, planted by Jay Smith just for the perverse thrill of it.

It wasn't even the pin identical to Karen Reinert's that had been found in that car, nor the letters from Jay Smith to Bill Bradfield.

It was probably the letter *within* a letter wherein Jay Smith asked his dying wife to clean the Capri *thoroughly,* writing, "I can't stress the importance of this: clean out and then clean up."

And that the downstairs rug in a house they'd already sold *must* go, as he explained: "Every time I walk on that rug something new pops out."

Jay Smith, already imprisoned, was *not* worrying about a couple of marijuana seeds in his former house.

It was an even more damaging letter after Martray and Montione described his obsession with forensics.

····

The mother and father of Edward Hunsberger, now missing for eight years, attended the Jay Smith trial whenever they could. In the William Bradfield trial they'd driven two hours to and from Harrisburg every day because they couldn't afford a hotel room.

During this Jay Smith trial Dorothy Hunsberger testified that back on June 25, 1979, when Jay Smith showed up for sentencing on the theft case, he'd arrived very late and that his hair was mussed. She said that he'd felt in his pockets and then smoothed his hair down with his hands.

Well, maybe. And maybe Mrs. Hunsberger saw and remembered what she now wanted to remember, this tragic woman, nearly seventy, haunting courtrooms for any clue to the fate of her only child.

Bill Costopoulos didn't cross-examine her. The jury knew *nothing* of Edward Hunsberger and Jay Smith's missing daughter.

····

Without a doubt, the most memorable witness in the Jay Smith murder trial was Rachel, the ice maiden. The entire corps of reporters as well as both counsel tables were waiting for the person they had called "the mystery woman" in the William Bradfield trial. Cynics said that the greatest mystery about her was how she could *still* be a loyal Bradfield woman, but she was.

The reporters were not disappointed when she took the long walk to the witness box. Now in her mid-thirties, she *was* Charlotte Brontë. Rachel was as tiny as Susan Reinert. Her hair was very dark and straight, parted in the middle and combed severely down behind her ears. She wore a long black skirt suit and a pale, high-throated blouse with a tiny black necktie. And flat shoes, of course. She wore no makeup and no jewelry. Color her black, white and gray.

The precision with which she spoke was startling, so much so that she made each lawyer work at phrasing the questions carefully.

After Guida got past the preliminaries, he said to his witness, "At the time you formed a romantic interest with Mister Bradfield, did you know that he was living with a woman by the name of Sue Myers?"

"Yes, I did," she answered.

"And what did Mister Bradfield tell you about his relationship with Sue Myers?"

"They shared living quarters, but there was not a romantic relationship between them at the time."

"Is that what he told you?"

"Yes, it is."

"In the summer of 1979, did you know that Mister Bradfield had been married?"

"No, I don't believe so."

"In terms of the fall of 1978 and spring of 1979, did he ever mention a woman by the name of Susan Reinert?"

"Yes, I do remember the name."

"What did he tell you about Susan Reinert with regard to any romantic interest?"

"I understood that she was interested in dating him, but that he wasn't interested."

"Did you ever meet Susan Reinert?"

"No, I did not."

"Did you ever meet Sue Myers?"

"Yes, I believe I met her once."

"During the school year of 1978 to 1979, were you studying at that time?"

"Yes, I was a graduate student at Harvard University."

"Now, on the Thanksgiving weekend of 1978, did you receive a visit from Mister Bradfield while living in Cambridge?"

"Yes."

"I'm going to refer you to the spring of 1979: did you visit the city of Philadelphia?"

"I was down twice."

"Did you see Mister Bradfield on that first occasion?"

"Yes."

"When was the second visit?"

"I came down after the end of the school term that semester. Sometime at the end of May."

"How did you register at the hotel on that occasion?"

"Mister and Mrs. Bradfield."

"And who made the reservation for that particular room?"

"Mister Bradfield did."

"Could you tell the jury why you used the name Mister and Mrs. Bradfield, as opposed to your own name?"

"Well, it was a center city hotel that was somewhat seedy but inexpensive, and I felt slightly more comfortable staying at a place identified as a couple. Instead of a single woman staying alone."

"How long did you stay at the hotel?"

"Something like three weeks, but I might be slightly off on that."

"When did you leave the hotel?"

"It was on a Tuesday morning. I'm sure you could fill me in on the date."

"Was this when you drove to New Mexico with Mister Bradfield's car to meet him there in Santa Fe?"

"Yes, it was."

"Did he ever mention to you a man by the name of Jay C. Smith?"

"Yes, I knew the name."

"Did he ever mention any threats that Mister Smith may have made against Susan Reinert?"

"No."

"When was the last time you saw Mister Bradfield prior to his leaving for the shore on Friday, June twenty-second, 1979? Do you remember?"

"No, I don't."

"The testimony up until this time has been that Mister Bradfield was in Cape May for the entire weekend. What were you doing over the weekend when Mister Bradfield was away?"

"I was looking at architecture in Philadelphia. Getting to know the city."

"And had you done that prior to that weekend while you were living in that hotel?"

"Yes. That was one of the main purposes for my being in Philadelphia."

"Did you do anything with anybody, or do anything in terms of registering, to verify your whereabouts for that weekend?"

"Aside from the hotel, I can't think of anything offhand."

After she testified that a change in plans had necessitated her driving his VW Beetle with their belongings, Guida asked her, "Were you in any way upset that you had to drive alone across the country while your friend, Mister Bradfield, flew?"

"Well, it would have been nicer to have him in the car, but I wasn't worried about the drive across the country alone."

"When you arrived in New Mexico, what was your living arrangement?"

"I stayed in the same room as he did."

"Now, you indicated that in 1979 you had this romantic relationship with Mister Bradfield. Does that romantic interest continue today?"

"Yes, it does."

"Pass the witness."

Bill Costopoulos began by asking about the present relationship: "Because of your romantic interest that has continued until this day with Mister Bradfield, is it fair to say that you communicate with him now that he's in prison?"

"Yes."

"And how frequently do you communicate?"

"I see him probably twice a month and talk maybe twice a month with him on the telephone."

"Have you always kept him advised of the investigation that was going on in this matter?"

"Meaning?"

"When the police would come to talk to you, would you report that to him?"

It was one of the few times she hesitated. She said, "I would say he probably . . . I probably talked to him about it, yes."

"And in fact you'd tell him exactly what you were being asked about, wouldn't you?"

"There's a possibility. I don't remember specifically trying to tell him *everything* I'd been asked about."

"Do you remember resisting any cooperation with law enforcement after the weekend in question?"

"Resisting?"

"Not cooperating?"

"Not by *my* definition," she said.

With this, Rachel leaned forward in her witness chair and

folded her tiny hands and stared Bill Costopoulos right in the eye and answered questions as precisely as anything manufactured by IBM.

"Not by *your* definition," he said. "Well, when they would come to talk to you, would you talk to them?"

"No, not without my lawyer's permission and my lawyer's presence."

"And was it Bradfield's suggestion that you have a lawyer present when you were questioned?"

"No, it was my lawyer's."

"When was the last time you talked to Bradfield before coming here today?"

"I spoke with him on the telephone last night." Then she paused and said, "*Or* the night before."

"Did you tell him you were under subpoena?"

"Oh, yes. He knew that."

"When did you first learn that Bradfield was having a romantic relationship with Susan Reinert?"

The witness leaned forward a little more and the tone in her voice could have chilled a martini. She paused and said, "I don't believe he *was* having a romantic relationship with Susan Reinert."

"You don't believe that to this day?"

"That's correct."

"When did you find out that he was having a romantic relationship with Sue Myers?"

"Since I've known him, he *hasn't* had a romantic relationship with Sue Myers."

"All right, just so I'm clear, we're not having a definition problem about a romantic relationship, are we?"

"I don't think so," she said.

"Did he ever tell you that he was the named beneficiary to the tune of seven hundred and thirty thousand dollars in life insurance?"

"No."

"He never told you that?"

"No, he didn't."

"Did he tell you that he was the designated beneficiary of her estate by a will executed May fourth, 1979?"

"No."

"Did you ever learn of those possible facts?"

"Well, I learned of those *possible facts,* as you put it, after the death of Susan Reinert."

"Did Bradfield tell you after her death that he was shocked that Reinert would name him as beneficiary in that insurance policy?"

"Yes, he did."

"Now when you say you were looking at architecture for the three weeks before the weekend in question, what is it that you would do?"

"Wander around in Philadelphia, go to see specific buildings, go to see neighborhoods in general."

"Do you recall where you were on June twenty-second, 1979, in the evening hours?"

"June twenty-second was a Friday, I understand, from what Mister Guida has said?"

"Yes."

"No."

"You don't know. When was the first time you were asked that question by the authorities?"

"Probably the first time I spoke to them."

"Do you recall when that was?"

"No."

"The fact is, is it not, that on that Monday, June twenty-fifth, when the two of you were supposed to go to Santa Fe together, *that* was the day that he told you to drive because he was flying?"

"On that Monday?"

"Yes."

"That probably was the day that the plans were eventually clear that he would fly and I would drive."

"How far is Santa Fe?"

"Approximately two thousand miles."

"So, when he told you to drive two thousand miles in his car with his belongings, you really didn't even question that, did you?"

"Question it in what way?"

"Would you consider your act of driving that car two thousand miles an act of obedience?"

"I consider it an act of common sense."

"Would you consider it an act of loyalty?"

"No. We had to have the belongings and the car taken to New Mexico."

"How did you learn of Reinert's death?"

"When I was driving across the country, I spoke with him on the phone."

"When did he tell you about the children?"

"I don't remember if he had anything to say about them, or not."

"Did you ever ask him what he might know about her death and their disappearance?"

"No, I did not."

"When the two of you left Santa Fe to go to Boston there was a certain typewriter that he left in your custody and control, wasn't there?"

"That's correct."

"The authorities were interested in that typewriter, weren't they?"

"Yes, that's correct."

"You refused to give it to them for a long period of time, didn't you?"

"No, that's not precisely correct."

"What *is* precisely correct?"

"There was, I believe, an FBI agent who came and asked for it. My lawyer in Philadelphia and I didn't think that I should give up something without a subpoena or warrant of some sort. I told him to contact my lawyer, that I wasn't going to give it to them. And I contacted my lawyer for instructions."

"And he told you to give it to them?"

"That's correct."

"And you of course had talked to Bradfield before you gave it to them, didn't you?"

"I don't recall whether I did or not."

"The typewriter that you gave them had a ball on it, didn't it?"

"An element, yes."

"Did you give them the *same* ball element that was on the typewriter when Bradfield left it in your custody and control?"

"Yes, as far as I know."

"As far as you *know*?"

"I turned over the typewriter, as it existed, to them."

"What else did they ask you to give them?"

"What else? It seems to me that they never actually took the typewriter, but took the ribbon and the element, what *you* are calling the ball, from the typewriter. If my memory is correct."

"Directing your attention to Thanksgiving, 1978, he made some long-distance calls from where you were staying in Massachusetts. You are not aware by chance that he called Susan Reinert's mother's house in Ridgway, Pennsylvania, from where the two of you were staying that Thanksgiving, are you?"

"Not currently."

"After Susan Reinert was murdered, did you and Bill Bradfield develop a code system for communications?"

"No."

"What was the purpose of the Ezra Pound book?"

"I don't know what the purpose of the Ezra Pound book was."

"When did you receive immunity from the government?"

"I really don't recall the date. It was after that summer."

"Do you understand what immunity is?"

"I believe my lawyer explained it to me."

"Were you given immunity to the point where anything you said could *not* be used against you even if you had a role in the murder? Or was your immunity limited to anything you said, presupposing that you *didn't* have anything to do with the murder?"

"I don't really remember at this time."

"You've had how many years of schooling?"

"At that time?"

"Today."

Rachel paused, unclasped her hands, and glanced at the watery April sunbeams streaming through the skylight. Anybody else would probably have said, I have such and such degrees, but she answered the question precisely *as* it had been asked. The computer clicked a few times and then flashed the answer.

"Nineteen and a half," she said.

"And it was only after you got immunity that you gave any statements whatsoever, isn't that right?"

"I believe that's correct. Yes."

"When Bill Bradfield made a claim on the insurance policies

and the estate of Susan Reinert, your relationship was a romantic one, correct?"

"Yes, I suppose so."

"And it was a romantic one on the weekend in question, right?"

"That's correct."

"And it's a romantic one today?"

"That's correct."

"Is it your testimony that there were *no* letters in your possession from Bill Bradfield while you were in Boston? In code?"

"Yes, there were *no* letters in code."

"Was there anything in code in your possession from William Bradfield while you were in Boston at Harvard?"

"No."

"What is cryptology?"

"Cryptology? That's the study of codes."

"Did you study codes?"

"No, I haven't studied codes."

"Was there a letter from Bradfield to you *congratulating* you for becoming an expert in cryptology?"

"No."

"Was there a letter while you were in Boston, in code, instructing you to destroy, burn and scatter the ashes of the typewriter ball that was in your custody and control?"

"No."

"Do you understand enough about immunity that if you testify untruthfully under oath that you could be charged with perjury?"

"Yes, I understand that."

"When you were living in New Mexico did William Sidney Bradfield tell you that the newspapers in Philadelphia would draw a correlation between the murder of Reinert and Jay C. Smith?"

"I don't believe so."

Costopoulos got up and took a report to the witness box for Rachel to read. He stayed there, clearly intending to intimidate her. Guida did not request that he move away from this witness.

When she'd finished reading the report, she said calmly, "Well, it *doesn't* refresh my memory."

"My question is, did you ever tell Trooper Holtz that Bradfield told you that the newspapers would draw a correlation between the murder of Reinert and Jay C. Smith?"

"I don't remember."

And from this moment, witness and lawyer had a little power struggle that Guida did not interrupt, and during which Rachel didn't even blink.

"And of course if Bradfield told you *that,* you wouldn't remember asking him what he meant, would you?"

"I don't remember," she said.

"You don't remember *where* you were Friday night, June twenty-second, 1979?"

"That's correct."

"Or Saturday, June twenty-third, 1979? You don't remember?"

"Other than in Philadelphia, no."

"And of course you *don't* remember anything other than being in Philadelphia on Sunday, June twenty-fourth, 1979, do you?"

"That's correct."

"And you don't remember your whereabouts or your activities that Monday, June twenty-fifth, 1979?"

"Aside from being in Philadelphia, no."

"You don't remember whether you left the residence of Bradfield and Pappas when the authorities came down to Santa Fe in the early summer of 1979, do you?"

"No, I don't."

"You don't remember any coding system, and in fact you *deny* any coding system between you and Bradfield, don't you?"

"That's correct."

"And you don't remember that in Thanksgiving of 1978, Bradfield called Reinert's mother's house from where the two of *you* were staying, do you?"

"I don't remember. That's correct."

"Knowing Bradfield romantically for the years that you've known him, is there *anything* you can remember that would help the prosecution in their effort to learn anything about the murder of Susan Reinert and the disappearance of her two children?"

"I don't have anything to add."

"I have no further questions," Bill Costopoulos said, and sat down.

Bill Costopoulos hadn't intimidated Rachel. The hound of the Baskervilles couldn't have intimidated Rachel.

When that study in black and white and gray strode across the courtroom, a single word came to mind: *resolute*. She had the self-righteous cast of a true believer. But a true believer risks sounding less like Joan of Arc and more like Lucrezia Borgia.

Along with the "my danger conspiracy" letter to *V* in cipher was the following deciphered message on the reverse side, also explained to the jury by an FBI cryptanalyst.

> Miss you Hon. Love you terribly. Love you so much. Hurt for you. Hope I can see you soon, but lawyer says going up there now could be grounds for unlawful flight to avoid prosecution. Lawyers warn there will be FBI plant near you soon. Car bugged. Chris has been subpoenaed for grand jury. He will say nothing much. He must maintain this all the way up through possible (probable) trial. Hand on Bible et cetera or be in perjury five to ten years.
>
> If you're in same position, you know practically nothing about case and nothing at all about ~~Smith~~ P of D. You must maintain this all the way up through trial hand on Bible forever. Did we mention Smith to Pappas? Try to remember. We can't be inconsistent about what we told them. Perhaps you could write them and warn them. Will be visited by FBI. If they haven't yet. Ask them exactly what they remember about what we said. Love you. Remember that we made it. Love you. Wish I were lying next to you and holding you.
>
> Destroy this and ashes. Congratulations you're on way to becoming expert cryptologist. Can you take some more rules? Hope so. Lawyers assure us we are dealing with the best FBI has. So we better be fairly sophisticated, okay?
>
> When coding, use last number then first and so forth back and forth. Destroy messages after receiving them. Destroy them without being observed. Don't let anyone know you're receiving or destroying code. Repeat. Destroy completely. If ashes are left, destroy them also. Grind them underfoot or something.

It is perhaps noteworthy that neither Bill Bradfield's ex-wife Muriel nor Sue Myers, nor Shelly nor Rachel, had married in all the years since they'd known him. Things like romantic fantastic irrelevant letters resembling games of Scrabble might have had something to do with it. After you've been part of *his* madcap adventures it might be hard to settle down to domestic routine. Besides, it was probably great to have a mission in life.

If Bill Costopoulos didn't succeed with intimidation, he *did* succeed in his foremost aim. He'd demonstrated to the jury that Rachel, unlike Vince Valaitis, could be considered as a crime partner of William Bradfield. In fact, her performance was assessed during the jury deliberation. It was learned that one juror asked if they had the power to *convict* her of anything.

27

Ghosts

If the letter within a letter was the most legally damaging piece of physical evidence in the Jay Smith trial, the tiny green pin from the Philadelphia Museum of Art carried the emotional load.

The trial had been going on for three weeks and both sides had just about shot their bolts. Bill Costopoulos had been working eighteen hours a day and looked haggard. Rick Guida was so overloaded with nicotine he could have jump-started a DC-10.

The prosecutor said that he had no idea what to expect when he subpoenaed former classmates of Karen Reinert from Chestnutwold Elementary School who'd made that museum field trip in the sixth grade. He was hoping they wouldn't have green hair with pins through their noses.

♦♦♦♦

The first of them wore a blue blazer and a necktie and testified that back in the sixth grade they'd gone to the museum, all right. He remembered the colonial furniture. He planned to enter Temple University in the fall.

The second, similarly dressed, was a senior at Haverford High School and would be attending the Virginia Military Institute. He testified to getting the green pin with the white *P*.

The third was also a student at Haverford who would be transferring to William and Mary, and he remembered the pin and the trip.

The next was going to the University of Cincinnati, and yes, he remembered the pin and the trip.

Another had kept his pin and turned it over to the police for comparison.

Each young witness was handsome and wholesome and well dressed and polite. Finally, one was called who wasn't wearing a coat and tie. He was wearing jeans, but he was the jock of the crowd, another good-looking kid with college plans. He'd played in Michael's last cub scout game.

Guida asked him about the field trip and he testified that Karen Reinert had definitely been on the field trip at the museum that day in 1979.

When the prosecutor asked him how he could be sure, the young man said, "She was very cute. Lots of people at school had a crush on her. I was one of them."

The jurors smiled. The courtroom got very quiet. A couple of people took out handkerchiefs.

Costopoulos *couldn't* cross-examine. He had to wait until Jack Holtz again testified, in order to imply that all of the Bradfield people had been on the loose at that time and someone could have planted that pin in Jay Smith's car when it was parked at his brother's house in Delaware.

The defense knew what was coming next. The queue of bright wholesome kids had kept the courtroom utterly silent.

The look on the face of the defense lawyer said, *Why* can't this one look like Saturday night at Studio 54?

She looked like a Mormon missionary. The young woman entered timidly and after the judge reassured her with a kindly smile, she sat down and put her hands in her lap and waited.

"State your name for the record," Guida said.

"Elizabeth Ann Brook."

"And where do you work?"

"I work at the Chubb insurance company."

"How old are you?"

"Twenty-three."

"What is your grandmother's name?"

"Mary Gove."

"And where did your grandmother live in 1979?"

"She lived on Woodcrest Drive."

"And who was her next-door neighbor?"

"Susan Reinert."

"Who did Susan Reinert live there with?"

"Her two children, Karen and Michael."

"Now, Beth Ann, during 1978 and 1979, did you stay at your grandmother's house at all?"

"Yes, I did. Quite frequently."

"Just tell us how frequently."

"Sometimes once a week. Sometimes once every two weeks. My grandfather had just passed away and we were trying to keep someone with her as much as possible."

"Did you know Karen and Michael Reinert?"

"Yes, I did. Very well."

"Did you do anything for them while you were staying with your grandmother?"

"Yes, I was their baby-sitter."

"Now, I'm going to take you back to Friday night, June twenty-second, 1979. Were you at your grandmother's house?"

"Yes, I was."

"And do you recall a hailstorm that evening?"

"Yes, sir."

"And what happened after the hailstorm was over? What did you do?"

"My grandmother and I went out to the porch. Karen and Michael and Susan were coming out of their house. Michael went down and he was picking up the hailstones. And he brought them to us and he said, 'Oh, gosh! Look how big they are!' "

"Did Karen have a pin that she wore?"

"Yes."

"What kind of pin did she wear?"

"Well, it was a clip-on pin with the back bent over and clipped on to whatever you were wearing."

"What color was the pin?"

"Green."

"What did the pin have on it?"

"It had a white *P* on it."

"How often would you say she wore that pin?"

"Practically every time I saw her she had it on."

"Now, Beth Ann, how was Karen Reinert dressed that night while you were out collecting hailstones?"

"She had on a white shirt with a scoop neck, a pair of shorts and sneakers."

"Did she have anything on that shirt that you remember?"

"She had on the pin."

"The green pin with the white *P*?"

"The green pin with the white *P*."

Guida got up from the counsel table and approached the witness. He took a packet from the evidence box and said, "I'm going to show you what has been marked as commonwealth's exhibit number one hundred ten. Does that look familiar to you?"

"Yes, it does."

"And what is it similar to?"

"That's the pin Karen had on."

"Beth Ann, did you ever see Karen or Michael Reinert again after that night at nine o'clock?"

"No, sir."

"Cross-examine."

It was a subdued Bill Costopoulos at that point. A grueling trial was winding down to those bright and handsome reminders of Karen and Michael Reinert. He slouched in his chair. He didn't get up to approach the witness.

"Beth Ann," he began, "do you recall being interviewed by two federal agents in August of 1979?"

"Yes, sir."

"Have you had an opportunity to look over their report before you testified today?"

"No, sir."

Costopoulos was taking his last shot. He withdrew the FBI report from the file and approached the young woman, pointing to a paragraph in the report.

"Let me show you your report at *that* time to refresh your memory as to what you recalled Karen having on."

She read the report, nodded and said, "The peasant shirt would have been the scoop neck."

"I can't hear you," said Judge Lipsitt.

The witness said, "The peasant shirt in the description I gave that year. I said that she had on a yellow peasant top."

"A yellow peasant top?" said the judge.

"A yellow peasant top is what I described. The scoop neck would be made out of cotton almost like T-shirts are made of. A peasant's shirt is made out of a gauze. But it *does* have a scooped neck."

Costopoulos said, "Well, you admit there's no mention in here about any pin?"

"No, sir."

"When was the first time you were asked to recall if you saw a pin?"

"About four weeks ago."

"About four weeks ago?"

"Yes, sir."

"Who asked you?"

"Mister Holtz."

"Did he *show* you the pin?"

"No, sir. As a matter of fact, when he called he didn't say anything about the pin. He just asked me to think about what she had on again."

"Okay," Bill Costopoulos said. "I have no further questions."

It was only getting worse for Costopoulos. He could've pointed out that she couldn't know if it was that *particular* pin, but he wisely let her go.

A couple of jurors were dabbing at tears, and a couple of others were staring at Jay Smith. He was as impassive as if he were attending a meeting of the Parent-Teachers Association.

Essentially, the commonwealth's case was over, and Guida had demonstrated that he too had a sense of theater. The jurors kept glancing at the spectators, toward the classmates of Karen Reinert. The jurors kept looking for should-have-beens. Looking for ghosts.

••••

On the 29th of April, William Costopoulos made his closing argument to the jury.

He said, "May it please the court, Mister Guida, Mister Smith.

Ladies and gentlemen of the jury, very soon you will retire to deliberate the fate of Jay Smith, and in your hands lies the power of rendering the only appropriate verdict in this case based on the evidence. Which is not guilty. In your hands lies the power of life and death. It is the gravest responsibility our country imposes on its citizenry.

"During the course of the trial, you've been patient, and you've seen a lot of interaction between the attorneys, and often intentionally or unintentionally we interject our egos into these proceedings. No matter what your verdict is our egos will heal, but your verdict is forever.

"Judge Lipsitt will explain to you that a reasonable doubt means the kind of doubt that you would only entertain in acting in a matter of importance to yourself. Beyond a reasonable doubt means that we don't convict in this country on suspicion, on conjecture, on theory. We don't convict in this country on probabilities.

"Even if you would decide that Jay Smith was *probably* responsible in some way, or directly, the law says not guilty. Because in this country we would rather acquit nine guilty persons than convict one innocent man for something he didn't do. Let alone ask that he be put to death."

Bill Costopoulos described to the jury how the pieces of the prosecution's puzzle didn't fit, and how they'd tried to force them to make them fit.

He began at the beginning when a prosecution witness had testified that Susan Reinert had granules of sand between her toes, and that Susan Reinert had written "Cape May" on a note in her car.

He proceeded to Mary Gove, the next-door neighbor of Susan Reinert, who had belatedly testified that she saw Susan Reinert wearing blue slacks the night she disappeared, to account for the two blue fibers stuck to her body.

As to her granddaughter belatedly testifying to the pin, he said that it must run in the family. He implied that the prosecution was "responsible" for that belated testimony.

He claimed that the defense hair and fiber experts had demolished the entire hair and fiber evidence of the prosecution, reiterating that his witness said the brown hair could belong to any brunette in the world, and the red fibers could have come from any red rug.

He dealt as quickly as possible with Jay Smith's letter to his dying wife about getting rid of the downstairs carpet, saying that Jay Smith had been trying to fulfill an obligation to his realtor.

He turned his attention to William Bradfield and pointed out that he was a hundred different kinds of liar, and had seven hundred and thirty thousand good reasons to kill Susan Reinert.

As to his client, he said, "Motive? What motive did Jay Smith have to kill the woman and hurt her children? According to the commonwealth's theory, Bradfield committed perjury for him. Well, that's *Bradfield's* problem, not Jay Smith's. Jay Smith didn't even testify at the St. Davids trial. Motive. *What* motive? Are the two links going to hold together that Bradfield did in fact commit perjury, and in payment Jay Smith savagely and brutally assassinates a woman and two children on the weekend he's to report for sentencing?

"Use your common sense. Why in God's name would Jay Smith want the body to be left outside the Host Inn? In the very city within a mile or so of where he was to appear for sentencing? If there was any reason, *you* come up with it, I can't.

"And that woman wasn't just murdered for the purpose of collecting insurance proceeds. She was *disgraced*. She was left nude in the fetal position in the back of her car, and the hatchback was left up, three rows from the front door. Who, psychologically, had this character of disgracing and demeaning women? William Sidney Bradfield.

"And where was Rachel for thirty days prior to the murder? And Chris Pappas, ladies and gentlemen. I don't know *where* that guy's coming from. They practiced shooting silencers. They practiced tying each other up. Make no mistake about it, ladies and gentlemen, he knows more. Rachel knows more. Sue Myers knows more, and if the prosecution would quit defending them they might find out what happened on that weekend because *they* know more.

"Does Smith have an airtight alibi for that weekend? Not even close. But neither do I. And neither do you. And I can guarantee you that each and every one of you has a brown hair in your house on the floor that matches Susan Reinert's. And the chances are good that every one of you has red fibers in your house.

"But you see, ladies and gentlemen, Jay Smith didn't know he was going to *need* an alibi, and when he first gave his recollection of that weekend to a federal agent he wasn't real clear *where* he'd been three months earlier. Make no mistake about it, Grace Gilmore *was* there that weekend, Friday, Saturday *and* Sunday.

" 'I went to see my wife every day that weekend,' he told them. But they said no, he was too busy murdering Susan Reinert and chopping up her kids and throwing them in the ocean or burying them in the woods or throwing them in graves. That's hogwash!

"The alibi of William Sidney Bradfield going down to the shore with Chris Pappas, Sue Myers and Vince Valaitis is only a good one if you believe them *all*. But if you don't believe one of them, the alibi is done.

"And Sue Myers at one point in time turned over every scrap of paper to them, and by God, they came up with a receipt from the A and P in Phoenixville dated Saturday, June twenty-third, at six-eighteen P.M. And instead of grabbing all those people and starting all over, they lost the receipt.

"Then there's the letter to his brother. You've got to remember this guy's been in jail at that time for sixteen months. He's a self-proclaimed jailhouse lawyer. So he wrote his brother and told him to invoke the Fifth Amendment. He said to say as little as possible. And in his letter of October thirtieth he tells him that on Sunday, June twenty-fourth, 1979, 'You came sometime in the late morning and left in the early afternoon. I believe you had your granddaughter with you.' His brother said, 'Well, that's not true. I wasn't there. And I'm not testifying.'

"And if you want to believe that was Jay's recollection in 1980, fine. I'd *like* to believe that. I don't. It appears as though Jay was trying to tell his brother to say something for him about that Sunday morning. That's what they came up with, ladies and gentlemen, out of fifty-three files they took from that man when they arrested him on June twenty-fifth, 1985.

"Fifty-three files. They invaded his most sacred communications. They took his letters to his brother. They took his letters to his lawyer which is the most sacred privileged communication we sanction in this country, and they read them to you.

"Raymond Martray showed up in 1981 and said every time

Smith had conversations pertaining to the murder, they were in the grandstands of the prison. The first time Smith told Martray, 'I took care of her.' The second and third times Martray was told, 'I killed the fucking bitch.'

"They had problems with Raymond. Big problems. They turned him over to the FBI. Constant attempts were made to pin down Martray concerning specific statements made to him by Smith concerning the Reinert killing, and Martray became more and more general rather than specific in his answers.

"You heard those tapes yourselves. Jay Smith talked to you, ladies and gentlemen, and you learned what he knew and didn't know about the death of Susan Reinert.

"I was worried about the fact that the crime was a savage one. Everybody gets angry, and it was an ugly crime, but my concern was never over the evidence against Jay Smith because there *isn't* any. Once you get rid of Martray that leaves them back where they were in 1980. With this new comb. What's that prove? Nothing.

"There wasn't a trace linking her body to anyone. It was professionally done. We've got the pin and the car of Jay, wiped clean. We've got everything that Bradfield said before and after. But use your common sense. William Sidney Bradfield is the biggest liar that ever walked the face of this earth. The comb was clean. The pin was clean. The fibers and hair mean nothing.

"Ladies and gentlemen, you have the power to render the only appropriate verdict in this case based on the evidence we've all heard. And this is that Jay Smith is not guilty. It's in your hands. Thank you."

When Costopoulos got back to the defense table, he whispered to Jay Smith, "How'd I do, teach?"

Jay Smith said, "The semester's not over yet."

••••

In the afternoon session it was the turn of the prosecutor. Guida rose and said, "Thank you, Your Honor. Ladies and gentlemen, seven years ago, on a very cold summer morning, Trooper John Holtz left his bed and went to the Host Inn parking lot. Since that time, the most massive police effort in the history of Pennsylvania has been continuing to try to solve the Reinert murder case.

"Four and a half years ago I joined the office of the attorney general. My first assignment was this matter. Today it's over. Today, all of the effort expended by the prosecutor, by the defense, by the FBI, all comes down to you.

"In this case, the law is not complex. Mister Costopoulos said in his opening argument, and I agree with him, that this is a case of murder in the first degree, or it is nothing. The commonwealth is alleging that this defendant cold-bloodedly and brutally killed a woman and her two small children. Why? We'll talk about motive in a while.

"In this case the commonwealth has presented two types of evidence: direct and circumstantial. Direct evidence is someone coming into the courtroom and saying the defendant confessed to him. In this case we have a man by the name of Raymond Martray who says that.

"The rest of the commonwealth's case is what is called circumstantial evidence, a group of facts, none of which in and of themselves is sufficient to prove the defendant guilty.

"Let's wrap up the defense case. During the first day of the case a retired trooper took the stand. He's worked for the defendant's private investigator. On cross-examination he suddenly talks about her feet, about some grains of sand. Mister Costopoulos said it was like pulling teeth getting him to say it. It was more like pulling out dentures. A big smile came over his face. He said that gritty particles could have been sand.

"You found out that early in the investigation when the state police were exploring the possibility that Mrs. Reinert might have been to the shore, they called him to a meeting to determine that, and what did he say? Nothing. It's a sad commentary on what was a decent career with the state police. What value did his testimony have for the defense? Zero. Nothing. As a matter of fact, it might tell you something *else*.

"We came to hair and fibers. They brought their experts in, men who were paid to attend this hearing. It was said that the hair found on the floor of Jay Smith's basement was four and a half inches long and Susan Reinert's hair was seven inches long. It probably was Jay Smith's hair, he said.

"On cross-examination, what did I say? How long are the samples? He didn't want to answer that question. He wanted to say that her hairbrush had seven-inch hairs in it. I said, how long were the samples? He said four and a half inches long.

"The defense switched tacks and we went to a receipt from the grocery store turned over by Sue Myers with many other things. This receipt happened to be stamped June twenty-third, 1979. Well, we can't explain it to you. Is it possible that Bradfield would have given access to his apartment to the person that he was using to murder Susan Reinert?

"If Sue Myers had murdered Susan Reinert with William Bradfield, and had an alibi at the shore, would she be so stupid as to hand that receipt to the state police? Back to common sense.

"There's Vincent Valaitis. Never given immunity. Vince was there with these people all weekend. I think he was, as he appeared here to you, somewhat insecure. He needed a friend. Bradfield provided it and used him.

"There were more than three victims. There's Sue Myers. Sixteen years with the same man she loved. He's with Reinert, with Rachel, with Shelly. She didn't want to believe that she'd invested sixteen years of her life. She was obedient. She was weak. If anything, you can say to these people that they certainly look foolish. But I'm asking you, did Vincent Valaitis and Sue Myers appear to be the kind of persons who would murder a child?

"Christopher Pappas was cut from the same cloth as Vincent Valaitis. He needed a friend. Shelly was nineteen years old. She made a commitment that will haunt her for the rest of her life. But was she a murderess? Could she have cut up two children?

"Well, let's talk about Rachel. She's the only person that is unaccounted for on that weekend. The commonwealth isn't saying that Rachel *isn't* involved. We never said there were only two. What we said to you is that we could only *prove* two.

"The evidence against Rachel is that her whereabouts are unknown for that weekend, and that's it. With that kind of evidence, there can't be another chair at this table. We have to work on the evidence that we have. It's very possible that somebody followed the defendant to Harrisburg and helped him get back home. And it's possible that William Bradfield would want this person there because there was a lot of money at stake. That's possible.

"In some degree, the commonwealth's strength is in its subtlety. Do you think that Sue Myers, Vince Valaitis and Chris Pappas would plant a pin under Jay Smith's car seat and then *anticipate* that Beth Ann Brook would remember that Karen had it on that night? It's something that an adult throws away. Why didn't they just take Karen's finger after she was dead and roll it on there? What we have here isn't a normal murder case.

"We didn't introduce William Bradfield's statement to his friends to show the truth of the matters. This case involves a conspiracy within a conspiracy, a conspiracy with two separate motives. Bradfield knows he's going to be a suspect so before she's murdered he starts covering himself. He starts saying that Jay C. Smith might do it.

"Those friends are going to come, he believes, and support him by saying Bill was worried. Bill wanted to help her. Bill was a great guy. He didn't *want* the insurance.

"Well, he *wanted* the money. And he didn't want to give *any* of it to the defendant. He wanted to keep it himself. Keep in mind that the circumstance of how that body was found show that the co-conspirator knew the money was coming, and did it so Bradfield could get the money. And what can you infer from that? *He* was going to get something.

"But Bradfield doesn't want to give it to him. Bradfield knows he's a suspect, so Bradfield covers himself, but interestingly, very interestingly. In the Susan Reinert vehicle amongst McDonald's happy meal boxes, children's raincoats, umbrellas. In a messy car, very child oriented, what do we find? A dildo. And what does Bradfield say. Suddenly in New Mexico he said that Smith *didn't* do it. A kinky guy named Alex killed her.

"Why would Bradfield suddenly change his story? He didn't continue to say Smith did it. He was *scared* because those two kids were dead and he realized the newspapers *wouldn't* let him go, and now he had to back off. So suddenly Smith *didn't* do it.

"Raymond Martray told you that the defendant said 'I killed the bitch' on two occasions. That in and of itself is sufficient to convict the defendant if you believe it. The defense suggested that because Martray saw this was a big case he was going to come into this courtroom and perjure himself. What did Martray get? Nothing. Martray served his time. He got out on schedule. What did the commonwealth do?

"Charles Montione. April, 1983, Bradfield's arrested. Smith

says, 'We're going to escape.' Does an innocent man who's being investigated by the police want to kill police officers who are looking into the facts? Are those the actions of an innocent man?

"Then we move to Mister Smith's alibi. Mister Costopoulos said that if any of you were asked to recall where you were on a certain day you'd have difficulty. But keep in mind that Susan Reinert worked for the defendant. She was found in Harrisburg on the same day that he's to be sentenced, and he's late for sentencing. Now, wouldn't you think that a person in that situation would think that somebody might conclude that he was involved? And look back and say, 'Well, I was with so and so?'

"What did Grace Gilmore tell you about the Saturday? 'I went to the shore with my sister. I was there all day Friday. I was there all day Saturday. I came back late Sunday afternoon. I heard a noise downstairs and then I heard his car drive away.' Are we going to believe Grace Gilmore who never was in the lower level of Smith's house? Or are you going to believe what *he* wrote down? Does an innocent man fake his alibi?

"We *know* where this man was on August twenty-seventh, 1977, but what does Bill Bradfield do? He takes the witness stand and says, 'Nope, he was with me at the shore. Jay Smith couldn't have done that Sears theft.' Why? I submit to you the why is the quid pro quo, the first quid pro quo for this murder.

"We were interested in the note that the defense has described as a nice note to his wife when she was sick. We were interested in this note for two reasons. One, 'Clean up the Capri. Thoroughly.' Two, 'Get rid of the rug.' He says, 'When you get better, get up off your deathbed and throw away the rug.'

"So we asked the defendant to provide us with a handwriting exemplar. This innocuous note means nothing. He sees it. What does he do? *You* have the exemplar that Jay Smith gave to us for comparison. Do you need to be a handwriting expert to tell that he faked it? It doesn't look anything like his writing. Are these the actions of an innocent man? If they are not, another pebble on the pile. On the other side of that scale only the presumption of innocence.

"On the tape of September eighth from Smith to Martray, he stated: 'Now where are the two kids' bodies? See, he's gotta show all that stuff and he can't. The only way they can get me is if he gets on the stand and says Smith did it. Do you see the advantage in not telling your partner where you put the bodies?'

"The only person in the world who can speak with confidence and know for *sure* that William Bradfield couldn't walk in here and tell us where the bodies are, the *only* person that knows, is his partner. That's more like a rock than a pebble.

"Now we come to Jay Smith's car. Our last pebble. In this innocuous letter where Jay Smith had to fake a handwriting exemplar, it says, 'Clean out the Capri. Thoroughly.' Underlined twice. Well, we learned that on June twenty-second, 1979, Karen Reinert and her brother Michael were collecting hailstones. Karen was dressed in a scoop-neck blouse and a pair of shorts. She wore a green pin. Nothing special to an adult.

"Karen was an eleven-year-old girl. It was more like an emerald to her. It wasn't something insignificant. It was something she prized. And on that night Karen Reinert got into the car of her mother and it drove away. Into oblivion.

"There's an old children's story about children walking through the woods. They leave things behind on the ground so they can find their way back home. Karen Reinert on the night of June twenty-second, 1979, knew she wasn't coming back. Either that or the force that looks after little children left something for us. Not so Karen could find her way back home, but to tell us where she went and who sent her there. The last pebble is in.

"When I stop talking, the criminal investigation into the murders of Susan Reinert and her two children will have ended. I'm asking you now to do the right thing and I think you know what that is. Thank you."

◆◆◆◆

That afternoon the judge charged the jury as to the law and their duties. As to the jury not having heard the defendant speak, he said, "Now I want to say a word about the failure to testify because that very often is on the minds of a juror. This is what the law states and I emphasize it to you. It is entirely up to a defendant in every criminal trial whether or not to testify. He has an absolute right founded on the Constitution to remain silent. You must not draw any inference of guilt from the fact that the defendant did not testify, and so I leave that with you."

At 6 P.M. when the jury was being fed dinner, Rick Guida and the defense team were at Catalano's bar. Rick Guida, after a few drinks, was telling everyone that they'd done their best but he had very very bad feelings about this juror, or that one, or another one.

Jack Holtz said, "I'm not putting myself through *this* craziness," and went home to his son.

28

The Dance

The jury reached a verdict the next morning, April 30, 1986. Reporters and spectators reassembled in the courtroom at 10:48 A.M.

The heavy security was still present. Burly men in plainsclothes sat next to Jay Smith at the counsel table, and there were more in the rear of the courtroom, and one in the reporters' box scanning the spectators.

••••

Pete and Dorothy Hunsberger had spent the night in Harrisburg and were present in the second row. Mrs. Hunsberger's hands were gripping each other so hard they were dead white. The Hunsbergers had tracked Jay Smith longer than anyone. They looked as though they were praying.

After all that had gone into the Reinert murder investigation, it seemed somehow that this was just another interlude. For Jack Holtz and Lou DeSantis it didn't seem possible that they were hearing for the last time in this case the court clerk calling all to rise in the historic way:

"Oyez, oyez, oyez, all those having anything to do this day before the Honorable William W. Lipsitt draw near and they shall be heard. God save the commonwealth and this honorable court."

Two jurors had their arms folded. A bad sign for the defense. Bill Costopoulos slid down in his chair. He rested his head on the back. He knew something.

Judge Lipsitt said, "Good morning, ladies and gentlemen. The court has been informed that the jury has reached a verdict. Would the foreperson hand the verdict forms to the clerk, please."

The clerk took the forms from the woman selected and said, "In the case of *The Commonwealth* Versus *Jay C. Smith,* number 1677, the charge of murder, how do you find the defendant?"

"Guilty. Murder in the first degree," she said.

"In the case of *The Commonwealth* Versus *Jay C. Smith,* number 1677a, the charge of murder, how do you find the defendant?"

"Guilty, murder in the first degree," she said.

"In the case of *The Commonwealth* Versus *Jay C. Smith,* number 1677b, the charge of murder, how do you find the defendant?"

"Guilty, murder in the first degree," she said.

Costopoulos requested a jury poll and the courtroom heard "Guilty, murder in the first degree" thirty-three more times. Jay Smith didn't so much as twitch.

When they were finished, the clerk said, "Will you please rise. Hearken to your verdict as the court has it recorded. In *The Commonwealth* Versus *Jay C. Smith,* the charge of murder, you say guilty in the first degree. So say you all?"

"We do," they said.

Pete Hunsberger touched his wife's arm as each count was uttered. Pete and Dorothy Hunsberger heard two additional counts of murder that no one else heard.

◆◆◆◆

The lawyers immediately had a conversation at the sidebar where Bill Costopoulos reminded Judge Lipsitt that Judge Garb had precluded the penalty phase from going to the jury in the case of William Bradfield. He asked the court to adopt the same position.

Guida argued that in the Bradfield case Judge Garb had reasoned that William Bradfield was not convicted of the actual killings, but was an accomplice. Nor had the prosecution proven to the judge's satisfaction that he had contracted the murder. In this case, Guida argued, Jay Smith was the *actual* murderer.

Judge Lipsitt quickly denied the request of the defense and the penalty phase was ordered to begin.

"Members of the jury," the judge said, "you have now found this defendant guilty of murder in the first degree in connection with three cases. Your verdicts have been recorded. We are now going to hold a sentencing hearing during which counsel may present additional evidence and argument.

"You will decide whether the defendant is to be sentenced to death or life imprisonment. Whether you sentence the defendant to death or life imprisonment will depend upon what, if any, aggravating or mitigating circumstances you found present in this case."

When the judge had finished, the moment had at *last* arrived. Jay Smith stood and walked tall and erect. He took the stand and sat easily. He was a bit more pale and gaunt than he had been, but at the moment looked to be in far better emotional condition than his lawyer. His eyes had all the expression of a pair of hubcaps.

"Mister Smith, please state your full name for the record," Costopoulos began.

"My name is Jay Charles Smith."

"Your age, sir."

"I will be fifty-eight on June fifth of this year."

"Where were you born?"

"I was actually born in Ridley Park, but lived all my life in Chester, Pennsylvania."

"Do you have any brothers or sisters?"

"I have three brothers living, one brother dead, and one sister."

"For how many years were you married before your wife passed away?"

"Twenty-eight years."

"When did your wife pass away?"

"On August seventh, 1979."

"From the date of your imprisonment, what have you done in the institutional environment in which you live?"

"Well, I've been involved in a large number of activities. I don't know whether it was you or someone else who mentioned the jailhouse lawyer. I was known more as a jailhouse guidance counselor because a great amount of my activity was helping individuals with their personal letters and personal problems.

"I handled fifteen Vietnam veterans, the Agent Orange cases, to get these individuals their medical examinations and get them their proper discharges. I worked with a large number of Hispanics who couldn't speak English.

"I taught a class for inmates called 'How to Get a Job,' showing them how to make out applications and construct résumés and keep files.

"I worked a lot in the church activities, not that I'm an expert on it. I was more of an organizer. I was president of the God Squad for three years. When there was no minister I handled all the church activity at the prison. I would bring in ministers and set up the ceremony. I handled the Bible study.

"I did my regular prison job. I handled the dayroom, handled all the books and papers, kept it clean.

"I've worked for over four years on a criminal justice dictionary. That was my main writing activity."

"How does the request for two back issues of *Penthouse* tie in with that?"

"I've found that *Black's Law Dictionary* and *Ballentine's* do not cover criminal justice definitions very well. I had inmates bring up words that they know, then I went through about fifty or sixty sociology and criminology textbooks and began writing definitions in the criminal justice dictionary.

"There's nothing in *Black's Law Dictionary* about the Muslims. In prison the Black Muslims and the Muslim faith has grown tremendously. You have a great deal of trouble in the criminal justice system finding out about corrections, especially halfway houses, furloughs, leaves of absence. Most lawyers do not know very much about corrections."

"It's in that category, corrections . . ."

"The *Penthouse*. Let me answer how I got to the *Penthouse*. I found over the past five or six years a number of crimes involving battered wives and child abuse.

"If you look at those issues, you'll find that they have Yoko and John Lennon in there. John Lennon beat up Yoko. I was considering her as an example of a battered wife because John Lennon is known throughout the world.

"Also John Lennon in the article kicked his child, Sean. Yoko thought he was going to kill him. This was a child abuse item."

"Did your having possession of those two *Penthouse* magazines have anything to do with Charles Montione?"

"Nothing whatever."

He looked as banal as Adolf Eichmann. He'd just been convicted of murdering a woman and two children, and he was now describing to the jury how he was writing dictionary definitions of child abuse, as emotional as a grapefruit.

Then he went on to describe how he'd helped Charles Montione and Raymond Martray, who'd betrayed him with their false testimony. And just so he didn't disappoint anyone by failing to offer a sexual innuendo, he gave the jury a news flash: one of the witnesses against him was homosexual, even though Dr. Jay had always tried to "talk him out of it."

Bill Costopoulos asked, "Mister Smith, since your arrest for the death of Susan Reinert and the disappearance of her children what have your living conditions been?"

"I've been kept in the hole ever since."

"Explain to the jury what that means."

"I'm not allowed any communication or calls. I'm not allowed to visit with my relatives except one time every two weeks when they're behind a screen. I get no religious activity whatever. It's the only place in the United States where you're not permitted to have any church services."

"Did you want to testify before this jury during this trial?"

"Yes. It was my feeling to testify because I felt the jury was entitled to hear my side. You said if I didn't testify it couldn't work against me. I mentioned to you I didn't think they could bring up the previous conviction. That shows you how much of a jailhouse lawyer I am."

"Mister Smith, if this jury would spare your life, are you aware that you will spend the rest of your natural life in the prison system of this commonwealth?"

"I don't think there's any doubt about that."

"If this jury would spare you your life, what would you do within the prison system until your natural death?"

"I don't see any major changes. I would go on as I am, trying to help people when I could, trying to work as closely as possible with my family so they can get over the disgrace. Finish the criminal justice dictionary and work in the church.

"I guess I would complete the Agent Orange lawsuits against Dow Chemical. Probably I'd start teaching again. I volunteered to teach English and reading. I'm not permitted to teach subjects where they have a hired position although that's what I could really do best."

"Mister Smith, are you asking this jury to spare your life?"

"Absolutely. Of course."

••••

After Bill Costopoulos sat down, Rick Guida's first question was "Where are the bodies of Karen and Michael Reinert?"

"I do not know," said Jay Smith.

"You do not know?"

"I do not know."

"Where did you kill Susan Reinert?"

"I did not kill Susan Reinert or her children. I had nothing to do with Susan Reinert."

"In other words, what you're telling this jury is that they made a terrible mistake, isn't that right?"

"All my life I've lived in the American system. I think they've made their decision honestly on the basis of what they were given. We accept their judgment. They say I'm guilty; I'm guilty. You asked me if I think I really did it? I didn't do it. I respect their judgment."

"I didn't ask you if you *think* you did it. *Did* you do it or didn't you?"

"I said I did not."

"It's not a thinking process. You know you didn't do it and these people made a horrible mistake, but it's just the American system. Is that right?"

Costopoulos stood and said, "I object! He's arguing!"

"Yes," Judge Lipsitt said. "I don't think you should argue with him. You just ask him the questions and don't argue the point."

"Let me ask you this," Guida continued. "Are you telling us that you are not upset even though you've been unjustly convicted of three counts of murder in the first degree?"

"Yeah, I'm upset," Jay Smith said. "But I'm not the kind who falls apart. I've had enough military training. I can take whatever happens to me."

"Where were you during the weekend of June twenty-second, 1979, between ten o'clock at night and noontime on June twenty-fourth, 1979?"

"Your Honor, I'm going to object!" Bill Costopoulos said.

"I agree," said the judge. "You can't go back into the case."

"He's accepted the verdict!" said Costopoulos.

Guida was relentless. In all these years it was his first and last shot at the prince of darkness. He said, "Your Honor, may I explore who he was *with* during that time period?"

"I think I've sustained the objection. You have a jury verdict."

The prosecutor turned to *Penthouse* magazine.

"Mister Smith, on direct examination you indicated that you wanted issues of *Penthouse* so that you could write a legal dictionary, is that correct?"

"I am writing a legal dictionary, yes."

"What specific word did you define in your dictionary using the Yoko Ono article?"

" 'Battered wives.' I'm not saying that I completed the total entry. 'Child abuse' and 'battered wives' are the two terms I was going after."

"How long an entry in your dictionary did you plan for 'battered wives'?"

"I would say twenty-five words."

"In order to get twenty-five words for the dictionary to define the term 'battered wives,' you ordered two copies of *Penthouse,* is that right?"

"That's correct."

"The prison library has a lot of books, doesn't it?"

"The prison library has very few books, Mister Guida. I had purchased my own books. I had over one hundred and fifty books in my cell including a full encyclopedia set."

"You, of course, have a Ph.D. in education?"

"I'm a doctor of education."

"As part of that you did extensive research both in your master's and your doctoral theses, did you not?"

"Correct."

"Are you saying that given your educational background, your knowledge of libraries and books, and the places to find information, that the best place for you to get a definition of 'battered wives' was in the issues of *Penthouse* magazine?"

"On those two celebrities. Yes."

"In other words your dictionary was going to include a list of famous cases, is that right?"

"That's right."

"Were you also going to include the Ted Bundy case?"

"Absolutely."

"How about the Jeffrey MacDonald case from *Fatal Vision*?"

"I had those books in my cell."

"As a matter of fact, you had a lot of books on Ted Bundy."

"I had three. I consider him to be the first major serial murderer."

"Also, *Fatal Vision*. Correct me if I'm wrong. That's the man who killed his wife and two children?"

"Yes."

"A woman and two children?"

"No. It was his *wife* and two children."

"She's still a woman, isn't she?"

"Of *course*, she's a woman."

It was starting to look as though Guida never wanted this case to end—until he sensed that the jury had had enough. He ended abruptly.

Bill Costopoulos said, "Mister Smith, is there anything else that you wish to tell this jury, your peers, before they pass judgment on life or death?"

"The only thing I wanted to mention was that *comb*," Jay Smith said. "I spent twenty-eight years in the army reserves. Twenty-eight *years*. I spent every Wednesday night for twenty years doing reserve work. I'm the one who originated the idea for the comb.

"We had trouble getting into schools to talk about recruiting because it was very antimilitary back in the sixties. There was a television program called *77 Sunset Strip*. On that program there was a fellow who was a detective. He used to comb his hair. They had a song called 'Kookie, Kookie, Lend Me Your Comb.' That's where I got the idea to hand out combs with the

79th USARCOM decal inscribed on it. That comb now works against me.

"I did not kill Susan Reinert. I never had anything to do with Susan Reinert. Nothing whatever. Nothing. Never saw her off school property at any time. Never saw her children."

"Nevertheless," said Costopoulos, "you accept the judgment of your jury?"

"Of course. They're honest people. They made an honest decision. You accept it. That's the way it goes."

"No further questions," said Costopoulos.

"Nothing further," said Guida.

Jay Smith just gave a little shrug.

••••

"Let's hear arguments," said the judge.

Bill Costopoulos had said during the trial that he didn't even like to think of this eventuality, arguing for a man's life. He said the mere thought filled him with dread.

Only now was it possible to see just how *much* Bill Costopoulos dreaded this moment. He arose, faced the jury, and said, "May it please the court, Mister Guida, and Jay. Ladies and gentlemen of the jury, I, like Mister Smith, believe that this is the greatest system in the world. I'm not questioning the verdict that you twelve honest people have reached.

"Jay Smith has always maintained to me, as he has to this jury, that he did not murder Susan Reinert. He did not murder those children. I don't know, but I think you can appreciate the *frightening* position I'm in . . ."

It was a stunning moment in the trial. When Bill Costopoulos said the word "frightening" his voice cracked and broke. He *was* frightened. The tears started to roll down his cheeks and he continued his final argument while swallowing them back.

He said, "The Supreme Court of Pennsylvania has found capital punishment to be legal. Thus, in your deliberation on the question of punishment, you are to presume, if you sentence Jay Smith to death, that he *will* be executed.

"You are to presume, if you sentence Jay Smith to life imprisonment, that he will spend the rest of his life in prison. You will make no other presumptions.

"The life he will lead in prison is no life at all. For all practical purposes, he began his life term on June twenty-fifth, 1979. Since his arrest for murder in 1985, the man has lived in a hole. He lives by himself. He's got minimal contact. They transport him in handcuffs and shackles.

"He has elected between the two options of death and that kind of life, to die in our prison system. I'm asking you to let him do that. Thank you."

◆◆◆◆

It was an effective plea by a passionate lawyer. There were even a couple of reporters brushing at their eyes.

The prosecutor, as always, talked longer than the defense lawyer. He began by saying, "When we picked this jury a month ago, I told you that this day might come, and it's here.

"When I sat at lunch I think I probably felt exactly the way you're feeling right now. I'm not standing here to tell you I like the death penalty, or that I want people to die. I don't think that any one of you feel that way either. The question is not how we feel, but what the law requires. If we *liked* the death penalty, if we felt that we really wanted people to die, we wouldn't be at these chairs, we'd be at Mister Smith's."

After a long argument in which he described the aggravating circumstance in this terrible murder, he said, "You've made a determination. You've made a commitment to obey the law. It is now your obligation to do what the general assembly says is proper and what the community says is proper. Sympathy, bias, prejudice should not be part of your decision. For the children, I thank you."

◆◆◆◆

In actual deliberation time, the jury used only five hours for the guilt verdict, but needed six for the penalty verdict. It was probably a tribute to Bill Costopoulos in his plea for Jay Smith's life.

After seeing Jay Smith in action, no one could doubt his lawyer's decision *not* to let him testify. Even if there hadn't been the convictions in the Sears thefts which he would surely deny as he'd denied everything in his life except parking tickets, the man could not have taken the stand.

While his lawyer was being smothered by fear and dread of his awful responsibility, Jay Smith had just shrugged. *That's the way it goes.*

No matter how you'd try to package Jay Smith, no matter how placid and scholarly he tried to be, he still danced to his *own* tune. He'd do his own lonely jig, barely noticing the twelve people who were considering a sentence of death.

At least he'd revealed the music to which he danced on those lonely crags with his little goat feet: "Kookie, Kookie, Lend Me Your Comb."

••••

Rick Guida had celebrated his thirty-ninth birthday in the last days of the trial. Jack Holtz's thirty-ninth was coming up in May. These two bachelors were now facing their potential mid-life crises without the work that had consumed them.

Jack Holtz hoped he could return to Troop H and resume investigations. He wondered how he'd be received after so long away.

Rick Guida said he might quit the law and go to Denver and be a bartender.

Lou De Santis was going home to Philadelphia and just get back to living in a house instead of a hotel.

When the talk inevitably turned to the long deliberation, Jack Holtz said, "I don't particularly need the death verdict. If he gets it, I'll give up a day at the Penn State football game to witness the execution, but I don't *need* it. I like the idea of him living every day with the knowledge that Martray dimed him."

Rick Guida said, "I don't want Jay Smith. *God* wants him."

God had a long wait. The jury didn't return to the courtroom until 8:15 P.M. that night. The judge greeted the jurors after all were assembled and the clerk stepped forward. The jurors were *not* looking at Jay C. Smith.

"Have you reached a verdict of life or death?" he asked.

The woman in charge said, "We have reached a verdict of death."

The verdict was recorded at 8:18 P.M. and the clerk said, "Ladies and gentlemen, will you stand, please. Hearken to your verdict, as the court has it recorded. You say that Jay C. Smith should receive death. So say you all."

The standing jurors said, "We do."

While the defendant stood, as remote and impassive as ever, Costopoulos said, "The defense requests a poll of the jury, Your Honor."

Each juror was required to utter the verdict in the murders of Susan Reinert and Karen Reinert and Michael Reinert.

The first said "Death" three times.

The next said "Death" three times.

It was eerie hearing it uttered thirty-six times that night.

"Death."

"Death."

"Death."

Jack Holtz never took his eyes off Jay Smith. He saw the defendant's chin tremble just once.

Jack Holtz later said, "I loved it. I wanted to hear it thirty-six *more* times."

"Death."

"Death."

"Death."

29

Ghosts and Brothers

For her years with William Bradfield, Sue Myers had his thousands of books, most unopened, and that was all she had. By 1986 she at least was enjoying the company of a gentleman friend, and was still teaching at Upper Merion Senior High School

Christopher Pappas was working at a construction job in 1986 and might never pursue the profession to which he'd been led by his former mentor. He said he feared he might forever be thought of as a fool.

Vincent Valaitis who also still taught at Upper Merion said that before Bill Bradfield he never thought of missing mass on Sunday, but from his experience he learned that the world is a far more evil place than he'd ever dreamed. That knowledge weakened his faith. He told of a moment in recent years when he'd been reading a book and a memento fell out. It was a card from Michael Reinert thanking him for buying him a cub scout uniform. He wept.

Ken Reinert and Susan's brother, Pat Gallagher, still had not settled with the insurance company by 1986. It appeared that they would eventually get money, but only a fraction of her policies. Ken Reinert still was not able to talk about his ex-wife or their children.

All of the former friends of William Bradfield felt deep humiliation, but none admitted conscious guilt. Indeed, there were a great *many* people besides Sue Myers, Chris Pappas, Vince Valaitis and Shelly, who had heard awful tales of Jay Smith and his plot to murder Susan Reinert. None of those persons has been known to express guilt for not calling the police or notifying Susan Reinert of possible danger.

All of these people are put in a difficult position when a question is asked: "What would you have done if, according to Bill Bradfield, Jay Smith had been making those same terrible threats against Susan Reinert *and* the children?"

To say they would *then* have acted would of course be an admission that the life of Susan Reinert had been assigned a paltry value, by virtue of Bill Bradfield's assessment of her. No one could answer the question.

All of them—William Bradfield's friends and colleagues, his former students, his lovers, the families of his confidants, or their lawyers—*all* of them who had been told that there was a man named Jay Smith planning to murder Susan Reinert—all of them can ask themselves one question: "Did I *believe* Bill Bradfield that she was in danger?"

If the answer is yes, there are *three* ghosts that each of them might have to face from time to time. In the darkness.

••••

What of the strange partnership between William Bradfield and Jay Smith? Well, perhaps there was nothing strange about it, once it's stripped of picturesque settings and yes, *Gothic* trappings. Their partnership perhaps was not so different from those formed every day in center city Philadelphia by thousands of crime partners who have *not* earned certificates and titles from famous universities.

Perhaps it had nothing to do with sin and everything to do with sociopathy, that most incurable of human disorders because all so afflicted consider themselves *blessed* rather than cursed.

It may have been nothing more than an everyday moment

when one sociopath detects a flare of black light in the eyes of another. Seeing a potential mate. Seeing his own kind.

If Jay C. Smith ever does sit in the electric chair, it would not be out of character for him to say testily, "I hope you're all satisfied, because I never *was* a pervert, you know."

The electric chair can be a sociopath's greatest triumph if he thinks he can manipulate his audience to the end. To die in control is to die in ecstasy.

As to William S. Bradfield, Jr., he's housed in the state correctional institution at Graterford, Pennsylvania. Sue Myers said that he was taking correspondence courses from Villanova in Arabic and astronomy.

"He *loves* prison," she said. "He gets to tell his mother horror stories and scare her to death. At last, he's a poet in exile. Locked away like Ezra Pound."

His lawyer, Joshua Lock, said that people don't understand Bill Bradfield, and that it's true that he might prefer Graterford to a less austere prison.

Lock described Graterford prison as "almost Gothic."

William Bradfield can live a life of contemplation. What he *can't* do is define his life as Greek tragedy, not in Aristotelian terms where the tragic hero must change. The sociopath *can't* change. For the sociopath there is no third act.

••••

One might think that after it was over, after he'd successfully concluded an immense investigation that the FBI said was unsolvable, when Jack Holtz returned to Troop H he'd be welcomed as some sort of hero. But if one thinks *that,* one doesn't know as much about the policeman's lot as Gilbert and Sullivan did.

When he returned, it was to find that most of the investigators who'd been there back in 1979 were dead, or retired, or transferred to other assignments.

The first thing that was said to him was "Why in the hell did it take you *seven years* to clear a homicide?"

There was even talk of not being able to find a slot for him, and perhaps returning him to uniform and traffic duties.

Rick Guida was at last able to remove the pictures of Karen and Michael Reinert from his desk. His letdown at the conclusion of the case was more noticeable than Jack Holtz's. He spoke to the attorney general of Pennsylvania about getting Holtz assigned to his office to investigate major crimes.

Jack Holtz said that he'd do it, but he didn't want to work on white-collar crimes. He wanted to work homicides. Not too much to ask as a reward, one might think. Just to pursue murderers, on behalf of the commonwealth.

Epilogue

It seemed that after the most massive police investigation in Pennsylvania history had been concluded, the thing to do would be to return to the lovely countryside near Downingtown where the trees are bronze and fire in Indian summer, and wild flowers riot on the hillsides, and haystacks are molded into huge bread loaves. Where one can watch young geese spiraling toward the sun, their sapphire heads glistening in the rays.

Susan Reinert and her children had had some happy times in the old springhouse near Pennypacker Road, hearing the wings of young honkers cracking like spinnakers in the wind, watching the young birds bursting through pale plumes in the summer sky. It was not out of the question that the bones of Karen and Michael Reinert could be resting in a place like this. There was no harm in wishing it.

In the summer of 1986, Pat and Biv Schnure's younger daughter Caitlyn was four years old, and Molly was nine by then, very tall like her parents.

Molly still had an old-fashioned rubber doll with blue eyes that used to belong to another little girl. All her life Molly had called that doll Karen, but she'd forgotten why she'd named her that.

When her mother asked Molly if she remembered the little girl who gave her that doll, she tried to recall her doll's namesake. But Molly was growing up and dolls weren't so important anymore.

It was just too hard for her to remember the other Karen. It seemed like *such* a long time ago.